JOB READY GO®

JOB READY GO®

*Land your first role with
one of the leading modern
programming languages*

HAYTHEM BALTI
CO-AUTHORED BY KIMBERLY A. WEISS

WILEY

About the Authors

Haythem Balti, Ph.D., is an associate dean at Wiley Edge. He has created courses used by thousands of Software Guild and Wiley Edge (formerly mthree) alumni to learn Go, Java, Python, and other development and data science skills.

Kimberly A. Weiss is a Senior Manager of Curriculum Operations for Wiley Edge. She has worked with multiple universities as well as corporate training settings to develop interactive instructional content appropriate for the target learners and course goals, specializing in software development courses.

About the Technical Writer

Bradley Jones is the owner of Lots of Software, LLC. He has programmed in a variety of languages and tools ranging from C to Unity on platforms ranging from Windows to mobile (and includes the web as well as a little bit of virtual reality for fun). In addition to programming, he has authored books on C, C++, C#, Windows, the web, and many more technical topics as well as a few nontechnical topics. Bradley has been recognized in the industry as a community influencer and has been recognized as a Microsoft MVP, CODiE Judge, an international technology speaker, best-selling technical author, and more.

About the Technical Editor

Michael A. Jarvis is a software industry veteran with over thirty years of experience, working for companies ranging from small dot-com start-ups to large Fortune 100 enterprises. Michael has extensive experience programming in C, C++, Java, and Python, but has been enamored with Go ever since discovering the language back in 2015. Michael has contributed code to multiple open-source projects over the years, including the vim text editor and the fish shell, among others. Michael currently works as a lead software developer, on assignment with the vehicle cybersecurity group of a large automobile manufacturer, where he leverages his Go expertise toward automating security testing and validation of embedded vehicle components.

Acknowledgments

Although Kim and Haythem are the main authors of this book, this book would not have been possible without the hard work of the content development and instruction teams at The Software Guild and mthree. Haythem would also like to thank his mother, Samira: From buying my first computer when I was 13 years old to encouraging me to take a career in tech, she always played an instrumental part in where I am today. I am very thankful for you.

Contents at a Glance

Contents

Introduction

There are many programming languages a person can pick to create applications. Go, also known as Golang, is an open-source programming language that was designed at Google with a focus on simplicity and safety. Go first appeared to the public in 2009 and was officially released in 2012. Go is similar to the C programming language in the syntax and concepts that it uses. Go is a fast, small programming language that lets you focus on the solutions you want to build.

Go also provides features to make a developer's life easier. This includes garbage collection, memory safety, and structural typing. It also includes features such as built-in concurrency primitives, support of lightweight processes, an interface system, and more.

Whether you are looking to build standalone applications, build web apps, do concurrent programming, or perform a variety of other tasks, Go can help get you there. Other companies beyond Google are using Go, including Netflix, Ethereum, Splice, Twitch, and Uber. As result, Go has become a popular programming language.

> ## Go vs. Golang
> The programming language is Go, but some people call it Golang. The Golang name comes from the domain where Go used to be located, which was `golang.org`. Go is now hosted on go.dev.

A Go Course within a Book

This book contains a full-fledged Go course that is used by the mthree Global Academy and The Software Guild to train our alumni in Go and other topics, such as data analysis and data science.

Features to Make You Job Ready

As already stated, *Job Ready Go* provides an overview of the Go programming language, also known as Golang. It also teaches you how to leverage the basics of Go to create programs that can process and analyze data, and it goes beyond the basics to present advanced topics such as using REST APIs and gRPC with Go.

As you read through this book, enter the code listings. Try playing with the code. Get it to execute, make changes to it, and see what happens. This is a book about learning to write code using the Go programming language, and the best way to do that is to play with actual code. By taking a hands-on approach to working with the code and doing the exercises, you will be better able to take what you learned to the next level.

Most importantly, this book (as well as the *Job Ready* series) goes beyond what many books provide by including lessons that help you pull together everything you are learning in a way that is more like what you would find in the professional world. This includes building a more comprehensive example than what you get in the standard short listings provided in most books. If you work through the "Pulling It All Together" lessons, then you will be better prepared for many of those Go jobs that are available.

WHAT DOES THIS BOOK COVER?

As mentioned, this book is a complete Go programming course. It is broken into several parts, each containing a number of lessons. By working through the lessons in this book, you will not only learn Go programming, but you will be preparing yourself for a job using Go programming.

Part 1: The Basics of the Go Programming Language   The first part of this book focuses on getting you set up to use Go. This includes help for installing Go and setting up the tools you will need to work through this book. You will also be shown how to enter and run Go programs. This section also provides an overview of the basics of Go, including syntax, basic data types, and control statements.

Part 2: Organizing Code and Data in Go   The second part focuses on using the basic syntax learned in the first part and applying it to help organize your programming code using constructs such as functions, methods, and interfaces. It also focuses on working with and organizing data that is used in your application. This includes learning about data structures such as arrays, slices, maps, and structs.

Part 3: Creating Job Ready Solutions in Go   The third part focuses on going beyond the basics and learning about concepts you'll need to build job ready solutions. This includes learning how to handle errors, working with concurrency, and working with data in files outside of your application. You'll also explore existing code that will let you add functionalities such as dates, times, and sorting to your applications. Most importantly, you'll learn the details needed to build solid, reusable, complex programs.

Part 4: Advanced Topics for Go Development   In the last part of this book, we will focus on more advanced concepts that go beyond Go programming but that are important for Go programmers. This includes using test-driven development to build a Go application. It also includes working with REST APIs and gRPC to connect to and interact with processes and APIs that are outside of your own application.

READER SUPPORT FOR THIS BOOK
There are several ways to get the help you need for this book.

Companion Download Files

As you work through the examples in this book, you should type in all the code manually. This will help you learn and better understand what the code does.

However, in some lessons, download files are referenced. You can download the files from www.wiley.com/go/jobreadygo.

How to Contact the Publisher

If you believe you have found a mistake in this book, please bring it to our attention. At John Wiley & Sons, we understand how important it is to provide our customers with accurate content, but even with our best efforts an error may occur.

In order to submit your possible errata, please email it to our Customer Service Team at wileysupport@wiley.com with the subject line "Possible Book Errata Submission."

PART I

The Basics of the Go Programming Language

Lesson 1

Getting Started with Go

Go is an open source programming language developed and distributed by Google. In this lesson, we will walk through the steps of installing Go on a computer running Microsoft Windows 10 or later.

LEARNING OBJECTIVES

By the end of this lesson, you will be able to:

- Download and install Go on a local computer.
- Test the installation to verify it works.
- Create and run a Hello, World! program.
- Demonstrate basic troubleshooting steps.
- Use an online editor with Go.
- Ensure consistent formatting of your Go programs.

> **NOTE** There are also versions of Go for Apple macOS and Linux that you can download. The process should be somewhat similar to what is shown in this lesson.

INSTALLING GO

There are several requirements for installing Go. First, you must have administrative rights on your computer. If you own the computer, you should have no problems. If you are using a work or school computer, contact your IT department if you run into permission problems during the installation process.

> **NOTE** If you have used Go in the past and already have it installed on your computer, you can skip the installation instructions and go straight to the testing steps.

Alternatively, if you have an older version of Go that you would like to update, you might want to remove the existing version before installing the updated version.

You will also need a text or code editor to create Go programs. Go programs are written in plain text, so if you already have an editor you like, you can continue using it. If you have never used a code editor before or if you want to try a different one, you can use one of the following:

- **Visual Studio Code**

  (downloadable from https://code.visualstudio.com)

- **Atom**

  (downloadable from https://atom.io)

You can also find additional editors that support Go by going to the "Editor plugins and IDEs" page on the Go site. The page is found at https://go.dev/doc/editors.html. You can also use a plain-text editor such as Notepad if you prefer; however, an editor that supports Go, such as Visual Studio Code or Atom, will provide tools to help you with errors in your code.

Downloading the Installation Files

The first step is to download the most current version of the installation files. You can find the files on Go's Downloads page at https://go.dev/dl. The instructions shown in Figure 1.1 are for version 1.17.2 for Windows, but you will likely see a more recent version on the page.

Click the link for your operating system in the Featured Downloads section of the page. This will download the necessary installation file or package for your operating system.

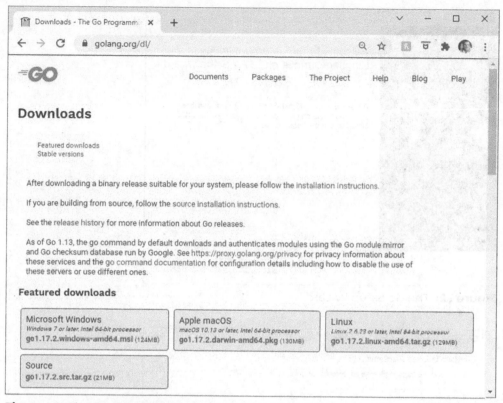

Figure 1.1: The Go Downloads page

Starting the Installation of Go

Once you have downloaded the installation file, open it from your computer. In Windows, you can open it by simply clicking the filename. This will start the Setup Wizard, as shown in Figure 1.2.

Click Next to begin the installation. The next screen displays the End-User License Agreement, as shown in Figure 1.3.

Go is distributed under an open source license. This means that you can modify and/or redistribute the code if you wish, but you must include the same copyright notice in any package you distribute.

You should read through the licensing agreement and then select the check box to accept it. Click Next to continue the installation. The next screen, shown in Figure 1.4, asks you to specify the destination folder where Go will be installed.

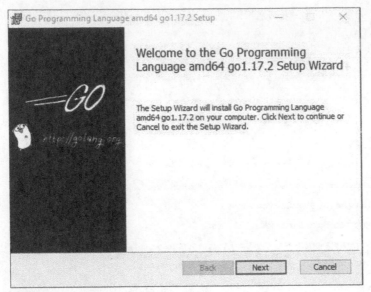

Figure 1.2: The Go Setup Wizard

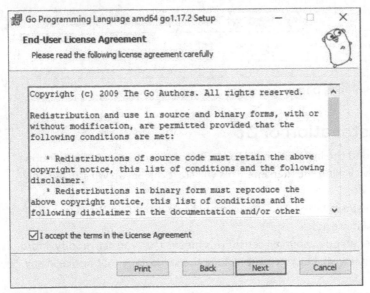

Figure 1.3: The Go End-User License Agreement

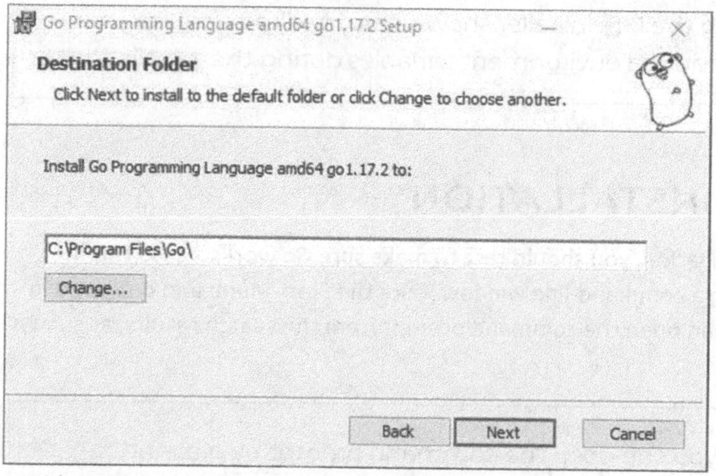

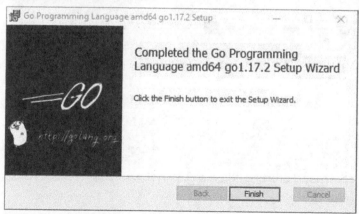

Figure 1.4: Specifying the folder where Go will be installed

You can either accept the default location or set a new location by entering the path to a folder or by clicking on Change to select a new location to install Go. Once you've entered the destination folder, click Next again. On the next screen, click the Install button to start the installation. Note that you might be prompted by Windows asking if you give permission to install the application. If so, you will need to indicate that it is okay.

When the installation is complete, you will see a confirmation message when the installation is complete, similar to what is shown in Figure 1.5. You can click the Finish button to close the wizard.

Figure 1.5: Confirmation that Go is installed

TESTING THE INSTALLATION

After completing the installation, you should test to make sure Go works. To do this in Windows, start by opening a command-line window. Click the Start Menu and type **cmd** in the search box. You can then open the command prompt from the search results, as shown in Figure 1.6.

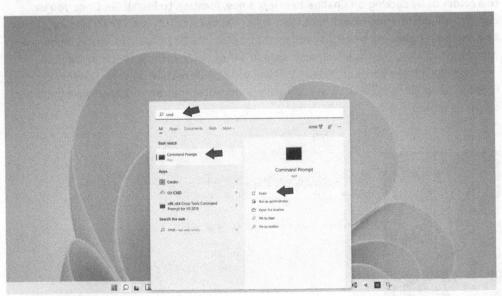

Figure 1.6: Running the command prompt (Microsoft Windows 11)

The command prompt will open in a new window similar to Figure 1.7. You should see a prompt that ends in your username.

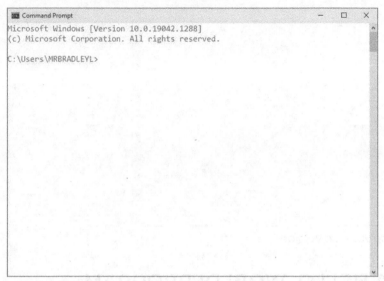

Figure 1.7: The command prompt

At the prompt, type the following command and press Enter:

```
go version
```

This command checks that Go is installed on your computer and displays the version number if it is. You should see a version that matches the one you just installed. Figure 1.8 shows version go1.17.2 installed.

If you get an error message instead of a version number, repeat the installation instructions and try again.

The default installation shown here used the MSI file. If entering the code snippet displayed the version number, then you should be ready to continue creating your first program, Hello World!.

If you downloaded a zip file instead of an MSI file, you will need to manually set up Windows environment variables before using Go. You can either delete the files created from the zip file and reinstall using the MSI file (which sets up the variables during the installation) or use the instructions provided in Go's Download and install page at `https://go.dev/doc/install`.

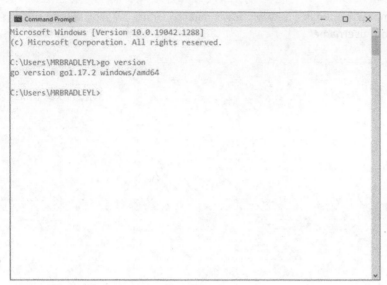

Figure 1.8: Displaying your Go version

CREATING A HELLO, WORLD! PROGRAM

With Go installed on your machine, you are ready to write and run your first Go program, Hello, World!. Using your preferred text or code editor (such as Atom or Visual Studio Code), create a file named **gotest.go** and save it to a known location, such as your Documents folder. In the example presented in Listing 1.1, the file is saved in Documents\GoLang. If you choose a different location, you will need to modify the instructions for compiling and running the program.

Make sure that the file has the filename extension .go. Most text or code editors will allow you to specify your own extension. Verify that the Save As box is set to All Files (or something similar) rather than a specific extension, such as .txt.

Add the code shown in Listing 1.1 to your new file.

LISTING 1.1

Hello, world!

```
package main
import "fmt"

func main() {
   fmt.Println("Hello, world!")
}
```

At this time, you are not expected to understand all the code presented in Listing 1.1; however, it is worth taking a closer look. You start by creating a `main` package to serve as the starting point for your program. You follow this by using the `import` statement to import Go's formatting package `fmt`. The `fmt` package contains code that allows text to be printed to the screen.

> **NOTE** The nice thing about using a package like `fmt` is that you can use it without having to worry about the code. In Listing 1.1, you can use `fmt.Println` without having to know what code is being used to actually do the printing.

You create a `main()` function in the third line of code, and you print the phrase "Hello, world!" by using `Println` from the `fmt` package you included. You don't need to understand how this works right now—just know that `fmt.Println("")` will print whatever is between the double quotes to the screen.

After entering the listing, make sure you save the file. You should leave the file open in your text editor in case you have problems running it. The compiler will read only the saved content in the file.

Compiling and Running the Program

The next step is to compile the file. *Compiling* is the process of converting human-readable code into machine-readable code. Use the `cd` command to navigate to the folder where `gotest.go` is saved:

```
cd Documents\GoLang
```

For our example, we created the file in a subfolder, GoLang, of the Documents folder, so we will change to that folder. If you saved your file in a different folder, then you should navigate to that folder. Figure 1.9 shows the `cd` command being used in the command prompt window to change to the Documents\GoLang folder. If you executed the command correctly, you will see the folder name at the end of the prompt.

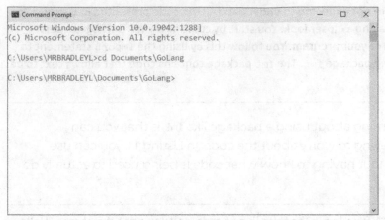

Figure 1.9: Using the cd command to change folders

Compile the program using the following command:

```
go build gotest.go
```

Simply enter this command at the command prompt and press Enter. The go build command will compile the file that is included, in this case, gotest.go. It may take a few moments to complete the compile, so as long as you don't see an error message, just wait. Eventually, the prompt will return, as shown in Figure 1.10.

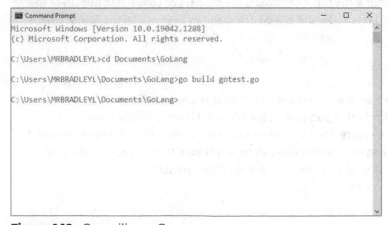

Figure 1.10: Compiling a Go program

While you don't see anything on the screen, if you list the files in the directory, you should now see that an executable file with an .exe extension called gotest.exe exists.

You can now run the program by entering the program name on the command line and pressing Enter:

```
gotest
```

If the program was written and compiled correctly, you will see "Hello, World!" displayed, as shown in Figure 1.11.

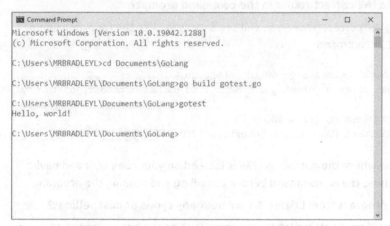

Figure 1.11: The output of the Hello, World! program

Alternate Run Option

The previous steps create and run a separate executable file using your program. The EXE file is useful if you want to share or run the program on a different computer. It is not necessary to create the EXE file if you simply want to test a program and don't plan to use the program somewhere else.

Another option is to compile and run the program in a single step, using this command:

```
go run program_name.go
```

You can try this using the same Hello, World! program. Verify that you are still in the correct directory in the command-line window (the directory where the gotest.go file is located) and run the command

```
go run gotest.go
```

You should see the following output immediately, without having to run a separate command to execute the program. This is the same output you saw before:

```
Hello, world!
```

Troubleshooting Hello, World!

If you had problems with this activity, you may have made one of the common mistakes many people make. Consider the following questions:

Did you navigate to the correct folder in the command prompt?

If you are not using the correct folder, you will see a message like the following when you run the go build command:

```
C:\Users\Student Name\Documents>go build gotest.go
can't load package: package gotest.go: cannot find package "gotest.go" in any
of:
        c:\go\src\gotest.go (from $GOROOT)
        C:\Users\Student Name\go\src\gotest.go (from $GOPATH)
```

Make sure you know where the gotest.go file is located on your computer and navigate to that location using the cd command before compiling and running the program.

Did you enter the program from Listing 1.1 without any typos or misspellings?

Most typing errors will be identified when you compile the program. If you see an error after running the go build command, read the error carefully to see where the problem is. As an example, consider the following error:

```
gotest.go:3:8: cannot find package "fnt" in any of:
        c:\go\src\fnt (from $GOROOT)
        C:\Users\Student Name\go\src\fnt (from $GOPATH)
```

In this example, fmt was misspelled as fnt in the 8th character on line 3 (3:8).

After correcting the error(s), save the file and try compiling it again.

Did you enter the commands on the command prompt line correctly?

Make sure you typed go build without any spelling mistakes. Also make sure you included the .go extension on your program filename.

Formatting Your Go Code

When you entered the code from Listing 1.1, you should have followed the format that was presented, including the spacing and the indentation of the code. Whether you indent with three spaces, four spaces, or a tab will not matter when it comes time to run your program; however, in most job environments there will be posted standards.

By providing consistency in how you format your listings, it makes it easier to go from one listing to the next. Additionally, in organizations with multiple programmers, consistent formatting helps make the code easier to read and maintain.

Unlike many programming languages, Go has tried to reduce the controversy over formatting issues. Debates on whether to use three or four spaces, or to use a tab instead, can all be eliminated by using an included formatting option. You can do the formatting using the go fmt command as follows:

```
go fmt mycode.go
```

This will remove or fix minor formatting concerns in mycode.go. Listing 1.2 presents the same "Hello, World!" listing you saw earlier; however, the formatting has been poorly done. Enter this listing and name it gotest2.go.

LISTING 1.2

goTest2.go: a poorly formatted Go listing

```
package main
import "fmt"
func main() {
fmt.Println("Hello, world!") }
```

With the listing created and named gotest2.go, enter the following at the command line:

```
go fmt gotest2.go
```

You will see the name of the program displayed when Go has finished running. If you then open gotest2.go in an editor, you will see that the file has been updated with clean formatting:

```
package main

import "fmt"

func main() {
        fmt.Println("Hello, world!")
}
```

MULTIPLE VERSIONS OF GO

Technically, you can have multiple Go versions installed on a single system. This is not only possible, but often very desirable, such as when you want to test specific code with multiple versions of the compiler. For example, you might want to make sure your open source package works with the latest compiler still being developed, but that it also works on the most recent stable version. It is beyond the scope of this book to cover installing multiple versions. You can, however, find instructions for doing this at `https://go.dev/doc/manage-install`.

ONLINE EDITOR FOR GO: THE GO PLAYGROUND

If you want to be "job ready" with Go, then we recommend you install a copy on your machine. You do, however, have the option to use Go without installing Go tools locally, as shown in this lesson. When you simply want to test a piece of Go code quickly, then you might find it easier to jump online and use the Go Playground.

The Go Playground can be found at `https://go.dev/play`. This online tool is shown in Figure 1.12. As you can see, it is primarily an open screen with line numbers down the left and a few buttons on the upper right.

You can enter a listing in the main box, next to the line numbers. In Figure 1.13, the "Hello, World!" code from Listing 1.1 has been entered but with a mistake. Additionally, after entering the code, the Format button on the upper right was clicked to format the code (similar to using the `go fmt` command shown earlier).

With the code entered into the Go Playground, the Run button can be clicked to run the listing. This results in the output shown in the lower part of the window.

You can also see in Figure 1.13 that the "Hello, World!" program does have an error on line 6. You can see this in the error message at the bottom of the screen as well as from the highlighted line number 6. The Go Playground makes it easy to locate the right line number to make a fix. In this case, the closing double quote is missing.

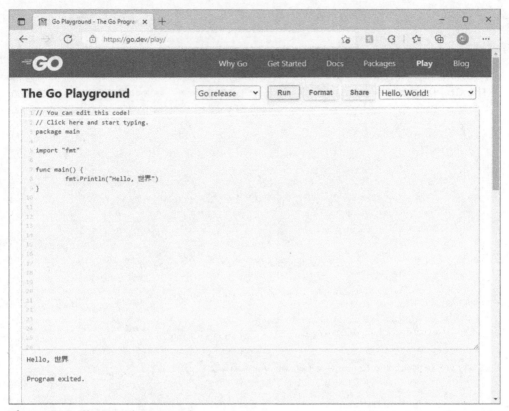

Figure 1.12: The Go Playground

> **NOTE** The Go Playground has limitations that are stated on the web page. You should, however, be able to use it for most of the lessons in the first three parts of this book.

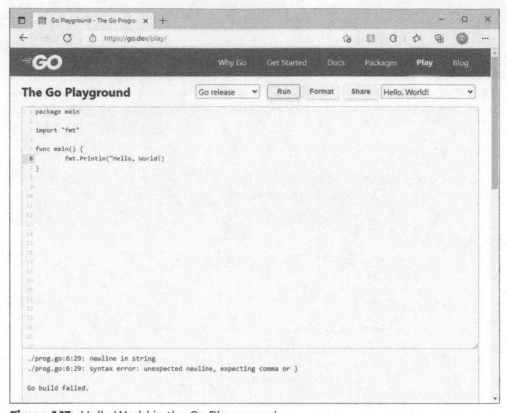

Figure 1.13: Hello World in the Go Playground

SUMMARY

In this lesson, the focus was on installing Go and confirming that it is ready to be used. When you are able to run the Hello, World! program successfully, you are ready to start coding with Go!

The following are a few useful online resources related to Go:

- `https://go.dev:` The official home page for Go
- `https://github.com/golang/go:` A GitHub-based learning wiki that includes many videos and exercises to help developers learn Go

EXERCISES

The best way to learn is by doing something rather than just by reading about it. If you've not already done so, enter, compile, and run the program presented in this lesson. To further help confirm your understanding of this process, you should complete the following exercises on your own. The exercises for this lesson are:

- **Exercise 1.1:** Counting Fun
- **Exercise 1.2:** Counting More Fun

Exercise 1.1: Counting Fun

Just as you did with Listing 1.1 in this lesson, enter the code presented in Listing 1.3 in your editor and save it as countingfun.go. Don't worry about the details of how the code works. Rather, focus on entering the code as presented in the listing.

LISTING 1.3

countingfun.go

```go
package main

import "fmt"

func main() {
    ctr := 0
    for ctr < 10 {
        fmt.Println("ctr: ", ctr)
        ctr += 1
    }
}
```

After entering the code in your editor and saving it, use the go run command to run the program:

```
go run countingfun.go
```

If you entered the code correctly, you should see the following output:

```
ctr:  0
ctr:  1
ctr:  2
ctr:  3
ctr:  4
ctr:  5
ctr:  6
ctr:  7
```

```
ctr:  8
ctr:  9
```

If you get an error, try the troubleshooting tips that we presented earlier in this lesson to determine what went wrong.

Exercise 1.2: Counting More Fun

Enter the code from Listing 1.4 and save it with the name `morecodingfun.go`.

LISTING 1.4

morecountingfun.go

```go
package main

import "fmt"

func main() {
   ctr := 0
   for ctr < 20 {
      fmt.Println("ctr: ", ctr)
      ctr += 2
   }
}
```

Can you find the changes? Compile and run the program to see the changes in action. When you run the code this time, the output should look like this:

```
ctr:  0
ctr:  2
ctr:  4
ctr:  6
ctr:  8
ctr:  10
ctr:  12
ctr:  14
ctr:  16
ctr:  18
```

You can continue to play with the numbers and the text in quotes to see what your changes do. Again, if you have trouble understanding what the code is doing, don't worry; we'll cover that in the rest of the lessons in this book.

Lesson 2
Understanding Go Basics

In this lesson, we will look at the basic building blocks of Go, including tokens, statements, comments, and identifiers. You will use these building blocks to create the code for your Go programs.

LEARNING OBJECTIVES

By the end of this lesson, you will be able to:

- Explain the concept of a token.
- Use line breaks and semicolons appropriately to end statements.
- Add comments to a program.
- Describe naming conventions and restrictions for identifiers.

> **NOTE** A lot of topics are covered in this lesson. Don't get overwhelmed if the information is new to you. We will cover most of the topics in this lesson in more detail in the next several lessons in this book. The intent of this lesson is to provide an introductory overview to help tie the upcoming lessons together.

UNDERSTANDING STATEMENTS AND TOKENS

A Go program is a series of statements. A Go statement is a series of tokens. In this context, a token refers to any meaningful object in a statement, including the following:

- **Keyword:** A reserved word used for special Go functionality
- **Operators and punctuation:** Symbols used to do mathematical operations and organize or perform special actions
- **Identifier:** Token used to identify things such as storage locations or functions that perform actions
- **Literal:** A specific value or number, such as 123 or "Hello, world"

We will look at each of these types of tokens in more detail in this and subsequent lessons. For now, consider the following statement from the Hello, World! example from the previous lesson:

```
package main
```

This statement includes two tokens: `package` and `main`. The token `package` is a keyword in Go. The token `main` is an identifier for the package. Another line from the Hello, World! example is included the following print statement:

```
fmt.Println("Hello, world!")
```

This statement includes the following tokens:

- `fmt`: This is an identifier that tells Go what library to use.
- `.`: The dot is a token that identifies a hierarchy. This tells Go that `Println` is part of `fmt`.
- `Println`: This is a keyword that references a function.
- `(...)`: Parentheses are operators that enclose the literal that the program will print.
- `"..."`: Quotes are operators that enclose the text string for the literal.
- `Hello, world!`: The literal that the `Println` function should display.

Each of these tokens is required for Go to understand the entire statement and understand how to interpret it.

STATEMENTS

As mentioned before, a program is a series of statements. There are a few things you need to know about statements. In Go, a statement must end in a semicolon or in one of the following tokens:

- an identifier
- an integer, floating-point, imaginary, rune, or string literal
- one of the keywords `break`, `continue`, `fallthrough`, or `return`
- an operator or punctuation, such as `++`, `--`, `)`, `]`, or `}`

Some statements have additional rules that supersede those given here. For example, when you declare a variable, the `var` statement must include the data type for that variable to indicate what types of values can be stored. These additional rules will become clearer as you work through future lessons in this book.

It is worth looking at a few statements to see how they are presented. Each of the statements in the program presented in Listing 2.1 ends with an appropriate final token.

LISTING 2.1

Example of final tokens

```
package main          // main  : identifier

import "fmt"          // "fmt" : identifier

func main() {         // {     : punctuation
    var x int         // int   : identifier
    x = 10            // 10    : integer
    fmt.Println(x)    // )     : punctuation
}                     // }     : punctuation
```

> **NOTE** The information to the right of each set of the double slashes (//) is a comment that is ignored. The statements end prior to the double slashes.

Given these rules for how statements must end, we would be able to change the fourth line to

```
var x
```

In this context, x is an identifier, and lines can end with identifiers. However, when we try to run the program, the compiler will produce an error (a *syntax error* to be more specific) because no type is specified for the variable:

```
.\main.go:6:9: syntax error: unexpected newline, expecting type
```

In this case, the program doesn't know what type of information can be stored in x because we didn't tell it. Don't worry, in Lesson 3, "Storing with Variables," you'll learn how to define types so that you can avoid this error.

Let's look at the Hello, World! program again. Many other programming languages use semicolons at the end of each statement to indicate the end. We originally wrote our Hello, World! program without semicolons. Listing 2.2 presents the Hello, World! program again.

LISTING 2.2

Hello, world!

```
package main

import "fmt"

func main() {
    fmt.Println("Hello, world!")
}
```

Each of the statements in this program ends with an appropriate token from the list presented earlier. We could, however, rewrite the program to include the formal semicolons at the end of each line, as shown in Listing 2.3.

LISTING 2.3

Hello, world! with semicolons

```
package main;
```

```
import "fmt";

func main() {;
    fmt.Println("Hello, world!");
};
```

The formal semicolon makes it clear that the statement has ended. With Go, however, these semicolons are not needed.

You might wonder why we would want to include a semicolon at the end. We can use a semicolon if we want to write several statements on a single line. For example, the program in Listing 2.3 could be written as a single line of code with semicolons at the end of each statement, as shown in Listing 2.4.

LISTING 2.4

A single line for Hello, world!

```
package main; import "fmt"; func main() { fmt.Println("Hello, World!");
fmt.Println("My name is John."); };
```

Because of the limited width of this book, the code is shown here on two lines; however, in your editor you can enter this on a single line. Going forward in this book, we will typically use line breaks instead of semicolons because using one statement per line makes the code more readable.

> **NOTE** A group of statements can be referred to as a *block* of code.

COMMENTS

Comments allow developers to properly document their code. When added correctly, the compiler will ignore comments. Comments are useful to document the life cycle of code development (by including the developers' names, dates, copyright information, and similar information), as well as to explain specific code to other developers. The Go language supports two comment formats: single-line or block.

Single-line Comments

Single-line comments can be included by using // followed by a space and then the comment. The compiler will ignore all text to the right of the double slashes on that line of code. Listing 2.5 shows a single-line comment being used on a line by itself.

LISTING 2.5

Single-line comments

```
package main

import "fmt"

func main() {
  // Display the message Hello World to the user
  fmt.Println("Hello, World!")
}
```

When you compile and run this listing, the line starting with // is ignored by the compiler and therefore has no actual impact on how your program runs. When using single-line statements, it is best to start a comment at the same indentation level as the statement that the comment refers to. As you can see in Listing 2.6, this helps with readability.

LISTING 2.6

Indentation of single-line comments

```
// Declare the main package
package main

// Import the fmt package
import "fmt"

// The main function
func main() {
  // Display the message Hello World to the user
  fmt.Println("Hello, World!")
}
```

In addition to single-line comments, you can add a comment at the end of a statement. You've seen examples of this type of commenting in earlier listings, including Listing 2.1. Listing 2.7 shows another example.

LISTING 2.7

End-of-line comments

```
package main

import "fmt"    // needed for Println

func main() {
   fmt.Println("Hello, World!") // Display the message Hello World
}
```

In this listing, everything starting from the double slashes to the right on any given line is ignored by the compiler.

The purpose of comments should be to help document and explain the code. They should bring clarity for someone new to the code or for someone who hasn't seen it in a while. As such, too many in-line comments can make code harder to read or even difficult to see the code itself. If you use standard syntax and well-named variables, comments should be used only to explain things that the code itself does not.

Block or Multi-line Comments

If you have comments that span multiple lines, you can either use // in front of each line or use block comments enclosed between /* and */. The compiler will ignore all text between these block comment markers. Listing 2.8 includes a block comment at the beginning of the listing.

LISTING 2.8

Multi-line comments

```
/* The purpose of this computer program is to display Hello, World!
   to the user.
```

continues

continued

```
    The program is written in Go and can be simply built using go
    build program.go. Additionally, you can run the program using
    go run program.go
*/

package main

import "fmt"

func main() {
  fmt.Println("Hello, World!")
}
```

When this listing is compiled, everything presented in the first several lines starting with /* and ending with */ is ignored. Even if Go statements are placed within this area, they will be ignored.

IDENTIFIERS

Identifiers are tokens that identify things like functions, types, and variables. In many cases, we will use existing identifiers, like functions included in imported packages. In other cases, we will create our own functions and variables, using Go's naming rules.

The naming rules for identifiers in Go are that they must start with a letter or an underscore, followed by a series of letters, underscores, or numeric digits. The following are valid identifiers in Go:

- Age
- age_15
- _age20

You can see how these identifiers are used by looking at Listing 2.9.

LISTING 2.9

Using identifiers

```
package main

import "fmt"

func main() {
```

```
    var Age int = 10
    var age_15 int = 15
    var _age20 int = 20

    fmt.Println(Age)
    fmt.Println(age_15)
    fmt.Println(_age20)
}
```

In this listing, three identifiers are being created and assigned values. These are Age, age_15, and _age20. They are assigned a value of 10, 15, and 20, respectively. The values are then printed by passing the identifier names to the Println function we've used before. If you enter and run this listing, you'll see the following output:

```
10
15
20
```

You should be careful to avoid using invalid identifiers. The following are examples of invalid identifiers:

- 0_age
- 1_age
- \#age
- $age

Listing 2.10 presents a version of the Hello, World! program that will not run because of invalid identifiers. Enter the code and run it to determine which identifiers are named incorrectly.

LISTING 2.10

Using identifiers

```
package main

import "fmt"

func main() {
    var ^output string = "Hello world!"
    var 2022 string = "The year is 2022."
    fmt.Println(^output, " ", 2022)
}
```

This listing creates two variable identifiers, which are assigned values. These values are then passed to a `Println` function to display on the screen with a space between them. When you run the program, you will see errors similar to the following:

```
.\TestScan.go:6:8: syntax error: unexpected ^, expecting name
.\TestScan.go:7:8: syntax error: unexpected literal 2022, expecting name
```

Try to correct the problems with the identifiers and run the code again to verify it works. When the identifiers have been corrected, you should see the following output:

```
Hello world!    The year is 2022.
```

You should have found that the first identifier, ^output, started with an invalid symbol. You can simply remove the symbol to have it work. The second identifier, 2022, is invalid because it starts with a number. To be used as an identifier, it needs to start with an underscore or a letter. You'll need to change these on the line where they are defined and assigned a value, as well as change them in the `Println` statement.

Case

Go is case-sensitive, so it is important to be consistent when you create identifiers. As an example, Listing 2.11 will not compile because it does not use the proper casing for the `fmt.Println` function.

LISTING 2.11

Misusing case

```
package main

import "fmt"

func main() {
    // The following statement will throw an error
    fmt.println("Hello, World!")
}
```

The compiler returns the following error:

```
.\main.go:7:4: cannot refer to unexported name fmt.println
.\main.go:7:4: undefined: fmt.println
```

This error is a result of using `println` instead of `Println`. If you capitalize the P in `println` and recompile the listing, it should work cleanly. Listing 2.12 illustrates that when creating identifiers, you must be consistent in the use of case. Because Go is case-sensitive, the names `Year` and `year` are not the same, as you can see by trying to compile and run Listing 2.12.

LISTING 2.12

Misusing case in multiple places

```
package Main

import "fmt"

func main() {
    var mainGreeting string = "Hello world!"
    var year string = "The year is 2022."
    fmt.println(MainGreeting, " ", Year)
}
```

Run the code to identify and correct the errors. After making all corrections, verify that the program runs as expected. A corrected version of this listing is provided at the end of this lesson.

Naming Conventions

Per Go's standards, if an identifier includes two or more logical human words, the identifier should use PascalCase (with each word capitalized) or camelCase (where the first word is lowercase but additional words are uppercase), without the use of underscores to separate the words. All the following use standard naming conventions in Go:

```
FirstName
firstName
LastName
lastName
HomeAddress
homeAddress
```

Because Go is case-sensitive, we recommend that you choose *one* of these options and use it consistently throughout your code. The use of camelCase seems to be gaining popularity at this time. If you are working with a team of developers, the team should agree on naming conventions to be certain that everyone is following the same guidelines.

> **NOTE** Most organizations that have more than one developer will have coding standards that they expect to be used. These standards should include, among other things, information such as naming and commenting guidelines for identifiers in code.

KEYWORDS

Keywords in Go language are reserved tokens that cannot be used as identifiers. The following list shows the keywords in Go language:

- break
- case
- chan
- const
- continue
- default
- defer
- else
- fallthrough
- for
- func
- go
- goto
- if
- import
- interface
- map
- package
- range
- return

- select
- struct
- switch
- type
- var

Because these keywords have special meaning in Go, they cannot be used to name a variable or a function that you create. For example, you can't create a function or variable called select because the select function already exists as part of the Go language. As you work through this book, you will learn what these keywords do.

SUMMARY

This lesson was a quick overview of a few key topics important for programming in Go. This included a brief look at tokens, statements, comments, and identifiers. You will use these building blocks to create the code for your Go programs. Starting in the next lesson, you'll begin to apply these building blocks as you learn how to create variables for storing information.

EXERCISES

The following exercises are provided to allow you to experiment with the tools and concepts presented in this lesson. For each exercise, write a program that meets the specified requirements and verify that the program runs as expected. The exercises are:

Exercise 2.1: Fixing Problems

Exercise 2.2: Making a Statement

Exercise 2.3: Go Is Fun!

Exercise 2.4: Printing Without Repeating

Exercise 2.5: Tagging Your Code

NOTE The exercises are for your benefit. The exercises help you apply what you learn in the lessons. You are also encouraged to experiment with the code as you complete the exercises.

Exercise 2.1: Fixing Problems

Each of the code blocks in Listing 2.13 through Listing 2.15 includes at least one error that will prevent it from running. Fix the errors and test to make sure the code runs as expected. Comments at the top of each block will tell you what the code should do.

LISTING 2.13

Code Block A

```
// output the text in quotation marks
package main

import "fmt"

func main() {
    fmt.println("Hello, world!")
}
```

LISTING 2.14

Code Block B

```
// display the text in quotation marks to an output block
// without moving any of the existing code to a different line
package main

import "fmt"

func main() {
  Println("Go is fun!") Println("Go is also easy.")
}
```

LISTING 2.15

Code Block C

```
// create separate variables for first name and last name
// print each name on a separate line
package main
```

```
func main() {
  var 1_Name string = "Rebecca" // first name
  var &_Name string = "Roberts" // last name

  fmt.Println("1_Name")
  fmt.Println("&_Name")
}
```

Exercise 2.2: Making a Statement

Using the Hello, World! program presented in Listing 2.2 as a pattern, write a program that displays the following text. Each item should be presented in a complete sentence on a separate line:

- Your name
- Your hometown
- Your favorite food

For example, the output of your program should look something like:

```
My name is Barbara Applegate.

I live in Augusta, Georgia.

My favorite food is apple pie.
```

Exercise 2.3: Go Is Fun!

Starting with the code provided in Listing 2.16, add to the code as needed to change the program so that it only outputs the text Go is fun! You should add necessary code, but you should not delete any of the existing code.

LISTING 2.16

Go is fun!

```
// Change this program so that it outputs only the text Go is fun!
// Do not delete any of the existing code
package main

import "fmt"
```

```
func main() {
  fmt.Println("Go is fun!")
  fmt.Println("Go is also easy!")
}
```

> **NOTE** There are several ways you can change the code in Listing 2.16 to accomplish the task. Try to solve the exercise in more than one way!

Exercise 2.4: Printing Without Repeating

Starting with what is provided in Listing 2.17, add the code needed to display the text that is presented in the quotation marks to output without reentering the text that is in the quotation marks. While you can add necessary code, you should not delete any of the existing code.

LISTING 2.17

Printing without repeating

```
// Add one line of code that displays the text in quotation marks to
// an output block without repeating the text in quotation marks.
package main

import "fmt"

func main() {
  var output string = "I love Go!"

}
```

> **NOTE** When declaring the variable output in Listing 2.17, we could remove string:
>
> ```
> var output = "I love Go!"
> ```
>
> This works because Go determines that what is on the right of the equal sign is a string and will infer that for the type for output.

Exercise 2.5: Tagging Your Code

Review the programs in this lesson. You should enter these programs into your editor and save them. You should then tag each listing by adding comments with the following information above the `package main` statement for each listing:

- Your name (single-line comment)
- The current date (single-line comment)
- A short description of the purpose of the program (multi-line comment)

Compile and run the program to ensure that there are no errors and that the comments do not appear in the output.

Solution: Listing 2.12

The following is the corrected version of Listing 2.12. Did you find all the case errors?

```go
package main

import "fmt"

func main() {
    var mainGreeting string = "Hello world!"
    var Year string = "The year is 2022."
    fmt.Println(mainGreeting, " ", Year)
}
```

Lesson 3
Storing
with Variables

L esson 2 presented a lot of topics. In this lesson, we'll begin to
dig deeper into some of those topics. Specifically, this lesson
provides an overview of creating variables in Go, including static
and dynamic types as well as global and local variables.

LEARNING OBJECTIVES

By the end of this lesson, you will be able to:

- Create string and integer variables.
- Display the memory address of a variable.
- Create variables using static and dynamic typing.
- Collapse variable declaration statements to streamline the code.
- Create local and global variables.
- Describe the number types that Go supports, including architecture-independent integers, implementation-specific integers, and floats.

VARIABLES

Variables in Go are identifiers. For example, we might need to store the email address of a client but also need to make sure it is valid. In this case, we can create a variable named email that stores the value of the email. The email address can be assigned to the email variable.

The variable references a memory address where the actual value assigned to the variable is stored. When the compiler needs the value of the variable, it uses the named memory address to retrieve it.

Whenever you create a variable, you must include its type, either by defining the type explicitly or by assigning a value with an identifiable type in the same statement. The basic syntax to create a variable looks like this:

```
var identifier type [= value]
```

The name of the variable is the identifier. In the case of the email address, we used the name email as the identifier. As mentioned in the previous lesson, the type indicates the type of information that will be stored, whether it be a number, letters, or other value. As an example, to create a variable that could store a simple whole number, we could make the following declaration:

```
var myNumber int
```

This creates a variable called myNumber and sets the type to int, which is used to store basic whole numbers.

NOTE In this lesson, we focus on setting up and storing information with some basic types. In Lesson 4, "Performing Operations," you will learn about the different types provided by Go for storing information.

In addition to setting the type of a variable, you can assign a value within the same statement. For example, the following declares our myNumber variable again, but also sets it to equal 42:

```
var myNumber int = 42
```

You also have the option to assign (or change) the value in a separate statement later in the program. After declaring myNumber, you could change its value by simply assigning a new value:

```
myNumber = 84
```

Listing 3.1 presents a complete listing that goes further by creating a variable that stores the string *Hello, World!* Enter this listing and run it to see the results.

> **NOTE** A string is simply a group of characters such as `Hello, World!`, John Doe, or 333–44–5555.

LISTING 3.1

Creating a variable to store a string

```
package main

import "fmt"

func main() {
    var message string = "Hello, World!"
    fmt.Println(message)
}
```

In this listing, you can see that a variable is declared with the identifier (name) of `message`. Additionally, you can see that the variable is assigned the string value that is presented after the equal sign, `"Hello, World!"` The variable's contents can then be printed, as is done in the next line of code using `fmt.Println`. The output from running this listing is:

```
Hello, World!
```

Naming Variables

Because variables are identifiers, they follow the same naming convention as identifiers in Go. That is, a variable name starts with a letter or underscore followed by a series of letters, numbers, or underscores. Listing 3.2 shows an example of an invalid variable definition.

LISTING 3.2

Using an invalid variable name

```
package main
```

continues

continued
```
import "fmt"

func main() {
    // the variable declaration below is invalid due to invalid
    // naming convention
    var 0_email string = "john@john.com"

    fmt.Println(0_email)
}
```

In this listing, you can see that a variable called 0_email is declared with a type of string. It is assigned the value of john@john.com. When you run this listing, the compiler will produce the following syntax error for the 0_email identifier:

```
syntax error: unexpected literal 0_e, expecting name
```

This variable name is invalid because an identifier must start with a letter or underscore.

Declaring and Initializing Variables

As mentioned, a variable in Go must have a type, which indicates the type of information that will be stored. More importantly, the type defines the amount of memory needed to store the data in the variable. We look at types in more detail in Lesson 4, but for now, we can continue to look at concepts that apply to variables independently of their type.

Declaring and Initializing One Variable

In the previous examples, we defined and initialized the variable in the same step. It is possible to split that into two steps, as shown in Listing 3.3.

LISTING 3.3

Declaring and initializing a variable

```
package main

import "fmt"

func main() {
    var message string      // declare the variable
```

```
    message = "Hello, World!" // assign a value to the variable

    fmt.Println(message)
}
```

Listing 3.3 has the same output as Listing 3.1, but instead of assigning a value to the identifier at the same time it is created, the listing does the process in two steps. You can see that in the first step, the variable named message is created as a string, then in the second step, "Hello, World!" is assigned. Each of these is done as a separate statement.

Declaring Multiple Variables

We can define multiple variables by simply creating a statement for each:

```
var message string   // declare variable called message as string
var email string     // declare variable called email as string
```

Additionally, we can define multiple variables of the same type in the same statement, as shown in Listing 3.4.

LISTING 3.4

Declaring multiple variables in one statement

```
package main

import "fmt"

func main() {
    var message, email string  // declare two string variables
    message = "Hello, World!"   // assign a value to one variable
    email = "john@john.com"     // assign a value to the second variable

    fmt.Println(message)
    fmt.Println(email)
}
```

In this listing, both message and email are being declared as string type variables in the same line. To declare multiple variables in the same line, you separate them by a comma. After declaring the two variables, the listing continues by assigning each a value and then printing their contents. When you enter and run this listing, you'll see that the output is:

```
Hello, World!
john@john.com
```

Declaring and Initializing Multiple Variables

We can also initialize multiple variables of the same type and assign a value to each variable in the same statement, as shown in Listing 3.5.

LISTING 3.5

Declaring and initializing multiple variables on one line

```
package main

import "fmt"

func main() {
    // initialize two string variables in the same statement
    var message, email string = "Hello, World!", "john@john.com"

    fmt.Println(message)
    fmt.Println(email)
}
```

This listing produces the same output as the previous listing. The difference in this listing is that the message and email variables are initialized in the same line they are declared. As you can see, the values used to initialize the variables are listed to the right of the equal sign. Values are assigned from left to right, so the first string, "Hello, World!", is assigned to the first variable on the left, message. The second string, "john@john.com", is assigned to the second variable, email.

STATIC VS. DYNAMIC TYPE DECLARATION

When we declare a variable with a specific type in Go, we create a static type variable. With a static type, the compiler does not have to determine the type associated with the variable. Listing 3.6 shows an example of static type declaration, with initialization in the same statement.

LISTING 3.6

Creating a statically typed variable

```
package main

import "fmt"

func main() {
    // initialize a variable and assign a value in the same statement
    var message string = "Hello, World!"

    fmt.Println(message)
}
```

You can see in the listing that a static type declaration happens because the variable named message is declared as a string type.

Go also supports dynamic typing. With dynamic typing, the compiler will infer the type based on the value that is assigned to the variable. Go uses the := operator for dynamic typing, using the syntax:

```
identifier :- initialValue
```

Listing 3.7 shows an example of a dynamic type declaration.

LISTING 3.7

A dynamically typed variable using the := operator

```
package main

import "fmt"

func main() {
    // dynamic declaration using the := operator
    email := "john@john.com"

    fmt.Println(email)
}
```

In this example, the compiler will infer that email is a string type because the value assigned to it is a string. Listing 3.8 provides another example.

LISTING 3.8

Dynamically typing the age variable

```
package main

import "fmt"

func main() {
    // dynamic declaration using the := operator
    age := 42

    fmt.Println(age)
}
```

Notice that this time, the variable declared is called age. The value assigned is not a string, but rather a number. Using dynamic typing, Go will set age to be an integer. The output from this listing is simply:

```
42
```

Mixing Types of Declarations

Go is reasonably flexible in type assignment as long as the compiler can clearly identify the identifier (the name of the variable) and the type associated with the variable. For example, the code block in Listing 3.9 shows the use of the = operator and the := operator in the same listing.

LISTING 3.9

Mixing types of declarations

```
package main

import "fmt"

func main() {
    var message = "Hello, World!" // initialize with a string value
    email := "john@john.com"      // initialize with a string value

    fmt.Println(message)
    fmt.Println(email)
}
```

In both the declaration of message and of email in this listing, a string is assigned. Because no type was stated, Go dynamically assigns the type of string to the variables.

It is important to note that you must use either the format of var ... = or :=. You cannot mix and match. Take a look at Listing 3.10. Neither of the variable declarations in the listing is supported.

LISTING 3.10

Invalid variable declarations

```
package main

import "fmt"

func main() {
    message = "Hello, World!" // missing var
    var email := "john@john.com" // cannot use var and := together

    fmt.Println(message)
    fmt.Println(email)
}
```

Take a look at the first case where message is assigned a value:

```
message = "Hello, World!"
```

In this case the var keyword was not included. Because message is not a keyword, Go cannot identify its purpose. As such, an error will be displayed.

In the second case, email is being assigned a value:

```
var email := "john@john.com"
```

This declaration and assignment will also cause an error because the use of var with := violates Go's syntax rules.

Mixing Type Declarations in a Single Statement

Several variables with different data types can also be declared in the same statement using dynamic type inference. In the code sample presented in Listing 3.11, a string and a number are defined in the same statement, using the = operator.

LISTING 3.11

Assigning multiple types in one declaration

```go
package main

import "fmt"

func main() {
    var message, year = "Hello, World!", 2022

    fmt.Println(message)
    fmt.Println(year)
}
```

As you can see, message and year are both declared in a single line. You can also see that values are assigned to each. The value of "Hello, World!" is assigned to message. Because the value is a string, message is declared as a string. The value of 2022 is assigned to year. Because the value is an integer number, year is dynamically declared as an integer. The output of this listing is simply:

```
Hello, World!
2022
```

VARIABLE SCOPE

Variable scope defines what components of a program can access the variable. In general, within computer programs, access to a variable might be made available across an entire program, or it might be restricted to only a certain area. Go supports local and global variable scope.

Local variables are only accessed within the block of code or function where the variable is defined. Listing 3.12 shows an example of a local variable defined within the main function that can only be accessed within the main function.

LISTING 3.12

Local variable scope

```go
package main

import "fmt"
```

```
func main() {
    // local variable
    var message string = "Hello, World!"

    fmt.Println(message)
}
```

While we can use the function itself to return a value that can be used elsewhere in the program, the program will not understand any reference to the variable called message outside of the main function.

Global variables are declared at the beginning of the program, outside of any block or function. These variables can be accessed anywhere in the program, and they are available throughout the life cycle of the program. Listing 3.13 shows an example of a global variable defined outside of the main block.

LISTING 3.13

Global variable scope

```
package main

import "fmt"

// global variable
var message string = "Hello, World!"

func main() {
    // local variable
    var email string = "john@john.com"

    fmt.Println(message)
    fmt.Println(email)
}
```

In this example, the message variable is outside of the main function. Because that makes it available everywhere in the program, the main function can access message and display its value as part of the function's activities.

It is hard to see the difference between local and global variables in an example listing that has only a single function. The value of local versus global scoping of variables will make more sense as our programs get larger. In Lesson 7, "Pulling It All Together: Income Tax Calculator," you will see the value of local versus global as you learn to organize your programs into functions.

For now, the thing to keep in mind is that unless you have a strong reason to use global variables, you should use local variables whenever possible. This limits what parts of the program have access to those variables and can make it easier to troubleshoot problems.

OBTAINING USER INPUT

In many programs, we want to allow the user to enter the value the program will use. While Go can accept a variety of data types for user input, we will use string input in this lesson. String is a very versatile data type, and a string value that contains only numeric characters can be easily converted into a number type later if necessary.

Memory Address

Before seeing how to obtain a value from a user and store it in a variable, it is important to understand a bit about variables and computer memory. As mentioned before, a variable is a type of identifier used to store data. When a variable is declared, enough memory is set aside to store the data based on the type we declared. The name of the variable is associated with an address within the computer's memory.

If we need to access the address of a variable, we can use the & operator along with the name of the variable. Listing 3.14 shows how to retrieve and display the memory address of two variables.

LISTING 3.14

Accessing a variable's address in memory

```
package main

import "fmt"

func main() {
    var myVar string = "Hello, World!"
    var myAge int = 99

    fmt.Println(myVar)
    fmt.Println(&myVar)
    fmt.Println(myAge)
    fmt.Println(&myAge)
}
```

You can see that two variables called myVar and myAge are declared and initialized in the same manner used previously in this lesson. To show that nothing mysterious is happening, the two variables are printed using the first two calls to fmt.Println. You can see the values displayed as expected in the output. The last two calls to fmt.Println, however, include the address-of operator, which returns the hexadecimal address of the memory location where myVar is and myAge are located. These addresses are printed by fmt.Println. The output will look similar to:

```
Hello, World!
0xc00010a050
99
0xc000100028
```

The actual value you see will be an address from your system.

Scanning for Values

There are also many different options for accepting input. Using the address-of operator is a part of using the fmt.Scanln function to obtain values from the user of a script. The pattern shown here is straightforward, but you may see others as you continue to work in Go. The basic syntax is

```
var variableName string
fmt.Scanln(&variableName)
```

The first line declares the variable as a string. The second line uses the Scanln function to read the input from the user and place it into the variable. The variableName can be any valid identifier name. It is important to note that we include the & symbol before the variable name when scanning in an item. & is the address-of operator, which helps Go know to place the input into the location of the variable that is named (variableName). Listing 3.15 provides an example that uses two input values.

LISTING 3.15

Inputting two variables

```
package main

import "fmt"
```

continues

continued

```go
func main() {
  fmt.Print("Enter your first name: ")    //Print function displays
                                          //output in same line
  var firstName string
  fmt.Scanln(&firstName)  // take input from user

  fmt.Print("Enter your last name: ")
  var lastName string
  fmt.Scanln(&lastName)

  fmt.Print("Your first name is: ")
  fmt.Println(firstName)

  fmt.Print("Your last name is: ")
  fmt.Println(lastName)
}
```

When this program is executed, the user is prompted to enter their first name and last name, which are then displayed back. You can enter any first and last name:

```
Enter your first name: Grace
Enter your last name: Hopper
Your first name is: Grace
Your last name is: Hopper
```

Let's review the code and make some observations. We've previously used Println to print output on a new line. In this listing, we use Print by itself. By using Print instead of Println, a new line is not generated after the statement is executed.

We use the print statements to display prompts. This is followed by using the Scanln function to essentially read in (or scan) the characters input by the user. These are then saved to the variable specified between the parentheses. You can see that we read in the first name and save it into the variable first_name. We read in the last name and save it into the variable last_name.

NOTE If you have trouble getting your code to work correctly, the first thing to check is to confirm that you included the address-of (&) operator before your variable name. Leaving it off will cause the program to not wait for the user to enter a value.

As you saw in Listing 3.15, `Print` and `Println` can be combined to control the output lines. We can also concatenate (or join) strings using the + operator, as shown in Listing 3.16, which is simply another version of the same program from the previous listing. In this new listing, the output is presented in a more concise manner using concatenation.

LISTING 3.16

Using concatenation on our strings

```
package main

import "fmt"

func main() {
  fmt.Print("Enter your first name: ")   // Print function displays output
                                         // in same line
  var firstName string
  fmt.Scanln(&firstName)  // take input from user

  fmt.Print("Enter your last name: ")
  var lastName string
  fmt.Scanln(&lastName)

  fmt.Println("Your name is: " + firstName + " " + lastName)
}
```

The output looks like this:

```
Enter your first name: Grace
Enter your last name: Hopper
Your name is: Grace Hopper
```

As a general rule of thumb, user prompts (like the text "Enter your first name:") should clearly explain what kind of input the program expects to get from the user. Because the user sees this text, it should also be free of spelling or grammar errors that can make your program look bad.

CONVERTING A STRING TO A NUMBER

When we accept user input using `fmt.Scan`, the input is stored as a string. The problem is that string values cannot be used in mathematical operations, so we have to convert the value to a number before we can use it as a number. The high-level view of this process includes the following steps:

1. Accept user input and store it in a string variable.
2. Convert the input into a number.
3. Store the converted value in a number variable.

We use the `fmt.Scan` or `fmt.Scanln` function to accept user input. For example, as shown in Listing 3.17, we might prompt a user to enter two separate numbers and then use the + operator to add the two input values together to get the sum.

LISTING 3.17

Attempting to add two values

```
package main

import "fmt"

func main() {
  var firstNumber string
  var secondNumber string

  fmt.Print("Enter the first integer: ") // user prompt
  fmt.Scan(&firstNumber)                  // store input

  fmt.Print("Enter the second integer: ")
  fmt.Scan(&secondNumber)

  fmt.Println(firstNumber + secondNumber) // addition of two strings
}
```

If you run the program and enter the values 3 and 7 at the prompts, the output will look like this:

```
Enter the first integer: 3
Enter the second integer: 7
37
```

While the user did enter two numbers, we have stored the input values as a string, so the result is concatenation rather than addition.

Because we cannot use `fmt.Scan` functions to accept numbers directly from the user, we must convert the input values into numbers as a separate step and store the converted values as separate variables. Go provides the `strconv` package specifically for this purpose. We can include this package by adding it to our `import` statement at the top of our listing:

```
import (
  "fmt"
  "strconv"
)
```

As you can see, we can add more than one package by adding parentheses after the `import` statement and then listing the packages.

When we convert our scanned string values, we will need to have new numeric variables for storing the converted values. We can add declarations to create two new variables of type `int`:

```
var firstInt int
var secondInt int
```

Once we've included the new package and declared our variables to store our converted values, we can then use the appropriate function in the `strconv` package to convert the string to an `int`. While there are several options to choose from, we will use the `Atoi` function in our example. This function takes two arguments—the original value that it will convert and an error notation:

```
originalValue, error = strconv.Atoi(integerValue)
```

Rather than define a specific error output, we will use _ as a nil error shortcut (which can also be called a "blank identifier"). As such, to convert the two strings (`firstNumber` and `secondNumber`) to integers (`firstInt` and `secondInt`), we would call `Atoi`:

```
firstInt, _ = strconv.Atoi(firstNumber) // convert to int
secondInt, _ = strconv.Atoi(secondNumber)
```

NOTE For more on handling errors and using a nil error shortcut, see Lesson 17, "Handling Errors."

Finally, we add an addition statement that uses the converted values. Listing 3.18 provides our updated code to convert the input values to integers. The values are then added together with the result being displayed.

LISTING 3.18

Converting strings to ints

```go
package main

import (
  "fmt"
  "strconv"
  )

func main() {
  var firstNumber string
  var secondNumber string

  var firstInt int
  var secondInt int

  fmt.Print("Enter the first integer: ") // user prompt
  fmt.Scan(&firstNumber)  // store input

  fmt.Print("Enter the second integer: ")
  fmt.Scan(&secondNumber)

  firstInt, _ = strconv.Atoi(firstNumber) // convert to int
  secondInt, _ = strconv.Atoi(secondNumber)

  fmt.Println(firstNumber + secondNumber) // addition of two strings

  fmt.Println(firstInt + secondInt) // addition of two ints
}
```

When you run this listing using the same values as before, the output should look like:

```
Enter the first integer: 3
Enter the second integer: 7
37
10
```

As you can see, the converted values are added together and the correct sum is displayed. You can use this same approach in future listings to obtain numeric values from the person running your program.

NUMERIC DATA TYPES

So far, we have touched on data types in Go but have not really dug deeply into the topic. When a variable is declared, its type is determined. We've been using integers and strings in our examples; however, Go offers a lot more than just these two types. Numeric types in Go include integers, floating-point numbers, and complex numbers.

While you can use dynamic typing to assign number types to variables, the type is assigned to the variable itself, rather than to the value in the variable. Once a variable type is defined, it cannot be changed.

> **NOTE** It is worth repeating: once a type is assigned to a variable, that variable's type cannot inherently change.

For example, if you declare a variable `quantity` using the `:=` operator like:

```
quantity := 100
```

Go will assign the type `int` to the `quantity` variable. We can check this using the following statement:

```
fmt.Printf("quantity type: %T\n", quantity)
```

The output will look like this:

```
quantity type: int
```

However, type is not dynamic on its own in Go. Once we assign a type to a variable, that variable's type cannot change. This means that if we later want to store a float value in the `quantity` variable, such as:

```
quantity = 99.5
```

the compiler will truncate the value to 99 and throw an error because it cannot store a float in a variable that was declared to hold an `int`. Listing 3.19 shows an example of trying to store a float in an integer.

LISTING 3.19

Trying to store a float in an integer

```go
package main

import "fmt"

func main() {
    quantity := 100          // assigns int type to variable
    fmt.Printf("quantity type: %T\n", quantity)
    quantity = 99.5          // store float in same variable: error
    fmt.Println(quantity)
}
```

If you build and run the code, it will generate an error. The output will look like this:

```
.\main.go:8:11: constant 99.5 truncated to integer
```

In Listing 3.19, the value of 100 was assigned to the variable quantity, which is dynamically generated as an integer variable since 100 is an integer. When the program tries to assign the floating-point value of 99.5 to quantity, the compiler knows that the types don't match. The program will stop running when it encounters this error and will not continue to the print statement.

Because data types cannot be inherently changed, it is important to understand the various types available in Go. This includes types for integers as well as floating-point values. It also includes understanding which types are architecture independent and which are implementation specific.

Architecture-Independent Integer Types

Go supports a variety of integer types, including both architecture-independent types and implementation-specific types. These types are considered *independent* because they do not depend on the architecture or implementation of the computer running the Go program. Using these data types makes Go programs more portable between different architectures. For instance, we can use int32 on a 32-bit machine or a 64-bit machine. Table 3.1 presents a list of the integer types available in Go.

Table 3.1 Integer data types in Go

Type	Description
uint8	The set of all unsigned 8-bit integers (0 to 255)
uint16	The set of all unsigned 16-bit integers (0 to 65535)
uint32	The set of all unsigned 32-bit integers (0 to 4294967295)
uint64	The set of all unsigned 64-bit integers (0 to 18446744073709551615)
int8	The set of all signed 8-bit integers (−128 to 127)
int16	The set of all signed 16-bit integers (−32768 to 32767)
int32	The set of all signed 32-bit integers (−2147483648 to 2147483647)
int64	The set of all signed 64-bit integers (−9223372036854775808 to 9223372036854775807)
byte	Alias for uint8
rune	Alias for int32

The byte type is equivalent to uint8, while rune is equivalent to int32.

Following number standards, unsigned types accept only positive values, whereas signed types can be positive or negative. The set of allowed values is the same length for both unsigned and signed, but the lower range and the upper range are different. Listing 3.20 shows examples of architecture-independent integers.

LISTING 3.20

Architecture-independent integers

```
package main

import "fmt"

func main() {
    var age int8 = 20              // signed 8-bit integer
    var port int16 = 80            // signed 16-bit integer
    var zipcode int32 = 90000      // signed 32-bit integer
    var phone int64= 7322335624    // signed 64-bit integer
    var phone2 uint64 = 7322335624 // unsigned 64-bit integer
    var score int64 = -1 // signed 64-bit integer w/ negative value
```

continues

continued

```
    // The next var is illegal because unsigned integers can
    // only represent positive integers

    // var score uint64 = -1

    fmt.Println("age int8",age)
    fmt.Println("port int16", port)
    fmt.Println("zipcode int32", zipcode)
    fmt.Println("phone int64", phone)
    fmt.Println("phone2 uint64", phone2)
    fmt.Println("score int64", score)
}
```

This listing simply uses a variety of architecture-independent data types to define example variables for things such as an age, zip code, and a score. The data types selected correspond to what should be large enough to hold values for the type of variable. For example, it is assumed the age will never be more than 127; thus an int8 is used. Similarly, a zip code of five digits would always fit in an int32 data type. The output should look like this:

```
age int8: 20
port int16: 80
zipcode int32: 90000
phone int64: 7322335624
phone2 uint64: 7322335624
score int64: -1
```

Out-of-Range Values

While the ability to choose the size of a data type gives you the advantage of improving the program's performance, the trade-off is that you run the risk of using values that exceed the defined range of the selected type. For example, the range of int8 is −128 to 127. This is ideal for a set of values that fall into that range, but if you try to add a value to an int8 variable that exceeds the range, you will see compilation errors like those that show up when you run Listing 3.21.

LISTING 3.21

Assigning a value out of range

```
package main

import "fmt"
```

```
func main() {
    // architecture-independent integers
    var age int8 = 200 // signed 8-bit integer
    fmt.Println("age int8:",age)
}
```

Running this listing will generate an error because you are trying to assign the value of 200 to a variable of type int8, which can only hold numbers up to 127. The error will look similar to the following:

```
.\main.go:7:6: constant 200 overflows int8
```

For this reason, you should use architecture-independent types only for scenarios where you are certain the values that will be assigned to a variable will not exceed the size of the variable. If you are not sure, you can use a larger type or an implementation-specific type.

Implementation-Specific Integer Types

Go also supports numeric types with implementation-specific sizes, which means that the data type size is dependent on the architecture running the program. Table 3.2 shows the implementation-specific integer types available in Go.

Table 3.2 Implementation-specific integer data types in Go

Type	Description
int	Same size as uint
uint	Either 32 or 64 bits
uintptr	An unsigned integer large enough to store the uninterpreted bits of a pointer value

The three data types in the table are implementation-specific sizes, meaning that the allowed range of values depends on the computer's architecture. For instance, the int type will be a 32-bit integer (with a range of −2147483648 to 2147483647) if the code is running on a 32-bit machine or a 64-bit integer (with a range of −9223372036854775808 to 9223372036854775807) if the code is running on a 64-bit machine.

You can use uint or int instead of specifying the bit size in most cases, unless you know you need to use a specific data size. For example, you may want to use int8 for cases where the numbers are likely to be small in order to improve processing time and reduce memory load.

If you use dynamic typing with the := operator, Go will automatically assign int to the variable if the initial value is an integer, regardless of the size of the number. Listing 3.22 provides examples of the uint and int types.

LISTING 3.22

Implementation-specific integer types

```
package main

import "fmt"

func main() {
    var aaa uint = 20; // unsigned implementation-specific data type
    fmt.Println("aaa uint:", aaa)

    var bbb int = -30; //signed implementation-specific data type
    fmt.Println("bbb int:", bbb)
}
```

In this listing, the variable aaa is declared as an unsigned integer (uint) that is implementation specific. The variable bbb is declared as a signed implementation-specific data type (int). The output from running the listing is:

```
aaa uint: 20
bbb int: -30
```

Float Types

A float type is one that may include a decimal value as part of the number such as 3.14. Float types are all architecture independent, meaning that you must specify the bit size for the value. Table 3.3 lists four floating-point types that can be used in Go programs.

Table 3.3 Float data types in Go

Type	Description
float32	The set of all IEEE-754 32-bit floating-point numbers
float64	The set of all IEEE-754 64-bit floating-point numbers
complex64	The set of all complex numbers with float32 real and imaginary parts
complex128	The set of all complex numbers with float64 real and imaginary parts

You can see that the table includes two types of numbers, float and complex. Floats are signed values that allow digits to the right of the decimal point. Complex numbers contain two parts: a real number and an imaginary number.

NOTE Complex numbers are useful for specific situations but otherwise not widely used. To find out more, see Cloudhadoop's page, Complex Types Numbers Guide With Examples, found at: www.cloudhadoop.com/2018/12/golang-tutorials-complex-types-numbers.html.

Listing 3.23 shows examples of variables defined using some of these architecture-independent types. Like previous listings, a couple of variables are declared with values being assigned. Those values are then printed.

LISTING 3.23

Using float types

```
package main

import "fmt"

func main() {
    var tax float32 = 0.065 // IEEE-754 32-bit floating point number
    var i float64 = 0.000006 // IEEE-754 64-bit float
    var cnumber complex64 = 1 + 4i //a complex number with float 32
    //real and imaginary numbers

    fmt.Println("tax float32:", tax)
    fmt.Println("i float64:", i)
    fmt.Println("cnumber complex64:", cnumber)
}
```

If you build and run this program, you will see the following output:

```
tax float32: 0.065
i float64: 6e-06
cnumber complex64: (1+4i)
```

SUMMARY

After going through this lesson, you should be able to store basic information within your programs both globally and locally using variables. By accessing the memory locations using the address-of operator, you also now know how to get data from the users of your applications by presenting them with a prompt and calling the `fmt.Scan` function. This lesson also covered how to convert a string input to a numeric value so that you can perform mathematical operations.

The lesson wrapped up by presenting a variety of numeric data types that are available for your use. In the next lesson, you'll learn how to use the data types you've created to do various operations within your Go programs.

EXERCISES

The following exercises are provided to allow you to experiment with the tools and concepts presented in this lesson. For each exercise, write a program that meets the specified requirements and verify that the program runs as expected. The exercises are:

Exercise 3.1: Fixing Problems

Exercise 3.2: Creating Variables

Exercise 3.3: Fewer Lines

Exercise 3.4: How It Is Assigned

Exercise 3.5: Conversions

Exercise 3.6: State Your State

Exercise 3.7: Where You Live

Exercise 3.8: Boxy Logic

Exercise 3.9: Assigning Types

NOTE The exercises are for your benefit. The exercises help you apply what you learn in the lessons. You are also encouraged to experiment with the code as you complete the exercises.

Exercise 3.1: Fixing Problems

The code in Listing 3.2 includes an error that will prevent it from running. Fix the errors and test to make sure the code runs as expected. Comments at the top of each block will tell you what the code should do.

Exercise 3.2: Creating Variables

Write a program in Go that includes three different variables:

- Your first name
- Your street address
- The year you were born

Practice using a variety of variable names to see what works and what doesn't. Use `fmt.Println` statements to print each value to the screen.

Exercise 3.3: Fewer Lines

Refactor the program you wrote in Exercise 3.2. It should still include the same three variables:

- Your first name
- Your street address
- The year you were born

In this version, collapse the string variables into a single statement. In this exercise, make sure you use an integer type (`int`) for the year you were born. Again, use `fmt.Println` statements to print each value to the screen.

Exercise 3.4: How It Is Assigned

Refactor the program in Exercise 3.3 to use the := operator in the declaration statement for each variable. Review the various listings throughout this lesson and rewrite them to also use the := operator if it wasn't already being used.

Exercise 3.5: Conversions

Starting with the code block in Listing 3.17, play with the code a bit. Consider the following:

- What happens if the user enters text instead of a number?
- What happens if the user enters a floating-point number instead of an integer? A floating-point number is one with a decimal value such as 3.14159.

Research options for converting string values into floats. Using the results of your research, update the code in Listing 3.17 to allow the user to input floats instead of integers.

Exercise 3.6: State Your State

Create a script that prompts the user for the name of the state where they were born and the name of the state where they live now. Save each value in its own variable and display the input values to the user.

Exercise 3.7: Where You Live

Write a program that collects the user's name and address as a series of discrete strings:

- First name
- Last name
- House number
- Street name
- City
- State abbreviation
- Zip code

Use this input to display the information in a standard address block. The final output should look like

```
Grace Hopper
4872 Main St
City ST 12345
```

Exercise 3.8: Boxy Logic

Write a program that prompts the user for a width, length, and height. Make sure to convert these from strings to integers as you learned in this lesson.

Once you've converted the values, use them to determine the total volume of the box. To calculate the volume, you would use the multiplication operator, which is an asterisk (*). The operation would be width * length * height.

Exercise 3.9: Assigning Types

Create a program that defines and displays at least five number variables that could be used in the same scenario. You may choose any type-appropriate variables you wish for your selected scenario. Here are some sample scenarios:

- A banking application that tracks the amount of money in a savings or investment account

- A payroll application that includes employee salaries and wages, as well as benefits like retirement account deposits and health plans
- A fantasy sports application that tracks users, teams, players, wins, losses, and overall ranking

Experiment with using signed and unsigned types, as well as architecture-independent and implementation-specific integers.

Lesson 4
Performing Operations

The previous lesson covered variables, along with the basic data types. In this lesson, you'll learn how to manipulate values and variables using operations. We'll also review some of the operations that you can use with each data type.

LEARNING OBJECTIVES

By the end of this lesson, you will be able to:

- Use number values in arithmetic and relational operations.
- Work with a variety of math functions.
- Use Boolean types and complex Boolean operations.

The Go programming language supports a variety of operations similar to other programming languages. These include arithmetic operations, relational operations, assignments, and more.

ARITHMETIC OPERATIONS

Go supports most arithmetic operations on all numeric types, including binary and unary operations:

- A binary operator requires two operands.
- A unary operator requires one operand.

Arithmetic operations allow you to do common math calculations such as adding, subtracting, multiplying, and dividing. Table 4.1 presents common arithmetic operators available in Go.

Table 4.1 Common arithmetic operators

Operator	Description
+	Adds two operands
-	Subtracts second operand from the first
*	Multiplies both operands
/	Divides the numerator by the denominator
%	Modulus operator; gives the remainder after an integer division
++	Increment operator; increases the integer value by 1
--	Decrement operator; decreases the integer value by 1

When writing coding statements for arithmetic operations, spaces are optional before and after the operators. In this book, we will generally include spaces before and after the operators to improve readability.

The best way to understand how to use the arithmetic operators is to see them in action. Listing 4.1 shows a variety of arithmetic operations in action.

LISTING 4.1

Using the arithmetic operators

```
package main

import "fmt"

func main() {
    var a, b, c int32 = 20, 10, 8
```

```
        fmt.Println("a =", a)
        fmt.Println("b =", b)
        fmt.Println("c =", c)
        fmt.Println("a + b =", a + b)  // addition (20 + 10 = 30)
        fmt.Println("a - b =", a - b)  // subtraction (20 - 10 = 10)
        fmt.Println("a * b =", a * b)  // multiplication (20 * 10 = 200)
        fmt.Println("a / b = ", a / b) // division (20 / 10 = 2)
        fmt.Println("a % c =", a % c)  // modulus (20 % 8 = 4)

        a++ //increment by 1
        fmt.Println("a++ =", a)  // a + 1 = 20 + 1 = 21

        b-- //decrement by 1
        fmt.Println("b-- =", b)  // b - 1 = 10 - 1 = 9
}
```

This program creates three simple variables of type `int32` called a, b, and c. As part of the declaration, the values of 20, 10, and 8 are assigned to the variables. These values will be used in the operations.

Using `fmt.Println`, the values for each of the variables are displayed on the screen to allow you to see what each contains. The `fmt.Println` function is then used to display the output from a variety of operations. Note that the operation will be executed, and the result will be displayed. The output for this program is

```
a = 20
b = 10
c = 8
a + b = 30
a - b = 10
a * b = 200
a / b = 2
a % c = 4
a++ = 21
b-- = 9
```

NOTE You should note that the increment and decrement operators can only be used on the right side of a variable name, as shown in Listing 4.1 with a++ and b--. Because it happens on the right side, they can be referred to as *postfix operators*. In other programming languages such as C, C++, and C#, you can also use these operators on the left side as *prefix operators*. Go, however, does not support a prefix version of these operators. Trying to use them on the left as a prefix operator will generate an error in Go.

Mixing Number Types

In Listing 4.1, the three variables used for the operations were all the same type. Go does not accept calculations using different data types. This is true even when you try to use different but equivalent types of integers with each other. For example, given the variables

```
a int = 10
b int32 = 20
c byte = 15
```

each of the following statements will throw an error:

```
fmt.Println(a + b)
fmt.Println(b + c)
fmt.Println(a + c)
```

You also cannot use expressions that mix an integer with a float. Given the same variables with a new float variable

```
a int = 10
b int32 = 20
c byte = 15
d float32 = 0.05
```

each of the following statements will throw an error:

```
fmt.Println(a + d)
fmt.Println(b * d)
fmt.Println(c / d)
```

To try this for yourself, create the program presented in Listing 4.2.

LISTING 4.2

Mixing data types in operations

```
package main

import "fmt"

func main() {
    var a int = 10
```

```
    var b int32 = 20
    var c byte = 15
    var d float32 = 0.05

    // fmt.Println(a + b) // int & int32
    // fmt.Println(b + c) // int32 & byte
    // fmt.Println(a + c) // int & byte
    // fmt.Println(a + d) // int & float32
    // fmt.Println(b * d) // int32 & float32
    // fmt.Println(c / d) // byte & float32
}
```

Uncomment each of the print statements one at a time. Save and run the program after each change to see the error messages. Do any of the print statements work?

If you uncomment all the lines and run the listing, you will see errors similar to the following:

```
.\Listing0401.go:11:19: invalid operation: a + b (mismatched types int
and int32)
.\Listing0401.go:12:19: invalid operation: b + c (mismatched types int32 and
byte)
.\Listing0401.go:13:19: invalid operation: a + c (mismatched types int and
byte)
.\Listing0401.go:14:19: invalid operation: a + d (mismatched types int and
float32)
.\Listing0401.go:15:19: invalid operation: b * d (mismatched types int32 and
float32)
.\Listing0401.go:16:19: invalid operation: c / d (mismatched types byte
and float32)
```

Experiment with changing the data types for the variables to see if you can get any (or even all) of the statements to work without changing any of the initial values.

Type Casting Numbers

You might think that one way to avoid getting type mismatch errors is to simply declare all your variables as something large such as float64. While this might sound like a simple solution, it isn't feasible. Floats require more memory than integers do, and as a result, a large program with lots of unnecessary floats will not be very efficient. There is a better solution.

When writing operations that include numbers of different types, we must use type casting to convert the numbers so that they are the same types when the program performs the calculations. This is easily done by simply naming the type you want to use when writing the operation.

For example, if we want to multiply a variable called num1 declared as an int with a variable called num2 declared as a float, the expression will look like the following:

```
result = float32(num1) * num2
```

The use of float32() converts the value in num1 to a float32 value. The converted value is then of the same type as num2, so the operation will succeed. Use the following guidelines when converting types:

- Convert integers to floats to avoid losing values to the right of the decimal point.
- Convert to the larger data type rather than the smaller type to ensure that all values fit in the selected type. For example, if you are using int8 and int16, convert int8 to the larger int16.

It's also a good idea to explicitly name the data type for each operand to be sure they are the same in the operation, even if one or more of the variables are already of that type. For example, we can write the previous statement as:

```
result = float32(num1) * float32(num2)
```

Listing 4.3 is a rewrite of Listing 4.2. In this case, you can see that by using the type casting, each operation works without giving an error.

LISTING 4.3

Converting data types for operations

```go
package main

import "fmt"

func main() {
    var a int = 10
    var b int32 = 20
    var c byte = 15
    var d float32 = 0.05

    fmt.Println( int32(a) + int32(b) )     // int & int32
    fmt.Println( int32(b) + int32(c) )     // int32 & byte
    fmt.Println( int(a) + int(c) )         // int & byte
    fmt.Println( float32(a) + float32(d) ) // int & float32
    fmt.Println( float32(b) * float32(d) ) // int32 & float32
    fmt.Println( float32(c) / float32(d) ) // byte & float32
}
```

Now when you run the listing, you should see the results of each of the operations:

```
30
35
25
10.05
1
300
```

> **NOTE** Unlike some other programming languages, Go has a strong type system. This means that it will not automatically convert types for you, but rather requires you to specify when you want a value's type converted. This requirement to explicitly state when you want a type converted is known as *explicit type conversion*. *Implicit type conversion*, also known as *coercion*, is when the compiler will automatically convert a type, which again, Go does not support. By forcing explicit type conversion, the chance of errors is reduced.

PEMDAS

Consider the following math operation:

```
3 + 2 * 5
```

The answer to this problem will be different depending on whether you do the multiplication or the addition first. If you add first, the result will be 25. If you multiply first, the result will be 13. As such, it is important to know the correct order to perform the operations.

Go, like many other mathematical systems, follows the rule of PEMDAS when evaluating statements that include more than one operation. PEMDAS refers to the order in which each operation is evaluated:

1. **Parentheses:** Any operations inside parentheses are evaluated first; if there are nested parentheses, Go starts with the innermost set of parentheses and works its way out.

2. **Exponents:** Exponents are calculated after any operations in parentheses and before any other operations.

3. **M**ultiplication and **D**ivision come next.

4. **A**ddition and **S**ubtraction are evaluated last.

If there are multiple operations of the same type, the compiler will evaluate them in left-to-right order after evaluating operations with a higher precedence.

Let's look at a couple of examples of PEMDAS in action. First, let's look at a plus b times c:

```
a + b * c
```

If we do not include parentheses, Go evaluates this expression in the order:

1. b times c

2. a plus the result of b times c

Based on this order of operation, we can calculate the result of $3 + 2 * 5$. Because multiplication happens before addition, 2 is multiplied by 5 to get 10. The value of 10 is then added to 3 to get the result of 13.

If we want Go to perform the addition first, that operation must be inside parentheses:

```
(a + b) * c
```

Another example is the remainder of a divided by b multiplied by c:

```
a % b * c
```

If we do not include parentheses at all, Go evaluates this expression from left to right: modulus is a type of division, and division has the same rank as multiplication:

1. The remainder of a divided by b

2. The result multiplied by c

If we want the program to perform the multiplication first, we must put that operation in parentheses:

```
a % (b * c)
```

The program will then perform the calculations in the following order:

1. Multiply b and c

2. Find the remainder of a divided by the result of the multiplication

Let's see how this works in a program. Listing 4.4 presents several operations.

LISTING 4.4

Showing PEMDAS in action

```go
package main

import "fmt"

func main() {
    var a, b, c int = 10, 20, 30
    fmt.Println("a =", a, "\nb =", b, "\nc =", c)

    var d, e, f, g int // create empty variables for results

    d = a - b * c
    fmt.Println("a - b * c =", d)

    e = (a - b) * c
    fmt.Println("a - (b * c) =", e)

    f = a % b * c
    fmt.Println("a % b * c =", f)

    g = a % (b * c)
    fmt.Println("a % (b * c) =", g)
}
```

This listing creates three integers to be used in the operations. The values are printed so you can see what they are. The listing then creates four additional integers that will be used to hold the results of the arithmetic operations. Each operation is performed before the output of the operation is displayed. You should review each of the operations in the listing using the PEMDAS order of operations to see if you get the same results. The final output will be:

```
a = 10
b = 20
c = 30
a - b * c = -590
a - (b * c) = -300
a % b * c = 300
a % (b * c) = 10
```

As a general rule, it is a good idea to include parentheses in longer mathematical statements even when they are not necessary. This will help you as a developer describe the math you want the program to perform, as well as make it easier for other people on your team to see what you intended the statement to do. Suppose you have a statement like:

```
a % b * c
```

Because modulus and multiplication have the same precedence, the compiler will evaluate the modulus operation first. However, to be clear that you know this will happen (and to help fellow developers), it would be better to write the statement as:

```
(a % b) * c
```

ASSIGNMENT OPERATIONS

You've seen the simple assignments in many of the listings presented up to this point. Go also supports several assignment operators, which are listed in Table 4.2.

Table 4.2 Basic Go assignment operators

Operator	Description
=	Simple assignment operator; assigns values from right operand or expression to left operand
+=	Addition assignment operator; adds right operand to left operand and assigns result to left operand
-=	Subtraction assignment operator; subtracts right operand from left operand and assigns result to left operand
*=	Multiplication assignment operator; multiplies right operand by left operand and assigns result to left operand
/=	Division assignment operator; divides left operand by right operand and assigns result to left operand
%=	Modulus assignment operator; finds the modulus of left operand and right operand and assigns result to left operand

Addition and Subtraction Assignment Operations

While the simple assignment operator assigns a value to the variable on the left of the equal sign, the other assignment operators do a bit more. Each of the other assignment operators perform a mathematical operation using the value in the variable on the left of the equal sign along with the operation that is to the right of the equal sign. For example, the addition assignment operator (+=) adds the value of the operation to the right of the equal sign to the variable on the left and then places the result into the variable on the left. For example:

```
x += 3
```

This statement would take the value of x, add 3 to it, and then place the result back into x. If x was 5 before this operation, then x would be equal to 8 after it is executed.

Listing 4.5 shows examples for using the addition and subtraction assignment operators. As you look at this code, notice how the values in a and b are changed.

LISTING 4.5

Using the addition and subtraction assignment operators

```
package main

import "fmt"

func main() {
    var a, b, c int = 100, 70, 50
    fmt.Println("a =", a, "\nb =", b, "\nc =", c)

    a += b   // a + b = 70 + 100 = 170 (a = 170)
    fmt.Println("a += b =", a)

    b -= c   // b - c = 90 - 50 = 20 (b = 20)
    fmt.Println("b -= c =", b)

    fmt.Println("\nc =", c)
}
```

Reviewing the code in the listing, you can see that a, b, and c are again assigned values to be used in mathematical operations. After being declared and initialized, the values stored in the variables are printed. This is then followed by the addition assignment operator being used to add the value of b to the variable a. You can see from the following Println statement that a is indeed changed from 100 to 170—an increase equal to the value stored in b.

The value stored in b is then updated using the subtraction assignment operator. The value in b is changed by subtracting the value of c from it. The result is that b decreases from 70 to 20, as can be seen when b is printed.

Finally, the listing prints the value of c. You can see from the output that c remains the same, as it should since nothing new was assigned to it. The full output is:

```
a = 100
b = 70
c = 50
a += b = 170
b -= c = 20
c = 50
```

Multiplication, Division, and Modulus Assignment Operations

Multiplication, division, and modulus assignment operations with the assignment operators work in the same way as the addition and subtraction operators. Listing 4.6 shows these operators in action.

LISTING 4.6

Using the multiplication, division, and modulus assignment operators

```
package main

import "fmt"

func main() {
    var a, b, c, d int = 100, 50, 25, 4
    fmt.Println("a =", a, "\nb =", b, "\nc =", c, "\nd = ", d)

    a *= b    // a * b = 100 * 50 = 5000 (a = 5000)
    fmt.Println("a *= b =", a)

    b /= c    // b / c = 50 / 25 = 2 (b = 2)
    fmt.Println("b /= c =", b)

    c %= d    // c % d = 25 % 4 = 1 (c = 1)
    fmt.Println("c %= d =", c)

    fmt.Println("d =", d)
}
```

This listing operates similarly to the previous listing, except that multiplication, division, and then the modulus operators are used. When you run this listing, you should see the following output:

```
a = 100
b = 50
c = 25
d = 4
a *= b = 5000
b /= c = 2
c %= d = 1
d = 4
```

WORKING WITH BOOLEANS

There is another type available in Go that we have not yet covered, but it is extremely important. This is a Boolean. A Boolean variable can hold a value of either true or false. Go supports Boolean types using the true and false constants, as shown in Listing 4.7.

LISTING 4.7

Using a Boolean type variable

```
package main

import "fmt"

func main() {
    var myBool bool = true
    fmt.Println("myBool =", myBool)

    var anotherBool bool = false
    fmt.Println("anotherBool =", anotherBool)
}
```

This listing is very straightforward. It starts by declaring a new variable called myBool as a type bool. This new variable is initialized to the value of true. Note that true (along with false) are keyword constants in Go that have been predefined for your use. When you run this listing, the value of myBool is printed, which will show equal to true:

```
myBool = true
```

A second Boolean variable named `anotherBool` is also declared, but this time it is initialized to `false`. You can see that when it is printed, it also shows its `false` value:

```
anotherBool = false
```

The full output you see when running the listing is

```
myBool = true
anotherBool = false
```

RELATIONAL OPERATIONS

Boolean variables are often used with the relational operators. Relational operators are generally used to compare values. Table 4.3 shows the binary relational operators that Go supports for numeric types.

Table 4.3 Go relational operators

Operator	Description
==	Checks if the values of two operands are equal or not; if yes, the operation returns `true`
!=	Checks if the values of two operands are equal or not; if the values are not equal, then the operation returns `true`
>	Checks if the value of left operand is greater than the value of right operand; if so, the operation returns `true`
<	Checks if the value of left operand is less than the value of right operand; if so, the operation returns `true`
>=	Checks if the value of left operand is greater than or equal to the value of right operand; if so, the operation returns `true`
<=	Checks if the value of left operand is less than or equal to the value of right operand; if so, the operation returns `true`

The result of a relational operator is either true or false. The code in Listing 4.8 shows the different relational operations applied to a variety of numeric types.

LISTING 4.8

Using relational operators

```go
package main

import "fmt"

func main() {
    var a, b int8 = 100, 70 // int8 cannot be larger than 128

    fmt.Println("a =", a)
    fmt.Println("b = ", b)
    fmt.Println("a == b:", a == b) //checks for equality
    fmt.Println("a != b:", a != b) //checks for inequality
    fmt.Println("a > b:", a > b)
    fmt.Println("a < b:", a < b)
    fmt.Println("a >= b:", a >= b)
}
```

This declares two variables, a and b, which will be used for the relational operations. After displaying the values of a and b, the first Println displays the result of using the equality operator (==). If a and b are equal, then this would print true. In this case, 100 does not equal 70, so false is printed.

The next statement uses the != operator. In this case, if a and b are not equal, then true will be printed. If they are equal, then the result is false. Because 100 does not equal 70, true is returned.

The next three statements check to determine if a is larger than b, if a is less than b, and then if a is greater than or equal to b. The resulting true or false is then displayed for each operation. The full output from running the listing is

```
a = 100
b = 70
a == b: false
a != b: true
a > b: true
a < b: false
a >= b: true
```

After running this the first time, change the values of a and b and run the listing again. Try giving a and b the same values and then compare the output when you run the listing.

Assigning Values to Boolean Variables

The reason we covered Booleans earlier in this section is because they work so well with relational operations. In fact, because the result of a relational operation is true or false, it can be assigned to a Boolean variable, as shown in Listing 4.9.

LISTING 4.9

Assigning to a Boolean variable

```
package main

import "fmt"

func main() {
    var n, m int = 2, 10
    a := n < m // assign the result of n < m to a
    fmt.Println("a =", a)
}
```

In this listing, the value of n is compared to m. If n is less than m, then the operation is true, and the value of true is placed in the Boolean variable a. If the value of n is not less than m, then false is placed in the variable a. You can see in this case, the value of n is 2, which is less than the value of m, which is 10, so true is assigned to a. When a is printed, we see that indeed it is true as confirmed by the output:

```
a = true
```

Using Mismatched Types in Relational Operations

As with arithmetic operations, you cannot compare variables of different types in a relational operation. Listing 4.10 illustrates this.

LISTING 4.10

Type mismatch in a relational operation

```
package main

import "fmt"
```

```
func main() {
    var a int8 = 100 // architect-specific type
    var b int = 70 // implementation-specific type

    fmt.Println("a =", a)
    fmt.Println("b =", b)
    fmt.Println("a == b:", a == b) //checks for equality
    fmt.Println("a != b:", a != b) //checks for inequality
}
```

When you try to compile and run this program, you get the following errors indicating that there is a type mismatch:

```
.\main.go:12:16: invalid operation: a == b (mismatched types int8 and int)
.\main.go:15:16: invalid operation: a != b (mismatched types int8 and int)
```

We can compare mismatched types in relational operations the same way we are able to use them in arithmetic operations—we can cast the variables to be the same types. Listing 4.11 updates Listing 4.10 to type cast the values so that they are the same. When you run this listing, you will see that it works as expected, without changing the initial types of the variables.

LISTING 4.11

Type casting in relational operations

```
package main

import "fmt"

func main() {
    // do not change the variable declarations
    var a int8 = 100 // architect-specific type
    var b int = 70 // implementation-specific type

    fmt.Println("a =", a)
    fmt.Println("b =", b)
    fmt.Println("a == b:", int(a) == b) //checks for equality
    fmt.Println("a != b:", int(a) != b) //checks for inequality
}
```

As you can see, this time we type cast a to be an `int` value to match the type of b. When you run the listing, the output is no longer an error:

```
a = 100
b = 70
a == b: false
a != b: true
```

> **NOTE** Type casting works in relational statements just as it does in arithmetic operations.

BOOLEAN OPERATIONS

Go supports operations on Boolean types, including AND, OR, and NOT, using the Boolean operators shown in Table 4.4.

Table 4.4 Go Boolean operators

Operator	Description
&&	AND: A binary statement where both values must be true for the operation to evaluate as true. Otherwise, the operation evaluates as false.
||	OR: A binary statement where either or both values must be true for the operation to evaluate as true. The operation evaluates as false only if both values are false.
!	NOT: A unary statement that returns the opposite of the original value.

The Boolean AND and OR operators are used on two values and return a value of true or false:

```
a && b
a || b
```

When using the Boolean AND (&&) operator, if both values being compared are true, then the overall result is true. When using the OR (||) operator, if *either* value is true, then the result is true.

The Boolean NOT (!) operator is used on just one value. This operator returns the opposite of original value.

The result of using any of the Boolean operators is a value of true or false. Listing 4.12 provides an example of each of the Boolean operators in action.

LISTING 4.12

Using the Boolean operators

```go
package main

import "fmt"

func main() {
    var a bool = true
    fmt.Println("a =", a)
    var b bool = false
    fmt.Println("b =", b)

    fmt.Println("a && b =", a && b) // AND operator
    fmt.Println("a || b =", a || b) // OR operator
    fmt.Println("!a =", !a) // NOT operator
}
```

The last three statements in the listing are important. You can see that in the first the AND operator (&&) is used with the variables a and b. In this case, a is true and b is false. Therefore, because both are not true, the result of the operation will be false. When using the OR (||) operator, however, the result will be true, because at least one of the variables contains true. In the last statement, the NOT (!) operator is used. Because a is set to true, the operation returns the opposite, which is false. The full output from the listing is:

```
a = true
b = false
a && b = false
a || b = true
!a = false
```

> **NOTE** You will learn the true value of the Boolean operators in the next lesson, "Controlling Program Flow with Conditional Statements." At that time, you'll be able to use the relational operators along with the Boolean operators to control what your program does. For example, you could do something special for those who are older than 16 with a credit rating score better than 599:

```
if (age > 16 && rating > 599 ) {
    // do something...
}
```

MATH FUNCTIONS

Go includes a math package for standard mathematical functions such as rounding, power, and square root. Some of the common functions included in the math package are shown in Table 4.5.

Table 4.5 Common Go math functions

Function	Use
Abs	Returns the absolute value of a given number
Ceil	Rounds a decimal value up to the next integer
Floor	Rounds a decimal value down to the next integer
Exp	Returns the exponential representation of a number
Sqrt	Returns the square root of a number
Trunc	Returns the integer of a decimal value
Round	Returns the closest integer of a decimal value
Round(a, b)	Rounds a decimal value a to b decimal place(s)
Pow(a, b)	Returns a to the power of b

By simply importing the math package into your Go application, you can get these functions without the need to write any additional code. Listing 4.13 shows an example of various functions of the math package.

LISTING 4.13

Using the math package

```
package main

import (
    "fmt"
    "math"
)
```

```go
func main() {
    var a, b, c float64 = -30.5, 45.6, 4
    fmt.Println("a =", a, "\nb =", b, "\nc =", c)

    fmt.Println("math.Abs(a) =", math.Abs(a))      // \|30.5\|
    fmt.Println("math.Ceil(b) =", math.Ceil(b))    // 46
    fmt.Println("math.Floor(b) =", math.Floor(b))  //45
    fmt.Println("math.Exp(a) =", math.Exp(a))      // exponential of 46.6
    fmt.Println("math.Sqrt(c) =", math.Sqrt(c))    // 2
    fmt.Println("math.Trunc(a) =", math.Trunc(a))  // -30
    fmt.Println("math.Round(a) =", math.Round(a))  // -31
    fmt.Println("math.Pow(b,c) =", math.Pow(b,c))  // b to the power of c
}
```

This code starts by importing the fmt and math packages. We could have used two separate import statements instead, like this:

```go
import "fmt"
import "math"
```

Instead, a collapsed import statement was used. As you include more packages in larger programs, this collapsed version of importing makes your code easier to read.

Within the main function, a few variables are declared, initialized, and then printed. This is followed by using several calls to the Println function to display the results obtained by using a variety of math functions. You can see that to use the math functions, you include the function name after the math package name with a dot separating the two. Thus, in the first call, the Abs function is called using math.Abs(a). In this case, the absolute value of a will be returned to Println to be printed. The full output of this program is:

```
a = -30.5
b = 45.6
c = 4
math.Abs(a) = 30.5
math.Ceil(b) = 46
math.Floor(b) = 45
math.Exp(a) = 5.675685232632723e-14
math.Sqrt(c) = 2
math.Trunc(a) = -30
math.Round(a) = -31
math.Pow(b,c) = 4.3237380096e+06
```

You can find a full list of the math package functions on Go's math package page at `https://pkg.go.dev/math`.

BITWISE OPERATIONS

Within Go, you can also do bitwise operations. These are operations that operate at the bit level. A bit is the smallest unit of storage that is generally considered on (true) or off (false). The bitwise operators that are supported by Go are listed in Table 4.6.

Table 4.6 Go bitwise operators

Operator	Description
&	Binary AND operator; copies a bit to the result if it exists in both operands
|	Binary OR operator; copies a bit if it exists in either operand
^	Binary XOR operator; copies the bit if it is set in one operand but not both
<<	Binary left shift operator; the left operand's value is moved left by the number of bits specified by the right operand
>>	Binary right shift operator; the left operand's value is moved right by the number of bits specified by the right operand

NOTE Use of bitwise operators is considered a more advanced topic, so if you are unfamiliar with bits, then the important thing to know at this time is that these operators are available should the time come that you need them. It is beyond the scope of this book to go into the details of bit manipulation.

The bitwise operators are used like many of the other operators. Listing 4.14 shows samples of using the bitwise operators.

LISTING 4.14

Using the bitwise operators

```
package main

import "fmt"
```

```
func main() {
    var a, b int16 = 10, 200
    fmt.Println("a =",a)
    fmt.Println("b =",b)

    fmt.Println("a & b:", a & b)    // binary AND
    fmt.Println("a | b:", a | b)    // binary OR
    fmt.Println("a ^ b:", a ^ b)    // binary XOR
    fmt.Println("a << b:", a << b) // binary left shift
    fmt.Println("a >> b:", a >> b) // binary right shift
}
```

The output looks like:

```
a = 10
b = 200
a & b: 8
a | b: 202
a ^ b: 194
a << b: 0
a >> b: 0
```

RANDOM NUMBERS

It is often useful to be able to generate random numbers to use in a program. We can use the math/rand package to create a variety of random numbers. Listing 4.15 creates three random numbers: an integer and two floats of different sizes.

LISTING 4.15

Creating random numbers

```
package main

import (
    "fmt"
    "math/rand"
)

func main() {
    fmt.Println(rand.Float32())
    fmt.Println(rand.Float64())
    fmt.Println(rand.Int())
}
```

The functions for obtaining random numbers are available within the math/rand package, so this will need to be imported at the beginning of the listing. Once imported, you can call the functions within rand that generate the random numbers. This includes Float32(), Float64(), and Int(), which each generate a random number of the corresponding type. The output should look something like this:

```
0.6046603
0.9405090880450124
6129484611666145821
```

Note that random float values will always be between 0 and 1, while a random integer will be any integer over 0, unless specified otherwise.

Run Listing 4.15 again. When you do, you should notice that Go will generate the same set of values, which seems counterintuitive for a supposedly random number. However, while you may want a random number in a program, it is very useful if the program always generates the same "random" number. We'll look at how to generate more randomized values later in this lesson.

Limiting the Possible Value

In the previous example, we used the Int function to generate any integer, and the actual values can be quite large. If we want to handle a smaller range of possible values, we can use Intn, as shown in Listing 4.16, to define a specific upper limit.

LISTING 4.16

Using Intn to limit integer value

```
package main

import (
    "fmt"
    "math/rand"
)

func main() {
    fmt.Print(rand.Intn(100))
}
```

In this example, we limit the highest possible value to 99 (1 less than 100). This is done by passing 100 to the Intn() function when we call it. When you build and run this program, you should see an integer displayed that is 100 or less, or more specifically from 0 to 99.

Does the output change if you run the program multiple times? Try changing the upper limit to higher and lower values to see the effect on the output.

Seeding the Random Number Generator

By default, Go uses the value 1 as the seed for any random integer. A seed is the starting point of the random number generator. While each rand function will generate a different random number using the same seed, any given instruction will always generate the same number for each "random" value.

When we want a program to generate numbers at random, we must create custom seeds for the random number generator. Changing the seed means that we will get different numbers.

To create a seed for this purpose, we can use the rand.NewSource function with an int64 number (see Listing 4.17). If we simply assign a number to NewSource, we will get the same output each time the program runs, just as we did with the default seed value of 1. To change the seed each time we run the program, we can use the current time in Unix nano format, which uses an int64 value to represent the current system time.

LISTING 4.17

Using a seed when generating random numbers

```
package main

import (
    "fmt"
    "math/rand"
    "time"
)

func main() {
  ns := rand.NewSource(time.Now().UnixNano())
  generator := rand.New(ns)

    fmt.Println(generator.Intn(100))
    fmt.Println(generator.Intn(100))
}
```

There are a few new things happening in this listing. First, we included the time package, which contains the routine we will need to grab the current time to be used as the seed for our random number generation. We will get the time using the `Now()` function, which is part of the time package.

`Now()` reads the current system time from the computer running the program, and we use `UnixNano()` to format the time value as an `int64`. Because the time changes constantly, we effectively generate a new seed each time the program runs, thereby generating values that appear more random.

We use `rand.NewSource` to generate a new seed value that the program will use to generate the random values. We only need to generate the new seed once in the program, regardless of the number of random numbers the program will generate.

Create the program provided in Listing 4.17 and run it to see the output values. You should see two integers displayed that are from 0 to 99. If you run the program multiple times, you should see different outputs as a result of using the time to seed the random number generator.

This listing passes 100 to `Intn` to limit the possible results. You can change 100 to another number. You can use the time to generate a seed for when you are wanting random floating-point numbers as well.

After verifying that the program works as expected, play with the code.

NOTE For more information about random values in Go, see Flavio Copes's article, "Generating random numbers and strings in Go," found at https://flaviocopes.com/go-random.

SUMMARY

The key focus of this lesson was on the operators available to you in Go. You learned about the arithmetic, assignment, relational, and other operators. You also got to see a number of math functions that have been provided in the math packages. At the end of the lesson, you covered what it takes to create and use random numbers.

In the next lesson, you will continue to build on what you've learned. You will learn how to control the flow of your programs.

EXERCISES

The following exercises are provided to allow you to experiment with the tools and concepts presented in this lesson. For each exercise, write a program that meets the specified requirements and verify that the program runs as expected. The exercises are:

Exercise 4.1: Resulting in 0

Exercise 4.2: Truncating

Exercise 4.3: Current Value of Deposit

Exercise 4.4: Simple Interest

Exercise 4.5: True and False

Exercise 4.6: Functioning Math

Exercise 4.7: Five Times the Basic Math

Exercise 4.8: Using Relational Operators

Exercise 4.9: Random Limits

> **NOTE** The exercises are for your benefit. The exercises help you apply what you learn in the lessons. You are also encouraged to experiment with the code as you complete the exercises.

Exercise 4.1: Resulting in 0

Update the code block in Listing 4.18 so that the output is 0, without changing the order of the numbers or operators in the output statement.

LISTING 4.18

Exercise 1

```
// The program should output 0
package main

import "fmt"
```

continues

continued

```
func main() {
  // do not change the order in which the numbers and operators appear
  fmt.Println(5 + 3 % 2 * 9)
}
```

Exercise 4.2: Truncating

Create a computer program that prompts the user for a float number and returns the integer portion of the floating number.

Exercise 4.3: Current Value of Deposit

Write a computer program that calculates and displays the current value of a deposit for a given initial deposit, interest rate, number of times interest is calculated per year, and number of years since the initial deposit.

The program should prompt the user for each of the values and use the following formula to calculate the current value of the deposit:

```
V = P(1 + r/n)^nt
```

where:

- V – value
- P – initial deposit
- r – interest rate as a decimal (e.g., 0.05)
- n – the number of times per year interest is calculated
- t – the number of years since the initial deposit

The program should display each of the values entered to the user in a meaningful way (so that the user can easily see what each value represents), along with the results of the calculation.

Exercise 4.4: Simple Interest

Write a computer program that prompts the user for a principal amount, the rate of interest, and the number of days for a loan and then calculates and returns the simple interest for the life of the loan. Use the formula

```
interest = principal * rate * days / 365
```

Exercise 4.5: True and False

Create a computer program that displays three statements that evaluate to True and three statements that evaluate to False. For example:

```
a = 0
b = 1
```

Example output:

```
a < b = True
```

Exercise 4.6: Functioning Math

Create a computer program that prompts the user for a number and calculates the following:

- The Boolean of the number entered
- The binary equivalent of the number entered
- The square root of the number entered

The program should display the following to the user:

- The number the user entered, in a phrase like, "You selected *value*."
- The Boolean of the number, in a phrase like, "The Boolean of your number is *value*."
- The binary equivalent of the number, in a phrase like, "The binary equivalent of your number is *value*."
- The square root of the number, in a phrase like, "The square root of your number is *value*," with the value rounded to three decimal places.

Exercise 4.7: Five Times the Basic Math

Create a computer program that completes the following tasks:

- It prompts the user for a series of five integers.
  - The user must be prompted for five numbers.
- After the fifth entry, the program stops prompting for values and performs the following calculations:
  - The product of the integers
  - The average of the integers
  - The sum of the integers

- After performing the calculations, the program should display the following to the user:
  - The values the user entered
  - Each of the calculations, using a phrase that identifies the value

Exercise 4.8: Using Relational Operators

Identify places where you would want to compare values to each other and write relational statements that output either true or false based on those comparisons. For example, in a bank scenario, it would be important to know if a customer's balance goes below a predefined value, and in a fantasy sports scenario, you need to be able to compare player statistics to other players.

After updating the code, run it to verify that the relational operations work without error and as expected.

Exercise 4.9: Random Limits

Create a program that prompts the user for an integer. Generate and display a random number that is between 0 and the number entered by the user. As a hint, you can store the number entered by the user into a variable that can be passed to the rand.Intn() function.

Make sure you seed your random number generator so that a new number is generated each time, even if the same number is entered by the user.

Lesson 5

Controlling Program Flow with Conditional Statements

Without specific instructions, a program executes
statements linearly, one after the other, until the program
ends or until an error causes the program to fail. In most cases
a solution will need to include places where the program can
change direction, either to react to a defined condition at a
specific place in the program or to repeat a set of instructions until
a desired goal is met.

   In this lesson, we will focus on the use of conditional statements
to control the flow of a program based on specific conditions

during runtime. In the next lesson, the focus will be on how to use loops to repeat a set of instructions.

LEARNING OBJECTIVES

By the end of this lesson, you will be able to:

- Use conditional statements to change the flow of your program.
- Switch the flow of your program based on the value of a variable.
- Nest conditions within other conditions.

CONDITIONAL STATEMENTS

In every programming language, it is important to be able to execute an appropriate block of code depending on some condition. That is the purpose of conditional statements. Go supports a variety of conditional statements, including the following:

- `if` statements
- `if-else` statements
- Nested `if` statements
- `switch` statements
- `select` statements

In this lesson, we will cover the first four of these. You will see how each can be used to change the flow of your Go programs. The `select` statement works similarly to the `switch` statement, but is generally used with communications, so we won't cover it in this lesson.

USING AN *IF* STATEMENT

An `if` statement creates a basic conditional statement that executes a block of code if a condition is `true`, using the syntax

```
if condition {
    statement
}
```

In this model, `condition` is a statement that can evaluate to either `true` or `false`. If the condition evaluates as `true`, Go will execute the statement that follows. If the condition evaluates as `false`, Go will skip that statement and go on to the next set of instructions.

In some cases, we want to test if the condition is `false` rather than only testing for `true`. For this reason, we often explicitly state the outcome of the condition. For example, we can use the statement:

```
if condition == true
```

if we explicitly want to test for `true`, or if we want to test for `false`, we can use:

```
if condition == false
```

We frequently use flowcharts to create a visual representation of the steps a program will follow when there is an `if` statement, using a diamond to represent the condition, as shown in Figure 5.1. The diamond normally has one input, a question that evaluates to Yes (`true`) or No (`false`), with one output for each possibility.

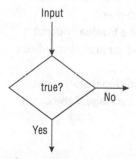

Figure 5.1: Visual representation of an `if` statement

> **NOTE** You do not have to use flowcharts if you don't want to, but they can be very useful to help you step through a program, both before you start to write the code and to troubleshoot programs that produce unexpected results.

The code in Listing 5.1 shows an example of an `if` statement. In this case, we create a variable named `age`, test to see if `age` is greater than 16, and output a statement if it is.

LISTING 5.1

Using an `if` statement

```
package main

import "fmt"

func main() {
    var age int8 = 12;

    if (age > 16){
        fmt.Println("This person can open a bank account.")
    }
}
```

If age is greater than 16, the program will execute the code in the brackets after the `if` statement, which will print that the person can open a bank account. In this case, however, we have assigned the value of 12 to age. Because 12 is less than 16, the program skips what is between the brackets, which includes skipping the print statement.

The key point to remember is that conditional operators produce a Boolean output that is either true or false. This makes them very useful when setting up programs whose output depends on one or more conditions that exist at runtime.

In Listing 5.2, we create another short program with a single conditional statement. In this listing, we are using an `if` statement to print an appropriate message if the conditional statement is false.

LISTING 5.2

Using an `if` statement to check for a false condition

```
package main

import "fmt"

func main() {
    var accountBalance int = 0

    if ( (accountBalance > 0) == false ){
        fmt.Println("This person's bank account has no money.")
```

```
        }
        fmt.Println("Balance verification is complete.")
}
```

This example is evaluating a condition, which is to see if the accountBalance is greater than 0. The result of this condition is then checked to see if it is false. If it is false, then we know the account balance is 0 or less and so the if statement's body will be executed. If the account balance is greater than 0, then the body of the if statement is skipped and the program continues with the first line after the if statement, which prints the message that the balance verification is complete.

Because accountBalance is set to 0, the output when running this listing is:

```
This person's bank account has no money.
Balance verification is complete.
```

If you change accountBalance to a number greater than 0, the output is:

```
Balance verification is complete.
```

There are a few additional things to note about this listing. First is that the condition for an if statement can be as complex as you want as long as the end result evaluates to either true or false. Additionally, the condition in Listing 5.2 is more complicated than it needs to be. It could have simply been:

```
if condition {
```

or in this case:

```
if (accountBalance <= 0) {
```

Often there is more than one way to code a solution. In the end, it is best to focus on writing code that is the clearest for others to understand.

NOTE Criteria statements can be nested in the same way you can nest arithmetic operations, so a single statement can include multiple operators. Using parentheses, as was done in Listing 5.2, can help keep the order of evaluation clearer. The parentheses, however, are considered unnecessary when doing simple operations like the examples in this lesson. The use of go fmt will likely remove the parentheses as well.

WORKING WITH MULTIPLE CONDITIONS

When we want to compare two Boolean expressions in the same statement, we can use the following operators:

- && (AND): This produces a value of true only if both conditional statements are true; otherwise, the result is false.

- || (OR): This produces a value of true if either (or both) of the conditional statements is true. The result is false only if both conditional statements are false.

Listing 5.3 shows an example of an if statement that combines multiple conditions. In this case, we start with a username and password and then we test to see if the combination of username/password is correct.

LISTING 5.3

Using multiple conditions

```
package main

import "fmt"

func main() {
   var username string = "chris";
   var password string = "dsxscg34"

   if (username == "mary" && password == "dsxscg34"){
      fmt.Println("This person has the right credentials.")
   }

   if(username != "mary" || password != "dsxscg34"){
      fmt.Println("This person does not have the right credentials.")
   }
}
```

If you review this listing, you'll see that two variables are created and given values. These are for a username and password. They are each assigned a value. The program then presents two different if statements to validate the credentials:

- An AND statement (&&) is used to authenticate if both values are correct. The username must equal "mary" and password must equal "dsxscg34" in order for the body of the if statement to be executed.

- An OR statement (||) is used to deny authentication if either value is incorrect. In the second if statement, if either the username does not equal "mary" or the password does not equal "dsxscg34", then the body of the if statement will be executed.

Note that at most only one of the if statements can be true, so only one output is possible. However, Go will read and execute both statements. When you run the listing, you'll see that the first if statement evaluates to false and the body is skipped. The second if statement evaluates to true:

```
This person does not have the right credentials.
```

For fun, you should modify the listing so that the first if statement evaluates to true. There are at least two ways you can modify the code to make that happen.

> **NOTE** Obviously, Listing 5.3 is a sample program for learning and you would never hard-code a password into a computer program.

USING AN *IF-ELSE* STATEMENT

When we use a simple if statement, we evaluate a single condition and produce an outcome based on the state of that condition. While we can include a series of if statements (and even build complex conditions by comparing individual if conditions), this approach has the disadvantage that Go will evaluate each statement as it goes through the code, even if only one of the statements can logically be true.

Another approach is to use an if–else statement instead of two (or more) individual if statements. The advantage of if–else is that the else part of the statement will be evaluated only if the if condition is not met. If the initial condition is met, Go will skip the remaining code in the block, which can help speed up the runtime of the code. However, a standard if–else block supports only two outcomes: one for situations where the condition is true and the other for where the condition is false.

The basic syntax for an if–else statement is:

```
if (condition) {
    // output if true
} else {
    // output if initial condition is false
}
```

Note in particular that the else block starts immediately after the closing curly bracket (}) for the if block. You cannot put this on a separate line in Go. Listing 5.4 shows an example of an if–else statement that again works with a username and password.

LISTING 5.4

Using an if-else statement

```
package main

import "fmt"

func main() {

    var username string = "chris";
    var password string = "dsxscg34"

    if (username == "john"  && password == "dsxscg34"){
        fmt.Println("This person has the right credentials.")
    } else {
        // the else must follow the closing bracket of the if statement
        // and NOT appear on a new line
        fmt.Println("This person does not have the right credentials.")
    }
}
```

In this listing, you are again comparing a username and password to values. If the username is equal to "john" AND the password is equal to "dsxscg34", then the if statement evaluates to true and the text displays saying the person has the right credentials. In this case, the program then jumps to the first statement after the entire if–else statement. If, however, the username and password don't both equal "john" and "dsxscg34", respectively, then the statement in the else block displays, which in this case is the message that the person does not have the right credentials. When you run this listing, you can see the credentials don't match, so the else statement is executed:

```
This person does not have the right credentials.
```

You can change the values to get the if statement to evaluate to true. Again, there is more than one way to change the code to accomplish this.

> **NOTE** Unlike some other programming languages, in Go the `else` keyword must follow the closing bracket of the `if` statement and not appear on a new line.

CREATING NESTED *IF* STATEMENTS

While `if` and `if-else` are good ways to produce a specific outcome based on current conditions in a program, they are most useful for situations whose outcome is either black or white (`true` or `false`), and it is harder to include gray areas in the conditions.

In reality, though, we often need a computer program to choose between a variety of outcomes rather than just one or two. For example, we might have a program that gives us a specific statement based on a person's age, but we want to include options for age ranges—what (school) grade they should be in, for example, or to apply age-dependent discounts in a museum—or something that Go can display as an error message if the user enters a value that cannot represent an age (like a name or a date). The `else if` operator allows us to nest a series of conditions in a conditional block and produce one of several different options.

The basic syntax is:

```
if (condition_1){
    instruction_1
} else if (condition_2) {
    instruction_2
} else {
    instruction_3
}
```

If *condition_1* is true, Go executes the code at *instruction_1* and skips the rest of the code in the structure. If *condition_1* is false, then the `else` statement after *condition_1* is evaluated, which contains *condition_2*. If *condition_2* is true, then *instruction_2* is executed, and again the rest of the `if-else` structure is skipped.

Go continues to evaluate each `else if` statement individually until it finds a condition that is true. It then executes the instructions for that `else if` statement and skips the rest of the code in the structure. If none of the conditions is true, Go executes the instructions in the `else` block.

As with else, the else if block starts immediately after the closing curly bracket (}) for the if block (or for the previous else if block). You cannot put this on a separate line in Go.

A nested if statement must start with one if block at the end, and it has the option to end with an else block (for any situation where none of the conditions is true). It may contain as many else if blocks as needed to express all appropriate conditions. Listing 5.5 shows an example of a nested if statement.

LISTING 5.5
Nested if statement

```go
package main

import "fmt"

func main() {
    var color string = "Blue"

    if (color == "Blue" ){
        fmt.Println("Blue like the sky")
    } else if (color == "Red") {
        fmt.Println("Red like the sun")
    } else if (color == "Green"){
        fmt.Println("Green like the trees")
    } else {
        fmt.Println("Please choose a valid color.")
    }
}
```

In this listing, a string called color is set to the value of "Blue". The if and else if statements then check the value of color to see if it matches different colors.

The biggest advantage to a nested if-else statement over a series of individual if statements is that Go will read and execute only the instructions for the block whose condition is true, and it will skip any remaining else if or else blocks once it finds a true condition. In Listing 5.5, Go will stop after the Println instruction for Blue and skip over the rest of the conditional statements to reach the end of the program.

If you change the value of color to equal "Red", then the if statement will execute to check if the color is "Blue". Since it is not, the else if will execute and check to see if color is "Red". It is, so the block of code will be executed that prints the message "Red like the sun," and the rest of the else if and else statements will be skipped.

It is worth noting that there is a second way that if statements can be nested; however, the previous method is considered more readable. Listing 5.6 rewrites Listing 5.5 using if–else statements within the body of an if statement. You can see this code is not as nicely aligned as Listing 5.5.

LISTING 5.6

Embedded if statements

```
package main

import "fmt"

func main() {
    var color string = "Blue"

    if (color == "Blue" ){
        fmt.Println("Blue like the sky")
    } else {
        if (color == "Red") {
            fmt.Println("Red like the sun")
        } else {
            if (color == "Green"){
                fmt.Println("Green like the trees")
            } else {
                fmt.Println("Please choose a valid color.")
            }
        }
    }
}
```

One of the nice things about Go is that you can often do things in more than one way. Listing 5.6 does the exact same thing as Listing 5.5 and produces the same output. As you can see, however, there is a bit more indenting. There are also more curly brackets used. If this code was more complex, it would also likely appear harder to read. While both formats work for nesting if–else statements, Listing 5.5 is generally considered more readable.

USING A *SWITCH* STATEMENT

We often need to compare a variable against a set of predefined values. For instance, we can ask a customer for a color in a T-shirt printing shop and check the request against all the available colors. In this case, we can use nested else if statements, but Go also supports the use of switch statements.

A switch statement is another control flow statement that allows us to create a set of comparisons against a finite set of possible options. A switch statement uses much simpler code than nested if statements do. In Go, a switch statement has the following syntax:

```
switch(value){
    case condition_1:
        instruction_1
    case condition_2:
        instruction_2
    case condition_n:
        instruction_n
    default:
        instruction_last
}
```

In this syntax, you start with a value (often in the form of a variable) and compare that value to a series of other values. Go moves through each case statement until it finds a match to the initial value. It then performs the associated instruction set and skips the remaining statements in the switch.

The default statement defines the instruction set that Go should perform if the initial value does not match any of the case values. It is technically optional, but if there is a possibility that there are no matches for the initial value, you should include it as the default endpoint for the switch statement. Listing 5.7 shows a switch statement in action.

LISTING 5.7

Using a switch statement

```
package main

import "fmt"

func main() {
    var color string = "csgsf"

    switch(color){
    case "Blue":
        fmt.Println("Blue like the sky")
```

```
        case "Red":
            fmt.Println("Red like the sun")
        case "Green":
            fmt.Println("Green like the trees")
        default:
            fmt.Println("Please choose a valid color.")
    }
}
```

What this program does should look familiar. It provides the same functionality as the series of nested if statements you saw in the previous listing, but it uses more concise code in the process. In this example, the listing will take the value in color and compare it to what is listed with each case statement. When it finds the match, it will print the result. Because color was initially assigned "csgsf", it doesn't match any of the case statement values, so the default is printed:

```
Please choose a valid color.
```

If you change the value of color to "Blue", you'd see that the case for "Blue" prints:

```
Blue like the sky
```

Once a case or the default is executed, the program exits the switch statement and continues with the first line that follows.

The case statements within a switch do not have to be just a comparison against a simple value. While you can compare simple values as was done in the previous listing, you can do more with case statements. This includes

- Executing more than one case with fallthrough
- Using multiple expressions in one case
- Using a condition in a case

Each of these is worth a closer look.

Executing More than One Case with *fallthrough*

There might be times when you want your program to flow from your current case into the next case. The fallthrough keyword is intended especially for this. If the fallthrough keyword is included as the last line of a case, then the code in the following case will also be executed. Listing 5.8 shows a countdown that is accomplished by using a switch statement.

LISTING 5.8

Using fallthrough

```go
package main

import "fmt"

func main() {
    var number int = 4

    switch (number) {
        case 10 :
            fmt.Println("...", number, "...")
            number -= 1
            fallthrough
        case 9 :
            fmt.Println("...", number , "...")
            number -= 1
            fallthrough
        case 8 :
            fmt.Println("...", number, "...")
            number -= 1
            fallthrough
        case 7 :
            fmt.Println("...", number, "...")
            number -= 1
            fallthrough
        case 6 :
            fmt.Println("...", number, "...")
            number -= 1
            fallthrough
        case 5 :
            fmt.Println("...", number, "...")
            number -= 1
            fallthrough
        case 4 :
            fmt.Println("...", number, "...")
            number -= 1
            fallthrough
        case 3 :
            fmt.Println("...", number, "...")
            number -= 1
            fallthrough
```

```
        case 2 :
            fmt.Println("...", number, "...")
            number -= 1
            fallthrough
        case 1 :
            fmt.Println("...", number, "...")
            number -= 1
            fallthrough
        case 0 :
            fmt.Println("*** BOOM ***")
        default:
            fmt.Println("Try a number from 1 to 10!")
    }
}
```

In this listing, we start with an integer we called number. We pass this number to our switch statement, where we display the number between dots and then decrement it by 1. We then fall through to the next case, which effectively does the same thing. We keep falling through until we reach the case for 0, where we display "*** BOOM ***" instead. Our number is 4 initially, so our output is:

```
... 4 ...
... 3 ...
... 2 ...
... 1 ...
*** BOOM ***
```

You can see that if you change the value of number to something between 1 and 10, you will get the countdown. If you enter 0, there is no countdown, just a boom! Any other number will send you to the default case.

You should note that if you use the fallthrough keyword, it must be the last statement in your case. You will get an error if you try to place it elsewhere.

> **NOTE** While Listing 5.8 is fun and illustrates a countdown to an explosion, the case statements repeat a lot of the same code. In the next lesson, you'll learn how to use loops, which makes doing a program like Listing 5.8 a lot easier and with fewer lines of code. There are instances, however, where you will find that the fallthrough keyword is a perfect solution.

> **NOTE** `switch` statements operate differently in Go than in languages such as C++, C#, and Java. In these other languages you must explicitly include a break statement at the end of each case in a `switch` statement. Otherwise, the cases fall through by default.

Using Multiple Expressions in One Case

More than one value can be used in a `case` statement. For example, Listing 5.9 continues with the color theme; however, this time we are using a `switch` statement to take the same action for primary colors, but a different action for a variety of other colors. To use multiple expressions in one case, each expression is separated by a comma.

LISTING 5.9

Using multiple expressions in a case

```
package main

import "fmt"

func main() {
   var color string = "Yellow"

   switch(color){
   case "Red", "Blue", "Yellow":
      fmt.Println(color, "is a primary color")
   case "Orange", "Green", "Violet":
      fmt.Println(color, "is a secondary color")
   default:
      fmt.Println(color, "is not a primary or secondary color.")
   }
}
```

In this listing, you can see that there are three values for each of the case statements. If the value being passed to `switch(color)` matches any of the colors in the case, then the code for that case will be executed. In this example, "Yellow" matches the first case, so the following is printed:

```
Yellow is a primary color
```

It is worth noting that the formatting can be adjusted in Listing 5.9. Sometimes it is more readable to include the case values on separate lines, as shown in Listing 5.10. This listing operates exactly like the previous one but may be a little easier to read for many programmers.

LISTING 5.10

Presenting case values on separate lines

```
package main

import "fmt"

func main() {
    var color string = "Yellow"

    switch(color){
    case "Red",
        "Blue",
        "Yellow":
        fmt.Println(color, "is a primary color")
    case "Orange",
        "Green",
        "Violet":
        fmt.Println(color, "is a secondary color")
    default:
        fmt.Println(color, "is not a primary or secondary color.")
    }
}
```

Using Conditions in Switch Cases

The case statements can also be more complex than just a value. Specifically, they can contain expressions. Consider the switch statement in Listing 5.11 that is used to determine grades.

LISTING 5.11

Using conditions in a switch to determine grades

```
package main

import "fmt"
```

continues

continued

```go
func main() {
    var score int = 88
    var grade string

    switch {
    case score > 90 :
        grade = "A"
    case ( score > 80 ) && ( score <= 90 ) :
        grade = "B"
    case ( score > 70 ) && ( score <= 80 ) :
        grade = "C"
    case ( score > 60 ) && ( score <= 70 ) :
        grade = "D"
    case  score <= 80 :
        grade = "F"
    default:
        grade = "unknown"
    }

    fmt.Println("Your grade is: ", grade )
}
```

This listing takes a score such as what a student would get on a test and converts it to a letter grade ranging from "A" to "F". In this case, the score of 88 is converted to a grade of "B". The output is:

```
Your grade is: B
```

If you look closely at this listing, you should notice that the switch statement does not include a value being passed:

```
switch {
```

Rather than passing a value to the switch, conditionals are being used in the cases. Because no value is received, each case statement will be evaluated to determine if it is true or false. If true, then the code in the case will execute.

> **NOTE** If more than one case evaluates to true, only the first will be executed. Once the case completes, the program flow will exit the switch statement.

SUMMARY

In this lesson, you've learned about controlling program flow using a variety of conditional statements. You not only learned about the forms of the `if`, `if-else`, and `else if` statements, but also how to use the `switch` statement to control program flow in a variety of ways.

In the next lesson, you will learn more about controlling program flow. Rather than redirecting based on conditions, you will learn how to repeat (loop) blocks of code.

EXERCISES

The following exercises are provided to allow you to experiment with the tools and concepts presented in this lesson. For each exercise, write a program that meets the specified requirements and verify that the program runs as expected. The exercises are

Exercise 5.1: Are You Rich?

Exercise 5.2: Cat vs. Dog

Exercise 5.3: Quiz

Exercise 5.4: Seasons

Exercise 5.5: Switching the Seasons

Exercise 5.6: Quiz Generator

Exercise 5.7: Coffee Shop

> **NOTE** The exercises are for your benefit. The exercises help you apply what you learn in the lessons. You are also encouraged to experiment with the code as you complete the exercises.

Exercise 5.1: Are You Rich?

Write a program that asks the user how much money they have in their wallet. The program should output "You're rich!" if the user inputs $20 or more and "You're broke!" if the input is less than $20.

Exercise 5.2: Cat vs. Dog

Write a program that performs the following steps:

- Ask the user if they have any cats. (Yes/No answer)

- Ask the user if they have any dogs. (Yes/No answer)

- If the user responses indicate that they have both cats and dogs, output "You must really love pets!"

- Otherwise, the output should be "Maybe you need more pets."

Write two different versions of this program, one that uses only if statements and another that uses if-else statements.

Exercise 5.3: Quiz

Create a computer program that asks the user a few questions to which the user will respond either True or False. Display all the questions with the correct answer and the user's answers at the end of the program. Also display a score for the user that shows their correct response rate (number of questions answered correctly/number of questions).

Exercise 5.4: Seasons

Write a program that uses nested if statements to produce five different possible outcomes based on a single user input.

- Ask the user what season it is (fall, winter, spring, or summer).

- If the user enters fall, output "I bet the leaves are pretty there!"

- If the user enters winter, output "I hope you're ready for snow!"

- If the user enters spring, output "I can smell the flowers!"

- If the user enters summer, output "Make sure your AC is working!"

- If the user enters a value that does not correspond to a season, output "I don't recognize that season."

The user should be able to enter the name of the season in any case and the program will still work.

Challenge: After you have the program working as described above, modify the program so that the user can enter either "fall" or "autumn" and get the same result.

Exercise 5.5: Switching the Seasons

Refactor the last activity to use a `switch` statement instead of nested `if`s.

Exercise 5.6: Quiz Generator

Expand the quiz you created in Exercise 5.3 to create a program that mimics a more robust quiz generator.

- The program will ask the user a series of questions and accept the user's answers as input.
- The program must provide feedback to the user for each question, including:
  - Whether the answer was correct or not
  - How many questions the user has answered to that point
  - The overall accuracy of the user's answers to that point
- The program must stop asking the user for answers after all questions have been answered or the user provides three consecutive incorrect answers.

  - If the user has answered all questions, end the program and display the overall stats (number of questions, correct/incorrect, and percentage correct), along with an appropriate congratulatory message for answering all questions.
  - If the user gives three consecutive incorrect answers, end the program and display the overall stats, with an appropriate feedback message to let them know why the program ended early.

Exercise 5.7: Coffee Shop

This exercise asks you to practice skills covered in all the lessons up to this point. You may find it useful to plan out the program using a flowchart or pseudocode before you start building the program itself. Write the program in the code editor or IDE of your choice and run the program to make sure there are no errors.

Write a program that will calculate the cost of a custom cup of coffee at a gourmet coffee shop, based on the size of the cup, the type of coffee selected, and flavors that can be added to the coffee. It should complete the following steps:

1. Ask the user what size cup they want, choosing between small, medium, and large.
2. Ask the user what kind of coffee they want, choosing between brewed, espresso, and cold brew.

3. Ask the user what flavoring they want, if any. Choices include hazelnut, vanilla, and caramel.

4. Calculate the price of the cup using the following values:

   - Size:
     - Small: $2
     - Medium: $3
     - Large: $4
   - Type:
     - Brewed: no additional cost
     - Espresso: 50 ¢
     - Cold brew: $1
   - Flavoring:
     - None: no additional cost
     - All other options: 50 ¢

5. Display a statement that summarizes what the user ordered.

6. Display the total cost of the cup of coffee as well as the cost with a 15% tip, in phrases that explain the values to the user. Round the cost with tip to two decimal places.

   - For example, if the user asks for a medium-sized espresso with hazelnut flavoring, the total should be $4; the total with a tip should be $4.60.

The following is an example of what the user might see when they run this program:

```
Do you want small, medium, or large? small
Do you want brewed, espresso, or cold press? espresso
Do you want a flavored syrup? (Yes or No) yes
Do you want hazelnut, vanilla, or caramel? vanilla
You asked for a small cup of espresso coffee with vanilla syrup.
Your cup of coffee costs 3.0
The price with a tip is 3.45
```

The following are some tips as you look at this exercise:

- Build the program one condition at a time, checking that each condition works as expected before adding the next condition.

- Include the user's options in the prompt so the user knows what the acceptable answers to each question are.

- Test all possible answers to make sure they work and produce the expected outcome.

- Use meaningful variable names to clearly identify the values in the program.

- The user should be able to enter text values using any letter case without causing errors.

- All output should be clear and meaningful to the user.

Lesson 6
Controlling Program Flow with Loops

As you learned in the previous lesson, without specific instructions, a program executes statements linearly until the program ends or until an error causes the program to fail. You also saw how to change the flow of your programs based on conditions.

In this lesson, you will learn how to repeat a line of code or set of instructions. We will look at the use of looping to control the flow of a program during runtime as well as cover a few related items for adjusting the flow of a program from within a loop.

LEARNING OBJECTIVES

By the end of this lesson, you will be able to:

- Learn how to repeat sections of code.
- Explore the for keyword.

- Understand how to stop or exit a loop.
- Discover how to loop through a string.
- Explore the concept of a never-ending infinite loop.

LOOPING STATEMENTS

In every programming language, it is important to be able to repeat statements without having to write the statements over and over. For example, Listing 6.1 uses only what you've learned so far to print the values 1 to 10 using a single variable.

LISTING 6.1

Counting to 10 linearly

```
package main

import "fmt"

func main() {
    var ctr int = 1
    fmt.Println(ctr)
    ctr += 1
    fmt.Println(ctr)
    ctr += 1
    fmt.Println(ctr)
    ctr += 1
    fmt.Println(ctr)
    ctr += 1
    fmt.Println(ctr)
    ctr += 1
    fmt.Println(ctr)
    ctr += 1
    fmt.Println(ctr)
    ctr += 1
    fmt.Println(ctr)
    ctr += 1
    fmt.Println(ctr)
    ctr += 1
    fmt.Println(ctr)
}
```

When you run this listing, you create a variable called `ctr` and assign it a starting value of 1. You then print the value. After printing, you add 1 to `ctr` and print its value again. You then add 1 to `ctr` and print it again. You continue to repeat this process until you've printed the numbers up to 10 as shown:

```
1
2
3
4
5
6
7
8
9
10
```

As you can see by looking at the listing, it is rather long and contains a lot of redundant code. If you were to change the listing to print to 100 instead of just 10, the code would grow to be roughly 10 times longer. Additionally, you'd have to keep track of how many times you add and print to determine when you get to 100.

There is, of course, a better way. That is the purpose of *looping statements*. In general, you will use the `for` statement to accomplish looping in your programs.

FOR LOOPS

In any programming or scripting language, it is important to be able to repeat a block of code several times based on some condition. This is done using repetition statements. Go supports only one repetition statement, which is the `for` loop.

The basic structure of a `for` loop is to use the `for` keyword followed by an initialization expression, a condition expression, and a post-argument expression:

Initialization Expression This is the starting point of your loop. It is executed once at the beginning of the loop.

Condition Expression This condition is tested every time the loop iterates. If the condition evaluates to false, then the loop will stop. If the condition evaluates to true, the loop will continue iterating.

Post Expression The post-expression is an expression that gets executed at the end of every iteration. It can contain an increment expression, which when executed can trigger the condition expression to evaluate to false and terminate the loop.

These are then followed by a block of code that will be repeated with the looping:

```
for initialization; condition; post_expression {
    // Instruction set
}
```

Listing 6.2 shows the basic structure of a for loop. This listing does the same task as the previous listing, but with the use of a loop.

LISTING 6.2

A basic for loop

```
package main

import "fmt"

func main() {
    for ctr := 1; ctr <= 10; ctr++ {
        fmt.Println(ctr)
    }
}
```

When you run this listing, we see that it indeed prints the same output as the previous listing, the numbers 1 to 10; however, it accomplishes this task with substantially fewer lines of code. If you change the value of 10 in the listing to 100, you see that the loop is repeated 100 times. Unlike Listing 6.1, we don't need additional lines of code to count to a higher number.

Let's look more closely at the code to see how it is accomplishing the looping and counting. In Listing 6.2, the for statement takes three arguments:

- In the first argument (the *initialization* argument), we initialize the ctr variable to 0. We use dynamic typing so that Go treats it as a number.

- In the second argument (the *condition*), we compare ctr to a fixed value, in this case, 10. If this statement is true, Go will execute the instruction set in the for loop.

- In the third argument (the *post_expression*), we increment the ctr by 1.

The *initialization* argument is only executed when the for loop initially starts. After the *initialization*, Go will check the *condition*. If at that time the *condition* is true, then the loop will begin, and the code in the body of the for statement will be executed. If the *condition* is not true at this time, then the body of the for statement will not be executed.

Assuming the *condition* was true, then after executing the body, Go will execute the *post_expression*. The *condition* is then checked again to see if it is still true. The looping will then continue executing the statement in the body of the for statement until the *condition* statement is no longer true. In the case of Listing 6.2, it will continue until ctr is no longer less than or equal to 10.

Because for loops are so important, it is worth showing a second example. Listing 6.3 is another basic for loop following the same structure as the previous listing. This time the code uses a loop and an if statement to print only even numbers.

LISTING 6.3

A basic for loop that prints even numbers

```
package main

// we import the strconv package which allows us to parse data
// between different data types
import (
    "fmt"
    "strconv"
)

func main() {
    for a := 0; a < 10; a++ {
        if (a % 2 == 0){
            // the Itoa function converts the int into its
            // equivalent string (UTF-8) value
            fmt.Println(strconv.Itoa(a) + " is an even number")
        }
    }
}
```

When you execute this listing, you see the following printed:

```
0 is an even number
2 is an even number
4 is an even number
6 is an even number
8 is an even number
```

Let's look more closely at the code. As noted in the comments, you use the strconv package here. This will allow you to compare a number variable to another number and then include the number value in a string statement. Specifically, you use the Itoa function, which converts an int into its corresponding UTF-8 code.

In this example, the for statement also takes three arguments:

- In the first argument, you initialize the variable (called a) to 0 again using dynamic typing so that Go treats it as a number.

- In the second argument, you compare the variable called a to the fixed value of 10. You check to see if a is less than 10. As long as this expression is true, Go will execute the instruction set in the for loop.

- In the third argument, you increment the variable a by 1.

You then use an if statement to determine if the variable's value is even. If so, Go will execute the instructions in the if block. If not, Go ends the if statement and returns to the for statement. Go stops looping through the for statement when the conditional statement a < 10 is no longer true.

Optional Items in a *for* Loop

Both the initialization and post-argument expression are optional in a for loop. Either or both can be left off, as shown in Listing 6.4.

LISTING 6.4

Dropping the initialization and post-argument expression

```
package main

import (
    "fmt"
    "strconv"
)

func main() {
    var a int = 0

    for ; a < 10; {
        if (a % 2 == 0){
            fmt.Println(strconv.Itoa(a) + " is an even number")
        }

        a++ // we have to increment manually in this case
    }
}
```

The output from this listing matches that of the previous listing. The code in this listing is also very similar to the code in the previous listing, with the following differences:

- You initialize the variable called a as an int with the value 0 at the start of the program, rather than doing this in the for block.

- You increment the variable's value after completing the if block and before restarting the for block, rather than incrementing it before entering the if block.

- Note the use of the semicolon after the for keyword. This informs Go that the *initialization* statement is not included (because we initialized the variable earlier in the program).

Go's *while* Is *for*

In most other programming languages, there is a while loop that can be used that takes a condition and repeats the loop until the condition is true. Go does not use the while keyword; however, we can perform the same type of loop using for.

As you saw in the previous listing, the only argument a for statement must include is the conditional statement. You had to include a semicolon in the previous example only because you put a semicolon after the conditional statement. However, you can create something akin to a while statement by removing the semicolons completely, as shown in Listing 6.5.

LISTING 6.5

Go's equivalent of a while loop

```
package main

import (
    "fmt"
    "strconv"
)

func main() {
    var a int = 0

    for a < 10 {   // remove the semicolons here
        if (a % 2 == 0){
```

continues

continued

```
        fmt.Println(strconv.Itoa(a) + " is an even number")
        }

    a++
    }
}
```

This listing operates exactly like the previous listing. This includes displaying the same output:

```
0 is an even number
2 is an even number
4 is an even number
6 is an even number
8 is an even number
```

Let's look at another example using for to create a while loop. The code in Listing 6.6 calculates the powers of 2 for numbers between 1 and 10.

LISTING 6.6

Powers of 2

```
package main

import (
    "fmt"
    "strconv"
)

func main() {
    var power2 int64 = 1
    var a int64 = 1
    for a < 10 {
        fmt.Println("2 to the power of " + strconv.FormatInt(a,10) +
                    " is equal to " + strconv.FormatInt(power2,10))
        power2 += power2
        a++
    }
}
```

When you execute this listing, the following output is displayed:

```
2 to the power of 1 is equal to 1
2 to the power of 2 is equal to 2
2 to the power of 3 is equal to 4
2 to the power of 4 is equal to 8
2 to the power of 5 is equal to 16
2 to the power of 6 is equal to 32
2 to the power of 7 is equal to 64
2 to the power of 8 is equal to 128
2 to the power of 9 is equal to 256
```

Of note here is that we again use the `for` keyword and include only a comparison statement. The variables are initialized before the `for` loop and incremented at the end of the `for` loop. In this case, we use `int64` instead of `int` for the variables. This means we must use the `FormatInt` function to convert the number to a string for the output statements:

```
strconv.FormatInt(power2,10)
```

The `FormatInt` function takes the value you want to convert to an integer and the base of that number. Since you are working with standard numbers, the base is base 10. You specify that the number is base 10 in the second parameter.

NOTE When using `for` loops, it's easy to get carried away and overflow the variable. Update the code in Listing 6.6 to use a `< 100` instead of a `< 10`. Run the program to see what happens.

Infinite Loops

A potential problem that can happen when looping is the creation of an infinite loop: a `for` statement whose conditional statement can never be true. Take a look at Listing 6.7. Can you identify the problem in the code?

LISTING 6.7

Code with a problem

```
package main

import (
```

continues

continued

```go
        "fmt"
        "strconv"
)

func main() {
    var power2 int64 = 1
    var a int64 = 1

    for {
        fmt.Println("2 to the power of " + strconv.FormatInt(a,10) +
                    " is equal to " + strconv.FormatInt(power2,10))

        power2 += power2
        a++
    }
}
```

Create the program in Listing 6.7 and run it to see what happens. You will find that it does, indeed, run without a compiler error. In fact, it will run, and run, and run....

> **NOTE** You can stop an executing program using Ctrl+C.

If you hadn't noticed, there is no condition in the code to stop the loop, so the `for` loop will continue running. It is imperative that if you don't want the loop to be infinite, you include a condition that will end the loop.

LOOPING THROUGH A STRING

There are a multitude of uses for loops. One use is to loop through a string and remembering that a string is really a set of individual characters. The example in Listing 6.8 shows the most basic way to iterate through a string one byte/character at a time.

LISTING 6.8

Looping through a string one character at a time

```go
package main

import "fmt"

func main() {
```

```
    var message string = "HELLO WORLD"

    fmt.Println(message)

    for idx := 0; idx < len(message); idx ++ {
        fmt.Println(string(message[idx]))
    }
}
```

In this example, you treat the message as a collection of characters, using the length of the collection as the stopping point for the loop. The start of the string (the first character) is in position 0, and the last character of the string is in the position that is 1 less than the length of the string.

You get the length of the string by using the `len` method. In this case, `len(message)` will return the length of your message string, which is 11. The space also counts as a character.

To get to each letter, you use the offset (which is an index value) within square brackets after the name of the string:

```
message[idx]
```

In this case, `message[0]` would be the first character, which is H. The second character (E) would be in `message[1]`. Using the `for` statement, the listing loops through the index values to retrieve and display each of the individual letters. The result is the printing of the characters in the `message` variable. Because we are using `Println` to print, each character is displayed on its own line:

```
H
E
L
L
O

W
O
R
L
D
```

NOTE In Lesson 9, "Accessing Arrays," we present this topic in more detail as we cover arrays and indexing.

THE *RANGE* FUNCTION

You can also leverage the range keyword to create indexes on a string so that you can iterate through it. Listing 6.9 gives a brief example of using range. We'll cover this keyword in more detail in Lesson 9, when arrays are presented.

In Listing 6.9, we convert the message into a range and then iterate through the message, where we print each index value and each character in the range.

LISTING 6.9

Using range

```
package main

import "fmt"

func main() {
    var message string = "HELLO WORLD"
    fmt.Println(message)

    for idx, c := range message {
        fmt.Println(idx) //index
        fmt.Println(string(c)) //value
    }
}
```

In this listing, you again create a string variable called message and assign it the text "HELLO WORLD". You print the value of message so that it can be seen.

You then use the range version of a for loop:

```
for idx, c := range message {
```

The first expression in the for loop is an index value that will be used in looping. The second expression is assigning a value to a variable (in this case called c). What is being assigned is the value within message at the location of the index (idx). In this case, it will be the character at that index location within the string.

There are two Println statements in the loop. The first one prints out the index value (idx). This will be the counter for the loop. The second line prints the value that is at the offset at that location. Because Println will treat a character as a numeric value, you use the `string` function to convert the character to a string before printing. When you run this listing, you will see each index value printed followed by the character:

```
HELLO WORLD
0
H
1
E
2
L
3
L
4
0
5

6
W
7
0
8
R
9
L
10
D
```

Note that if you comment out the first `Println`, then the output will match the previous listing.

LOOP CONTROL STATEMENTS

Go supports three different statements that allow you to deviate the flow of execution within a loop. For instance, you might want to search for a word in a list of words. Once you find the first occurrence, you do not want to continue iterating through the list. Rather, you might simply want to stop the loop and display that the word was found. There is no need to continue the loop and the search once the word has been found. The three options Go provides are:

- `break` statements
- `continue` statements
- `goto` statements

Let's look at an example of each.

The *break* Statement

Go provides the break keyword to end a loop. Once a break statement is encountered, program flow goes to the first statement after the loop. In the example in Listing 6.10, you will use the powers of 2 program again.

LISTING 6.10

Using break

```
package main

import (
    "fmt"
    "strconv"
)

func main() {
    var power2 int64  = 1
    var  a int64 = 1

    for {
        if (a >= 10){
            break // exit the loop when we reach 10
        }

        fmt.Println("2 to the power of " + strconv.FormatInt(a,10) +
                    " is equal to "+ strconv.FormatInt(power2,10))

        power2 += power2
        a++
    }
}
```

In this version, you use a break statement to stop the for loop when the value of a reaches 10. Other than the if statement that checks to see if a is greater than 10, this listing is just like Listing 6.6. The output is as follows:

```
2 to the power of 1 is equal to 1
2 to the power of 2 is equal to 2
2 to the power of 3 is equal to 4
2 to the power of 4 is equal to 8
2 to the power of 5 is equal to 16
```

```
2 to the power of 6 is equal to 32
2 to the power of 7 is equal to 64
2 to the power of 8 is equal to 128
2 to the power of 9 is equal to 256
```

The *continue* Statement

The continue keyword is used to immediately return control back to the beginning of a
loop. This doesn't restart the loop from the beginning, but rather starts the next iteration
of the loop. Listing 6.11 prints odd numbers between 0 and 10 by using continue to tell
Go to skip even numbers.

LISTING 6.11

Using continue to print odd numbers

```go
package main

import (
    "fmt"
    "strconv"
)

func main() {
    for ctr := 0; ctr < 10; ctr ++{

        if (ctr % 2 == 0){
            continue // continue to next iteration; i.e., ignore even values
        }

        fmt.Println(strconv.Itoa(ctr) + " is an odd number")

    }
}
```

Looking at the code, you can see that a simple for loop is used. ctr is set to 0 at the
beginning of the loop and incremented with each iteration until ctr is no longer less than
10. Within the body of the for statement, the value of ctr is checked to see if it is even. If
dividing ctr by 2 returns a value of 0, then you know it is even, so the continue statement

is called to immediately start the next iteration of the loop. When the `if` statement fails, then the rest of the statements in the body of the `for` loop are executed, which in this case is just the print statement to print the number. The final output is as follows:

```
1 is an odd number
3 is an odd number
5 is an odd number
7 is an odd number
9 is an odd number
```

The *goto* Statement

Another loop control statement supported by Go is goto. The goto keyword sends the program flow to a different location identified by a label. This jump is done without any conditions. While a goto statement can be used anywhere, Listing 6.12 presents an example within an `if` statement.

LISTING 6.12

Using goto

```go
package main

import (
    "fmt"
    "strconv"
  )

func main() {
   var a int = 20
   var b int = 30
   fmt.Println("a = " + strconv.Itoa(a))
   fmt.Println("b = " + strconv.Itoa(b))

   if (a > b){
      goto MESSAGE1 //this will jump the execution to where MESSAGE1 is defined
   } else {
      goto MESSAGE2
   }
```

```
MESSAGE1: // We define a label that we can use in a goto statement
    fmt.Println("a is greater than b")

MESSAGE2:
    fmt.Println("b is greater than a")
}
```

In this example, you use two goto statements. Each statement references a different labeled code block. You then use if-else to define which code block should run, depending on whether the initial condition is true or false. In this case, when the program runs, a is not greater than b, so the else statement executes, which uses a goto statement to send the program flow to MESSAGE2 where a message is printed:

```
b is greater than a
```

Although goto statements can be useful, they should generally be avoided. If they are not used properly, they can cause issues with the flow of the program, and because the executed code is separate from the loop itself, troubleshooting is more complicated.

> **NOTE** If you change the code in Listing 6.12 so that it checks for a < b instead of a > b, then the goto statement will go to MESSAGE1 instead of MESSAGE2. In this case, you will see that both messages will be printed, which might not be what you would expect. Such possibly unexpected results are a reason the goto statement is generally avoided by programmers.

SUMMARY

We've now covered the primary program control keywords in Go. In the previous lesson, you learned how to control flow based on conditions. In this lesson, you expanded your knowledge to understand how to repeat lines of code via looping using for statements.

You also went further by learning additional keywords that allow for controlling loops, which include the continue and break commands. You also learned about the goto keyword that lets you jump to a new location unconditionally. Of course, goto should be used with caution as it can lead to hard-to-find errors in code.

EXERCISES

The following exercises are provided to allow you to experiment with the tools and concepts presented in this lesson. For each exercise, write a program that meets the specified requirements and verify that the program runs as expected. The exercises are:

Exercise 6.1: The Alphabet

Exercise 6.2: Sum It Up

Exercise 6.3: Fifty

Exercise 6.4: Numeric Breakout

Exercise 6.5: Reverse It

Exercise 6.6: Length Without len

Exercise 6.7: Guessing Game

Exercise 6.8: URL Shortener

Exercise 6.9: Validating Phone Numbers

Exercise 6.10: Validating Email Addresses

Exercise 6.11: Fizz Buzz

NOTE The exercises are for your benefit. The exercises help you apply what you learn in the lessons. You are also encouraged to experiment with the code as you complete the exercises.

You should notice that this lesson has more exercises than previous lessons. It is important to understand the Go keywords you've learned so far along with those that control program flow using conditions and loops. Using what you've learned so far, you can do quite a bit. These exercises not only help demonstrate and confirm your learning, but also show you some of the things you can already do with what you've learned in six lessons. Of course, there is still a lot to learn.

Exercise 6.1: The Alphabet

Using for loops and string functions, create a computer program that displays the alphabet from A to Z.

Exercise 6.2: Sum It Up

Create a program that computes the sum of all numbers between 0 and 100.

Exercise 6.3: Fifty

Write two programs, each of which displays all numbers divisible by 50 between 100 and 1,000 (inclusive). Both programs should have identical output.

- Use the range keyword with for in one program.
- Use for without range in the other program.

Exercise 6.4: Numeric Breakout

Create a program that prompts the user for an integer and then displays the following information about that number:

- The number of digits in the value entered
- The first and last digits of the number
- The sum of the digits in the number
- The product of the digits in the number
- Whether or not the number is prime
- The factorial of the number

Exercise 6.5: Reverse It

Write a program that asks the user for an input integer and then computes the reverse of that number. For example:

- Input: 12456
- Output: 65421

Exercise 6.6: Length Without *len*

Write a program that computes the length of a string without using the len function.

Exercise 6.7: Guessing Game

Write a program that generates a random integer between 0 and 10 and asks the user to guess what the number is.

- If the user's guess is higher than the random number, the program should display "Too high, try again."

- If the user's guess is lower than the random number, the program should display "Too low, try again."

- If the user's number is the same as the random number, the program should display "That's right. You guessed the number!"

The program should use a loop that repeats until the user correctly guesses the random number.

Exercise 6.8: URL Shortener

Create a program that mimics a URL shortener. The program will take a URL as input from the user, and it will return a short version of the URL. For example, if the user inputs the URL

```
www.thisisalongurl.com/somedirectory/somepage
```

The program will generate a short URL, like this:

```
http://surl.com/se04
```

The requirements for this program are the following:

- Use your own imaginary domain but keep it short.

- Generate a four-character identifier for the page:
  - Use the first and last character of the original page name.
  - Assign a random two-digit number.

- Include comments to explain the logic of how to shorten the URL.

Exercise 6.9: Validating Phone Numbers

Create a program that validates a phone number. The program should satisfy the following requirements:

- The program should accept a string that the user inputs as a phone number.

- It should check if the input value is appropriate for a U.S. phone number.

- If it is not valid, it should display a message with information about the problem it found.
- If it is valid, it should display the phone number in a normalized format, using the representation *999-999-9999*.

Exercise 6.10: Validating Email Addresses

Create a program that validates an email address. The program should satisfy the following requirements:

- The program should accept an email address as string input.
- The program should check that the address is formatted as a valid email address and provide appropriate feedback.
- After accepting the email, the program should output the following (with appropriate output messages):
  - The domain of the email address.
  - The identifier of the email address.

For example, given the input someperson@somedomain.com, the output should look something like:

```
Valid format: True
Domain: somedomain
Identifier: someperson
```

Challenge

Set up the program so that if the user enters an invalid string as an email address, the program informs the user of the problem and prompts them to reenter the address before continuing.

Exercise 6.11: Fizz Buzz

Write a program that loops through a series of values and uses those values to determine the output shown to the user. The program should perform the following steps:

1. Ask the user for a number.
2. Output a count starting with 0.
   - Display the count number if it is not divisible by 3 or 5.
   - Replace every multiple of 3 with the word "fizz."

- Replace every multiple of 5 with the word "buzz."

- Replace multiples of both 3 and 5 with "fizz buzz."

3. Continue counting until the number of integers replaced with "fizz," "buzz," or "fizz buzz" reaches the input number.

4. The last output line should read "TRADITION!!"

For example:

```
How many fizzing and buzzing units do you need in your life? 7
0
1
2
fizz
4
buzz
fizz
7
8
fizz
buzz
11
fizz
13
14
fizz buzz
TRADITION!!
```

Pulling It All Together: Income Tax Calculator

I n this lesson, we pull together many of the concepts from the previous lessons. Instead of presenting new information on Go, we will walk you through a real-world application that uses what you've already learned. In this lesson, we will walk through the steps to create a calculator that determines a person's income tax based on their income.

IMPORTANT!

NOTE The information in this lesson is based on U.S. tax law for the year 2020. If you choose to update this calculator for a different year, you should find current values for the year you want to use. However, this specific calculator will work only for individuals with relatively simple income based only on wages and tips. A more advanced calculator would be needed for more complicated returns, including other forms of income and tax credits or deductions. Consult a tax expert or business analyst for more advanced tax return requirements.

LEARNING OBJECTIVES

By the end of this lesson, you will be able to:

- Demonstrate understanding of basic Go tools, including using syntax basics, defining variables, and accepting user input.
- Explain basic Go data types and describe the differences between each data type.
- Use numbers and number operations in a Go application.
- Use Boolean values in a Go application, especially in the use of conditional statements.
- Use conditional statements to determine the outcome of a program.

GETTING STARTED

To complete this lesson, you will need an IDE that supports Go, such as one of the following:

- GoLand
- Visual Studio

Although you can use an online tool like Replit to test small blocks of code, we recommend that you get in the habit of using an installed IDE for larger programs.

As you work through this lesson, make sure that you understand each step before going on to the next one. For steps that involve writing code, all code should work before you go to the next step. Run the code frequently to check for problems and fix problems as soon as you find them.

STEP 1: GATHER REQUIREMENTS

Before you begin to write code for any program, you should take the time to identify the requirements and expected use of that application. When you are working with a client, agree on the requirements early in the process, to ensure that you understand what the client expects and that your final program meets those expectations.

In this case, the client wants a simple income tax calculator that will calculate the tax obligation for an individual, single filer, based only on income from wages and tips, as reported on a U.S. W-2 form. Remember that for many people, calculating income tax can be complicated by other forms of income, such as dividends and interest payments, so if you want to create a calculator for more complicated returns, you should consult a tax expert to understand how other forms of income can affect a tax return.

Values in Use

For this example, we are using values from U.S. tax law for the year 2020. If you want to calculate income taxes for another year, you will need to update the values used in the calculations.

Specifically, we are assuming the following values to calculate taxable income based on gross income:

Table 7.1 2020 tax rates

Rate	Income for single individuals
10%	Up to $9,875
12%	$9,876 to $40,125
22%	$40,126 to $85,525
24%	$85,526 to $163,300
32%	$163,301 to $207,350
35%	$207,351 to $518,400
37%	$518,401 or more

- All taxpayers are allowed a $12,200 standard deduction.
- For each dependent, a taxpayer is allowed an additional $2,000 deduction.

U.S. tax rates vary based on the amount of money earned. For 2020, the values in Table 7.1 are used to calculate a person's income tax based on their taxable income.

User Interface

We want the program to accept the following input values from the user:

- Gross income
- Number of dependents

At this point, we will also assume that the user will access the program through a terminal window rather than a form.

Other Standards

The number standards are as follows:

- Gross income must be entered to the nearest cent.

- The taxable income is expressed as a decimal number.

- The tax due is expressed as an integer.

All text that appears to the user should use correct grammar and spelling.

STEP 2: DESIGN THE PROGRAM

After finalizing what the program will do, you should take time to design the program. Designing a program can include pseudocode or flowcharts. Let's start with pseudocode that describes the actions the program will perform:

```
User Input: gross income
User Input: number of dependents

taxable income = gross income - $12,200 - ($2,000 * number of dependents)
tax due = amount calculated from tax table

print tax due
```

You may find it useful to create a flowchart for yourself that identifies these steps. Remember that you only need a pencil and paper to create a flowchart, but it can help you visualize what the program will do and identify the required steps in the program.

STEP 3: CREATE THE INPUTS

When writing a program, it is good practice to break it up into smaller pieces. You can then build the pieces individually, testing that they work as expected as you go. If you try to write an entire program in one go (even a relatively short program like the one we are working on here), you may end up with errors that are hard to trace. If you get each piece working without error before going on to the next piece, it is easier to troubleshoot problems when they happen.

For this lesson, you are using $35,987.65 for the gross income value, with two dependents, except where stated otherwise. When you test the code with input values, you can use different values to see what happens.

Let's start by creating the user inputs. You know that you want the user to enter their gross income and you need to save the input in a variable, as shown in Listing 7.1. You will also include a print statement so that you can verify that the correct value was stored.

LISTING 7.1

Prompting for the income

```
package main

import "fmt"

func main() {

    // ask user for the gross income
    fmt.Print("Enter your gross income from your W-2 for 2020:")

    var grossIncome float64
    fmt.Scanln(&grossIncome) // take input from user
    fmt.Print("Your gross income is: ")
    fmt.Println(grossIncome)
}
```

Add the code in Listing 7.1 to your IDE and run the program. It should prompt you for a value and display that value immediately after you have entered it.

```
Enter your gross income from your W-2 for 2020: 35987.65
35987.65
```

Once this code works, you can create the prompt for the number of dependents and add it to your code, as shown in Listing 7.2.

LISTING 7.2

Adding another prompt

```
package main

import "fmt"
```

continues

continued
```go
func main() {

    // ask user for the gross income
    fmt.Print("Enter your gross income from your W-2 for 2020:")

    var grossIncome float64
    fmt.Scanln(&grossIncome) // take gross income input from user
    fmt.Print("Your gross income is: ")
    fmt.Println(grossIncome)

    fmt.Print("How many dependents are you claiming? ")
    var numDep int
    fmt.Scanln(&numDep) // take number of dependents input from user
    fmt.Print("Your claimed number of dependents is: ")
    fmt.Println(numDep)
}
```

The output should now look like this:

```
Enter your gross income from your W-2 for 2020:35987.65
Your gross income is: 35987.65
How many dependents are you claiming? 2
Your claimed number of dependents is: 2
```

STEP 4: CALCULATE THE TAXABLE INCOME

We know from the planning step that the formula for taxable income is:

```
taxable income = gross income - $12,200 - ($2,000 * number of dependents)
```

The values $12,200 and $2,000 come from U.S. tax calculations for the year 2020.

Remember that using variables not only saves values to a named memory location, but if you name them correctly, they can help you better map a formula to an operation. In Listing 7.3, the variables grossIncome and numDep have been plugged into the statement, and the result of the calculation has been assigned to a new variable. We can also print the result to help us make sure that the value is appropriate.

LISTING 7.3

Adding the taxable income formula

```go
package main
```

```
import "fmt"

func main() {

    // ask user for the gross income
    fmt.Print("Enter your gross income from your W-2 for 2020:")

    var grossIncome float64
    fmt.Scanln(&grossIncome) // take gross income input from user
    fmt.Print("Your gross income is: ")
    fmt.Println(grossIncome)

    fmt.Print("How many dependents are you claiming? ")
    var numDep int
    fmt.Scanln(&numDep) // take number of dependents input from user
    fmt.Print("Your claimed number of dependents is: ")
    fmt.Println(numDep)

    //calculate taxable income

    var taxableIncome float64
    taxableIncome = grossIncome - 12200 - (2000 * numDep)
    fmt.Print("Your taxable income is: ")
    fmt.Println(taxableIncome)
}
```

However, if you run this program, Go will return an error:

```
# command-line-arguments
./main.go:24:40: invalid operation: grossIncome - 12200 - 2000 * numDep
(mismatched types float64 and int)
```

The issue is that the numDep variable is defined as an int and the grossIncome variable is defined as a float, which results in a type mismatch. To overcome this error, you will need to convert the numDep variable into a float prior to compute the taxable income.

Let's update the code to include these conversions and to use the new variables. Listing 7.4 shows the updated listing.

LISTING 7.4

Adding conversions

```
package main

import "fmt"
```

continues

continued

```
func main() {

    // ask user for the gross income
    fmt.Print("Enter your gross income from your W-2 for 2020:")

    var grossIncome float64
    fmt.Scanln(&grossIncome) // take gross income input from user
    fmt.Print("Your gross income is: ")
    fmt.Println(grossIncome)

    fmt.Print("How many dependents are you claiming? ")
    var numDep int
    fmt.Scanln(&numDep) // take number of dependents input from user
    fmt.Print("Your claimed number of dependents is: ")
    fmt.Println(numDep)

    //calculate taxable income

    var taxableIncome float64
    taxableIncome = grossIncome - 12200 - (2000 * float64(numDep))
    fmt.Print("Your taxable income is: ")
    fmt.Println(taxableIncome)
}
```

Notice that the `float64` function is used to convert the `numDep` from `int` to `float64` before computing the taxable income. You should get the following value, if you use the same inputs that we used earlier in the lesson:

```
19787.65
```

STEP 5: CALCULATE THE TAX RATE

The next step is to calculate the tax due for the person whose values you are using. You know that the income tax rate is dependent on the taxable value itself, using the values from Table 7.1 presented in step 1.

Here's where things get complicated, though. In U.S. tax law, the taxable income is sliced into values that match the tax table presented in Table 7.1, and each slice uses the appropriate tax rate for that slice. For example, if a person's taxable income is $80,000, the tax due is calculated as follows:

1. The first $9,875 is taxed at 10 percent:

    9875 * .1 = 987.6

2. The amount from $9,876 through $40,125 is taxed at 12 percent:

```
40145 - 9875 = 30270
30270 * .12 = 3632.4
```

3. The remainder is taxed at 22 percent:

```
80000 - 40125 = 39875
39875 * .22 = 8772.5
```

4. You then add the three values to get the total tax due:

```
taxDue = 987.6 + 3632.4 + 8772.5
taxDue = 13392.5
```

Let's look at how to code this, breaking it up into slices (or *tiers*). The first tier is for taxable incomes of less than $9,875. Because this is the first tier, you simply multiply the taxable income by 10 percent to calculate the tax due. Add that to your program, as shown in Listing 7.5.

LISTING 7.5

Adding the first tier of the tax calculation

```go
package main

import "fmt"

func main() {

    // ask user for the gross income
    fmt.Print("Enter your gross income from your W-2 for 2020:")

    var grossIncome float64
    fmt.Scanln(&grossIncome) // take gross income input from user
    fmt.Print("Your gross income is: ")
    fmt.Println(grossIncome)

    fmt.Print("How many dependents are you claiming? ")
    var numDep int
    fmt.Scanln(&numDep) // take number of dependents input from user
    fmt.Print("Your claimed number of dependents is: ")
    fmt.Println(numDep)

    //calculate taxable income
```

continues

continued

```
    var taxableIncome float64
    taxableIncome = grossIncome - 12200 - (2000 * float64(numDep))
    fmt.Print("Your taxable income is: ")
    fmt.Println(taxableIncome)

    // calculate tax due

    var taxDue float64
    taxDue = taxableIncome * 0.1
    fmt.Print("Your tax due is: ")
    fmt.Println(taxDue)
}
```

If you test this with a gross income of $20,000 and two dependents, you should get the following output:

```
Enter your gross income from your W-2 for 2020:20000
Your gross income is: 20000
How many dependents are you claiming? 2
Your claimed number of dependents is: 2
Your taxable income is: 3800
Your tax due is: 380
```

Add a Conditional Statement

Now that you understand the math, you can make the program more flexible. Specifically, you want it to look at the taxable income, determine the correct tax rate for that value, and use that tax rate to calculate the tax due. That requires you to use conditional statements. Because this step is a bit complicated, we're only going to look at the taxable income for now. Once you understand what's going on, you can incorporate the code into the earlier version of the program.

Create a new program that includes the basics of calculating the tax due based on the taxable income but ignores the deductions at this point. Start with $4,000, as shown in Listing 7.6, which is in the 10 percent tier.

LISTING 7.6

Taxing 4000

```
package main

import "fmt"
```

```
func main() {

    var taxableIncome float64 = 4000
    var taxDue float64 = taxableIncome * 0.1
    fmt.Print("Your tax due is: ")
    fmt.Println(taxDue)
}
```

This should give you a result of `400.0`, which is the $4,000 in income multiplied by the 0.1 tax rate.

Now update the code to calculate a taxable income that is in the 22 percent tier. In this case, you first need an `if` clause for the 10 percent tier:

```
if taxableIncome <= 9875 {
        taxDue = taxableIncome * 0.1
}
taxDue = (9875 * .1) + ((taxableIncome - 9875) * .12)
```

The calculation is a bit complicated. You first calculate 10 percent of the first $9,875:

```
9875 * .1
```

You then subtract 9875 from the taxable income and calculate 12 percent of that value:

```
(taxableIncome - 9875) * .12
```

You then add those values together to calculate the tax due:

```
taxDue = (9875 * .1) + ((taxableIncome - 9875) * .12)
```

Update your code in Listing 7.6 to include this calculation, and use a taxable Income value that falls into the 22 percent tier. Listing 7.7 shows the updated code.

LISTING 7.7

Adding the second-tier logic

```
package main

import "fmt"

func main() {
```

continues

continued

```
    var taxableIncome float64 = 35000
    var taxDue float64

    if taxableIncome <= 9875 {
        taxDue = taxableIncome * 0.1
    } else {
    taxDue = (9875 * .1) + ((taxableIncome - 9875) * .12)
    }
    fmt.Print("Your tax due is: ")
    fmt.Println(taxDue)
}
```

If you start with a taxable income value of 35000, the result should be:

```
4002.5
```

Now that you understand the math from one tier to the next, you can add the next tier.

Create Nested Conditionals

To handle more than two options in a conditional construction, you use nested conditionals. Because the tax table is a series of "up to" values, you can simply use less than or equal to (<=) conditional statements that correspond to the highest value on the current tier.

In Go, you use else if to create nested conditions between the initial condition and the else value. Let's start by making the 12 percent tier an else if statement, as shown in Listing 7.8.

LISTING 7.8

The second tier using an else if statement

```
package main

import "fmt"

func main() {

    var taxableIncome float64 = 35000
    var taxDue float64
```

```
if taxableIncome <= 9875 {
    taxDue = taxableIncome * 0.1
} else if taxableIncome <= 40125 {
    taxDue = (9875 * .1) + ((taxableIncome - 9875) * .12)
}

fmt.Print("Your tax due is: ")
fmt.Println(taxDue)
}
```

Run the code to make sure you get the same result you saw before:

```
4002.5
```

Now add the 22 percent tier, as shown in Listing 7.9.

LISTING 7.9

Adding the 22 percent tier

```
package main

import "fmt"

func main() {

    var taxableIncome float64 = 50000
    var taxDue float64

    if taxableIncome <= 9875 {
        taxDue = taxableIncome * 0.1
    } else if taxableIncome <= 40125 {
        taxDue = (9875 * .1) + ((taxableIncome - 9875) * .12)
    } else if taxableIncome <= 85525 {
        taxDue = (9875 * .1) + ((40125 - 9875) * .12) + ((taxableIncome -
40125) * .22)
    }

    fmt.Print("Your tax due is: ")
    fmt.Println(taxDue)
}
```

Now our program is getting even more complicated, so look at the code to make sure you understand it.

To calculate the tax for values between 40125 and 85525, you perform the following steps:

1. Calculate 10 percent of the first tier's maximum value:

   9875 * .1

2. Calculate 12 percent of the second tier's maximum value:

   (40125 - 9875) * .12

3. Calculate 22 percent of what's left:

   (taxableIncome - 40125) * .22

4. Add the three values together.

Now, do the same thing for the 24 percent tier, as shown in Listing 7.10.

LISTING 7.10

Adding the 24 percent tier

```go
package main

import "fmt"

func main() {

    var taxableIncome float64 = 140000
    var taxDue float64

    if taxableIncome <= 9875 {
        taxDue = taxableIncome * 0.1
    } else if taxableIncome <= 40125 {
        taxDue = (9875 * .1) + ((taxableIncome - 9875) * .12)
    } else if taxableIncome <= 85525 {
        taxDue = (9875 * .1) + ((40125 - 9875) * .12) + ((taxableIncome -
40125) * .22)
    } else if taxableIncome <= 163300 {
        taxDue = (9875 * .1) + ((40125 - 9875) * .12) + ((85525 - 40125) * .22)
+ ((taxableIncome - 85525) * .24)
```

```
        }

        fmt.Print("Your tax due is: ")
        fmt.Println(taxDue)
}
```

Note that you're seeing a lot of repetition here. You know that 10 percent of 9,875 is always 987.5, and you keep reusing values like 40124 and 9875. In fact, you likely copied and pasted code from one else if to the next and then updated as necessary.

Whenever you see repetition like that, you should also see the opportunity to introduce variables. Using variables will not only simplify our code by removing repetition, but the variables themselves will also make the code easier to read. Variables can also make the code more flexible.

In 2020, you have fixed ranges for each tier, but it's possible that those ranges will be different in other years. If you use variables instead of constants, you only have to update those values in one place rather than replacing every instance of each value with a new value.

Start by creating variables that reference the highest value in each tier. Create them above the if block, as shown in Listing 7.11, so that you can use them in the calculations.

LISTING 7.11

Declaring high-range value variables

```
var taxableIncome float64 = 140000
var max10 float64 = 9875
var max12 float64 = 40125
var max22 float64 = 85525
var max24 float64 = 163300
var max32 float64 = 207350
var max35 float64 = 518400

var taxDue float64

if taxableIncome <= max10 {
    taxDue = taxableIncome * 0.1
}
// etc
```

You can also calculate the maximum tax due for each tier and assign those values to variables, as shown in Listing 7.12. Again, this is not a complete listing, so the code won't run.

LISTING 7.12

Using variables calculating maximum tier taxes

```
var taxableIncome float64 = 140000
var max10 float64 = 9875
var max12 float64 = 40125
var max22 float64 = 85525
var max24 float64 = 163300
var max32 float64 = 207350
var max35 float64 = 518400

var tier10_tax float64 = max10 * .1
var tier12_tax float64 = tier10_tax + ((max12 - max10) * .12)
var tier22_tax float64 = tier12_tax + ((max22 - max12) * .22)
var tier24_tax float64 = tier22_tax + ((max24 - max22) * .24)
var tier32_tax float64 = tier24_tax + ((max32 - max24) * .32)
var tier35_tax float64 = tier32_tax + ((max35 - max32) * .35)

var taxDue float64

if taxableIncome <= max10 {
    taxDue = taxableIncome * 0.1
}
```

Here, you calculate the maximum tax due for each tier by adding the maximum for the previous tier and calculating the remaining tax rate based on the current tier.

Now you can replace the hard-coded values in the calculations with the appropriate variables, as shown in Listing 7.13.

LISTING 7.13

Updating tax calculations with variables

```go
package main

import "fmt"

func main() {

    var taxableIncome float64 = 140000
    var max10 float64 = 9875
    var max12 float64 = 40125
    var max22 float64 = 85525
    var max24 float64 = 163300
    //var max32 float64 = 207350
    //var max35 float64 = 518400

    var tier10_tax float64 = max10 * .1
    var tier12_tax float64 = tier10_tax + ((max12 - max10) * .12)
    var tier22_tax float64 = tier12_tax + ((max22 - max12) * .22)
    //var tier24_tax float64 = tier22_tax + ((max24 - max22) * .24)
    //var tier32_tax float64 = tier24_tax + ((max32 - max24) * .32)
    //var tier35_tax float64 = tier32_tax + ((max35 - max32) * .35)

    var taxDue float64

    if taxableIncome <= max10 {
        taxDue = taxableIncome * 0.1
    } else if taxableIncome <= max12 {
        taxDue = tier10_tax + ((taxableIncome - max10) * .12)
    } else if taxableIncome <= max22 {
        taxDue = tier12_tax + ((taxableIncome - max12) * .22)
    } else if taxableIncome <= max24 {
        taxDue = tier22_tax + ((taxableIncome - max24) * .32)
    }

    fmt.Print("Your tax due is: ")
    fmt.Println(taxDue)
}
```

It should be easy to see that the code is much simpler, but it's also worth taking the time to examine the code to see what it's doing. First, each of the if–else clauses references the maximum value for that tier. The appropriate maximum value is also used to calculate the amount of taxable income for the current tier:

```
else if taxableIncome <= max24 {
    taxDue = tier22_tax + ((taxableIncome - max24) * .32)
}
```

Second, most of the math required for each of the else if results is already done for you when you define the tier tax values, because those expressions calculate the highest possible tax due for each tier. You can then include that value in the next tier when you calculate the tax due:

```
else if taxableIncome <= max24 {
    taxDue = tier22_tax + ((taxableIncome - max24) * .32)
}
```

Finally, should the maximum value for a given range be changed in the future, we only have to change the values assigned to the max variables, which is much more efficient than having to replace every instance where that value is used in the code.

Now, finish the code with the remaining tiers. Try to do it on your own, and then check your code against the code shown in Listing 7.14.

LISTING 7.14

Tax calculation with remaining tiers added

```
package main

import "fmt"

func main() {

    var taxableIncome float64 = 2000000
    var max10 float64 = 9875
    var max12 float64 = 40125
    var max22 float64 = 85525
    var max24 float64 = 163300
    var max32 float64 = 207350
    var max35 float64 = 518400

    var tier10_tax float64 = max10 * .1
    var tier12_tax float64 = tier10_tax + ((max12 - max10) * .12)
```

```
var tier22_tax float64 = tier12_tax + ((max22 - max12) * .22)
var tier24_tax float64 = tier22_tax + ((max24 - max22) * .24)
var tier32_tax float64 = tier24_tax + ((max32 - max24) * .32)
var tier35_tax float64 = tier32_tax + ((max35 - max32) * .35)

var taxDue float64

if taxableIncome <= max10 {
    taxDue = taxableIncome * 0.1
} else if taxableIncome <= max12 {
    taxDue = tier10_tax + ((taxableIncome - max10) * .12)
} else if taxableIncome <= max22 {
    taxDue = tier12_tax + ((taxableIncome - max12) * .22)
} else if taxableIncome <= max24 {
    taxDue = tier22_tax + ((taxableIncome - max22) * .24)
} else if taxableIncome <= max32 {
    taxDue = tier24_tax + ((taxableIncome - max24) * .32)
} else if taxableIncome <= max35 {
    taxDue = tier32_tax + ((taxableIncome - max32) * .35)
} else if taxableIncome > max35 {
    taxDue = tier35_tax + ((taxableIncome - max35) * .37)
}

fmt.Print("Your tax due is: ")
fmt.Println(taxDue)

}
```

Note that the last else if block uses only a greater-than symbol rather than less-than or equal to. This is because any income above $518,400 is taxed at the 37 percent rate. There is no maximum value set on this range, so you can't compare it to a highest possible value (which is also why you didn't initialize a max37 variable).

Test your code with a variety of taxable incomes in each range. For testing purposes, your results should match those shown in Table 7.2.

Table 7.2 Taxes due based on tier

Taxable income	Tax due
$9,000	$900.00
$35,000	$4,002.50
$50,000	$6,790.00
$100,000	$18,079.50
$200,000	$45,015.50
$400,000	$114,795.0
$700,000	$223,427.00

STEP 6: UPDATE THE APPLICATION

Now that you have the tax due calculations finalized, you can incorporate them into our original program. Because you used the same tax_income variable in the calculations, you simply need to add the new code to the existing program, replacing the original tax due calculation, as shown in Listing 7.15.

LISTING 7.15

Tax program with updated tax calculation

```go
package main

import "fmt"

func main() {

    var max10 float64 = 9875
    var max12 float64 = 40125
    var max22 float64 = 85525
    var max24 float64 = 163300
    var max32 float64 = 207350
    var max35 float64 = 518400

    var tier10_tax float64 = max10 * .1
    var tier12_tax float64 = tier10_tax + ((max12 - max10) * .12)
    var tier22_tax float64 = tier12_tax + ((max22 - max12) * .22)
    var tier24_tax float64 = tier22_tax + ((max24 - max22) * .24)
    var tier32_tax float64 = tier24_tax + ((max32 - max24) * .32)
    var tier35_tax float64 = tier32_tax + ((max35 - max32) * .35)

    // ask user for the gross income
    fmt.Print("Enter your gross income from your W-2 for 2020:")

    var grossIncome float64
    fmt.Scanln(&grossIncome) // take gross income input from user
    fmt.Print("Your gross income is: ")
    fmt.Println(grossIncome)

    fmt.Print("How many dependents are you claiming? ")
    var numDep int
```

```
fmt.Scanln(&numDep) // take number of dependents input from user
fmt.Print("Your claimed number of dependents is: ")
fmt.Println(numDep)

//calculate taxable income

var taxableIncome float64
taxableIncome = grossIncome - 12200 - (2000 * float64(numDep))
fmt.Print("Your taxable income is: ")
fmt.Println(taxableIncome)

// calculate tax due

var taxDue float64

if taxableIncome <= max10 {
    taxDue = taxableIncome * 0.1
} else if taxableIncome <= max12 {
    taxDue = tier10_tax + ((taxableIncome - max10) * .12)
} else if taxableIncome <= max22 {
    taxDue = tier12_tax + ((taxableIncome - max12) * .22)
} else if taxableIncome <= max24 {
    taxDue = tier22_tax + ((taxableIncome - max22) * .24)
} else if taxableIncome <= max32 {
    taxDue = tier24_tax + ((taxableIncome - max24) * .32)
} else if taxableIncome <= max35 {
    taxDue = tier32_tax + ((taxableIncome - max32) * .35)
} else if taxableIncome > max35 {
    taxDue = tier35_tax + ((taxableIncome - max35) * .37)
}

fmt.Print("Your tax due is: ")
fmt.Println(taxDue)
}
```

Note that in this listing you added the variables at the beginning of the application. It is common practice to define variables early in an application to ensure that they are available when they are needed in the application itself. Grouping them together like this can also help with debugging in case you need to look at how a variable was originally declared and initialized.

After updating the code, test it a couple more times to make sure it produces the expected results. Remember that the complete code starts with gross income and calculates deductions to determine the taxable income.

What About Negative Taxable Incomes?

Another problem that our tax calculator doesn't solve is situations where the taxable income is less than 0. For example, if a person earns $10,000 gross income and has two dependents, their taxable income is –$6,200. Note that this is a logic error, not a syntax error. Entering the values 10000 and 2 for the initial income values in our program will not cause Go to throw an error. In fact, it will clearly tell you that the person owes –$620, an amount that doesn't really make sense.

In U.S. tax law, a person whose taxable income is less than 0 owes no taxes at all. You can update our program to take this into account, as shown in Listing 7.16.

LISTING 7.16

Adjusting for low incomes

```
package main

import "fmt"

func main() {

    var max10 float64 = 9875
    var max12 float64 = 40125
    var max22 float64 = 85525
    var max24 float64 = 163300
    var max32 float64 = 207350
    var max35 float64 = 518400

    var tier10_tax float64 = max10 * .1
    var tier12_tax float64 = tier10_tax + ((max12 - max10) * .12)
    var tier22_tax float64 = tier12_tax + ((max22 - max12) * .22)
    var tier24_tax float64 = tier22_tax + ((max24 - max22) * .24)
    var tier32_tax float64 = tier24_tax + ((max32 - max24) * .32)
    var tier35_tax float64 = tier32_tax + ((max35 - max32) * .35)

    // ask user for the gross income
    fmt.Print("Enter your gross income from your W-2 for 2020:")

    var grossIncome float64
    fmt.Scanln(&grossIncome) // take gross income input from user
    fmt.Print("Your gross income is: ")
    fmt.Println(grossIncome)
```

```
fmt.Print("How many dependents are you claiming? ")
var numDep int
fmt.Scanln(&numDep) // take number of dependents input from user
fmt.Print("Your claimed number of dependents is: ")
fmt.Println(numDep)

//calculate taxable income

var taxableIncome float64
taxableIncome = grossIncome - 12200 - (2000 * float64(numDep))
fmt.Print("Your taxable income is: ")
fmt.Println(taxableIncome)

// calculate tax due

var taxDue float64

if taxableIncome <= 0 {
    taxDue = 0
} else if taxableIncome <= max10 {
    taxDue = taxableIncome * 0.1
} else if taxableIncome <= max12 {
    taxDue = tier10_tax + ((taxableIncome - max10) * .12)
} else if taxableIncome <= max22 {
    taxDue = tier12_tax + ((taxableIncome - max12) * .22)
} else if taxableIncome <= max24 {
    taxDue = tier22_tax + ((taxableIncome - max22) * .24)
} else if taxableIncome <= max32 {
    taxDue = tier24_tax + ((taxableIncome - max24) * .32)
} else if taxableIncome <= max35 {
    taxDue = tier32_tax + ((taxableIncome - max32) * .35)
} else if taxableIncome > max35 {
    taxDue = tier35_tax + ((taxableIncome - max35) * .37)
}

fmt.Print("Your tax due is: ")
fmt.Println(taxDue)
}
```

Run the program with a few lower numbers to make sure it produces the correct results without errors.

Does Code Compare to Standards?

As a final check on the code, compare what you have to the expected standards. Specifically, the number standards are as follows:

- Gross income must be entered to the nearest cent.

- The taxable income is expressed as a decimal number.

- The tax due is expressed as an integer.

You do allow the user to enter a float value for the gross income, and you do have the program express the taxable income as a decimal number. However, you should have noticed at least one example where the tax due included a value after the decimal point.

You can fix this by converting the calculated value to an integer. In Go, this conversion will cause the number to use standard rounding procedures (rounding up for values where the decimal value is .5 or higher and rounding down otherwise). Update the Print statement for the tax due:

```
fmt.Print("Your tax due is: ")
fmt.Println(int(taxDue))
```

Run the code a few times with different inputs to ensure that the tax due is expressed as an integer.

STEP 7: ADDRESS THE UI

Once you have the program working as you expect, you should take time to improve the user interface (UI). You've done this a little by clearly stating what data the user should enter, but you also want to clean up the output a little.

In this case, you want the program to clearly state what values were input as well as the calculated values, using phrases that identify the values. At this point, you can uncomment the earlier print statements you used for testing and embellish them to make them more meaningful:

```
fmt.Print("Your gross income is: $")
    fmt.Println(grossIncome)


fmt.Print("Your claimed number of dependents is: ")
    fmt.Println(numDep)
```

Here you include the $ symbol as part of the first print statement so that the symbol appears in front of the number and the result looks like money. The output statements should look like the following:

```
Your gross income is: $100000
Your claimed number of dependents is: 2
```

You also want to clearly state the taxable income:

```
fmt.Print("Your taxable income is: $")
    fmt.Println(taxableIncome)
```

Now do something similar with tax due:

```
fmt.Print("Your tax due is: $")
    fmt.Println(int(taxDue))
```

Next, let's finalize the program with all the print statements in a logical order at the end of the program, as shown in Listing 7.17. This isn't absolutely necessary, but it helps keep the code more organized. It's also easier to update a program if similar pieces of code are grouped together.

LISTING 7.17

Our completed tax program

```
package main

import (
    "fmt"
)

func main() {

    var max10 float64 = 9875
    var max12 float64 = 40125
    var max22 float64 = 85525
    var max24 float64 = 163300
    var max32 float64 = 207350
    var max35 float64 = 518400
```

continues

continued

```go
var tier10_tax float64 = max10 * .1
var tier12_tax float64 = tier10_tax + ((max12 - max10) * .12)
var tier22_tax float64 = tier12_tax + ((max22 - max12) * .22)
var tier24_tax float64 = tier22_tax + ((max24 - max22) * .24)
var tier32_tax float64 = tier24_tax + ((max32 - max24) * .32)
var tier35_tax float64 = tier32_tax + ((max35 - max32) * .35)

// ask user for the gross income
fmt.Print("Enter your gross income from your W-2 for 2020:")

var grossIncome float64
fmt.Scanln(&grossIncome) // take gross income input from user

fmt.Print("How many dependents are you claiming? ")
var numDep int
fmt.Scanln(&numDep) // take number of dependents input from user

//calculate taxable income

var taxableIncome float64
taxableIncome = grossIncome - 12200 - (2000 * float64(numDep))

// calculate tax due

var taxDue float64

if taxableIncome <= 0 {
    taxDue = 0
} else if taxableIncome <= max10 {
    taxDue = taxableIncome * 0.1
} else if taxableIncome <= max12 {
    taxDue = tier10_tax + ((taxableIncome - max10) * .12)
} else if taxableIncome <= max22 {
    taxDue = tier12_tax + ((taxableIncome - max12) * .22)
} else if taxableIncome <= max24 {
    taxDue = tier22_tax + ((taxableIncome - max22) * .24)
} else if taxableIncome <= max32 {
    taxDue = tier24_tax + ((taxableIncome - max24) * .32)
} else if taxableIncome <= max35 {
    taxDue = tier32_tax + ((taxableIncome - max32) * .35)
} else if taxableIncome > max35 {
    taxDue = tier35_tax + ((taxableIncome - max35) * .37)
}
fmt.Print("Your gross income is: $")
fmt.Println(grossIncome)
fmt.Print("Your claimed number of dependents is: ")
```

```
    fmt.Println(numDep)
    fmt.Print("Your taxable income is: $")
    fmt.Println(taxableIncome)
    fmt.Print("Your tax due is: $")
    fmt.Println(int(taxDue))
}
```

Using an income of $100,000 and two dependents for the input values, the output should look like the following:

```
Enter your gross income from your W-2 for 2020:100000
How many dependents are you claiming? 2
Your gross income is: $100000
Your claimed number of dependents is: 2
Your taxable income is: $83800
Your tax due is: $14226
```

ON YOUR OWN

Once you have the program working from this lesson, check results using different input values—both lower and higher. Feel free to use a calculator to spot-check results for accuracy.

Also consider that tax rates and the tax table can change from one year to the next. We looked at using variables to store the maximum value for each tier as well as the maximum tax due for each tier, but there are still some hard-coded values that could potentially change and that are repeated throughout the program. For example:

- Can you refactor the program to use variables for the percentages for each tier?
- Can you refactor the program to use a variable for the personal deduction and the dependent deduction values?
- How could you handle changes to the range or percentage tax value for each tier?

Also keep in mind that code style can vary drastically from one developer to the next. The program here shows one solution, but there are many other ways to approach a problem like this one and at least as many ways to solve it. The important take-aways here are

- Understand what you want the code to do to solve the problem at hand.
- Understand how the code solves that problem.
- Write code so that it is easy to read, especially by other developers.
- Write code that is reasonably free of repetition or reused values and calculations.

SUMMARY

In this lesson we pulled together many of the concepts you've seen in the previous lessons into a working application. We walked you through the steps to create a calculator that determines a person's income tax based on their income. You added variables to make it easier for you to update the program in the future for different tax rates.

PART II

Organizing Code and Data in Go

Lesson 8
Using Functions

Functions are an important aspect of any programming language in that they allow us to create reusable blocks of code that can use a variety of input values. You've used functions in previous lessons, including the functions `main` and `Println`. In this lesson, you will take a closer look at functions and learn to create your own.

LEARNING OBJECTIVES

By the end of this lesson, you will be able to:

- Create your own functions.
- Pass arguments to functions.
- Use the return values from a function as well as skip them when you don't need them.
- Work with variadic functions.
- Assign a function to a variable and use closures.

DEFINING A FUNCTION

A function is a block of organized, reusable code that uses one or more Go statements to complete a single, related action. You use functions to help with code reusability, increased readability, and redundancy checking (making sure that you do not use the same lines over and over within an application).

Go provides many built-in functions, such as the `fmt.Println()` function that you've been using throughout this book; however, you are also allowed to create or define your own functions. A function that you define yourself in a Go program is known as a user-defined function.

As you progress through this lesson, here are a few key terms you should know:

- Functions are blocks of organized, reusable code.
- User-defined functions are functions defined by the user. These functions use the `def` keyword to define them.
- Built-in functions are functions that are built into Go.
- Arguments are pieces of information passed into functions. An argument is the value sent to the function when called upon.

Functions allow you to organize snippets of code that can then be used (called) to perform specific functionality. One of the core values of functions is that you can write the code once and then call it as many times as you would like.

You define a function using the keyword `func`, and you can define any values you need for the function as parameters of that function. The basic syntax to define a function is:

```
func funcName (arg1 type, arg2 type) returnType {
    [function instructions]
}
```

A function can take zero or more parameters, depending on what you want it to do, so it is possible to define a function without any parameters at all, as in `main()`. Let's look at a simple function that adds two numbers. A function called `add` is presented in Listing 8.1.

> **NOTE** Note that an *argument* is a value passed to a function when you call that function. A *parameter* is a variable defined by a function that receives a value when the function is called. An argument is a value passed to a parameter, which is generally a variable.

LISTING 8.1

A simple add function

```
package main

import (
```

```
    "fmt"
)

//  add takes as input a and b of type int and returns an int
func add(a int, b int) int {
    return a + b
}

func main() {
    fmt.Println("add function results:", add(4, 6))
}
```

There are two areas of Listing 8.1 that are worth a close look. First is the definition of the add function. You see this definition starting with the func keyword, followed by the name of the new function being defined, add. You then see that the function has two parameters called a and b that are both defined as type int. At the end of the function declaration line, you see that the type of int is listed, which means that the add function is expecting to return an integer value.

The body of the add function is contained between a set of brackets ({ }). In the case of the add function, the body is only a single line of code:

```
return a + b
```

This simple line of code adds the values that are in a and b and returns the result. Note that a and b are parameters, so they are expected to be provided when the add function is called. Similarly, the return statement returns the result of the addition to the code that called the function.

In fact, you can see that the add function is called from within the Println function that is in the main function of the listing. As expected, you can also see that the values of 4 and 6 are passed as arguments to the function. The returned value from the call to add is then used within the Println statement. The resulting output is:

```
add function results: 10
```

Note that the add function is created outside the main function. This makes it a global function that can be accessed from inside the main function or from anywhere else within our program listing.

Using Multiple Functions

A program can include multiple functions, and you can use the same values in multiple functions. Listing 8.2 is a variation of the previous program, with a simplified add2 function and a new multiply function.

LISTING 8.2

Using multiple functions

```go
package main

import (
    "fmt"
)

// add takes as input a and b of type int and returns an int
func add(a int, b int) int {
    return a + b
}

// add2 is a short version of add
func add2(a, b int) int {
    return a + b
}

// multiply takes as input a and b of type int and returns an int
func multiply(a int, b int) int {
    return a * b
}

func main() {
    c := 5
    d := 6
    fmt.Println("c =", c)
    fmt.Println("d =", d)

    fmt.Println("add result:", add(c, d))
    fmt.Println("add2 result:", add2(c, d))
    fmt.Println("multiply result:", multiply(c, d))
}
```

When you execute this program, the following output is displayed:

```
c = 5
d = 6
add result: 11
add2 result: 11
multiply result: 30
```

In this case, the add2 function has a simpler signature than the original add function. Specifically, you use (a, b int) to define the function's parameters. You can do this only because both parameters are of the same type. If the function used parameters of different types, you would have to use the syntax in the add function.

You also use variables instead of hard-coded values in the main function. This allows you to easily reuse the numbers in multiple functions. Here, you used the values of c and d in each of the functions.

> **NOTE** It is worth reviewing the use of the := operator in this listing:
>
> ```
> c := 5
> d := 6
> ```
>
> In these statements, you are using the := operator to declare the c and d variables as well as initialize them. Go will determine the type for c and d based on the values being assigned, in this case ints. This shortcut method of declaring and initializing is a useful feature of the Go programming language.

Functions with No Return Values

In the functions created in the previous two listings, you returned a single calculated value. You don't have to return a value in a function, especially if the function provides output already.

In Listing 8.3, the function converts a string to uppercase and prints the results as part of the function. Note that the listing includes the package called strings, which contains functions you'll use in the new function being created.

LISTING 8.3

Using a function with no return value

```
package main

import(
  "fmt"
  "strings"
)
```

continues

continued

```go
func DisplayUpper(x string) {
  fmt.Println("Original text:", x)
  fmt.Println("Revised text:", strings.ToUpper(x))
}

func main() {
  a := "elizabeth"

  DisplayUpper(a)
}
```

In this listing a new function called `DisplayUpper` is created that takes a string called `x`. You can see that there is no return type listed after the parameter, so nothing is expected to be returned. The function itself simply prints the original text, then uses the `ToUpper` function in the `strings` package to convert the string to uppercase. When this listing is executed, the following output should be displayed:

```
Original text: elizabeth
Revised text: ELIZABETH
```

You can change the value of `a` from `elizabeth` to any other string and run the program again. You can also pass a string literal to our new function to convert it as well.

Functions with Multiple Return Values

You've now seen how to return a single value from a function as well as how to create a function that does not return a value. You can also create functions that return multiple values.

To return a single value, you include the returned data type in the function declaration:

```go
func funcName (arg1 type, arg2 type) returnType {
```

In this case, *returnType* is the type of the data to be returned. To return more than one value, you can place each of the return types in parentheses separated by a comma:

```go
func funcName (arg1 type, arg2 type) (returnType, ..., returnType) {
```

The created function will then need to return all the values with the `return` statement. Each value should be separated by a comma, as shown in Listing 8.4.

LISTING 8.4

Using a function with multiple return values

```
package main

import "fmt"

func rectStuff(length int, width int) (int, int) {
   a := length * width
   c := length + length + width + width
   return a, c
}

func main() {
  area, perimeter := rectStuff(3, 5)

  fmt.Println("area:", area)
  fmt.Println("perimeter:", perimeter)
}
```

While this is not the best application of using a function, it provides a simple illustration of returning multiple values. The function rectStuff is declared to receive two arguments (length and width). More importantly, it also returns two integer values. Looking within the function, you can see that two variables are declared and assigned values determined based on what was passed to the function. Calculations are performed and the results are assigned to the variables a and c. A single return statement then returns both of these values back to the calling function.

Looking in the main function, you can see that the rectStuff function is called with the two arguments of 3 and 5. To the left of the assignment operator, you see that there are two variables separated by a comma that are ready to receive the two integer values that will be returned.

When this listing is executed, the following output should be displayed:

```
area: 15
perimeter: 16
```

Returning Different Types

When returning multiple values from a function, it is not mandatory that they be the same. In Listing 8.4, both data types were of type int. You could use other data types as well.

The important thing is that you must return values of the types you indicate. Listing 8.5 presents a function that returns two different data types.

LISTING 8.5

Using a function with different return types

```
package main

import "fmt"

func circleStuff(radius int) (int, float32) {
    d := radius * 2
    c := 2 * 3.14 * float32(radius)
    return d, c
}

func main() {
    diameter, circumference := circleStuff(5)

    fmt.Println("diameter:", diameter)
    fmt.Println("circumference:", circumference)
}
```

This time, instead of determining characteristics of a rectangle, the listing determines a diameter and circumference of a circle. Looking at the `circleStuff` function details, you can see that a value of type `int` and a value of type `float32` are returned, in that order. The function itself simply calculates the diameter (d) and the circumference (c) and then returns the results in a single `return` statement. You should note that because you are calculating a floating-point number using an integer, you do need to use a cast function on the radius to avoid a type mismatch error. The results of running this listing when passing a radius of 5 are:

```
Diameter: 10
Circumference: 31.400002
```

> **NOTE** In Listing 8.5, we used the value of 3.14 for pi. If we wanted to be more accurate, we could import the Go math package, which includes a constant defined as `math.Pi`:
>
> ```
> c = 2 * math.Pi * float32(radius)
> ```

Returning Named Types

In Go you can also define the names of the return values. In Listing 8.6, the `circleStuff` function has been rewritten to use named return values.

LISTING 8.6

Returning named types

```
package main

import (
    "fmt"
    "math"
)

func circleStuff(radius int) (d int, c float32) {
    d = radius * 2
    c = 2 * math.Pi * float32(radius)
    return
}

func main() {
    diameter, circumference := circleStuff(5)

    fmt.Println("diameter:", diameter)
    fmt.Println("circumference:", circumference)
}
```

When the return values are named, those names are then usable within the function. You can see in the listing that the `circleStuff` function returns two values, one of type `int` and one of type `float32`. More importantly, you can see that each return value is given a name prior to the type. The return variable `d` is defined as the `int`, and the return variable `c` is defined as the `float32`. You are also using `math.Pi` instead of 3.14, so your output will be more accurate.

Within the code, values are assigned to these return variables. Because the return variables have already been identified, there is no need to list them after the `return` statement. The output from running Listing 8.6 is similar to the previous listing:

```
Diameter: 10
Circumference: 31.415928
```

Skipping a Return Value

When calling a function that returns multiple values, you have the option to skip the use of some of the values. In fact, you can use the blank identifier (_) to indicate you do not need a value returned. Listing 8.7 is a modification of Listing 8.6. In this case, only the diameter is needed, so the circumference is skipped.

LISTING 8.7

Skipping a return value

```
package main

import (
    "fmt"
    "math"
)

func circleStuff(radius int) (d int, c float32) {
    d = radius * 2
    c = 2 * math.Pi * float32(radius)
    return
}

func main() {
    diameter, _ := circleStuff(5)

    fmt.Println("diameter:", diameter)
}
```

When you run this listing, the output is

```
diameter: 10
```

Notice that within the `main` function, the blank identifier was used instead of a variable for circumference. This allowed the diameter to be retrieved without getting the circumference.

You might wonder why you don't simply include a placeholder variable when you call the listing. The reason is because Go will give an error if you declare a variable and don't use it.

VARIADIC FUNCTIONS

In general, functions are designed to accept a fixed number of parameters, but there are cases where you may not know ahead of time how many parameters you need, especially if you are working with data structures like arrays and maps that can be of different lengths. When you're using a *variadic* function (a function with a variable number of parameters), all parameter values must be of the same type. You define the parameter using this syntax:

```
func funcName (parameterName ... type) [returnType] {
    // function instructions
}
```

Listing 8.8 presents a function called sumN that accepts a variable number of inputs. The function adds the values of all the arguments received and returns the sum.

LISTING 8.8

A variadic function to sum integers

```
package main

import (
    "fmt"
)

// this function accepts a variable number of input values
func sumN (numbers ... int) {
  sum := 0
  for i, num := range numbers {
    // display values to the user
    fmt.Println("Current element:", num, "; Current index:", i)
    sum += num
  }
```

continues

continued

```
    // print sum of all input values
    fmt.Println("Sum of values:", sum)
    return
}

func main() {
    sumN(4, 6, 5)
    sumN(4, 6, 5, 6, 7, 8)
}
```

The output is

```
Current element: 4 ; Current index: 0
Current element: 6 ; Current index: 1
Current element: 5 ; Current index: 2
Sum of values: 15
Current element: 4 ; Current index: 0
Current element: 6 ; Current index: 1
Current element: 5 ; Current index: 2
Current element: 6 ; Current index: 3
Current element: 7 ; Current index: 4
Current element: 8 ; Current index: 5
Sum of values: 36
```

In this example, the sumN function accepts a range of values rather than a fixed number of values, and it returns no value. It includes a for loop that uses range to iterate through the values provided, adding each value to the current total, printing each value and its index number as it cycles through the loop.

Finally, it prints the sum of the numbers provided when the function is called. In the first case, it has only three numbers to work with, but in the second case, it has six numbers.

RECURSION

Go also supports recursive functions. A recursive function is one that calls itself. Listing 8.9 shows one of the most common uses of recursion, which is calculating the factorial of a given number.

LISTING 8.9

Recursion

```
package main

import "fmt"

func factorial(n int) int {
    if n == 0 {
        return 1
    }
    return n * factorial(n-1)
}

func main() {
    a := 5

    fmt.Println(factorial(a))
}
```

In this example, you create a function named factorial, and this function calls itself in the process of calculating the factorial of a given number. Looking closer, you can see that the function receives an integer. If that integer is 0, then the value of 1 is returned. If the number passed to the function is not 0, then the function is called again when the return statement is executed.

The main function passes the value of 5 to the factorial function. The resulting output is the number 120.

FUNCTION AS A VALUE

In Go, you can assign a function to a variable and then reference the variable when the function is needed. In Listing 8.10, you use the circleStuff function described earlier, but this time, instead of defining the function outside of the main function, you create a variable named circleStuff and assign the function to that variable.

LISTING 8.10

Using a function as a value

```
package main

import (
    "fmt"
    "math"
)

func main() {

    circleStuff := func(radius int) (d int, c float32) {
        d = radius * 2
        c = 2 * math.Pi * float32(radius)
        return
    }

    fmt.Println(circleStuff(5))
}
```

This program works identically to the earlier version, with exactly the same output:

```
10 31.415928
```

Once you define the variable, you can use it to reference the function anywhere in the main function.

CLOSURES

Go supports anonymous functions. An *anonymous function* is a function that does not have a name. In some cases, you simply want the function to run once as part of the main program; you don't need to name it because you don't plan to reuse it. Alternatively, you can assign the anonymous function to a variable or use it as part of a larger function and then call the function through the variable or parent function instead of calling it directly.

A *closure* is a special type of anonymous function that references variables declared outside of the function itself. In a normal function, you use either constants or variables in the main program and pass those values to the parameters defined in the function. The function itself uses its own parameters as the variables.

In a closure, however, you simply reuse the variables you initialized elsewhere and call them directly in the closure. As an example (see Listing 8.11), let's go back to the simple add function you used earlier and use it as an anonymous function.

LISTING 8.11

A simple anonymous add function

```go
package main

import (
    "fmt"
)

func main() {
    a := 4
    b := 10

    add := func() int {
        return a + b
    }

    fmt.Println(add())
}
```

In this program, you create an anonymous function that adds two values, and you assign the function to a variable. The function itself is a closure because it calls the variables defined in the main function, and it does not have any defined parameters of its own.

You use the variable add to call the function. Because the function already knows what values to use, you do not need to provide those values when you call the function.

Listing 8.12 includes a closure as part of the passGenerator function.

LISTING 8.12

An embedded function

```go
package main

import (
    "fmt"
    "math/rand"
```

continues

continued
```go
)

func passGenerator() func() string {
    length := 10
    return func() string {
        pwd := ""
        for i := 0; i < length; i++ {
            // generate a number between 0 and 255 and convert it
            // into its equivalent in UTF-8
            randomChar := string(rand.Intn(256))
            pwd += randomChar
        }
        return pwd
    }
}

func main() {
    passGen := passGenerator()
    fmt.Println(passGen())
    fmt.Println(passGen())
    fmt.Println(passGen())
}
```

The passGenerator function is configured to generate a password using a series of randomly generated characters. The resulting password is saved to the pwd variable, a variable that is defined outside of the anonymous function that generates the password.

> NOTE Because this program generates characters based on UTF-8, you may not see the characters correctly if you are using a Windows CLI to run the program. You can use the web-based Go Playground found at https://go.dev/play instead.

SUMMARY

In this lesson you learned about one of the important features for organizing your code. As you write programs using Go, it is important to organize functionality. You can do so with functions.

Not only did you learn how to create your own functions, but you also learned how to pass items to a function in a variety of ways as well as how to return and receive information from the functions you create. The lesson ended by covering a couple of more advanced topics, including recursion, assigning a function to a variable, and closures.

In the next lesson, you'll start to dig into special data structures that can be used to hold information. You will be learning about arrays!

EXERCISES

The following exercises are provided to allow you to experiment with the tools and concepts presented in this lesson. For each exercise, write a program that meets the specified requirements and verify that the program runs as expected. The exercises are:

Exercise 8.1: Creating Your Own Functions

Exercise 8.2: Spheres

Exercise 8.3: What Does the Fox Say?

Exercise 8.4: Using Recursion

Exercise 8.5: Fibonacci Function

Exercise 8.6: A Calculator

> **NOTE** The exercises are for your benefit. The exercises help you apply what you learn in the lessons. You are also encouraged to experiment with the code as you complete the exercises.

Exercise 8.1: Creating Your Own Functions

Write a program that uses at least two customized functions to perform operations on at least two values input by the user. As an example, you could create a function that compares an input value to a fixed value to determine if the values are the same. As a more complicated approach, you could create a login function that compares an input username and password to a known username and password and displays appropriate feedback based on whether or not both input values match the known values.

Exercise 8.2: Spheres

Rename the `circleStuff` function presented in the lesson to `sphereStuff`. Modify the function to also return the area of the sphere in addition to the circumference and diameter.

Exercise 8.3: What Does the Fox Say?

Create a new function called petSound. The function should take the name of a pet as the parameter. The function should return a string that indicates the sound the pet makes.

For example, if the function were called with dog in the following manner:

```
fmt.Println("A dog says", petSound("dog"))
```

then, the return value would be woof and the output would be

```
A dog says woof
```

Exercise 8.4: Using Recursion

Research other problems that can use recursion to find the solution. Write a program that includes a recursive function for at least two other examples.

Exercise 8.5: Fibonacci Function

Implement a Fibonacci function that returns a function (a closure) that returns successive Fibonacci numbers (0, 1, 1, 2, 3, 5, ...).

> **NOTE** You can learn more about Fibonacci numbers at https://mathworld.wolfram.com/FibonacciNumber.html.

Exercise 8.6: A Calculator

Create a calculator application that runs from the command line. The calculator should perform the following tasks:

- Accept a word like quit or exit at any prompt to end the program.
- Accept two numeric values from the user.
- Allow the user to choose a mathematical operation using the two input values, including at least addition, subtraction, multiplication, modulus (%), square root, and factorial. You may include other operations if you wish.

- Display the output as a complete mathematical statement. For example, if the user wants to add two numbers, the output should look like

  8 + 9 = 17

- Prompt the user to start over after completing a calculation.

Additional requirements:

- Use and call appropriate functions in the code.
  - Each operation should be a separate function.
  - Include additional functions as appropriate.
- If the user enters an unexpected/invalid value at a prompt or the output causes an error (such as dividing by 0), the program should display appropriate feedback and prompt the user to try again.
- The program should be as user-friendly as possible, by giving the user clear options for each prompt and letting them know how to exit the program when they wish.

Lesson 9
Accessing Arrays

You learned about storing basic data types in Lesson 3, "Storing with Variables," by using variables. There are times when you want to store several of the same things together, such as a list of numbers, names, or contacts.

An *array* is a data structure that holds a finite number of elements. In Go, all values in an array must be of the same data type, and the size of the array is part of the array's type. In this lesson, we will look at the use of arrays in your Go programs.

LEARNING OBJECTIVES

By the end of this lesson, you will be able to:

- Declare your own arrays.
- Initialize arrays.
- Change the values in an array.
- Use looping to access elements in an array.
- Understand how to use Range with an array.
- Work with multidimensional arrays.
- Duplicate an array.
- Compare similar arrays.

NOTE Arrays are just one construct that can be used to store similar data. In Lesson 12, "Accessing Slices," you will also learn about slices, which are related to arrays but are more flexible. For now, however, it is important to understand arrays and how they can be used in Go.

DECLARING AN ARRAY

As a general rule in Go, it is not possible to change the data type of any declared variable. Because an array's data type includes both the value type and the size, you cannot change the type or how many values are in a defined array. As you will learn later in this lesson, you can, however, change the individual values in the array.

When declaring an array, you can specify the number of values the array will hold and the data type for those values. This number is included after the array name between square brackets. For example, the following statement would create an array that can hold five integers:

```
var array_1 [5]int
```

You can see the format for declaring an array is similar to that of a regular variable with the addition of the brackets and the number of elements the array can hold. If you wanted to declare a variable to hold a name, you would type:

```
var name string
```

To declare a variable to hold an array of names, you'd type:

```
var names [10]string
```

Assigning a Value to an Array Element

Once you have declared the array, you can access the values within it. Each value in the array is identified by an index value, with the first value indexed as 0. You can use these indexes to assign a specific value to each slot in the array. For example, the following statement assigns the value 143 to the first slot in array_1:

```
array_1[0] = 143
```

> **NOTE** A common mistake Go programmers make is to forget that the first element of an array uses an index of 0, not 1. An index of 1 gives you the second element. Remember that arrays start with 0!

Listing 9.1 creates an array of integers and adds three values to the array. It then prints the array in the last instruction.

LISTING 9.1

Declaring an array

```
package main

import "fmt"

func main() {
  // create an array of three integers
  var numbers [3]int

  // assign a value to each position in the array
  numbers[0] = 1
  numbers[1] = 34
  numbers[2] = 3455

  // display the array
  fmt.Println(numbers)
}
```

In this example, you create an empty int array called numbers that has three slots. You then add values to each index in the array. When Println runs, you see the three numbers displayed:

```
[1 34 3455]
```

You can see in the output that because the array was passed to Println, the numbers were printed inside brackets to indicate it is an array. You could access and print each number in the array using the individual indexes, as shown in Listing 9.2.

LISTING 9.2

Printing individual array elements

```
package main

import "fmt"

func main() {
  // create an array of three integers
  var numbers [3]int

  // assign a value to each position in the array
  numbers[0] = 1
  numbers[1] = 34
  numbers[2] = 3455

  // display the array
  fmt.Println(numbers[0], numbers[1], numbers[2])
}
```

The only difference in this listing is the `fmt.Println` statement. Instead of passing the entire array, each element is passed with its index. You can see the same number displayed when running the listing this time; however, each is printed individually without the brackets around them:

```
1 34 3455
```

Basic Rules of Arrays

The code in Listing 9.1 and Listing 9.2 declare an array with three elements of type `int`. There are several observations to be gained by experimenting with this listing by making some changes.

For example, the code in the listings add values to the array in sequential order. Does the order have to be sequential? What if you add a value to index 2 before adding a value to index 1? Would this matter? Try changing the three assignment statements in Listing 9.2 to the following and rerun the listing:

```
numbers[2] = 3455
numbers[0] = 1
numbers[1] = 34
```

What you will find is that *the order you assign values to the indexes does not matter.* But what happens if you do not fill all the slots in the array? What if you were to leave one of the values unassigned? Listing 9.3 repeats Listing 9.2, but it fails to assign a value to numbers[1]. What do you think will happen when you try to run this code?

LISTING 9.3

Failure to add a value to an array element

```
package main

import "fmt"

func main() {
  // create an array of three integers
  var numbers [3]int

  // assign a value to each position in the array
  numbers[0] = 1

  numbers[2] = 3455

  // display the array
  fmt.Println(numbers[0], numbers[1], numbers[2])
}
```

As you can see, numbers[0] and numbers[2] are assigned values, but there is no assignment of a value to numbers[1]. numbers[1], however, is included in the printed output. The result is that the value of 0 is printed for numbers[1]. *When the array is declared, it is initialized to default values.*

There is another thing to consider regarding arrays. What happens if you add more values than the array is defined to hold? In the previous listings, you have assigned three values to the numbers array. You've put a value in each of the three elements. Listing 9.4 assigns extra values to our index. Will the index simply grow to accommodate the values, or is something else going to happen?

LISTING 9.4

Assigning extra index values

```
package main

import "fmt"

func main() {
    // create an array of three integers
    var numbers [3]int

    // assign a value to each position in the array
    numbers[0] = 1
    numbers[1] = 34
    numbers[2] = 3455
    numbers[3] = 30
    numbers[4] = 40
    numbers[99] = 990

    // display the array
    fmt.Println(numbers[0], numbers[1], numbers[2])
}
```

You might think that this will simply increase the size of the array to hold the added values; however, that would be incorrect. Running this listing will give you errors:

```
.\ Listing0904.go:13:11: invalid array index 3 (out of bounds for 3-element array)
.\ Listing0904.go:14:11: invalid array index 4 (out of bounds for 3-element array)
.\ Listing0904.go:15:11: invalid array index 99 (out of bounds for 3-element array)
```

Remember, one of the things mentioned earlier is that *when an array is declared, the type and the size cannot be changed.*

> **NOTE** Another common mistake made by Go programmers is to use the wrong index value to access the last element of an array. If you declare an array of *n* elements, the last element will use an index of *n*–1. So, the last element of an array of 10 elements will be 9.

Similarity of an Array Element and Variable

In addition to the basic rules mentioned in the previous section, there are a couple of other things to consider when working with arrays:

- What happens if you add a different value to the same index?
- What happens if you add a string value to a number array (or vice versa)?

The answer to these questions is that the same thing happens that would happen if you were working with regular variable types. If you assign a value more than once to a regular variable, what happens? If you try to assign a string to an integer variable (or vice versa), what happens?

Assigning a value to the same element more than once does not cause an issue. Rather, just like a variable, the last value assigned will overwrite any previously entered values, as shown in Listing 9.5.

LISTING 9.5

Assigning a value to the same array index more than once

```
package main

import "fmt"

func main() {
    // create an array of three integers
    var numbers [3]int

    // assign a value to each position in the array
    numbers[0] = 1
    numbers[1] = 34
    numbers[2] = 3455

    numbers[0] = 999
    numbers[0] = 50000

    numbers[1] = numbers[2]

    // display the array
    fmt.Println(numbers)
}
```

This listing modifies Listing 9.1 to include three additional assignment statements. You can see that numbers[0] is assigned a second value of 999 and then is reassigned again to the value of 50000. The array element numbers[1] is assigned numbers[2]. This assigns the value stored within numbers[2] to numbers[1]. The final output from this listing is:

```
[50000 3455 3455]
```

As you can see, the values can be overwritten just like regular variables, but what about the type? If you try to assign a variable of a different type, such as a string to an int array, you will get the same error you would get when doing the assignment to a variable of a basic data type, as shown in Listing 9.6.

LISTING 9.6

Assigning a different data type

```
package main

import "fmt"

func main() {
    // create an array of three integers
    var number int
    var numbers [3]int

    // assign a value to the basic variable
    number = "one"
    // assign a value to each position in the array
    numbers[0] = "one"
    numbers[1] = "two"
    numbers[2] = "three"

    // display the int
    fmt.Println(number)
    // display the array
    fmt.Println(numbers)
}
```

When you run this listing, you see that assigning strings results in the same type of error for both number and numbers:

```
.\List0906.go:11:11: cannot use "one" (type untyped string) as type int in
assignment
```

```
.\List0906.go:13:15: cannot use "one" (type untyped string) as type int in
assignment
.\List0906.go:14:15: cannot use "two" (type untyped string) as type int in
assignment
.\List0906.go:15:15: cannot use "three" (type untyped string) as type int in
assignment
```

DECLARING AND INITIALIZING AN ARRAY

In the previous examples, you created an empty array and then added values to it. You can also choose to add values when you declare the array. As you saw in the previous section, when an empty array is declared, Go assigns a default value to each slot in the array. The default value depends on the data type:

- For numbers, the default is 0.

- For strings, the default is an empty string (often referred to as *null*).

Listing 9.7 shows different ways to declare and initialize an array in a single statement.

LISTING 9.7

Declaring and initializing an array

```
package main

import "fmt"

func main() {

    // declare an empty array
    var empty [6]int

    // declare an int array and initialize its values
    var numbers = [5]int {1000, 2, 3, 7, 50}

    // declare an array without the var keyword
    words := [4]string {"hi","how","are","you"}

    fmt.Println(empty)
    fmt.Println(numbers)
    fmt.Println(words)
}
```

For the first array called `empty`, you create an array, but you do not add any values to it anywhere in the program. Go will assign a default value to each item in the array, based on the data type assigned to the array. For integers, the default is 0, so the array looks like this:

```
[0 0 0 0 0]
```

For the second array called `numbers`, you use the `var` keyword and include a set of integers after declaring the array. The values are added to the array from left to right, so the final array looks like this:

```
[1000 2 3 7 50]
```

In the last array called `words`, you use the `:=` operator instead of the `var` keyword and include a set of string values to be added to the array. You can see that the array is defined to hold four elements. When the `words` array is printed, you see it contains these values:

```
[hi how are you]
```

NOTE Remember, the `:=` operator both declares the type and assigns values to the variable on the left side of the statement. The type is inferred from the type of the data used on the right. When using the `:=` operator to declare and initialize an array, make sure all of the values on the right are of the same type.

INFERRING ARRAY SIZE

When you declare and initialize an array in the same statement, you can choose to leave out the size of the array. In this case, Go will create an array whose size is equal to the number of values added to the array when it is initialized.

Listing 9.8 does not specify the size of the array when you declare it. Because you initialize it with four values, the array's size will be 4.

LISTING 9.8

Inferring an array's size

```
package main

import "fmt"

func main() {
   numbers := [...]int {5, 6, 7, 9}

   fmt.Println(numbers)
   fmt.Println(len(numbers))
}
```

Note the following:

- You include a placeholder for the size of the array: [. . .]
- At the end of the program, you use the len function to identify the number of elements in the array (its length).

Even when the array's size is not explicitly declared, however, the array's size is fixed. After creating the numbers array In this listing, you cannot add a fifth value to the array.

There is also a difference between this option and the option of initializing only some of the values in a longer array. For example, the following statement will create an array that contains five items but the last item will have the default value of 0:

```
numbers := [5] int {5, 6, 7, 9}
```

USING A *FOR* LOOP TO DEFINE AN ARRAY

Instead of adding values individually to an array, you can use a for loop to assign values to an empty array. Listing 9.9 first defines an int array and then uses a for loop to sequentially add numbers to the array.

LISTING 9.9

Defining an array with a for loop

```
package main

import "fmt"
```

continues

continued

```go
func main() {
    var numbers [20]int

    for x := 0; x < 20; x++ {
        numbers[x] = x
    }

    fmt.Println(numbers)
}
```

In this code, you initialize x as 0. You compare x to the number of values in the array (20 in this example) to control the loop, and you increment x after each iteration of the loop. Within the loop, you assign the value of x to the array element with an index value of x, so the result is:

```
[0 1 2 3 4 5 6 7 8 9 10 11 12 13 14 15 16 17 18 19]
```

USING RANGE WITH AN ARRAY

In the previous listing, you knew that the array contained 20 elements and you were able to use that in the for loop. You can use the len function mentioned earlier to get the length of an array, as shown in Listing 9.9, and then use that value to iterate through an array. There is, however, another option.

The range function, shown in Listing 9.10, iterates through a defined collection of elements and can be used to retrieve index values or stored values. When used in a for loop, range effectively limits the number of loops based on the number of items in the array collection.

LISTING 9.10

Using range

```go
package main

import "fmt"

func main() {
    numbers := [4] int {1,3,5,7}

    fmt.Println("Printing numbers:")
    fmt.Println(numbers)
```

```
    fmt.Println("Starting for loop...")
    for index, value := range numbers{
        fmt.Println(index)
        fmt.Println(value)
        fmt.Println("---")
    }
}
```

In this example, you create an array called numbers that contains four integers. You first print the numbers array so that the values can be seen. You then use range to iterate through the array to output the index value (stored in index) for each item in the array, as well as the values themselves (stored in value). The full output is as follows:

```
Printing numbers:
[1 3 5 7]
Starting for loop...
0
1
---
1
3
---
2
5
---
3
7
---
```

Listing 9.10 used the names index and value in the for loop; any name can be used for them. These names were, however, selected for these variables because they represent what they hold.

CREATING MULTIDIMENSIONAL ARRAYS

Go supports multidimensional arrays. A multidimensional array is a data structure that includes at least one array nested inside another array. In essence, you can use arrays as values inside a larger array. Listing 9.11 creates a two-dimensional array—a single large array whose values are themselves arrays.

LISTING 9.11

Two-dimensional array

```
package main

import "fmt"

func main() {
    // declare a two-dimensional array with two sizes instead of one
    matrix := [3][3]int {
        {1, 2, 3},
        {4, 5, 6},
        {7, 8, 9},
    }

    fmt.Println(matrix)
    fmt.Println(matrix[0][0])
    fmt.Println(matrix[1][2])
}
```

Look at the code:

- To create both dimensions, you include two size values when you declare the array. You are declaring an array of three elements that will hold arrays that also contain three elements.

- As with any other array, all values in a multidimensional array must use the same data type. In this example, you use int.

At the end of the program, you display the array itself. The output looks like this:

```
[[1 2 3] [4 5 6] [7 8 9]]
```

You also retrieve and display two values from the array, using a pair of indexes for each value. The first value in the pair identifies which nested array the value is in, and the second value identifies the index value from the nested array itself. For the first pair ([0][0]), you retrieve the first value in the first array. For the second pair ([1][2]), you retrieve the third value from the second array. Figure 9.1 shows the index positions of each element in the matrix you created in Listing 9.11.

In this example, each of the nested arrays has the same size, but the nested arrays can be different sizes. Again, however, they must all be of the same type.

	column 0	column 1	column 2
row 0	matrix[0][0]	matrix[0][1]	matrix[0][2]
row 1	matrix[1][0]	matrix[1][1]	matrix[1][2]
row 2	matrix[2][0]	matrix[2][1]	matrix[2][2]

Figure 9.1: The index positions of matrix

NOTE We've shown the use of a two-dimensional array in this lesson. You can expand an array to be more than two dimensions by adding additional brackets. A three-dimensional array would be in the form of matrix[][][]. In general, however, the more dimensions you use, the more complicated your code will appear. As such, it is often good practice to try to limit the number of dimensions when possible.

DUPLICATING AN ARRAY

Arrays in Go are value types in their own right. This means that if you assign an array to a new variable, Go creates a new copy of the array. Listing 9.12 creates a duplicate of an array and then changes one of the values in the new array.

LISTING 9.12

Duplicating an array

```
package main

import "fmt"

func main() {
   numbers_1 := [3]int {5, 6, 7}
   fmt.Println(numbers_1)

   // copy the array to a new variable
   numbers_2 := numbers_1
   fmt.Println(numbers_2)
```

continues

continued

```
    // change a value in the new array
    numbers_2[0]=100

    // output both arrays
    fmt.Println(numbers_1)
    fmt.Println(numbers_2)
}
```

In this listing, you can see that an array called numbers_1 is created and assigned the values of 5, 6, and 7. A second array called numbers_2 is created, and it is set equal to numbers_1. Because arrays are value types, the numbers in numbers_1 are copied to numbers_2. This is important because it means that when the value in numbers_2 is changed to 100, it does not impact the values stored in numbers_1. They each have their own copy of the values, as you can see by the output from the last two print lines of the listing:

```
[5 6 7]
[100 6 7]
```

This clearly shows that updating the value in the copy of the array does not affect the values in the original array.

COMPARING ARRAYS

In most programming languages, to compare two arrays to see if they are the same, you would iterate through the arrays and compare each element in the same position to see if they matched. In Go, you can directly compare two arrays of the same size and type for equality without having to iterate through them. Listing 9.13 uses the matrix array from earlier and compares it to two other arrays.

LISTING 9.13

Comparing arrays

```
package main

import "fmt"

func main() {

    matrix := [3][3]int {
        {1, 2, 3},
```

```
        {4, 5, 6},
        {7, 8, 9},
    }

matrix_2 := [3][3]int {
        {1, 2, 3},
        {4, 5, 6},
        {7, 8, 9},
    }

matrix_3 := [3][3]int {
        {9, 9, 9},
        {9, 9, 9},
        {9, 9, 9},
    }

    // Compare matrix to matrix_1
    if( matrix == matrix_2 ) {
        fmt.Println("matrix equals matrix_2")
    } else {
        fmt.Println("matrix does NOT equal matrix_2")
    }

    // Compare matrix to matrix_3
    if( matrix == matrix_3 ) {
        fmt.Println("matrix equals matrix_3")
    } else {
        fmt.Println("matrix does NOT equal matrix_3")
    }

    // Print out the three arrays
    fmt.Println(matrix)
    fmt.Println(matrix_2)
    fmt.Println(matrix_3)
}
```

You can see that matrix and matrix_1 are the same, so when compared, the result is a value of true. When matrix is compared to matrix_2, the values are not the same, so the output is false:

```
matrix equals matrix_2
matrix does NOT equal matrix_3
[[1 2 3] [4 5 6] [7 8 9]]
[[1 2 3] [4 5 6] [7 8 9]]
[[9 9 9] [9 9 9] [9 9 9]]
```

It is important to remember that this comparison only works if the arrays are of the same size and type. If they are not, you will get an error.

SUMMARY

In this lesson, we covered arrays, including how to declare, initialize, and use them. Now that you've completed this lesson, you should be able to change values in an array, loop through an array, duplicate an array, and even compare two similarly sized and typed arrays. You also learned how to work with multidimensional arrays.

EXERCISES

The following exercises are provided to allow you to experiment with the tools and concepts presented in this lesson. For each exercise, write a program that meets the specified requirements and verify that the program runs as expected. The exercises are:

Exercise 9.1: Two Arrays

Exercise 9.2: Three Arrays

Exercise 9.3: For Evens

Exercise 9.4: Moving from One to Another

Exercise 9.5: Forward and Backward

Exercise 9.6: Two Dimensions of Four

Exercise 9.7: Duplicating

Exercise 9.8: Personal Data

> **NOTE** The exercises are for your benefit. The exercises help you apply what you learn in the lessons. You are also encouraged to experiment with the code as you complete the exercises.

Exercise 9.1: Two Arrays

Create a program with two different arrays. Create the arrays, add the values, and print both arrays:

- The first array should include at least 10 different integers.
- The second array should include at least five different string values.

Exercise 9.2: Three Arrays

Write a program that includes at least three separate arrays. The program should do the following using working examples:

- Declare an array in one statement and assign values to the array in a separate statement.
- Declare an array with a defined size and assign values to the array in the same statement.
- Declare an array without specifying the size and assign values to the array in the same statement.

You may use whatever arrays you wish, including reusing arrays from the listings in this lesson. For each array, display the array itself and its length.

Exercise 9.3: For Evens

Starting with the code in Listing 9.9, create an array that includes 10 values, where each value is an even number between 1 and 20. You must use a for loop in your solution, but you can use a different variation on a for loop if you prefer.

Exercise 9.4: Moving from One to Another

Write a program that includes an array with at least 10 values in it. The program should also include a second, empty array with 10 values. Use a for loop and the range function to populate the second array with the values in the first array.

Challenge: Update the program so that the second array contains the values in the first array, but in the reverse order. For example, if the original array is [5 6 7], the second array should be [7 6 5].

Exercise 9.5: Forward and Backward

Create a program that iterates through the values of an array and replaces the original values with the same values in the reverse order. For example, if the original array is [5 6 7], the updated array (with the same name) should be [7 6 5].

Exercise 9.6: Two Dimensions of Four

Create a program with a two-dimensional array that is at least 4×4 (an array with at least four array values, where each nested array also includes at least four values). The completed program should display the following:

- The values of the main array, as well as the length of the main array

- The values in the second nested array, as well as the length of the second array
- The last value in the last nested array

Exercise 9.7: Duplicating

Create a program that includes an array with at least six integers. Duplicate the array and update it so that every other value in the new array is updated to match the value immediately ahead of it.

For example, if the original array is [7 5 10 15 30 50], the final version of the new array is [7 7 10 10 30 30]. Do not make any changes to the original array.

Exercise 9.8: Personal Data

Create a program that performs the following tasks:
- Prompt the user to answer a series of 5–10 questions about themselves, such as their name, their birthday, where they live, their favorite hobby/sport, etc.
  - Include at least 10 questions but give the user the option to quit after answering at least five questions.
- Save the answers in an array.
- Display the results to the user in a user-friendly format.
  - For example, if one of the questions is "What is your name?," the output for that response should look like "Your name is Mary."
- After displaying all answers, prompt the user to change one or more of the answers.
- Update the array with the new answers and redisplay the results.
- Allow the user the option to exit the program at any time.

Lesson 10
Working with Pointers

G o supports pointers. A *pointer* is a variable that stores the
memory address of another variable where the data is stored,
rather than storing a value itself. In this lesson, we will look at the
use of pointers.

LEARNING OBJECTIVES

By the end of this lesson, you will be able to:

- Declare your own pointers.
- Dereference a pointer to view a value.
- Use a pointer to change the value of another variable.
- Compare pointers to determine if they are the same.
- Create an array of pointers and assign it values.
- Pass pointers to functions.

CREATING A POINTER

All variables in Go other than maps and slices are value types. What that means is that if
you have a variable that you are passing to a function and you want to make changes to

the variable outside of the function, you can't change the variable directly. A copy gets passed in whenever you send it to a function.

If you want to modify the variable, the general approach is to use a *pointer to the memory address* instead of trying to affect the variable itself. In other words, you can pass in a pointer to the address of the variable, rather than passing a copy of the value itself. When you pass in a pointer, both the original value and the value used in the function are pointing to the same part of memory. Because they're pointing to the same spot in memory, when you change one value, both variables are changed.

Pointers are also used to pass in larger variables. If you have a large struct, then your application would take time and memory to copy the struct and all of its fields over to a function when passed, whereas if you pass in a pointer, the function will just receive the memory address of the struct. The memory address is going to be much smaller than the struct, so the application will be more efficient.

> **NOTE** Although we mention them here, you will learn the details of structs in Lesson 11, "Organizing with Structs"; of slices in Lesson 12, "Accessing Slices"; and of maps in Lesson 13, "Manipulating Maps."

The syntax used to define a pointer is:

```
var pointerName *dataType
```

The *pointerName* is the name of the variable that will hold the pointer. The *dataType* is the type that is associated with the value stored in the pointer. In Listing 10.1, you create two variables:

- The variable a is a normal int variable, to which you assign the value 20.
- The variable b is an int pointer, as designated by *int.

LISTING 10.1

Declaring two variables

```
package main

import "fmt"
```

```go
func main() {
    var a int = 20 // a stores the value 20
    var b *int // create a pointer variable b

    fmt.Println(a)
    fmt.Println(b)

}
```

When you run the code, the output is:

```
20
<nil>
```

Nothing has been assigned to the b variable, so it is empty. While Go does assign the default value of 0 to an int variable, it does not assign any value at all to a pointer. As a result, you will see that it is shown to be equal to nil.

NOTE It is worth noting that nil is a special value that only applies to pointers. In other languages such as Java and C++, you can assign 0 or a null value to a pointer to have it point at nothing; however, that is not done in Go.

Initializing a Pointer

Once you define a pointer, you can initialize it to point to the memory address of another variable by using the syntax:

pointerName = &*variableName*

In Listing 10.2, the pointer b points to the memory address of variable a.

LISTING 10.2

Initializing a pointer

```go
package main

import "fmt"
```

continues

continued

```go
func main() {
    var a int = 20 // a stores the value 20
    var b *int     // create a pointer variable b
    b = &a         // b stores the memory address of variable a

    fmt.Println(a)
    fmt.Println(b)
}
```

Running the program now gives you this output:

```
20
0xc0000100b0
```

The second value is the hexadecimal address of the memory where the value for a is stored. This value will likely be different each time you run the program, depending on available memory blocks.

Declaring and Initializing a Pointer

You can also combine the definition and initialization of a pointer in one step. Listing 10.3 shows your pointer b being declared and assigned the address of a within one statement.

LISTING 10.3

Declaring and initializing a pointer in one statement

```go
package main

import "fmt"

func main() {
    var a int = 20  // a stores the value 20
    var b *int = &a // b stores the memory address of variable a

    fmt.Println(a)
    fmt.Println(b)
}
```

You again declare a as an int and store the value of 20 within it. You then declare b as a pointer to an int. Within the declaration, you then assign the address of a to the pointer b. When you run this listing, you see output similar to the previous listing. Again, the address printed in the second print statement will vary:

```
20
0xc0000aa058
```

Using Dynamic Typing

You can also create a pointer variable using dynamic typing in the same way you can declare other types of variables. As you may recall, dynamic typing is when you create a variable and assign a value without specifying its type. Listing 10.4 illustrates dynamic typing, where variable b is defined without a type. The compiler will infer the type based on the initial value.

LISTING 10.4

Dynamic typing

```
package main

import "fmt"

func main() {
   var a int = 20 // a stores the value 20
   var b = &a      // b stores the memory address of variable a

   fmt.Println(a)
   fmt.Println(b)
}
```

This listing operates identically to the previous listings. The only difference is that the compiler will infer that b is a pointer to an int.

Pointers of Different Types

Up to this point, you've used a pointer to an int. You can use pointers to any other data types in the exact manner, as illustrated in Listing 10.5.

LISTING 10.5

Pointers of various types

```go
package main

import "fmt"

func main() {
    var a int = 20  // a stores the value 20
    b := &a         // b stores the memory address of variable a

    var c float32 = 10.3
    var d *float32 = &c

    var e string = "My string"
    var f *string = &e

    var g uint = 42
    var h *uint = &g

    fmt.Println(a)
    fmt.Println(b)
    fmt.Println("-------------")
    fmt.Println(c)
    fmt.Println(d)
    fmt.Println("-------------")
    fmt.Println(e)
    fmt.Println(f)
    fmt.Println("-------------")
    fmt.Println(g)
    fmt.Println(h)
    fmt.Println("-------------")
}
```

This listing simply adds declarations to the previous listing to define variables of types float32, string, and uint along with pointers to each. When you run this listing, you see that the values of the variables are printed, and each pointer variable has a unique address:

```
20
0xc000014098
-------------
10.3
```

```
0xc0000140b0
-------------
My string
0xc00003a230
-------------
42
0xc0000140b8
-------------
```

Looking at Listing 10.5, you can see that the type declared for each pointer matches the type being assigned. What happens if you try to assign a variable of one type to a pointer of a different type, such as trying to assign a variable of type float32 to a pointer to an int? Modify Listing 10.5 to assign the value in the variable c (a float32 value) to the pointer called h, which is defined as a pointer to an uint. What happens when you do this? Listing 10.6 shows this modification.

LISTING 10.6

Using a pointer to a different type

```go
package main

import "fmt"

func main() {
    var a int = 20 // a stores the value 20
    b := &a         // b stores the memory address of variable a

    var c float32 = 10.3
    var d *float32 = &c

    var e string = "My string"
    var f *string = &e

    var g uint = 42
    var h *uint = &c  // Assigning a type float32 value to *uint

    fmt.Println(a)
    fmt.Println(b)
    fmt.Println("-------------")
    fmt.Println(c)
    fmt.Println(d)
    fmt.Println("-------------")
```

continues

```
    fmt.Println(e)
    fmt.Println(f)
    fmt.Println("-------------")
    fmt.Println(g)
    fmt.Println(h)
    fmt.Println("-------------")
}
```

If you make the change and run the new listing, you will get an error:

```
# command-line-arguments
.\Listing1006.go:16:9: cannot use &c (type *float32) as type *uint in
assignment
```

While a pointer might hold an address, the value stored in the pointer needs to still match the defined type.

ACCESSING THE STORED VALUE OF A POINTER

In order to access the value stored in the memory address stored in a pointer, you can use the * operator (the *dereferencing operator*), as shown in Listing 10.7.

LISTING 10.7

Accessing a pointer's stored value

```
package main

import "fmt"

func main() {
    var myVar int = 20
    b := &myVar

    fmt.Println(b) // print the memory address
    fmt.Println(*b) // print the value stored in the memory address
}
```

In this listing, a variable of type int called myVar is declared and set to the value of 20. A second variable called b is also declared and it is set to the address of myVar. Because a type is not included when b is declared, the compiler will dynamically type b to be a pointer to type int.

After your two variables are declared, two print statements are executed. You first print out the value of b, which will be the memory address where myVar is located. In the second print statement, you pass *b instead of b. Instead of the address being printed, the dereferencing operator provides the value stored in the variable called b to be retrieved and printed, which is the value stored in myVar. Based on this dereferencing, the output this time looks like this:

```
0xc0000100b0
20
```

> **NOTE** You might notice that the dereferencing operator is the same character as the multiplication operator. Go infers whether you are using the asterisk for multiplication versus dereferencing based on the context of your code.

UNDERSTANDING *NIL* POINTERS

You saw earlier that when we define a pointer without initializing it, it contains a nil value by default. Listing 10.8 declares a pointer but does not initialize it.

LISTING 10.8

Creating a nil pointer

```
package main

import "fmt"

func main() {
    var b *int // create a pointer variable b

    fmt.Println(b)
}
```

The output for this program is:

```
<nil>
```

The nil value means that the pointer itself is empty and contains no real value. In other words, it doesn't point to anything. What would happen if you added a print statement to dereference the value stored in b?

```
fmt.Println(*b)
```

If you try to access the value in a nil pointer, you will get an error similar to the following:

```
panic: runtime error: invalid memory address or nil pointer dereference
[signal 0xc0000005 code=0x0 addr=0x0 pc=0x2ec5d5]
```

To avoid this error, you can use an if statement to verify that a pointer doesn't equal nil. Listing 10.9 checks to see if the pointer called b is nil before trying to access its value.

LISTING 10.9

Checking for nil

```
package main

import "fmt"

func main() {
   var b *int // create a pointer variable b

   fmt.Println(b)
   if b == nil {
      fmt.Println("b is nil")
   } else {
      fmt.Println(*b)
   }
}
```

You can see that to make sure b has a value, it is simply compared to the Go keyword nil. If b is equal to nil, then you know it doesn't point to anything, so you can avoid doing something that would cause an error.

USING POINTERS TO CHANGE VARIABLES

Because the dereferencing operator (∗) assigns a variable's value to a pointer, you can also use it to assign new values to the variables themselves. Listing 10.10 illustrates this.

LISTING 10.10

Changing a variable's value via a pointer

```go
package main

import "fmt"

func main() {
    var a int = 20
    b := &a

    fmt.Print("The value stored in a: ")
    fmt.Println(a)  // print a

    fmt.Print("Memory address: ")
    fmt.Println(b)  // print the memory address

    fmt.Print("Value stored in a (via pointer): ")
    fmt.Println(*b)  // print the value stored at the memory address

    *b = 30  // use the *b to change the value stored at the
             // memory address (or in variable a)
    fmt.Print("New value of a: ")
    fmt.Println(a) // see that the value changed
}
```

In this listing, you assign a value of 20 to the variable a. You create a variable called b as a pointer to a. The listing prints a, b (the memory address), and ∗b (the value stored at the address stored in b, which is the value of a).

After printing these values, the following line is executed:

```go
*b = 30
```

This statement changes the value stored at the memory address in b. As a result of using * on the pointer variable b, you change the value assigned to a. You can confirm this by reviewing the output from the listing:

```
The value stored in a: 20
Memory address: 0xc0000ae058
Value stored in a (via pointer): 20
New value of a: 30
```

Again, the memory address will be different, but you can see that the value of a was changed from 20 to 30.

COMPARING POINTERS

You can use the == operator to check if two pointers are equal. Pointers are equal if they point to the same storage location, which typically implies that they point to the same variable. In Listing 10.11, you create two pointers that refer to the variable a, as well as a nil pointer.

LISTING 10.11

Comparing pointers

```go
package main

import "fmt"

func main() {
    var a int = 20
    b := &a
    c := &a
    var x *int

    fmt.Print("Is c == b? ")
    fmt.Println(c == b) // compare c and b

    fmt.Print("Is x == b? ")
    fmt.Println(x == b) // compare x and b
}
```

Both b and c are declared as pointers that contain the address of a. You also declare a pointer called x as a pointer to an int. You do not assign x a value, so it will contain nil.

You then compare the pointers to each other. First, you compare c to b. You then compare x to b. The output is:

```
Is c == b? true
Is x == b? false
```

> **NOTE** Don't confuse comparing pointers with comparing the values stored at pointers. Comparing pointers will compare the addresses stored in the pointers. You can use the dereferencing operator (*) to compare the value pointed to by pointers as well.

WORKING WITH AN ARRAY OF POINTERS

In the previous lesson, you learned about arrays. In Go, you can also create an array of pointers. Each element of such an array contains an address to a value stored in memory. You can use an array like this in the same way you use traditional arrays. Listing 10.12 illustrates the use of an array of pointers.

LISTING 10.12

Creating an array of pointers

```
package main

import "fmt"

func main() {
  // create a simple array
  numbers := []int{100,1000,10000}

  // print each value in the array
  var ctr int
  for ctr = 0; ctr < len(numbers); ctr++ {
    fmt.Println(numbers[ctr])
  }
```

continues

continued

```
  // create an array of pointers
  var numbersptr [3] *int;

  // assign a pointer to each value in the original array and
  // store them in the new array
  for  ctr := 0; ctr < len(numbersptr); ctr ++ {
    numbersptr[ctr] = &numbers[ctr]
  }

  fmt.Println(numbersptr) // print the pointer array

  // print the values the pointers point to
  fmt.Println(*numbersptr[0])
  fmt.Println(*numbersptr[1])
  fmt.Println(*numbersptr[2])
}
```

In this example, you create an int array called numbers that contains three elements: 100, 1000, and 10000. You then use a for loop to print these values.

You then create a second array called numbersptr that holds three pointers to variables of type int:

```
  var numbersptr [3]*int
```

You use a second for loop to assign a pointer to each value in the original array. This assignment is done using the same index offset:

```
  numbersptr[ctr] = &numbers[ctr]
```

Once these assignments are done, you print the new array, which displays the addresses of the pointers in your numbersptr array.

Finally, you print the individual values the pointers in the array point to. You do this by using the * operator. The output from the complete listing is:

```
  100
  1000
  10000
  [0xc00000a3c0 0xc00000a3c8 0xc00000a3d0]
  100
  1000
  10000
```

Changing Values in an Array

You can manipulate the values of an array using an array of pointers. The code in Listing 10.13 takes the previous example and refactors it to use the pointer to update a value in the original array.

LISTING 10.13

Changing values in an array

```
package main

import "fmt"

func main() {
  // create a simple array
  numbers := []int{100,1000,10000}

  // print each value in the array
  var ctr int
  for ctr = 0; ctr < len(numbers); ctr++ {
    fmt.Println(numbers[ctr])
  }

  // create an array of pointers
  var numbersptr [3] *int

  // assign a pointer to each value in the original array and
  // store them in the new array
  for  ctr := 0; ctr < len(numbersptr); ctr++ {
    numbersptr[ctr] = &numbers[ctr]
  }

  fmt.Println(numbersptr) // print the pointer array

  *numbersptr[0]=200   // change value of first element in array
  fmt.Println(numbers) // view the current array
}
```

Most of this listing is the same as the previous one. However, instead of printing the individual elements of the array of pointers, you assign the value of 200 to the dereferenced pointer in the first element of the numbersptr (position 0):

```
*numbersptr[0]=200
```

You can then see in the output that the value stored in the first element of the numbers array has indeed changed from 100 to 200:

```
100
1000
10000
[0xc00000a3c0 0xc00000a3c8 0xc00000a3d0]
[200 1000 10000]
```

USING POINTERS WITH FUNCTIONS

You can pass pointers to functions. By passing a pointer to a function, you are able to access and use the value stored in the variable the pointer references. Listing 10.14 includes a function called isupper that accepts a pointer to a string as input and returns true if the string is in uppercase and false otherwise.

LISTING 10.14

Checking case

```
package main

import(
    "fmt"
    "strings"
)

// create a function that main will call
// function checks that string is uppercase
func isupper(x *string) bool {
    if strings.ToUpper(*x) == *x {
        return true
    }
    return false
}
```

```
func main() {
    var message string = "HELLO WORLD"
    messageptr := &message

    // return true if string is all uppercase
    fmt.Println(isupper(messageptr))
}
```

Here, instead of passing the message variable directly to the function, the isupper function is set up to accept a pointer to that variable, as indicated by the *string argument. Because the original string stored in message is in all caps, the program returns true.

As a side note, this listing imports strings, which includes routines for working with and manipulating strings. In this case, the strings.ToUpper method is used, which takes a string as a parameter and returns a copy of the string in all uppercase letters. For this listing, the copy of the string in all uppercase is then compared to the original string (*x) to see if they are the same.

> **NOTE** Because the original string is not changed in the isupper function, you might wonder why we didn't simply pass the string by value. We mentioned earlier reasons for using a pointer instead of passing by value. In this case, the pointer is likely using less memory than most strings that would be passed to the function, thus making for a more efficient program.

Changing Values from a Function

We mentioned before that variables are passed by value to a function, which means a copy of the variable is passed. You just saw that by passing a pointer to a function, you are able to access and use the value of a variable. The previous example retrieved a value stored in memory without changing that value. However, as you have seen, you can also use pointers to change the value stored in a variable.

Listing 10.15 converts a string to uppercase. The function (called upper in this listing) is again defined to use a pointer as an argument rather than the variable's value itself. This time, however, the function replaces the variable's value with an uppercase version of the original string.

LISTING 10.15

Converting a string to uppercase

```go
package main

import(
    "fmt"
    "strings"
)

// create a function that main will call
// upper function takes as input a pointer of string
func upper(x *string) {
    *x = strings.ToUpper(*x)
}

func main() {
    var message string = "hello world"

    messageptr := &message

    upper(messageptr)

    fmt.Println(message)
}
```

In this code, you initialize message with a string in lowercase. You then use messageptr in the upper function to convert the string to uppercase. The final output (HELLO WORLD) shows that the variable's value has been changed, rather than just presenting the original string in uppercase.

SUMMARY

In this lesson you learned about pointers, which are variables that contain the memory address of another variable or nil if the pointer is unassigned. Not only did you learn how to declare and initialize pointers, but you also saw how to use them to access and manipulate the values in other variables. You even went further and saw how to use pointers in arrays as well as how to use them with functions. You learned that by passing a pointer to a function, you are able to change values in variables outside of the function.

EXERCISES

The following exercises are provided to allow you to experiment with the tools and concepts presented in this lesson. For each exercise, write a program that meets the specified requirements and verify that the program runs as expected. The exercises are:

Exercise 10.1: Name, Age, and Gender

Exercise 10.2: User Input

Exercise 10.3: Playing with Pointers

Exercise 10.4: Full Name

Exercise 10.5: What's It Doing?

Exercise 10.6: Reverse

Exercise 10.7: Sort

NOTE The exercises are for your benefit. The exercises help you apply what you learn in the lessons. You are also encouraged to experiment with the code as you complete the exercises.

Exercise 10.1: Name, Age, and Gender

Create a program that contains three variables: name, age, and gender. Assign values to each. Make each of these variables a different data type. Create pointers that point to each variable. Use fmt.Println statements to print the values from each of the three variables both by using the original variables and by dereferencing the pointers.

Exercise 10.2: User Input

In a previous lesson, you prompted the user to enter values. You used the fmt.Scanln function for this. Enter and run Listing 10.16, which prompts the user to enter a name, age, and gender:

LISTING 10.16

Getting user input

```
package main

import "fmt"

func main() {
  fmt.Print("Enter your name: ")

  var name string
  fmt.Scanln(&name)

  fmt.Print("Enter your age: ")
  var age string
  fmt.Scanln(&age)

  fmt.Print("Enter your gender: ")
  var gender string
  fmt.Scanln(&gender)

  fmt.Print("Your first name is: ")
  fmt.Println(name)

  fmt.Print("Your age is: ")
  fmt.Println(age)

  fmt.Print("Your gender is: ")
  fmt.Println(gender)
}
```

After running the listing, change it to use pointers to each of the three variables instead of directly passing the address of each.

Exercise 10.3: Playing with Pointers

Enter and run the program in Listing 10.14 if you haven't already. Make the following changes to the listing and review what happens. Try to predict what will happen before making the changes.

- Change the value assigned to message to be "Hello World". What is the output?

- Change the value assigned to message to be "HELLO 123 WORLD". What is the output?

- What happens if the function uses message instead of messageptr in the last line of code?

```
fmt.Println(isupper(message))
```

Exercise 10.4: Full Name

Create a function that takes three parameters. The first should be a pointer to a string variable that will hold a full name. The second and third parameters should be strings that contain a first name and a last name, respectively. The function should first combine the first and last name strings with a space between to create a full name, which should be applied to the variable in the location of the pointer passed to the function.

In addition to writing the function, create a main program that creates the full name variable and a pointer to the full name. Pass these along with first and last name strings to the function. After calling the function, print the full name.

Exercise 10.5: What's It Doing?

Take a look at Listing 10.17. Most of this code is similar to what you saw in this lesson. Without running the code, what do the last three statements in the listing do?

LISTING 10.17

What's it doing?

```
package main

import "fmt"

func main() {
  numbers := []int {123,111,333,777, 222,999,555,888,666,444}

  // print each value in the array
  var ctr int
  for ctr = 0; ctr < len(numbers); ctr++ {
    fmt.Println(numbers[ctr])
  }
```

continues

continued

```
var numbersptr [10] *int;
for  ctr := 0; ctr < len(numbersptr); ctr ++ {
  numbersptr[ctr] = &numbers[ctr]
}

tmp := *numbersptr[9]
*numbersptr[9] = *numbersptr[0]
*numbersptr[0] = tmp
}
```

Exercise 10.6: Reverse

Expand the listing in Exercise 10.5 so that you use the pointers to change the order of the array. Using the pointers, reverse the values so that when the array is displayed, the results are:

```
[444 666 888 555 999 222 777 333 111 123]
```

Exercise 10.7: Sort

Rewrite the listing in Exercise 10.6 so that you use the pointers to change the order of the array. This time, use the pointers and the values to which they point to sort the list from highest to lowest.

Lesson 11
Organizing with Structs

U p to this point, you've used a variety of individual variables. When it has come to grouping or relating variables, you've learned about arrays, which group a number of values of the same type under a single variable name. There are also times when you want to associate a number of different variables to a single group. For instance, you can create a bank account item with fields that represent information about a bank account, such as an account holder, an account number, and a balance.

A *struct* is a data structure that includes a list of fields. Structs are an important aspect of any programming language in that they allow you to organize a group of variables into a related unit such as an account. This lesson takes a close look at the use of structs in Go.

By the end of this lesson, you will be able to:

- Understand how a struct can be used.
- Create your own structs.
- Retrieve elements from a struct.
- Modify the values in a struct.
- Use functions (methods) with a struct.
- Compare structs.

DECLARING AND INITIALIZING A STRUCT

Structs allow you to create complex data types. A struct in Go can contain one or more fields. Each field in the struct must have a data type. You can use the struct keyword to create a struct using syntax like this:

```
type structName struct {
    field1 string
    field2 float64
[…]
}
```

Listing 11.1 creates a struct named account with two fields, accountNumber and balance, and assigns a value to each of those fields.

LISTING 11.1

Creating a struct

```
package main

import "fmt"

// create the struct
type account struct {
    accountNumber string
    balance float64
}
```

```
func main() {
    var a account

    a.balance = 140
    a.accountNumber = "C14235345354"

    fmt.Println(a)
}
```

Let's look at the code. You define a struct by using the `type` keyword followed by the name of the struct and then the keyword `struct`. You use the keyword `type` because you're creating a new data type that you can use in the listing. The data type you're creating in this case is an account struct, named `account`. In the `account` struct, `accountNumber` represents the account number, defined as a string, and `balance` represents the current account balance, using `float64`.

In the `main` function of this listing, you define a variable using the account type you've defined. You declare a variable named `a` in the same way you would any other variable; however, in this case you use `account` as the type:

```
var a account
```

To access the individual fields of the new struct you created, you use the `.` operator (a period). More specifically, you use the name of the struct followed by the period, followed by the name of the field. In order to access and assign values to the fields in your account struct called `a`, you do the following:

```
a.balance = 140
a.accountNumber = "C14235345354"
```

Finally, you print the struct, which displays the values of the fields within the struct:

```
{C14235345354 140}
```

Retrieving Values from a Struct

You could've also printed the individual fields in the struct by using the same format you used to assign values. This is illustrated in Listing 11.2, which adds two print statements to the previous listing.

LISTING 11.2

Retrieving values from a struct

```
package main

import "fmt"

type account struct {
    accountNumber string
    balance float64
}

func main() {
    var a account

    a.balance = 140
    a.accountNumber = "C14235345354"

    fmt.Println(a)

    fmt.Println("The account number is", a.accountNumber)

    fmt.Println("The current balance is", a.balance)
}
```

In this example, you use a.number to retrieve only the account number, whereas a.balance retrieves only the account balance. The output is as follows:

```
{C14235345354 140}
The account number is C14235345354
The current balance is 140
```

Initializing a Struct When Declaring

As with other variables, you can declare and initialize a struct variable in a single statement. Listing 11.3 uses the *struct literal* to assign values to the fields in the struct. In a struct literal, you simply assign values inside curly brackets ({}) when you declare the variable.

LISTING 11.3

Using a struct literal to initialize a struct

```
package main

import "fmt"

type account struct {
    accountNumber string
    balance float64
}

func main() {
    var a = account{"C14235345354",140}

    fmt.Println(a)
}
```

In this example, the values in the curly brackets are assigned to the struct's field in the order they appear in the struct itself. As such, C14235345354 will be assigned to the accountNumber string and 140 will be assigned to balance. When this listing is executed, the output looks like this:

```
(C14235345354 140}
```

Using the Short Assignment Operator

Another option is to use the short assignment operator (:=) with the struct literal. You've used this operator in the same manner when declaring basic variables of basic data types as well. Listing 11.4 shows the short assignment operator being used with a struct.

LISTING 11.4

Using the short assignment operator

```
package main

import "fmt"
```

continues

continued

```
type account struct {
    accountNumber string
    balance float64
}

func main() {
    a := account{"C13242524", 140.78}
    fmt.Println(a)

    b := account{}
    fmt.Println(b)
}
```

This listing again creates the account struct with a string and `float64` value. The struct is then used in the `main` function to declare two new variables. Using the short assignment operator, the first variable called `a` is defined to be an account and the values `C13242524` and `140.78` are assigned to its fields. You see these values printed in the first line of the output.

The second variable called `b` is also created using the short assignment operator, which declares and initializes the struct. You should notice that there are, however, no values between the curly brackets. This means that default values will be assigned to the fields. By default, these fields are assigned 0, which is a blank for a string. You can see this also from the second line of the output:

```
{C13242524 140.78}
{ 0}
```

> **NOTE** As a reminder, the following are the default values assigned by Go:
>
> - A numeric variable will be defaulted to a value of 0.
> - A string variable will be assigned an empty string ("").
> - A Boolean variable will be defaulted to a value of false.

USING KEY-VALUE PAIRS WITH STRUCTS

When initializing values in a struct by passing a value between curly brackets, you must make sure that the values are listed in the same order as the struct fields. Additionally, all fields must be initialized. Consider your previous struct for an account:

```
type account struct {
    accountNumber string
    balance float64
}
```

When you initialize this, let's see what happens if you pass the balance first and the account number second:

```
a := account{140.78, "C13242524"}
```

In this case, a number is being assigned to a string and a string to a number, so errors will occur:

```
# command-line-arguments
.\listing.go:11:17: cannot use 140.78 (type untyped float) as type string in
field value
.\listing.go:11:25: cannot use "C13242524" (type untyped string) as type
float64 in field value
```

If you were to create an account with an account number but not assign a balance, you might be tempted to do the following:

```
a := account{"C13242524"}
```

In this case the account number is provided, but there is no balance. While you might assume that this would default the balance to 0, that is not the case. Instead, this produces an error indicating there are too few elements:

```
# command-line-arguments
.\listing.go:11:17: too few values in account{...}
```

In a small struct with two fields, it is easy to make sure things are in order and all fields are assigned; however, as programs get more complex and structs get larger, this might not be the case. Go provides a way to get around these two restrictions by using *key-value pairs*.

When you use key-value pairs to initialize a struct, fields can be initialized in any order and not all fields have to be initialized. A key-value pair is simply the name of a field followed by a colon (:) and then the value being used to initialize the field:

```
field : value
```

Each key-value pair is separated by a comma. Listing 11.5 once again presents the account struct to illustrate the use of key-value pairs.

LISTING 11.5
Using key-value pairs

```go
package main

import "fmt"

type account struct {
    accountNumber string
    balance float64
}

func main() {

    a := account{ balance: 140.78, accountNumber: "C13242524"}

    b := account{ accountNumber: "S12212321"}

    fmt.Println(a)
    fmt.Println(b)
}
```

The unique part of this listing is the creation and initialization of the account structs called a and b. In the first declaration, a is initialized using key-value pairs. You can see that the field names are listed, followed by a colon, then by the value you want to assign. The order of the assignments in this case is reversed so that the balance is passed first and the account number second. When the a struct is printed, you can see that the fields are initialized correctly:

```
{C13242524 140.78}
```

In the creation of the struct called b, only the account number is assigned. You can see that there is no initialization of the balance. As such, by default the balance will be set to 0. This can also be seen when the b struct is printed:

```
{S12212321 0}
```

USING THE *NEW* KEYWORD

It is also possible to create a struct using the new keyword. Listing 11.6 shows the use of the new keyword to declare the same account struct you've been using.

LISTING 11.6

Creating a struct using new

```go
package main

import "fmt"

type account struct {
    accountNumber string
    balance float64
}

func main() {
    a := new(account)
    a.accountNumber = "C14235345354"
    a.balance = 140

    fmt.Println(a)
}
```

In this listing, you can see that the new keyword is used to create a new struct to assign to a variable. The type of struct to be created (the struct's name) is passed within parentheses after the new keywords. In this case, a new account struct is being created and assigned to the variable named a. Everything else about the listing, including how values are assigned, is done in the same manner shown before.

> **NOTE** You can also use the following format to declare a struct using the new keyword:
>
> ```go
> var a = new(account)
> ```

It is important to note that the new keyword is returning a pointer to the struct that is being created. This means that if the struct a in Listing 11.6 were to be passed to a function, the function would not be using a copy of the struct, but rather would be referencing the original object that was created. Listing 11.7 illustrates this by making a change to the account number within a function.

> **NOTE** The built-in function `new()` dynamically allocates the storage for the variable at runtime, zeroes it, and returns the pointer to that variable. This is different from other programming languages such as Java or C++.

LISTING 11.7

Passing a struct created with `new`

```
package main

import "fmt"

type account struct {
    accountNumber string
    balance float64
}

func closeAccount(CurrentAccount *account) {
  CurrentAccount.accountNumber = "CLOSED-" + CurrentAccount.accountNumber;
}

func main() {
    var a = new(account)

    a.accountNumber = "C13242524"
    a.balance = 140.78

    fmt.Println(a.accountNumber)

    closeAccount(a)

    fmt.Println(a.accountNumber)
}
```

In this listing, you're again using the same account struct within your `main` function. You're creating a new account called a, which is assigned an account number and balance. The account number is printed and looks just like you've seen before:

```
C13242524
```

This listing also includes a function called `closeAccount` that receives an account struct as an argument. This struct is called `CurrentAccount` within the function. What you can see, however, is that `CurrentAccount` is a pointer that points to an account.

Within the function, `CurrentAccount` is used in the same way that you've been using the account struct objects up to this point. The account number is being assigned a new value, which is the original value with the text "CLOSED-" concatenated to the front.

Program flow returns to the `main` function after calling `closeAccount` passing the struct called a. When the value of `a.accountNumber` is printed, you can see that the struct was indeed passed by reference and not by value, because the account number has been updated:

```
CLOSED-C13242524
```

> **NOTE** When a struct is created without using the `new` keyword, the name of the struct is not a pointer. Therefore, passing such a struct to a function would be done by value—a copy of the struct would be passed. See Exercise 11.3 at the end of this lesson for an example of this.

POINTERS AND STRUCTS

In the previous section you saw that the `new` keyword can be used to create a pointer to a struct. It is possible to create a pointer in the same way you did in Lesson 10, "Working with Pointers." Listing 11.8 creates a pointer that can access and update values in the fields in an account struct.

LISTING 11.8

Creating a pointer to a function

```go
package main

import "fmt"

type account struct {
    accountNumber string
    balance float64
}
```

continues

continued

```
func main() {
    a := account{"C21345345345355", 15470.09}
    p := &a

    (*p).balance = 220
    fmt.Println(a)

    p.balance = 320
    fmt.Println(a)
}
```

In this listing, you create a struct called a and assign values to it. You then declare a variable called p and assign it the address of a, which means p will be created as a pointer to a struct, or more specifically a pointer to an account struct. You then use the rest of the listing to assign a value to the balance of your struct, which is then printed.

Note that both of the following statements work to assign a value to the field:

```
(*p).balance = 220
```

and:

```
p.balance = 320
```

In the first version, you explicitly represent p as a pointer, using *. However, because you have already defined p as a pointer, you can simply reference it in the same way you would reference the struct itself. The second version uses simpler code to perform the same task. When this listing is executed, you see the balance was indeed assigned and printed in both ways:

```
{C21345345345355 220}
{C21345345345355 320}
```

NESTED STRUCTS

Go supports nested structs, which allow you to create structs and then use those structs as data type fields for other structs. In the example presented in Listing 11.9, you create a new entity struct that represents a person or business that owns an account. You then include an entity struct in your original account struct.

LISTING 11.9

Using nested structs

```go
package main

import "fmt"

type account struct {
    accountNumber string
    balance float64
    owner entity
}

type entity struct{
    id string
    address string
}

func main() {
    e := entity{"000-00-0000", "123 Main Street"}
    a := account{}
    a.accountNumber ="C21345345345355"
    a.balance = 140609.09

    // assign the entity struct as a value in the account struct
    a.owner = e

    fmt.Println(a)
}
```

Within the main function of this listing, you create an entity struct called e, which is initialized with values when declared. You then create an account struct called a. You assign values to the fields in a individually. Note that when you assign the owner value to the account struct, you simply reference the variable that represents the entity struct:

```go
a.owner = e
```

The output from printing the struct called a includes the nested struct:

```
{C21345345345355 140609.09 {000-00-0000 123 Main Street}}
```

It is worth noting that if you wanted to print just the id that is stored in the entity struct within your account, you would need to include the account (called a in the listing), owner (which is the name of the entity struct within the account struct), and the field name, which is called id. To print the value, you would use this:

```
fmt.Println(a.owner.id)
```

ADDING METHODS TO A STRUCT

Up to this point, we've shown structs that contain fields that tend to define the properties of an object created by a struct. A struct can also contain functions, which can also be referred to as methods.

> **NOTE** Methods in a struct are similar to methods used in classes in object-oriented programming. The Go language does not have a "class" construct that many other programming languages have. The way methods are added to a struct is different from how methods are added to classes in other programming languages.

Listing 11.10 adds a method to your account class. You create the HaveEnoughBalance method, which you can use in the main function to check if the account has enough money to be withdrawn.

LISTING 11.10

Using a function in a struct

```
package main

import "fmt"

type account struct {
    accountNumber string
    balance float64
    owner entity
}
```

```
type entity struct{
   id string
   address string
}

// method uses value from account struct
func(acct account) HaveEnoughBalance(value float64) bool{
   if acct.balance >= value{
      return true
   }
   return false
}

func main() {
   e := entity{"000-00-0000","123 Main Street"}
   a := account{}
   a.accountNumber = "C21345345345355"
   a.balance = 140609.09
   a.owner = e

   // check if the account has 150 dollars to withdraw
   fmt.Println(a.HaveEnoughBalance(150))
   fmt.Println(a)
}
```

In this listing, the account struct is again being created and includes the entity
struct you saw in the previous listing. Where this listing differs is in the inclusion of the
HaveEnoughBalance method. You know this is a function because of the use of the func
keyword. Overall, the method should look very similar to what was seen in Lesson 8,
"Using Functions."

What is different is that within the function's declaration, there is a *receiver type* of
account Included in the method declaration:

```
func(acct account) HaveEnoughBalance(value float64) bool{
   if acct.balance >= value{
      return true
   }
   return false
}
```

This tells Go that the method is bound to the account struct and thus will be available
to any account structs that are created. Within the method, you can then have access to

the fields in the struct that have been created. In this case, the method compares the provided value called value (which contains 150 in the main function) to the current value in the account struct (acct.balance) to determine the outcome. In this case, because the account balance is greater than 150, the output is:

```
true
{C21345345345355 140609.09 {000-00-0000 123 Main Street}}
```

Within the main function, the HaveEnoughBalance method is called by using the name of the struct followed by the dot operator and then the method name. The appropriate parameters are also passed, in this case, simply a value of 150:

```
a.HaveEnoughBalance(150)
```

Note that just as 150 is associated and passed to the value argument in your HaveEnoughBalance method, the struct called a is associated to the acct receiver type in your method.

NOTE In the example in Listing 11.10, you used a comparison operator in the function. You could also perform other operations within the function, including mathematical operations and string operations. For example, a method could be set up to accept a deposit amount and update the account balance to include that deposit.

TYPE AND VALUE

By importing the Go reflect package, you can check the type and value of a struct using the TypeOf and ValueOf functions. The code in Listing 11.11 shows these functions in use.

LISTING 11.11

Type and value

```
package main

import (
    "fmt"
    "reflect"
)
```

```
type account struct {
    accountNumber string
    balance float64
    owner entity
}

type entity struct{
    id string
    address string
}

func(a account) HaveEnoughBalance(value float64) bool{
    if a.balance >= value{
        return true
    }
    return false
}

func main() {
    e := entity{"000-00-0000","123 Main Street"}
    a := account{}
    a.accountNumber = "C21345345345355"
    a.balance = 140609.09
    a.owner = e

    fmt.Println("Type and value of a:")
    fmt.Println(reflect.TypeOf(a))
    fmt.Println(reflect.ValueOf(a))

    fmt.Println("\nType and value of e:")
    fmt.Println(reflect.TypeOf(e))
    fmt.Println(reflect.ValueOf(e))
}
```

Remember that the struct keyword is used to create structs, which are considered new types. In this listing, you update the previous listing and add calls to the TypeOf and ValueOf functions from the reflect package. You use these to print the type and value of the variables a and e that were defined in the listing. You can see that these print the type and value of both structs. The output is:

```
Type and value of a:
main.account
{C21345345345355 140609.09 {000-00-0000 123 Main Street}}

Type and value of e:
main.entity
{000-00-0000 123 Main Street}
```

COMPARING STRUCTS

You can use the == operator to compare two structs. Using this operator, each element within a struct will be compared to verify if they are the same. In Listing 11.12, three different variables are created using the entity struct, and then they are compared to each other.

LISTING 11.12

Comparing structs

```
package main

import (
    "fmt"
)

type account struct {
    accountNumber string
    balance float64
    owner entity
}

type entity struct{
    id string
    address string
}

func main() {
    e1 := entity{"000-00-0000", "123 Main Street"}
    fmt.Println(e1)

    e2 := entity{"000-00-0000", "123 Main Street"}
    fmt.Println(e2)

    fmt.Println(e1 == e2)

    e3 :=entity{"000-00-0000", "124 Main Street"}
    fmt.Println(e3)

    fmt.Println(e1 == e3)
}
```

Because both values assigned to e1 and e2 are the same, the first comparison statement returns true:

```
{000-00-0000 123 Main Street}
{000-00-0000 123 Main Street}
true
```

However, you have a slightly different address in e3, so e1 is different from e3:

```
{000-00-0000 124 Main Street}
false
```

Simplifying Boolean Expressions

Within this lesson and many others throughout this book, Boolean expressions are being used. In many cases, the expressions could be simplified from what is being shown. For example, consider the following code that was used in this lesson:

```
if accountBalance >= value {
        return true
}

return false
```

Because the expression accountBalance >= value returns a Boolean, you could simply return the result of the expression rather than doing the if statement. The previous four lines of code could be reduced to one:

```
return accountBalance >= value
```

For most who are learning a new programming language, the four lines of code give a clear indication of what is happening. The difference in execution speed between the four lines of code and one line of code has no discernible impact.

Similarly, the if statement:

```
if value == true {
```

could be simplified to:

```
if value {
```

The code, however, is clearer for a newer developer to include the comparison to true.

SUMMARY

In this lesson you've learned how to associate a group of fields and methods into a package that can then be used to create new types. Using structs, you should be able to better organize the information used within your programs.

You should now be able to create your own structs (including nested structs) as well as use them within the code you create. You should be able to add, update, and display values from a struct as well as determine their types, compare them, and even create pointers to access them.

> **NOTE** Developers use a variety of terminology. A variable included in a struct can also be called a field or a property. Methods are functions that are part of a struct. A struct can be considered a "user-defined type" that can be used to create a variable just like the base types. A variable created by a struct might also be referred to as an object.

EXERCISES

The following exercises are provided to allow you to experiment with the tools and concepts presented in this lesson. For each exercise, write a program that meets the specified requirements and verify that the program runs as expected. The exercises are:

Exercise 11.1: Addressing an Envelope

Exercise 11.2: Name

Exercise 11.3: Full Name

Exercise 11.4: Address Book

Exercise 11.5: Passing a Struct

Exercise 11.6: Nesting Practice

Exercise 11.7: Burger Shop

> **NOTE** The exercises are for your benefit. The exercises help you apply what you learn in the lessons. You are also encouraged to experiment with the code as you complete the exercises.

Exercise 11.1: Addressing an Envelope

Create an address struct that contains the following items:

- First name
- Last name
- Address line 1
- Address line 2
- City
- State
- Country
- Zip code/postal code

Write a program that creates and initializes a variable using the struct. Assign values and then use `fmt.Print` and `fmt.Println` to display the address in a manner that would look good on an envelope. Include logic to avoid printing address line 2 if it is blank and to add a comma between the city and state. For example:

```
John Doe
123 My Street
Chicago, IL  12345
```

Exercise 11.2: Name

Create a struct to hold a name. It should include a first name, last name, and middle name. Rewrite your solution from Exercise 11.1 to use this name struct (nested) instead of the individual fields.

Exercise 11.3: Full Name

Update the struct you created in the previous listing that holds a name. Add a method to your name struct called `GetFullName` that doesn't take any parameters but returns a string from the struct that contains the full name of the person in the current name struct. The full name should be formatted as first name, middle initial, a period, then last name. If there is no middle name, then the period should not be included.

Exercise 11.4: Address Book

Using the address struct you've created in the previous listings, create an array of addresses called `AddressBook`. Assign at least four addresses to the array. Print the resulting addresses in a format that would look appropriate for an envelope.

Exercise 11.5: Passing a Struct

Compare Listing 11.13 to Listing 11.7 within the lesson. What are the differences? Before running Listing 11.13, predict what the final value of a.accountNumber will be. Enter the code and see if you are correct.

LISTING 11.13

Passing a struct

```
package main

import "fmt"

type account struct {
    accountNumber string
    balance float64
}

func closeAccount(CurrentAccount account) {
    CurrentAccount.accountNumber = "CLOSED-" + CurrentAccount.accountNumber;
}

func main() {
    var a account

    a.accountNumber = "C13242524"
    a.balance = 140.78

    fmt.Println(a.accountNumber)

    closeAccount(a)

    fmt.Println(a.accountNumber)
}
```

Exercise 11.6: Nesting Practice

Consider a different scenario where it makes sense to nest a struct in another struct. Using that scenario, create a struct that contains at least one nested struct. Using the structs, write a program that creates and displays at least two different variables using the structs.

Examples include:

- A bank customer with multiple accounts
- A student taking multiple courses
- A course with multiple students

Exercise 11.7: Burger Shop

In this activity, you will create an online ordering system for a burger shop. This exercise will require using what you've learned in the book up to this point. The program will perform the following tasks:

- Take an order from a user, including a burger, a drink, a side, or a combo.
- Customize selected items, including toppings for the burger.
- Display the completed order to the user.
- Calculate and display the order total.
- Allow the user to cancel the order and exit the program at any prompt.
- If the user enters an unexpected value, provide appropriate feedback and prompt them to try again.

The program must include the following features:

1. Create a struct that represents a burger with the following attributes:
   - **Bun:** Boolean (True if you want the burger with bun, False otherwise)
   - **Price:** float64
   - **Dressed:** Boolean (True if you want the burger fully dressed, False otherwise)
   - Do a basic Boolean option for the first pass. You can add other options after the main program works as expected.

2. Create a struct that represents a drink with the following attributes:
   - **Price:** float64
   - **Type:** string

3. Create a struct that represents a side with the following attributes:
   - **Price:** float64
   - **Type:** string

4. Create a nested struct called Combo that represents a burger, side, and drink combo:
   - Burger
   - Side

- Drink
- Price: The price of the combo is the price of the three items with a 20% discount.

5. Next, implement the following functions:

- A function called `user_input_burger` that asks the user how they want their burger and stores it in a struct type. The price of the burger is computed as follows:
  - Burger with bun: 7
  - Burger without bun: 6
  - Dressed has no impact on price.

- A function for `user_input_drink`, which asks the user for their drink. Provide the user with a limited number of drink options to choose from (include 3–4 choices).
  - The price of water is $1.
  - The price of any other drink is $2.

- A function for `user_input_side`, which asks the user for their side. Provide the user with a limited number of side options to choose from, such as fries, onion rings, a salad, and coleslaw.

- The price of fries is $2.

- The price of any other option is $3.

- A function for `user_input_combo`, which asks the user for their combo preferences.

- A function called `take_order_from_user`
  - Ask the user for a name for the order.
  - Repeat taking the order until the user is done.
  - Display order details.
  - Display a thank you message.

Challenges

Once the basic program outlined here works as expected, consider refactoring it to improve it. For example:

- Allow the user to choose specific toppings on the burger, including items such as cheese, lettuce, tomato, onion, pickles, mustard, and ketchup, and/or offer a choice of buns.

- Allow non-burger options, such as a fish sandwich, tacos, or personal pizza.

- Allow the user to choose a drink size, with appropriate pricing.

- Allow user-specific customization, such as low-salt or extra pickles.

- Add a dessert menu.

Lesson 12

Accessing Slices

The data type of an array includes the size of the array. This means that once you have created an array, you cannot change its size. In some cases, though, having fixed-size arrays can be limiting.

Go supports variable-sized data structures through the use of *slices*. Unlike arrays, the slice data type does not depend on its length, so a slice is a dynamic and powerful tool, with more flexibility than an array. Essentially, a slice is a subset of values in an array. In this lesson, we will dive into slices to understand how they work.

LEARNING OBJECTIVES

By the end of this lesson, you will be able to:

- Create a slice.
- Explain the difference between slices and arrays.
- Change values within a slice.
- Iterate through a slice.
- Append values to a slice.
- Copy a slice.

HOW SLICES WORK

A slice is an abstraction built on top of the array type. This means that it allows you to use the same logic you would with an array, but with more powerful features and flexibility.

A slice is a subset of an array. In other words, you can formally create an array and then create a slice that references only some elements of that array. Because each element of an array must be the same data type, it follows that each element of a slice must also be the same data type.

A slice consists of a pointer to an element in an array, the length of the segment, and its capacity (the maximum number of elements the slice can hold, which depends on the underlying array). To understand these three factors, consider the visualization in Figure 12.1.

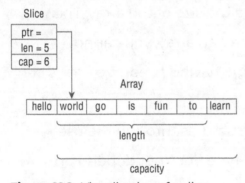

Figure 12.1: Visualization of a slice

In Figure 12.1, we start with an array that includes seven string elements, whose index values are 0–6. The slice references that array with three values:

- The pointer (ptr) points to a specific element in the original array, using the index value for that element. In the figure, its value is 1, so it points to the second element in the array.

- The length (len) of the slice is 5. This means that it references five elements in the array (1–5), starting at the pointer's value.

- The capacity (cap) refers to the largest size of the slice based on the pointer value and the size of the array. In this case, because the array includes seven elements and the slice starts at the second element, the capacity is 6.

SLICE AN ARRAY

To understand the relationship between a slice and an array, let's look at an example where you first create an array and then create a slice of that array. Listing 12.1 creates an array of seven integers. It then creates a slice of that array, using the values in positions 0 through 4 of the original array.

LISTING 12.1

Slicing an array

```
package main

import (
    "fmt"
    "reflect"
)

func main() {
    // define an array with 7 elements
    numbers := [7]int{0,1,2,5,798,43,78}
    fmt.Println("array value:", numbers)
    fmt.Println("array type:", reflect.TypeOf(numbers))

    // define a slice s based on the numbers array
    s := numbers[0:4]
    fmt.Println("slice value:", s)
    fmt.Println("slice type:", reflect.TypeOf(s))
}
```

This listing starts by defining an array called numbers that contains seven ints, which are assigned on the declaration. This array is then printed, followed by using the TypeOf method in the reflect package to show that numbers is indeed an array:

```
array value: [0 1 2 5 798 43 78]
array type: [7]int
```

The listing then declares s to be equal to a slice of the numbers array using the following line of code:

```
s := numbers[0:4]
```

The slice includes the pointer 0 (referencing the first element in the array) and the next three elements. With the slice defined, you then use two more print statements. This time you print the values in s followed by the type of s:

```
slice value: [0 1 2 5]
slice type: []int
```

Notice in the output that the array type explicitly includes the size of the array (7), while the size is not included in the slice type. The full output from the listing is:

```
array value: [0 1 2 5 798 43 78]
array type: [7]int
slice value: [0 1 2 5]
slice type: []int
```

Using *len* and *cap*

We mentioned that the length of the s slice in Listing 12.1 is 4; however, we didn't mention the capacity. You can use the len and cap functions to compute the length and capacity of the slice. Listing 12.2 uses these functions to determine the length and capacity of a slice.

LISTING 12.2

Using len and cap

```
package main

import (
    "fmt"
)

func main() {
    // define an array with 7 elements
    numbers := [7]int{0,1,2,5,798,43,78}
    fmt.Println(numbers)

    // define a slice mySlice based on numbers in the array
    mySlice := numbers[1:5]
    fmt.Println(mySlice)

    fmt.Println("Length of slice:", len(mySlice))

    fmt.Println("Slice capacity:", cap(mySlice))
}
```

In this case, the slice called mySlice starts with the second element in the array and includes four elements starting from that point:

- The pointer is 1 because that is the first element you include from the original array.

- The length is 4 because you specifically include four elements. You start at index position 1 of the array and go to index position 5. Five minus 1 is 4.

- The capacity is determined by the size of the array itself. In this case, you exclude the first element in the array because you started the slice with index position 1, so the capacity is 6 because the array includes 7 elements.

The output confirms these statements:

```
[0 1 2 5 798 43 78]
[1 2 5 798]
Length of slice: 4
Slice capacity: 6
```

Using Shortcuts

You can use shortcut notations to define the size and elements of a slice. The basic syntax includes both a pointer and a length, but Go has a default value for each. Listing 12.3 presents three ways to define a slice.

LISTING 12.3

Ways of defining slices

```
package main

import (
    "fmt"
)

func main() {
    numbers := [7]int{0, 1, 2, 5, 798, 43, 78}
    fmt.Println("Numbers array:", numbers)

    // define a slice with the first 4 elements
    slice_1 := numbers[0:4]
    fmt.Println("slice_1:", slice_1)
```

continues

continued

```
    // define slice from the second element through the end of the array
    slice_2 := numbers[1:]
    fmt.Println("slice_2:", slice_2)

    // define a slice with the first 5 elements
    slice_3 := numbers[:5]
    fmt.Println("slice_3:", slice_3)
}
```

This listing presents three separate ways or options for creating a slice by creating three separate slices. Let's look at the slices that were created:

- slice_1: The notation [0:4] was used, which tells Go to go to the item at index position 0 and take all the elements up to, but not including, the item in index position 4. This is a total of 4 items, at index positions 0, 1, 2, and 3. (The pointer is 0.)

- slice_2: The notation [1:] defines the pointer as 1, so the slice starts with the second element in the original array (which is index position 1 of the array). Because you do not define the length, Go will use all remaining elements in the array, through *len – 1.*

- slice_3: If no pointer is defined, Go will use 0 by default. The notation [:5] tells Go to start at index position 0 of the array and retrieve 5 values.

When you execute this listing, the following output is generated:

```
Numbers array:  [0 1 2 5 798 43 78]
slice_1: [0 1 2 5]
slice_2: [1 2 5 798 43 78]
slice_3: [0 1 2 5 798]
```

> **NOTE** For *slice[low : high]*, the length of the slice is the value obtained by subtracting low from high:
>
> *length = high – low*

CHANGING THE SIZE OF A SLICE

Because a slice is not defined by its size in the same way an array is, you can create slices of different lengths from the original array. In the example in Listing 12.4, you create a slice called s from the numbers array, using four elements from the original array. You then replace the slice with a slice whose length is equivalent to the capacity of the original slice.

LISTING 12.4

Changing the size of a slice

```
package main

import (
    "fmt"
)

func main() {
    // define an array with 7 elements
    numbers := [7]int{0,1,2,5,798,43,78}
    fmt.Println(numbers)

    // define a slice s based on the numbers array
    s := numbers[1:5]
    fmt.Println(s)

    fmt.Println("Length of slice:", len(s))
    fmt.Println("Slice capacity:", cap(s))

    s = s[:cap(s)]
    fmt.Println("Revised slice:", s)
    fmt.Println("Length of slice:", len(s))
}
```

The first part of this listing is similar to the previous listings in defining the array of numbers and an initial slice from those numbers. The initial slice starts with position 1 and goes through position 5, so it contains four values. You can see this when you print the initial array and the slice along with the length and capacity of the slice:

```
[0 1 2 5 798 43 78]
[1 2 5 798]
Length of slice: 4
Slice capacity: 6
```

After you print this information, a new value is assigned to your slice using the following line of code:

```
s = s[:cap(s)]
```

Note here that the pointer of the slice did not change when you redefined the slice because you did not include a pointer value when you updated it. In the original slice, you defined the pointer as the second element in the original array (the element with index 1). When you redefined the slice, you did not change the pointer; you simply redefined how many elements the slice should include. In this case you use cap(s) to determine the highest index value of the array you were pointing to. This successfully changes the length of the slice from 4 to 6, which can be verified by looking at the last two lines of the full output:

```
[0 1 2 5 798 43 78]
[1 2 5 798]
Length of slice: 4
Slice capacity: 6
Revised slice: [1 2 5 798 43 78]
Length of slice: 6
```

ITERATING THROUGH A SLICE

You can use a for loop to iterate through the elements of a slice. Listing 12.5 creates an array and then creates a slice based on that array. A for loop is then used to print the values of the slice.

LISTING 12.5

Iterating through a slice

```go
package main

import (
    "fmt"
)

func main() {
    numbers := [7]int{0,1,2,5,798,43,78}
    fmt.Println(numbers)

    s := numbers[0:4]
    fmt.Println(s)

    for i := 0; i < len(s); i++{
        fmt.Println("Element", i, "is", s[i])
    }
}
```

In this listing, a simple `for` loop is used to print each element of the array on a separate line. This is done after print statements are used to print the entire array and the slice. The output is:

```
[0 1 2 5 798 43 78]
[0 1 2 5]
Element 0 is 0
Element 1 is 1
Element 2 is 2
Element 3 is 5
```

It is important to note that the index used to access individual items in the slice starts at 0. You can change the slice in Listing 12.5 to the following:

```
s := numbers[2:4]
```

When you run the listing with the slice using `[2:4]`, the output becomes:

```
[0 1 2 5 798 43 78]
[2 5]
Element 0 is 2
Element 1 is 5
```

You can see that `s[0]` contains the first item in the slice.

THE *MAKE* FUNCTION

As we covered earlier, a slice always depends on an array; thus, each element in a slice must have the same data type. Additionally, while you define the initial size of the slice when you declare it, the size is not a fixed part of the definition.

Two or more slices can reference the same conceptualized array. If you assign one slice to another slice, both slices will refer to the same array, even in the absence of a formally defined array.

Go also allows you to simply create a slice without having to first create an array by using the built-in `make` function. When you use the `make` function, the compiler creates an array internally and then creates a slice that refers to that array, as shown in Listing 12.6.

LISTING 12.6

Creating a slice with make

```
package main

import (
    "fmt"
)

func main() {
    s := make([]int, 10)

    fmt.Println(s)
}
```

In this listing, an int slice named s is created with 10 elements. The slice is created using make. In this case, make receives two arguments. The first is the array type associated with the slice ([]int), and the second is the length of the slice (10). After the slice is created, it is printed:

```
[0 0 0 0 0 0 0 0 0 0]
```

Because you did not assign any values to the slice elements and because the type is int, Go automatically assigns the default value of 0 to each element in the slice.

CREATING A SLICE VARIABLE WITH *VAR*

We can also use var to create a slice variable, using the syntax:

```
var variableName []dataType
```

In Listing 12.7, you create an empty slice variable and then display the slice and its type. You do this using var.

LISTING 12.7

Creating a slice variable

```
package main

import (
```

```
    "fmt"
    "reflect"
)

func main() {
   var s []int      // define a slice
   fmt.Println(s)   // display an empty slice
   fmt.Println("Slice type:", reflect.TypeOf(s)) // type of the slice
}
```

The output is:

```
[]
Slice type: []int
```

Go does not assign default values to slices, and because you do not define a length for the slice, the slice itself is empty. You must, however, include a data type for the slice. That data type is reflected in the slice's type. In this case, even though the slice is technically empty, you could only add integer values to the slice because of the slice's data type.

> **NOTE** Remember from earlier that the way you can tell a slice from an array is that the array will include the length when you print its type.

WORKING WITH SLICE ELEMENTS

While a slice depends on an array (explicitly or implicitly), each element in the slice is identified using an index value based on that slice, where the first element is index 0, regardless of the index values in the original array.

As with other data structures, you can identify individual elements by referencing their index values in the slice. You saw this illustrated earlier in Listing 12.5, when the values of the slice named s were printed.

Replacing an Element in a Slice

Accessing individual elements within a slice allows you to make changes to them. This includes being able to replace the values of individual elements in a slice, as shown in Listing 12.8.

LISTING 12.8

Replacing a slice element

```
package main

import (
    "fmt"
)

func main() {
    s := make([]int, 10)
    fmt.Println("Original slice:", s)

    s[0]=99
    fmt.Println("Updated slice:", s)
}
```

In this listing, you create a slice called s using the make function. The slice is created to include 10 integer elements. Because you defined the slice as int, Go assigns the default value of 0 to each element. Once the slice is defined, you print the values stored in the slice:

```
Original slice: [0 0 0 0 0 0 0 0 0 0]
```

You then replace the first value with a different value. In this case, you assign the value 99. After the update is made in index 0, the slice uses the value of 99 for the first element. The full output is:

```
Original slice: [0 0 0 0 0 0 0 0 0 0]
Updated slice: [99 0 0 0 0 0 0 0 0 0]
```

Working with Empty Slices

It's worth mentioning that if the slice is empty, you cannot add elements to it using indexes. In Listing 12.8, you specified that the slice should include 10 elements, so the slice is not empty. If you do not specify the number of elements in a slice, the slice remains empty until you add something to it, as illustrated in Listing 12.9.

LISTING 12.9

Using an `empty` slice

```
package main

import (
    "fmt"
)

func main() {
    var s []int      // create an empty slice
    fmt.Println(s)
    s[0]=10          // this won't execute
}
```

You can see that s is created as an empty slice that will hold int values. When you try to add a value to the slice (even using index 0), the program throws a runtime error. This can be seen in the output presented when the listing is run:

```
[]
panic: runtime error: index out of range [0] with length 0
```

Working with a Section of a Slice

You've seen how to print a single element from a slice using the slice name and an index value. For example, the following prints the first element in mySlice:

```
fmt.Println(mySlice[0])
```

You can also print a section of elements in a slice by including the starting element and ending element indexes, separated by a colon. For example, the following prints the elements from index positions 0 up to but not including 3 of mySlice:

```
fmt.Println(mySlice[0:3])
```

> **NOTE** Technically, in the previous Println statement, the code is creating an unnamed slice from mySlice[0:3]. This unnamed slice is then printed and discarded. This is equivalent to doing the following; however, Go takes care of doing the added step for you:
>
> ```
> newSlice := mySlice[0:3]
> fmt.Println(newSlice)
> ```

Listing 12.10 creates a slice of strings. Within this listing, the entire slice is printed, then a single element, and finally a range of elements.

LISTING 12.10

Printing a section of a slice

```
package main

import (
    "fmt"
)

func main() {
    mySlice := make([]string, 8)

    mySlice[0] = "Happy"
    mySlice[1] = "Sneezy"
    mySlice[2] = "Grumpy"
    mySlice[3] = "Bashful"
    mySlice[4] = "Doc"
    mySlice[5] = "Sleepy"
    mySlice[6] = "Dopey"
    mySlice[7] = "Fred"

    fmt.Println(mySlice)
    fmt.Println(mySlice[2])
    fmt.Println(mySlice[2:5])
}
```

This listing illustrates what has been shown before. It uses make to create an empty slice that can contain eight strings. Values are then assigned individually to elements within the slice before printing. The first print shows all the values in the slice. The second print shows an individual element—the element at mySlice[2], which is "Grumpy". Finally, the third print uses [2:5], which displays a section of the slice that starts with the element in the second index position up to, but not including, the element in the fifth position. The full output is:

```
[Happy Sneezy Grumpy Bashful Doc Sleepy Dopey Fred]
Grumpy
[Grumpy Bashful Doc]
```

Using *range* with Slices

In Listing 12.5 you looped through the elements of a slice called numbers and printed each value. You used the length of the slice to determine when the looping should end. You can also use the range keyword to loop through a slice, as shown in Listing 12.11.

LISTING 12.11

Looping through a slice with range

```
package main

import (
    "fmt"
)

func main() {
    numbers := [7]int{0,1,2,5,798,43,78}
    fmt.Println(numbers)

    s := numbers[0:4]
    fmt.Println(s)

    for i, v := range s {
        fmt.Println("Element", i, "is", v)
    }
}
```

You can see in this listing that the for loop has been simplified by using range. In this example, range returns two values, i and v. The variable i contains the index value of the slice element, and v will contain the value of the element.

> **NOTE** The following for loop would also work to capture only the returned index value from range:
>
> ```
> for i := range s {
>     fmt.Println("Element", i, "is", s[i])
> }
> ```

APPENDING TO A SLICE USING THE *APPEND* FUNCTION

While you cannot append a value to an array, you can append a value to a slice. The append function adds a new element to the end of a slice. If the slice is empty, the element will be placed in index 0. If the slice is not empty, it will add the value to the first available position. In Listing 12.12 you create an empty slice named s and then add two elements to it.

LISTING 12.12

Appending to a slice

```
package main

import (
    "fmt"
)

func main() {
    // create an empty slice
    var s []int
    fmt.Println(s)
    s = append(s, 10)
    fmt.Println(s)
    s = append(s, 11)
    fmt.Println(s)
}
```

The output is:

```
[]
[10]
[10 11]
```

As you can see in the output, the initial slice is empty. Each value you append to the slice adds a new element to the slice, changing the size of the slice.

COPYING A SLICE

The content of one slice can be copied into another slice by using the copy function. In Listing 12.13 you create one slice with two elements as well as an empty slice. You then copy the first slice into the second slice.

LISTING 12.13

Copying a slice

```
package main

import (
    "fmt"
)

func main() {
    var s = []int{10, 11}
    fmt.Println("Slice s: ",s)

    // create a destination slice
    c := make([]int, len(s))

    // copy everything in s to c
    num := copy(c, s) // returns the minimum number of elements in the slices
    fmt.Println("Number of elements copied:", num)
    fmt.Println("Slice c:", c)
}
```

The output is:

```
Slice s:  [10 11]
Number of elements copied:  2
Slice c:  [10 11]
```

Note that when you create the second slice, you specify that its length should be equal to the length of the first slice:

```
c := make([]int, len(s))
```

You could use a hard-coded value (like 2) instead, but this approach guarantees that the new slice is large enough to hold the copied elements. If this value is too low (including even an empty slice with a length of 0), the copy operation will not work as expected.

The copy function itself performs two separate tasks:

- It copies the elements from one slice to another.
- It returns the number of elements successfully copied, which is equivalent to the lowest value of the length of the two slices.

In this case, the copy function copies two elements and then returns the value 2. However, if the length of the destination slice is lower than the length of the original slice, then only the lower number of elements will be copied. For example, if you use the following instruction to create the destination slice:

```
c := make([]int, 1)
```

Go will copy only the first element from s to c:

```
Slice s: [10 11]
Number of elements copied: 1
Slice c: [10]
```

CREATING A SLICE USING THE *NEW* KEYWORD

It is also possible to create a slice using the new keyword. In this case, you can use the following statement:

```
var newSlice = new ([capacity] type)(startingElement:length)
```

For example, the following code creates a pointer to a slice with a capacity of 10 int elements and a length of five elements:

```
var mySlice = new([10]int)[0:5]
```

With this declaration, the elements in the slice will have default values assigned. In this case, because the elements are of int type, all the elements of the slice will have the value 0.

Assigning and using the slice is similar to what you have seen before. You can assign values to the first two elements of the slice using the index value:

```
mySlice[0] = 1
mySlice[1] = 2
```

Additionally, you can print the slice using Println by passing the name of the slice:

```
fmt.Println(mySlice)
```

Listing 12.14 is similar to Listing 12.10. The only difference is that, instead of using make, the new keyword is used to declare mySlice.

LISTING 12.14

Using the new keyword

```
package main

import (
  "fmt"
  "reflect"
)

func main() {
    var mySlice = new ([10]string) [0:8]
    mySlice[0] = "Happy"
    mySlice[1] = "Sneezy"
    mySlice[2] = "Grumpy"
    mySlice[3] = "Bashful"
    mySlice[4] = "Doc"
    mySlice[5] = "Sleepy"
    mySlice[6] = "Dopey"
    mySlice[7] = "Fred"

    fmt.Println("slice type:", reflect.TypeOf(mySlice))
    fmt.Println(mySlice)
    fmt.Println(mySlice[2])
    fmt.Println(mySlice[2:5])
}
```

In this listing, mySlice is creating a new slice of string elements. This is confirmed by using the reflect.TypeOf function to print the slice's type in the output. The slice is defined to have a capacity of 10. The slice, however, starts in position 0 of that capacity and contains eight elements. These elements are assigned just as they were in the previous listing, and various portions of the slice are also printed the same as before with Listing 12.10. The full output is:

```
slice type: []string
[Happy Sneezy Grumpy Bashful Doc Sleepy Dopey Fred]
Grumpy
[Grumpy Bashful Doc]
```

As you should recall, in Lesson 11, "Organizing with Structs," you used the new keyword to create structs. At that time, you learned that the new keyword actually created a pointer to the struct that is created. The same is true with using the new keyword to create a slice.

The new keyword is returning a pointer to the slice that is being created. This means that if the slice is passed to a function, the function would not be using a copy of the slice, but rather would be referencing the original slice that was created.

REMOVING AN ITEM FROM A SLICE

There is a not a built-in function in Go that allows an item from a slice to be easily removed. Instead, you can use the concept of re-slicing. That is, you construct a new slice from the original slice, while removing the item you don't want or need.

Let's first consider the following function, RemoveIndex. The function takes as input a slice inSlice and an index (the index of the element you want to remove) and returns a new slice:

```go
func RemoveIndex(inSlice []int, index int) []int {
    return append(inSlice[:index], inSlice[index+1:]...)
}
```

Within the function, you are simply using the append function to concatenate two slices. The first slice is the one defined as inSlice[:index], which will contain all the elements prior to the element you want to remove. The second slice is defined as inSlice[index+1:], which contains all the elements after the element you want to remove. When you use the append function, a new slice will be created and then returned by the RemoveIndex function.

Listing 12.15 uses the RemoveIndex function. In this case, an element from the middle of a slice is removed.

LISTING 12.15

Removing an element from a slice

```go
package main

import (
    "fmt"
)

func main() {
var mySlice = new([10]int)[0:5]
    mySlice[0] = 1
    mySlice[1] = 2
```

```
    mySlice[2] = 3
    mySlice[3] = 4
    mySlice[4] = 5

    fmt.Println(mySlice)
    newSlice := RemoveIndex(mySlice, 2)
    fmt.Println(newSlice)
}

func RemoveIndex(slice []int, i int) []int {
    return append(slice[:i], slice[i+1:]...)
}
```

In this listing, you create a new slice called mySlice and assign different values to its five elements. Next, you use the RemoveIndex function to remove the third element from the slice (index 2). You print the slice before and after the call to RemoveIndex to show that the correct element is indeed removed. As you can see, the new slice does not include the third element of the original slice:

```
[1 2 3 4 5]
[1 2 4 5]
```

> **NOTE** For more details on slices in Go, see the Go Blog's article, "Go Slices: usage and internals," found at https://go.dev/blog/slices-intro.

SUMMARY

In this lesson you learned about slices and how they differ from arrays. You learned several ways to create slices as well as how to manipulate the data within them. This includes adding, removing, and changing values. You also learned about using the new keyword to create a pointer to a slice. Finally, you learned how to remove an element from a slice.

EXERCISES

The following exercises are provided to allow you to experiment with the tools and concepts presented in this lesson. For each exercise, write a program that meets the specified requirements and verify that the program runs as expected. The exercises are:

Exercise 12.1: Alphabet

Exercise 12.2: Count the Letters

NOTE The exercises are for your benefit. The exercises help you apply what you learn in the lessons. You are also encouraged to experiment with the code as you complete the exercises.

Exercise 12.1: Alphabet

Create an array that contains the entire alphabet. After creating the array, create two slices. In the first slice, place all the consonants from the alphabet array. In the second, place all the vowels.

Exercise 12.2: Count the Letters

Create two functions using the slices from Exercise 12.1. The functions should take a string and return either the number of vowels or the number of consonants that the string contains. You can determine the number by comparing each letter in the string to the values stored in either the consonant or vowel slices.

Create a program to prompt the user to enter a string. Print the number of characters, vowels, and consonants that are in the string.

Exercise 12.3: An Average Word

Create a program that prompts the user for a series of a fixed number of words and store each word in an array. You may choose the length of the initial array, but its size should be at least 10. After obtaining the array of words, do the following:

- Calculate the average length of each word in the array.

- Identify all words that are longer than the average length and store the results in a slice.

- Identify all words that are shorter than the average length and store the results in a slice.

- Display the original collection of words as well as both slices, with appropriate feedback to the user.

Additional requirements:

- All output words should be in lowercase, regardless of the case used to enter the initial values.

- Use functions where appropriate.

Exercise 12.4: Student Names

Create a program that prompts a user to enter names. Use the append function to add these names to a slice. Continue to add names until the user enters **Quit**.

Exercise 12.5: No Blanks

Add the following code to a program:

```
mySlice := make([]string, 8)

mySlice[0] = "Happy"
mySlice[1] = "Sneezy"
mySlice[2] = "Grumpy"
mySlice[3] = "Fred"
mySlice[4] = "Doc"
mySlice[5] = "Sleepy"
mySlice[6] = "Dopey"
mySlice[7] = "Bashful"
```

This code creates a slice and adds eight values to it. Within your program, write the code necessary to remove "Fred" from the slice. More importantly, also remove any blank elements from the slice.

Exercise 12.6: Slicing Numbers Together

Create a program that includes the following features:

- A function that creates a slice with a collection of random numbers between 0 and 100

- A function that sorts a slice in place (ascending and descending depending on an input parameter)

- A function that takes as input two sorted slices and combines the slices into a single sorted slice

- In the main function:

  - Create two slices.
  - Sort the two slices.
  - Combine and sort the two slices.

Additional requirements:

- Display all slices to the user, with appropriate feedback to identify each slice.
- Do not use any built-in functions.

Lesson 13
Manipulating Maps

In the previous lessons, several methods for organizing and accessing data have been presented, including arrays, structs, and slices. Another common structure for storing data is a hash map, or simply a map. In this lesson, we will look at the use of maps and how to program them using Go.

LEARNING OBJECTIVES

By the end of this lesson, you will be able to:

- Declare a map.
- Describe the limitation of an empty map.
- Add key-value pairs to a map.
- Access values in a map.
- Determine if a key-value exists in a map.
- Remove items from a map.

DEFINING A MAP

Most major programming languages support maps as they are arguably one of the most important data structures for storing data. A map is a collection of paired values, where one value in each pair is a key that identifies the other value in the pair.

You can use maps to reference values through their key as a way of avoiding referencing the value itself. You can also use maps to change one value that is associated with another value.

Go supports maps through the built-in map data type, using the basic structure:

map[*KeyType*]*ValueType*

The key type and the value type can be different, but all keys must be of the same type and all values must be of the same type. The values in a map can be of any type (even another map). Map keys can be any of the following types:

- Boolean
- Numeric
- String
- Pointers
- Structs or arrays that contain the previous types listed
- Channels (more on this later)
- Interface types (more on this later)

Because the keys are the identifiers in a map, each key must be unique within the map. While the same value can be used in multiple pairs, the same key cannot be used in more than one pair.

You can use map literals to define and initialize a map with values. Listing 13.1 is a simple example of storing the number of times words might occur in a document.

LISTING 13.1

Defining and initializing a map

```
package main

import (
    "fmt"
)

func main() {
    FreqOccurrence := map[string]int{
        "hi": 23,
        "hello": 2,
        "hey": 4,
```

```
        "weather": 1,
        "greet": 35,
    }

    fmt.Println("Map value:", FreqOccurrence)
}
```

The output from running this listing includes a series of key-value pairs:

```
Map value: map[greet:35 hello:2 hey:4 hi:23 weather:1]
```

In the listing, you can see that a map named FreqOccurrence is being declared and initialized. You know this is a map based on the use of the map keyword. Additionally, you can see that the declaration follows what was shown earlier. The map is declared with a key type of string and a value type of int.

You can also see that curly brackets are used to initialize a number of map elements. Each element is defined with the key first, a colon, and then a value. Each element is ended with a comma. You can see that the first key defined is the string "hi" and that its associated value is 23. The second key is "hello" with an associated value of 2. The output presented earlier confirms the full list of key-values that were initialized.

NOTE The order in which items are stored in a map might not match the order in which they were initialized.

Maintaining Type

As with using other data structures in Go, you need to be careful using maps as well. For example, take a look at Listing 13.2. This listing generates an error. Can you determine the error before running the listing?

LISTING 13.2

Defining and attempting to initialize a map

```
package main

import (
    "fmt"
)
```

continues

continued

```go
func main() {
    FreqOccurrence := map[string]int{
        "hi": 23,
        "hello": 2,
        "hey": 4,
        "weather": 1.5,
        "greet": 35,
    }

    fmt.Println("Map value:", FreqOccurrence)
}
```

If you look closely at this listing, you can see that "weather" is assigned a value of 1.5, which is a floating-point number rather than an integer. As mentioned, a map must contain values that are all of the same type. The 1.5 will cause an error.

Duplicating Keys

One of the aspects of a map that is important to remember is that the keys must be unique. Listing 13.3 attempts to duplicate a key.

LISTING 13.3

Duplicating a key in a map

```go
package main

import (
    "fmt"
)

func main() {
    FreqOccurrence := map[string]int{
        "hi": 23,
        "hello": 2,
        "hey": 4,
        "weather": 1,
        "greet": 35,
        "hi": 10,
    }

    fmt.Println("Map value:", FreqOccurrence)
}
```

If you look closely at this listing, you can see that "hi" is used twice as a key. When you run this listing, you will receive an error indicating that this duplication is not allowed:

```
# command-line-arguments
.\Listing1303.go:14:7: duplicate key "hi" in map literal
        previous key at .\ Listing1303.go:9:7
```

EMPTY MAPS

As with other data types, you can create empty maps, but doing so is not as useful. Let's look at how to create an empty map and why you wouldn't want to. Listing 13.4 creates a simple map using the var keyword.

LISTING 13.4

Creating an empty map

```
package main

import (
    "fmt"
)

func main() {
    var m map[string]int
    fmt.Println(m)
}
```

In this example, you create an empty map called m that contains string keys and int values. The output is simply:

```
map[]
```

The map data type is a reference type like pointers and slices in Go. This means that when you create a map using the syntax in Listing 13.4, the map is defined with the default value, nil.

You can create this empty map with a default nil, and you can read it. Listing 13.5, however, illustrates the issue with this empty map.

LISTING 13.5

Writing to an empty map

```
package main

import (
    "fmt"
)

func main() {
    var m map[string]int

    fmt.Println(m) // (Reading) Displays the nil map as empty
    m["Hi"] = 1    // (Writing) Throws an error
}
```

Like in Listing 13.4, in Listing 13.5 you also declare an empty map called m, which you then print. The output of printing m is the empty map. You also, however, add another line of code in this listing:

```
m["Hi"] = 1
```

This line attempts to create a new key-value pair within m. In a normal map, this statement would add the value 1 along with the key "hi" to the map m. When you attempt to do this with an empty map, you get the following output:

```
map[]
panic: assignment to entry in nil map
```

As you can see, you get an error when you try to add a value to an empty map. You can read a nil map, but you cannot write to one, so there isn't much point in doing this.

CREATING A MAP USING *MAKE*

While you can declare and initialize a map in the same step, there are times when you may want to define a map for which you do not yet have any content, but as you've seen, you can't declare a map as an empty variable and add values to it later using the standard syntax.

For these situations, you can use the make function to initialize a map. The make function effectively creates a virtual hash map structure that you can add value pairs to later. In Listing 13.6 you use make to initialize a map and then you add two key-value pairs to the map.

LISTING 13.6

Creating a map using make

```go
package main

import (
    "fmt"
)

func main() {
    m := make(map[string]int) // define and initialize a map
    fmt.Println("Map value:", m)

    // add key-value pairs to the map
    m["Hi"] = 20
    m["How"] = 245

    fmt.Println("Updated map:", m)
}
```

In this listing, make is used to declare a map again called m. You can see that the make function receives the map declaration as its parameter. This is the same declaration you saw earlier using the keyword map, followed by the key type in brackets and the value type. You are again creating a map with a key type of string and a value type of int:

```go
make(map[string]int)
```

After you declare your new map, its contents are printed. This is followed by two statements that are used to add key-value pairs to the map. You use the syntax [key] = value to create the elements in the map:

```go
m["Hi"] = 20
m["How"] = 245
```

In this case, you are adding a key of "Hi" with a value of 20 and a second key, "How", with a value of 245. The output from the second print shows that you successfully added the two key-value pairs to the map:

```
Map value: map[]
Updated map: map[Hi:20 How:245]
```

MAP LENGTH

The len function calculates the number of keys in a map (and by extension, the number of key-value pairs). Listing 13.7 uses len to display the size of the map.

LISTING 13.7

Length

```
package main

import (
    "fmt"
)

func main() {
    m := make(map[string]int)
    fmt.Println("Map value:", m)

    // add key-value pairs to the map
    m["Hi"] = 20
    m["How"] = 245
    fmt.Println("Updated map:", m)

    // calculate the map's length
    fmt.Println("Map length:", len(m))
}
```

This listing is similar to Listing 13.6. The difference is the addition of a print statement that calls the len function. You can see that when this listing is executed, the length of the m map is 2:

```
Map value: map[]
Updated map: map[Hi:20 How:245]
Map length: 2
```

RETRIEVING MAP ELEMENTS

Because the key is the identifier for each element in a map, you can use a key to retrieve its associated value. In Listing 13.8 you retrieve the value associated with a key and store the value in a variable.

LISTING 13.8

Retrieving a value from a map

```go
package main

import (
    "fmt"
)

func main() {
    m := make(map[string]int)
    fmt.Println("Map value:", m)

    // add key-value pairs to the map
    m["Hi"] = 20
    m["How"] = 245
    fmt.Println("Updated map:", m)

    // Retrieve a value based on its key
    var num int = m["Hi"]
    fmt.Println("Value of num:", num)
}
```

Because you are using a map, the expression m["Hi"] retrieves the value associated with Hi, rather than the word itself. This is also reflected in the fact that num is defined as an int variable. You can see that the value of 20 was stored in num and thus printed:

```
Map value: map[]
Updated map: map[Hi:20 How:245]
Value of num: 20
```

Note that you could also have printed the value associated with the "Hi" key directly by using a print statement such as the following:

```go
fmt.Println("Value associated to Hi:", m["Hi"] )
```

Whether assigning a phrase to a variable or using it directly, you can access any key in this manner. What happens, however, if you use a key that is not in the map? Listing 13.9 modifies the previous listing to try to retrieve a value from the m map using the key "BadKey". What do you think the result will be?

LISTING 13.9

Retrieving a value from a map with a bad key

```
package main

import (
    "fmt"
)

func main() {
    m := make(map[string]int)

    m["Hi"] = 20
    m["How"] = 245
    fmt.Println("Updated map:", m)

    // Retrieve a value based on its key
    var num int = m["BadKey"]
    fmt.Println("Value of num:", num)
}
```

In this case, you assign the value associated with m["BadKey"] to num and then print the value stored in num. Although you might expect an error, the result is actually the default value of an int, which is 0:

```
Updated map: map[Hi:20 How:245]
Value of num: 0
```

CHECKING FOR A KEY

Sometimes, you just need to know whether or not a key exists in a map, even if you don't necessarily want to use its value. For this, you can use a Boolean expression that looks for a given key and returns true or false. The following structure will check for a key:

```
value, okay := mapName[key]
```

In this case, if the *key* exists, its value will be assigned to *value* and *okay* will return true. If the *key* does not exist, *value* will have the default value for its type and *okay* will return false.

If you simply want to know whether or not the key exists without storing a value in *value*, you can replace the variable name with an underscore (a blank identifier):

```
_, okay := mapName[key]
```

In Listing 13.10 you check for a key-value pair and use an if-else statement to provide information about its existence to the user.

LISTING 13.10

Checking for a key

```
package main

import (
    "fmt"
)

func main() {
    m := make(map[string]int)
    m["Hi"] = 20
    m["How"] = 245
    fmt.Println("Map value:", m)

    // check to see if "Hi" exists
    val, ok := m["Hi"]
    fmt.Println("Value of val:", val)
    fmt.Println("Value of ok :", ok)

    if ok == true{
        fmt.Println("The key exists")
    } else{
        fmt.Println("The key doesn't exist")
    }
}
```

This listing creates the m map once again. You then use the syntax shown earlier to check to see if the key-value of "Hi" exists in the listing:

```
val, ok := m["Hi"]
```

This line of code retrieves the variables val and ok. After the assignment, val will contain the value associated with the "Hi" key or 0 if the key doesn't exist. The variable ok is a Boolean and will contain true if the key exists or false if the key does not exist. When you run the listing, the output is:

```
Map value: map[Hi:20 How:245]
----------------
Value of val: 20
Value of ok : true
The key exists
```

If you replace "Hi" with another word (such as "Bye"), the output will be:

```
Map value: map[Hi:20 How:245]
---------------
Value of val: 0
Value of ok : false
The key doesn't exist
```

ITERATING THROUGH A MAP

As with other data structures, you can iterate through the key-value pairs of a map using a for loop. In Listing 13.11 you iterate through the map using a range that is determined by the map size.

LISTING 13.11

Iterating through a map

```
package main

import (
    "fmt"
)

func main() {
    m := make(map[string]int)
    m["Hi"] = 20
    m["How"] = 245
    m["hi"] = 23
```

```
    m["hello"] = 2
    m["hey"] = 4
    m["weather"] = 2
    m["greet"] = 35

    for key, value := range m {
        fmt.Println("Key:", key, "Value:", value)
    }
}
```

In this listing, you again declare a map called m that takes a string for the key and an int for the value. You then assign a variety of values to keys. Again, you should note that each key is unique, even though the values don't have to be. As mentioned, you use a for statement that loops through the map and pulls the key and value for each element. These are then printed as shown:

```
Key: How Value: 245
Key: hi Value: 23
Key: hello Value: 2
Key: hey Value: 4
Key: weather Value: 2
Key: greet Value: 35
Key: Hi Value: 20
```

Because of how Go manages the keys in a dictionary, the order in which the key-value pairs appear in an iteration may be different from one run to the next, especially for longer maps. You can also see that there is a key called "hi" and a key called "Hi". Because strings are case-sensitive, these values are different.

DELETING MAP ELEMENTS

Go includes a delete function that you can use to delete key-value pairs from a map using this syntax:

```
delete(mapName, key)
```

The code in Listing 13.12 shows the delete function in action.

LISTING 13.12

Deleting a map element

```
package main

import (
    "fmt"
)

func main() {

    months := make(map[string]string)
    fmt.Println("Map value:", months)

    // add key-value pairs to the map
    months["Jan"] = "January"
    months["Feb"] = "February"
    months["Mar"] = "March"
    months["Apr"] = "April"
    months["May"] = "May"
    months["Jun"] = "June"
    months["Jul"] = "July"
    months["Bad"] = "BadMonth"
    months["Aug"] = "August"
    months["Sep"] = "September"
    months["Oct"] = "October"
    months["Nov"] = "November"
    months["Dec"] = "December"

    fmt.Println("Updated map:", months)

    // delete a key-value pair
    delete(months,"Bad")
    fmt.Println("Updated map:", months)
}
```

This listing creates a map called months that contains a string type for both the key and the value of each key-value pair. After creating the map, a number of key-value pairs are added. The code then deletes one of the pairs. You can see that the call to the delete function receives your map (months) and the key you are removing ("Bad"). In the output, you see the map once it is created, after adding the key-value pairs, and then finally after the call to the delete function:

```
Map value: map[]
Updated map: map[Apr:April Aug:August Bad:BadMonth Dec:December Feb:February
```

```
Jan:January Jul:July Jun:June Mar:March May:May Nov:November Oct:October
Sep:September]
Updated map: map[Apr:April Aug:August Dec:December Feb:February Jan:January
Jul:July Jun:June Mar:March May:May Nov:November Oct:October Sep:September]
```

You can see that "Bad" and "BadMonth" have been removed.

LITERAL DECLARATIONS IN MAPS

Just as with other variables, you can add literal values to your maps at the same time you declare them. Listing 11.13 rewrites Listing 11.12 using literal declarations at the time the months map is created.

LISTING 13.13

Using literal declarations for the months

```
package main

import (
    "fmt"
)

func main() {

    // add key-value pairs to the map
    months := map[string]string{
        "Jan": "January",
        "Feb": "February",
        "Mar": "March",
        "Apr": "April",
        "May": "May",
        "Jun": "June",
        "Jul": "July",
        "Bad": "BadMonth",
        "Aug": "August",
        "Sep": "September",
        "Oct": "October",
        "Nov": "November",
        "Dec": "December"}

    fmt.Println("Map value:", months)
```

continues

continued

```
    // delete a key-value pair
    delete(months,"Bad")
    fmt.Println("Updated map:", months)
}
```

As you can see in this listing, the primary difference is that when months is declared, you also initialize it with the key-value pairs for each of the 12 months (plus a bad month that gets removed). When you run this listing, the output is the same as the previous listing's output:

```
Map value: map[Apr:April Aug:August Bad:BadMonth Dec:December Feb:February
Jan:January Jul:July Jun:June Mar:March May:May Nov:November Oct:October
Sep:September]
Updated map: map[Apr:April Aug:August Dec:December Feb:February Jan:January
Jul:July Jun:June Mar:March May:May Nov:November Oct:October Sep:September]
```

SUMMARY

In this lesson we explored maps. Not only did we cover the structure of a map, but also how they can be created and used. This included learning how to add and remove key-value pairs, as well as how to assign values to a key. Iterating using a for loop was also discussed, as well as checking for the existence of a key within a map.

EXERCISES

The following exercises are provided to allow you to experiment with the tools and concepts presented in this lesson. For each exercise, write a program that meets the specified requirements and verify that the program runs as expected. The exercises are:

Exercise 13.1: Creating Your Own Map

Exercise 13.2: User Input

Exercise 13.3: Looping

Exercise 13.4: Does It Exist?

Exercise 13.5: State Populations

Exercise 13.6: Keyword Search

Exercise 13.1: Creating Your Own Map

Using the model in Listing 13.1, create a map that includes at least five key-value pairs. Once you have a working program that displays the map, play with the code. Experiment using different data types for both the key and the value.

After getting your program to work, update it to use the make keyword instead of the method shown in Listing 13.1.

Exercise 13.2: User Input

Create a program to prompt the user to enter the values for the map you created in Exercise 13.1. The user should be able to continue to enter values until they enter quit. Include descriptive prompts and check to make sure the values they enter are valid.

Make sure your program can handle possible problems caused by the user. For example, what happens if the user enters a key more than once?

Exercise 13.3: Looping

Create a map that includes at least five key-value pairs. Use a for loop to iterate through the map and run the program multiple times. Check to see if the results appear in the same order each time.

Exercise 13.4: Does It Exist?

Create a map with at least five key-value pairs. Add code that prompts the user to enter a key and then informs the user whether or not the key exists:

- If the key does not exist, the program should inform the user of that fact, display a list of available keys, and prompt the user to look for another key.
- If the key exists, the program should display the corresponding value and ask the user if they would like to delete it. If the user says yes, then delete the key-value pair.

Exercise 13.5: State Populations

Create a map that includes state abbreviations as a key and state populations as a value. You can make up populations for the values or research them online. Using your created map, write a program that determines the following:

- Iterate through the map and determine the state with the highest population.
- Iterate through the map and determine the state with the lowest population.
- Determine the average state population.

Exercise 13.6: Keyword Search

Write a program that includes a map with at least 10 key-value pairs. The pairs should make sense, but you can choose whatever you wish. Suggestions include produce categories (e.g., *apple: fruit* and *onion: vegetable*), animal categories (e.g., mammals, birds, fish), city populations, or word definitions. In your program, do the following:

- Prompt the user to input a search term.
- Display all key-value pairs that include the input search term, either in the key or in the value. For example, if the topic is *produce*, the user can enter either `apple` or `fruit` and see all matching map entries.
- If the value does not exist in the dictionary, display a user-friendly error message.
- Prompt the user to start over again or exit the program.

Lesson 14
Creating Methods

Go doesn't support classes like Java or C# does. However, Go offers some aspects of object-oriented programming (OOP) and ways to reuse code. For example, though Go doesn't support classes, it does support the concept of a method. You learned a little bit about methods in Lesson 8, "Using Functions." In this lesson, we return to the topic of methods and dive a little deeper.

LEARNING OBJECTIVES

By the end of this lesson, you will be able to:

• Understand the difference between methods and functions.

• Define your own methods.

• Call your own methods.

• Understand nonlocal receivers.

• Work with multiple methods of the same name.

• Work with passing values and pointers to methods.

WORKING WITH METHODS

Methods in Go are functions defined on a particular data type. The only difference between a function and a method is that a method has a special *receiver type* that it can operate on. To understand the difference between functions and methods, consider the code in Listing 14.1.

LISTING 14.1

Function vs. method

```
package main

import "fmt"

type Account struct {
    Number  string
    Balance float64
}

// HaveEnoughBalance is a method defined on the struct, Account.
// The receiver argument is (acct Account) which is separate from
// the input argument list (value).
func (acct Account) HaveEnoughBalance(value float64) bool {
    return acct.Balance >= value
}

// HaveEnoughBalance2 is a simple function
func HaveEnoughBalance2(acct Account, value float64) bool {
    return acct.Balance >= value
}

func main() {
    a := Account{Number: "C21345345345355"}

    // call the method defined on Account
    fmt.Println("Method result:", a.HaveEnoughBalance(150))

    // call the function
    fmt.Println("Function result:", HaveEnoughBalance2(a, 150))
}
```

In this code, you create a struct, account. You then define a function, HaveEnoughBalance, that takes as input a value and returns bool. If you look closely, after the func keyword, you see (acct account). This tells Go that the function is actually a method and that the receiver is an account type. In the same code, you then define a traditional function, HaveEnoughBalance2, that uses an account value as input rather than being a receiver.

Both `HaveEnoughBalance` and `HaveEnoughBalance2` have the same functionality except that one is a method with an account type receiver and the other is a function. The output is the same for both:

```
Method result: false
Function result: false
```

The difference between the function and the method is that the method includes a receiver argument (`acct account`), which instructs the compiler to execute the method through account types, whereas the function requires the account to be passed as an argument. The advantage of the method using a receiver argument is that the `HaveEnoughBalance` method can now be executed through the account type. You see this done in the print statement, where the method is called using the following syntax:

```
a.HaveEnoughBalance(150)
```

This is very similar to the object-oriented approach using classes (struct in this case) and methods. You can use methods in Go to create various routines that define the behavior of the receiver struct.

DEFINING A METHOD

You are not limited to defining methods on structs. In fact, you can define them on any other type if you wish. In Go, it is possible to create new types based on a built-in type using this syntax:

```
type identifier builtin_datatype
```

The `identifier` of a custom type must follow the same naming convention used for other identifiers. In the code in Listing 14.2, you use the keyword `type` to create a new type called `s` based on the existing `string` type. You then use the type as a receiver in a method.

LISTING 14.2

Defining a method on a custom type

```
package main

import "fmt"
```

continues

continued

```
// Use the type keyword to create a new type, "Text", based
// on the string type
type Text string

// This method has a receiver of type Text, as defined above
func (t Text) IsEmpty() bool {
    return len(t) <= 0
}

func main() {
    text := Text("Hi")

    fmt.Println("type value:", text)
    fmt.Println("method value:", text.IsEmpty())
}
```

The output for this listing is:

```
type value: Hi
method value: false
```

Why would you create a new data type that acts like a string instead of simply passing a string type to the method? As a rule, in Go, the definition of the receiver type must be in the same package as the method. This means that you cannot use the string as the receiver type because it is not in the same package as the method you are creating.

To see what happens when you try to use a string as the receiver for a method, consider the code in Listing 14.3.

LISTING 14.3

Using a nonlocal receiver

```
package main

import "fmt"

// method attempts to use the string variable as the receiver
func (t string) IsEmpty() bool {
    return len(t) <= 0
}

func main() {
    text := s("Hi")
```

```
    fmt.Println(text)
    fmt.Println(text.IsEmpty())
}
```

In this listing, you are creating a method with a receiver type of string. When executed, the output generates an error:

```
# command-line-arguments
.\main.go:6:5: cannot define new methods on nonlocal type string
.\main.go:14:12: undefined: s
```

In this version, the receiver of the method IsEmpty is of type string. This code won't work because the string type is not in the same package as the method IsEmpty.

USING POINTERS WITH METHODS

In the previous examples, you have used method receivers that are values (called *value receivers*) instead of pointers. When you pass values to methods, a copy of the value is made, and the method operates on a copy of the input. This could be an issue. To understand this problem, consider the code in Listing 14.4.

LISTING 14.4

Method and value receiver

```
package main

import "fmt"

type account struct {
    number string
    balance float64
}

// method with value receiver
func(acct account) withdraw(value float64) bool{
    if acct.balance >= value{
        acct.balance = acct.balance - value
        return true
    }
    return false
}
```

continues

continued

```
func main() {
   acct := account{}
   acct.number = "C21345345345355"
   acct.balance = 159

   fmt.Println(acct)
   fmt.Println(acct.withdraw(150)) // call the method defined on account
   fmt.Println(acct)
}
```

In this code, you create a struct, account, and a method, withdraw, which mimics a withdrawal from an account. The method receiver is a value receiver of type account. When we execute the code, the output is:

```
{C21345345345355 159}
true
{C21345345345355 159}
```

The Boolean part of the method executed correctly in that the original balance (159) is greater than the withdrawal amount (150), but the value of balance in the struct did not change as expected. This is because the method operated on a copy of acct, rather than using the values directly.

One work-around that will update the changes in the caller a properly is to return the new value acct and assign it to the old version of acct, as shown in Listing 14.5.

LISTING 14.5

Reassigning the value

```
package main

import "fmt"

type account struct {
   number string
   balance float64
}

func(acct account) withdraw(value float64) account {
   if acct.balance >= value {
      acct.balance = acct.balance-value
   }
   return acct
}
```

```go
func main() {
    acct := account{}
    acct.number = "C21345345345355"
    acct.balance = 159

    // Show initial values
    fmt.Println(acct)
    // assign the result of withdraw to acct
    acct = acct.withdraw(150)

    // The changes are now properly recorded in the caller acct
    fmt.Println(acct)
}
```

In this version, you reassign the copy created by the withdraw method to acct. The result includes the updated balance, as can be seen in the output:

```
{C21345345345355 9}
True
{C21345345345355 9}
```

Although the code in Listing 14.5 overcomes the issue with updating acct, there is a more elegant solution. This is accomplished by using pointers as receivers.

Instead of using value receivers and having to create work-arounds for the method's copy, you can use a *pointer receiver*. In other words, instead of passing the value as a receiver, you pass a reference to it (a pointer). This approach will directly change the value assigned to the caller acct by changing the value assigned to that memory block. Listing 14.6 is the same as the earlier example, except that the receiver is a pointer receiver.

LISTING 14.6

Using a pointer receiver

```go
package main

import "fmt"

type account struct {
    number string
    balance float64
}
```

continues

continued

```go
// the method uses a pointer to account
func(acct *account) withdraw(value float64) bool{
    if acct.balance >= value{
        acct.balance = acct.balance-value
        return true
    }
    return false
}

func main() {
    acct := account{}
    acct.number="C21345345345355"
    acct.balance=159

    fmt.Println(acct)
    fmt.Println(acct.withdraw(150))
    fmt.Println(acct)
}
```

In this listing, you can see that the primary change is that a pointer (*account) is being used in the receiver instead of just account for the type. Using a pointer receiver means that the method accesses the memory location of the stored value, rather than accessing the value itself. When it updates the value, the update is stored to the same location, allowing the original variable to retrieve the updated value.

By using the pointer, the output is now:

```
{C21345345345355 159}
true
{C21345345345355 9}
```

The choice to use value receivers or pointer receivers depends on the situation. If you want the changes that the method performs to be visible to the caller, you should use a pointer receiver. Otherwise, you can use a value pointer.

NAMING METHODS

In Go, you cannot create multiple functions with the same name. On the other hand, you can create several methods with the same name, using them to operate on different data types, an approach similar to the concept of overloading in object-oriented programming. This is another advantage of using methods over functions. Listing 14.7 illustrates this by creating a program with methods that mimic withdrawing funds from both checking and savings accounts.

LISTING 14.7

Two methods with the same name

```
package main

import "fmt"

type SavingsAccount struct {
  number string
  balance float64
}

type CheckingAccount struct {
  number string
  balance float64
}

func(acct *SavingsAccount) Withdraw(value float64) bool {
  if acct.balance >= value{
    acct.balance = acct.balance - value
    return true
  }
  return false
}
func(acct *CheckingAccount) Withdraw(value float64) bool {
  if acct.balance >= value{
    acct.balance = acct.balance - value
    return true
  }
  return false
}

func main() {
  acct := SavingsAccount{}
  acct.number="S21345345345355"
  acct.balance=159

  fmt.Println("savings balance", acct)
  fmt.Println("withdraw from savings:", acct.Withdraw(150))
  fmt.Println("new savings balance", acct)

  acct2 := CheckingAccount{}
  acct2.number="C218678678345345355"
  acct2.balance=2000
```

continues

continued

```
    fmt.Println("checking balance", acct2)
    fmt.Println("withdraw from checking:", acct2.Withdraw(150))
    fmt.Println("new checking balance", acct2)
}
```

In this listing, you create two struct types: one, called `CheckingAccount`, is for a checking account and the other, called `SavingsAccount`, is for a savings account. You then define the same method called `Withdraw` twice. These methods use the same signature other than the receiver type. The method mimics a withdrawal from a savings account and a checking account.

In the `main` function, you create a struct called `acct` using the `SavingsAccount` struct. You assign values and then call with the `Withdraw` method. You repeat the process, creating a struct called `acct2`, this time using the `CheckingAccount` struct, but also calling its `Withdraw` method. The output from the listing is as follows:

```
savings balance {S21345345345355 159}
withdraw from savings: true
new savings balance {S21345345345355 9}
checking balance {C218678678345345355 2000}
withdraw from checking: true
new checking balance {C218678678345345355 1850}
```

WORKING WITH VALUE RECEIVERS AND ARGUMENTS

Here's another difference between methods and functions:

- If a function accepts a value argument, it can only accept a value argument.
- If a method accepts a value receiver, it can accept either a value receiver or a pointer receiver.

To understand this difference, let's consider the code in Listing 14.8, which uses a method defined with a value receiver. Note that this method is defined to take a value receiver, but the listing passes a pointer.

LISTING 14.8

Using a method with a value receiver

```
package main

import "fmt"
```

```
type account struct {
    number string
    balance float64
}

// method defined with value receiver
func(acct account) withdraw(value float64) bool {
    if acct.balance >= value{
        acct.balance = acct.balance - value
        return true
    }
    return false
}

func main() {
acct := account{number: "C21345345345355", balance: 159.0}

    ptra := &acct // create a pointer

    fmt.Println("Before:", ptra)

    // This is ok because the method can accept both a value and a
    // pointer receiver
    ptra.withdraw(100)

    fmt.Println("After: ", ptra)
}
```

In this example, you use the withdraw method, and you provide a pointer receiver. The method accepts the receiver, and the output is:

```
Before: &{C21345345345355 159}
After: &{C21345345345355 159}
```

Although this does not throw an error, note that the balance value does not change; the output still reflects a balance of 159, even after the method supposedly subtracted 100 from that value. Using a pointer receiver for a method that accepts value receivers works, but it is important to remember that the method still copies the *passed* pointer and operates on the *copy*, rather than on the value itself. In order to see the changes in the caller, you still need to use pointer receivers.

If you update the main function to use a withdraw function rather than the method, the program will not run, as you can see if you try to run Listing 14.9.

LISTING 14.9

Passing a pointer to a value argument

```
package main

import "fmt"

type account struct {
    number string
    balance float64
}

// function defined with value receiver
func withdraw(acct account, value float64) account {
    if acct.balance >= value{
        acct.balance = acct.balance - value
    }
    return acct
}

func main() {
    acct := account{}
    acct.number="C21345345345355"
    acct.balance=159

    ptra :=&acct // create a pointer

    fmt.Println("Before: ", ptra)

    // This is not ok because the function accepts only value arguments
    // The withdraw statement won't execute and will throw an error
    withdraw(ptra,150)

    fmt.Println("After:" , ptra)
}
```

In this listing, withdraw has been changed to a standard function. You can see that instead of using a receiver type, the account is passed as a parameter. As in the previous listing, you create a pointer (ptra) that points to an account. This pointer is passed to the function. The output is an error:

```
.\Listing1409.go:29:11: cannot use ptra (type *account) as type account in
argument to withdraw
```

WORKING WITH POINTER RECEIVERS AND ARGUMENTS

The reverse is also true in regard to working with pointer receivers and pointer arguments:

- If a function accepts pointer arguments, it will only accept pointer arguments.
- If a method accepts a pointer receiver, it will accept both pointer and value receivers.

Listing 14.10 is similar to what you've been using; however, this time you use a method defined with a pointer receiver, but a value is defined and used in the main function.

LISTING 14.10

Sending a value to a pointer

```
package main

import "fmt"

type account struct {
    number string
    balance float64
}

// method defined with a pointer receiver
func(acct *account) withdraw(value float64) bool {
    if acct.balance>=value{
        acct.balance=acct.balance-value
        return true
    }
    return false
}

func main() {
    acct := account{number: "C21345345345355", balance: 159.0}


    fmt.Println("Before:", acct)

    // The acct.withdraw will be interpreted by compiler as
    // (&acct).withdraw(). This is ok because the method can
    // accept both value and pointer receivers
```

continues

continued

```
    acct.withdraw(100)

    fmt.Println("After:", acct)
}
```

You can see that the withdraw method receives a `float64` argument called `value`. Because this is a value type, the expectation might be that a copy of the value would be received, and the original value would not be impacted. The result of the program shows that this is not the case:

```
Before: {C21345345345355 159}
After:  {C21345345345355 59}
```

Because the method uses a pointer receiver, the account balance updates, even with a value provided.

Now let's look at the same example using a function with a pointer parameter instead of a value parameter. This is shown in Listing 14.11.

LISTING 14.11

Passing a value to a pointer argument

```
package main

import "fmt"

type account struct {
    number string
    balance float64
}

// Function defined with pointer parameter
func withdraw(acct *account, value float64) account {
    if acct.balance >= value{
        acct.balance = acct.balance - value
    }
    return *acct
}

func main() {
    acct := account{}
    acct.number="C21345345345355"
    acct.balance=159
```

```
ptra :=&acct // create a pointer
fmt.Println(&ptra)

fmt.Println("Before:", acct)
// This statement will not execute and will throw an error
withdraw(acct,150)
fmt.Println("After:", acct)
}
```

In this listing, the `withdraw` function accepts a pointer to an account. In the `main` function, you define a pointer, but you don't use it. Rather, you pass `acct`, which is an account struct, to `withdraw`. When you run the code, it throws the following error:

```
.\Listing1411.go:27:12: cannot use a (type account) as type *account in
argument to withdraw
```

You can change the call to `withdraw` to use a pointer:

```
withdraw(ptra,150)
```

In this case, the function gets the pointer it expects and thus works as expected:

```
0xc000006028
Before: {C21345345345355 159}
After: {C21345345345355 9}
```

The key to remember in this case, however, is that if the function expects a pointer, then a value type can't be sent.

SUMMARY

In this lesson, we returned to the topic of methods as well as functions. Not only were the differences between methods and functions mentioned, but some aspects of object-oriented programming were also covered, such as ways to reuse code. We know that Go doesn't support classes, but it does support the concept of a method, and you learned how methods with the same name can be used.

We also covered the use of pointers versus value types for method receivers as well as arguments and parameters. It is important to understand receiver type in order to get the results you expect. Keep the following rules in mind as you build your own methods and functions:

- If a function accepts a value argument, it can only accept a value argument.
- If a method accepts a value receiver, it can accept either a value receiver or a pointer receiver.

- If a function accepts pointer arguments, it will only accept pointer arguments.

- If a method accepts a pointer receiver, it will accept both pointer and value receivers.

EXERCISES

The following exercises are provided to allow you to experiment with the tools and concepts presented in this lesson. For each exercise, write a program that meets the specified requirements and verify that the program runs as expected. The exercises are:

Exercise 14.1: Functioning with Integers

Exercise 14.2: Methods with Integers

Exercise 14.3: Volume of a Solid

Exercise 14.4: Banking Terminal

> **NOTE** The exercises are for your benefit. The exercises help you apply what you learn in the lessons. You are also encouraged to experiment with the code as you complete the exercises.

Exercise 14.1: Functioning with Integers

Create a function that takes as input an int, n, and returns an array of length *n* with random integers between −100 and 100. Then implement a function for each of the following bullets. Test that each function will return an input array of 100 integers. Do not use the sort package or any built-in function (like min or max).

- Compute the max of an array of int.

- Compute the index of the max of an array of int.

- Compute the min of an array of int.

- Compute the index of the min of an array of int.

- Sort an array of int in descending order and return the new sorted array in a separate array.

- Sort an array of int in ascending order and return the new sorted array in a separate array.

- Compute the mean of an array.

- Compute the median of an array.

- Identify all positive numbers in the array and return the numbers in a slice.

- Identify all negative numbers in the array and return the numbers in a slice.

- Compute the longest sequence of sorted numbers (in descending or ascending order) in the array and return in a new array. For example, with input of [1 45 67 87 6 57 0], the output should be [1 45 67 87].

- Remove duplicates from an array of ints and return the unique elements in a slice.

Exercise 14.2: Methods with Integers

Modify the code you wrote for Exercise 14.1 so that you add methods to the array instead of creating standalone functions. The receiver type of your methods should be the integer array you create.

Exercise 14.3: Volume of a Solid

Create a program that will calculate the volume of a solid. Start with the following structs:

- Cube: Represents a cube with one attribute: length: float64

- Box: Represents a box with three attributes: length, width, height as float64

- Sphere: Represents a sphere with one attribute: radius: float64

Implement a volume method for each of the structs defined above. The volume method returns the volume of a cube, box, or sphere. Use the main function to create different shapes and compute their volume.

After verifying that the program meets the requirements and works correctly, add additional shapes. For example, you could add a cuboid, a cone, and a pyramid.

Exercise 14.4: Banking Terminal

In this exercise, you will create a banking terminal that allows a user to manage their bank account. Start by creating the following structs. Use an appropriate name for each struct.

Bank Account

Create a struct to represent the accounts. Include the following information:

- Account number: string

- Account owner: struct of type `entity` that includes:
  - ID
  - Address
  - Entity type: `string` (Individual or Business)
- Balance: `float64`
- Interest rate: `float64`
- Account type: `string` (checking, savings, or investment)

Wallet

Create a struct to group accounts by owner:

- Wallet ID: `string`
- Accounts: The different accounts in the wallet (choose appropriate data structure)
- Wallet owner: struct of type `entity`

Define the Methods

Implement the following methods for the `account` struct:

- `withdraw` method: Implement necessary logic to validate balance before performing a withdrawal.
  - Check that `balance` is greater than the amount to be withdrawn and that `balance` is not negative.
  - The `withdraw` method should take as input the amount to be withdrawn.
- `deposit` method: This method should take as input the amount to be deposited.
- apply `interest`: This method should apply an interest rate to the balance of the account as follows:
  - For individual accounts:
    - 1% APR for checking accounts
    - 2% APR for investment accounts
    - 5% APR for savings accounts
  - For business accounts:
    - 0.5% APR for checking accounts
    - 1% APR for investment accounts
    - 2% APR for savings accounts

- `wire`: This method should mimic wiring money to another account.

  - The accounts can be owned by the same entity or by different entities.
  - The method will need the source account and the target account.
  - The method will need the amount to be wired.
  - The method will deduct the amount from the source (after checking the validity of the amount) and add it to the target.

Implement the following method for the `entity` account:

- `change address`: Changes the address of the entity

Implement the following methods for the `wallet` struct:

- `display accounts`: Iterate and display the information from each account in the wallet.

  - The method should display the accounts in the following order:
    - The checking accounts first
    - The investment accounts second
    - The saving accounts last

- `balance`: Iterate through all accounts and return the overall balance in all accounts.

- `wire`: This method will mimic a wire from a source account to a target account.

  - The source account must be in the wallet.
  - The target account can be in the wallet or external.
  - If the balance in the account is too low, display an error message.

main Function

Create a `main` function that can:

- Create account, entity, and wallet types.
- Showcase the different methods implemented, based on the user interaction with the accounts.

Challenge

After you have the basic program working as expected, add the following updates:

- Create a nice banking terminal that allows users to:
  - View accounts
  - Interact with accounts (deposit, withdraw, etc.)

- View the wallet
- Interact with the wallet
- Identify at least one design change that will make the structs and your program more elegant and efficient, such as:
  - Adding new attributes
  - Adding new structs
  - Implementing new methods
- Instead of an error message, the `wire` method should recommend another account in the wallet that has enough of a balance to perform the transfer.
- Can you change the `account` and `wallet` structs so that you are able to compute the overall interest rate paid to all the accounts in the wallet?

  - You will need to store the interest amount somewhere each time you apply interest to a particular account.
  - Use appropriate data structures and logic to implement it.

Lesson 15
Adding Interfaces

In the previous lessons, we've covered a number of different types that Go supports. Go supports another type as well: *interfaces*. In its basic form, an interface in Go is a named collection of method signatures without any implementation.

LEARNING OBJECTIVES

By the end of this lesson, you will be able to:

- Create an interface.
- Use an interface with multiple types.
- Work with static and dynamic interface types.
- Apply multiple interfaces.
- Embed an interface.

CREATING AN INTERFACE

If you have worked with object-oriented languages before, then you might already be familiar with the concept of an interface. In Go we can define an interface type using the type and interface keywords:

```
type Name interface {
    // methods
}
```

After creating an interface, we can create variables based on that interface. The values stored in those variables implement the methods of the interface.

In other programming languages, such as Java, we normally use the `implements` keyword to implement an interface. In Go programming, we use the simple convention that the value of an interface type can only hold values of a type that implements the methods of the interface. To understand the concept of interfaces, consider the code in Listing 15.1.

LISTING 15.1
Creating an interface

```
package main

import "fmt"

type AccountOperations interface{
    // methods
    withdraw(value float64) bool
    deposit(value float64) bool
    displayInfo()
}

type account struct {
    number string
    balance float64
}

func (acct *account) withdraw(value float64) bool {
    if acct.balance >= value{
        acct.balance = acct.balance - value
        return true
    }
    return false
}

func (acct *account) deposit(value float64) bool {
    if value > 0 {
        acct.balance = acct.balance + value
        return true
    }
    return false
}
```

```go
func (acct *account) displayInfo() {
    fmt.Println("Account Balance:", acct.balance)
    fmt.Println("Account Number: ", acct.number)
}

func main() {
    var ao AccountOperations
    fmt.Println("initial value:", ao)

    // Assign a pointer to an account value that is created to ao
    // We can only do this because the account type implements
    // all the methods of AccountOperations interface

    ao = &account{"C13443533535",1500}

    //withdrawal amount
    ao.withdraw(150)
    ao.displayInfo()

    // deposit amount
    ao.deposit(1000)
    ao.displayInfo()
}
```

Go ahead and run this listing. You should see the following output:

```
initial value: <nil>
Account Balance: 1350
Account Number:  C13443533535
Account Balance: 2350
Account Number:  C13443533535
```

Let's take a closer look at what the code is doing.

First, you create an interface called AccountOperations with three method signatures: withdraw, deposit, and displayInfo. Here you simply list the methods the interface will use, without providing details about their implementation.

Next, you create a struct type account that includes two fields: number and balance. This represents a basic banking account.

You also define the three methods included in the interface, withdraw, deposit, and displayInfo, on the account struct. This is where you define each method's implementation. Note that you use a pointer receiver of type account for the three methods, which allows each method to change values in the struct directly. You could use value receivers instead, but you would have to add additional steps to update the values stored in the struct.

Finally, in the `main` function, you first create a variable named ao of type AccountOperations, which will initially hold the zero value of the interface type. As you see in the output, the default value for an interface is `nil`.

Once you create an interface variable, the variable can hold any type that implements the methods defined in the interface. In this case, because the account type implements all three methods, you can assign a pointer for an account value to the variable ao. You create the account type using an account number of C13443533535 and a balance of 1,500.

You can then execute the methods from the AccountOperations interface to update the account balance using `withdraw` or `deposit`. Using the `displayInfo` method, you can see that the balance in the struct updates to reflect the method used.

INTERFACES AND CODE REUSABILITY

Interfaces promote code reusability because you can use the same interfaces across different packages but allow each package to have its own implementation of the interface. To understand the power of interfaces in another example, consider the code in Listing 15.2.

LISTING 15.2

Code reusability

```
package main

import "fmt"

type AccountOperations interface{
    // Methods
    computeInterest() float64
}

type SavingsAccount struct {
    number string
    balance float64
}

type CheckingAccount struct {
    number string
    balance float64
}
```

```
func(acct *SavingsAccount) computeInterest() float64{
    return 0.005
}

func(acct *CheckingAccount) computeInterest() float64{
    return 0.001
}

func main() {
    acct := SavingsAccount{}
    acct.number="S21345345345355"
    acct.balance=159

    var ao1 AccountOperations
    ao1 = &acct
    fmt.Println("savings interest:", ao1.computeInterest())

    acct2 := CheckingAccount{}
    acct2.number = "C218678678345345355"
    acct2.balance = 2000

    var ao2 AccountOperations
    ao2 = &acct2
    fmt.Println("checking interest:", ao2.computeInterest())
}
```

In this listing, you create two structs that implement the same method in the
AccountOperations interface. This helps us ensure that both SavingsAccount and
CheckingAccount behave in the same way. This example includes only one method in the
interface, but you could include more. When you execute this listing, you'll see the following output:

```
savings interest: 0.005
checking interest: 0.001
```

In the main function of the listing, you create two variables, acct and acct2, of type
CheckingAccount and SavingsAccount, respectively. Using the same logic as the previous
example, you store the values of acct and acct2 in two interface variables, ao1 and ao2.
This allows you to execute the displayInterest method from the interface.

This is an example of how to use interfaces to enforce a certain behavior across different struct types as well as other types. In this case, you are making sure the different types
of accounts support similar methods.

STATIC VS. DYNAMIC INTERFACE TYPES

You are probably wondering at this point how an interface created with a specific type (AccountOperations, for example) can hold another type like SavingsAccount or CheckingAccount. The reason is that an interface in Go has two different types: one is static, and one is dynamic. The static type is the type of the interface itself. For example, the static type of the interface AccountOperations is AccountOperations. The dynamic type is the type that implements the interface.

Internally, an interface is represented by a tuple, which in turn represents the dynamic type of the interface and the value of that dynamic type. To see this internal representation, look at Listing 15.3.

LISTING 15.3

Internal representation of an interface

```
package main

import "fmt"

type AccountOperations interface{
    // Methods
    computeInterest() float64
}

type SavingsAccount struct {
    number string
    balance float64
}

type CheckingAccount struct {
    number string
    balance float64
}

func(a *SavingsAccount) computeInterest() float64{
    return 0.005
}

func(a *CheckingAccount) computeInterest() float64{
    return 0.001
}
```

```
func describe(ao  AccountOperations) {
    // we use %T to display the dynamic type of ao
    // and %v to display the dynamic value

    fmt.Printf("Interface type %T value %v\n", ao, ao)
}

func main() {
    acct := SavingsAccount{}
    acct.number = "S21345345345355"
    acct.balance = 159

    var ao1 AccountOperations
    ao1 = &acct
    fmt.Println("ao1 type:")
    describe(ao1)

    acct2 := CheckingAccount{}
    acct2.number = "C218678678345345355"
    acct2.balance = 2000

    var ao2 AccountOperations
    ao2 = &acct2
    fmt.Println("ao2 type:")
    describe(ao2)
}
```

This listing includes another function, display, which displays the internal representation of the interfaces ao1 and ao2. As the comments in the listing indicate, the describe function uses a call to Printf to display information about the interface that is provided. Note that this is using Printf, not Println. The Printf function allows you to add escape codes to your output. In this case, you use %T to display the dynamic type of ao and %v to display the dynamic value. The output looks like this:

```
ao1 type:
Interface type *main.SavingsAccount value &{S21345345345355 159 0}
ao2 type:
Interface type *main.CheckingAccount value &{C218678678345345355 2000 0}
```

You can see the following in the results:

- The dynamic type of ao1 is SavingsAccount.
- The dynamic type for ao2 is CheckingAccount.
- The dynamic value stored is essentially the value of acct and acct2.

EMPTY INTERFACES

An empty interface in Go is an interface without any methods, known as interface{}. By default, all types in Go implement the empty interface. Listing 15.4 shows an example.

LISTING 15.4

Empty interfaces

```
package main

import "fmt"

func main() {
    var s interface{}
    fmt.Println(s)
    fmt.Printf("s is nil and has type %T value %v\n", s, s)
}
```

In this listing, you define an empty interface called s. You then use Println to display the contents of the empty interface. Finally, you use Printf to show the type and value of s as well. In all cases, the type and contents are empty, as indicated by the value nil. The output is:

```
<nil>
s is nil and has type <nil> value <nil>
```

CHECKING AN INTERFACE TYPE

If you want to check the type of a variable, you can use the reflect package. In fact, Go supports switch statements on values (the usual switch), but it also supports the use of a switch statement to check against various data types (both built-in and custom).

In other words, you can use a switch statement to check the underlying type of an interface. This is illustrated in Listing 15.5 once again using our SavingsAccount and CheckingAccount structs with our AccountOperations interface.

LISTING 15.5

Checking an interface type

```go
package main

import "fmt"

type AccountOperations interface{
    // Methods
    computeInterest() float64
}

type SavingsAccount struct {
    number string
    balance float64
}

type CheckingAccount struct {
    number string
    balance float64
}

func(a *SavingsAccount) computeInterest() float64{
    return 0.005
}

func(a *CheckingAccount) computeInterest() float64{
    return 0.001
}

func CheckType(i interface{}) {
    switch i.(type) {
      case *SavingsAccount:
          fmt.Println("This is a savings account")
      case *CheckingAccount:
          fmt.Println("This is a checking account")
      default:
          fmt.Println("Unknown account")
    }
}

func main() {
    a := SavingsAccount{}
```

continues

continued

```
      a.number = "S21345345345355"
      a.balance = 159

      var ao1 AccountOperations
      ao1 = &a
      fmt.Println("Result for ao1")
      CheckType(ao1)

      b := CheckingAccount{}
      b.number = "C218678678345345355"
      b.balance = 2000

      var ao2 AccountOperations
      ao2 = &b
      fmt.Println("Result for ao2")
      CheckType(ao2)
}
```

Most of this listing is the same as the previous one; however, a new function was added called CheckType, which will be used by the main function to print the type of ao1 and ao2. Within CheckType, the received variable is used within a switch statement. The switch receives the type of the variable:

```
switch i.(type)
```

The cases within the switch are then pointers to the different types that you are interested in comparing against. In this listing, you are comparing the type of the passed-in value to a SavingsAccount and a CheckingAccount. The final output is:

```
Result for ao1
This is a savings account
Result for ao2
This is a checking account
```

Again, keep in mind that the statement i.(type) will only work within a switch statement and cannot be used on its own. If you want to check the type of a variable, you can use the reflect package.

MULTIPLE INTERFACES

A type in Go can implement multiple interfaces. Listing 15.6 shows the use of multiple interfaces with the same variable.

LISTING 15.6

Multiple interfaces

```go
package main

import "fmt"

// create first interface
type AccountOperations interface{
   computeInterest() float64
   displayInfo()
}

// create second interface
type UserOperations interface{
   changeANumber(number string)
}

// create a struct type
type SavingsAccount struct {
   number string
   balance float64
   interest float64
}

// implement method from first interface
func(a *SavingsAccount) computeInterest() float64{
   return 0.005
}

// implement method from first interface
func(a *SavingsAccount) displayInfo() {
   fmt.Println(a.number)
   fmt.Println(a.balance)
   fmt.Println(a.interest)
}

// implement method from second interface
func(a *SavingsAccount) changeANumber(number string) {
   a.number=number
}

func main() {
   // create a SavingsAccount variable
```

continues

continued

```
        acct := SavingsAccount{}
        acct.number = "S21345345345355"
        acct.balance = 159

        // Declare an interface variable for AccountOperations
        var ao1 AccountOperations

        // acct implements the method of interface AccountOperations
        ao1 = &acct
        fmt.Println("ao1 info:")
        ao1.displayInfo()

        fmt.Println("---------------")  // print divider for output

        // Declare an interface variable for UserOperations
        var uo1 UserOperations

        // acct also implements the methods of interface UserOperations
        uo1 = &acct
        // execute the account number change
        uo1.changeANumber("2345353453")

        fmt.Println("updated ao1 info:")
        ao1.displayInfo()
}
```

In this listing you again focus on creating a banking account. You create the SavingsAccount structure you created before with an account number and balance, but this time you add an interest rate. You then create two different interfaces that you'll use. The first is an AccountOperations interface that will compute the interest rate with the method computeInterest and display account information with the displayInfo method. The second is a UserOperations interface that will be used to change the account number using the method named changeANumber.

The main function creates a SavingsAccount called acct in the same way that you've used before. An account number and balance of 159 are assigned to acct. This is followed by declaring an interface called ao1 of type AccountOperations and applying it to your account. The displayInfo method of the interface is then called, which displays the account information. Up to this point, everything is exactly as you saw earlier in this lesson.

The listing then prints a simple dashed line to make it easier to see the before and after data. A second interface, uo1 of type UserOperations, is then created. In the same manner used for ao1, the interface uo1 is assigned to acct:

```
uo1 = &acct
```

With uo1, you can now access `changeANumber` to change the number of your account. You can still access the methods from the original interface, ao1, as can be seen by the call once again to `displayInfo`, which prints the account information. The full output of the listing is:

```
S21345345345355
159
0
0.005
-------------
X9999999999
159
0
```

The key thing to note is that multiple interfaces are being applied to acct at the same time. acct has both the `AccountOperations` (ao1) and the `UserOperations` (uo1) interfaces providing access.

EMBEDDED INTERFACES

Go supports a concept similar to inheritance in object-oriented programming through the use of embedded interfaces. That is, you can define interfaces using the definition of other interfaces. Listing 15.7 shows how this works.

LISTING 15.7

Embedded interfaces

```go
package main

import "fmt"

// create first interface
type AccountOperations interface{
    // Methods
    computeInterest() float64
    displayInfo()
}

// create second interface
type UserOperations interface{
    changeANumber(number string)
}
```

continues

continued

```go
// create a third interface that uses the first and second interface
type BankingOperations interface{
    AccountOperations
    UserOperations
}

// create a struct type
type SavingsAccount struct {
    number string
    balance float64
    interest float64
}

// implement method from interface 1
func(a *SavingsAccount) computeInterest() float64{
    return 0.005
}

// implement method from interface 2
func(a *SavingsAccount) changeANumber(number string) {
    a.number=number
}

// implement method from interface 1
func(a *SavingsAccount) displayInfo() {
    fmt.Println(a.number)
    fmt.Println(a.balance)
    fmt.Println(a.interest)
}

func main() {
    // create a SavingsAccount variable
    acct := SavingsAccount{}
    acct.number = "S21345345345355"
    acct.balance = 159

    // create a variable of type BankingOperations
    var ao1 BankingOperations
    // implement the methods in BankingOperations
    ao1 = &acct
    ao1.displayInfo()
    fmt.Println(ao1.computeInterest())
}
```

In this code, you first create two interfaces: AccountOperations and UserOperations. You then create a third interface, BankingOperations. Because the third interface calls the first two interfaces, its methods are the methods of the first two interfaces combined.

You then create a series of methods that execute the appropriate interface to handle the account defined in the struct.

In the main function, you use acct to implement the method of the BankingOperations interface, which effectively implements both AccountOperations and UserOperations. This then allows you to use displayInfo from AccountOperations without having to call it through an AccountOperations type. The output from running the listing is:

```
S21345345345355
159
0
0.005
```

Note that the use of multiple interfaces in this manner is similar to inheritance in object-oriented programming, where an inherited class includes all the properties of its parent's class, even if they aren't specified when the subclass is called.

SUMMARY

The use of interfaces is common in object-oriented languages. The Go language also supports interfaces. As you saw, an interface in Go is a named collection of method signatures without any implementation. In this lesson you learned how to create and use interfaces. This includes using multiple interfaces on a struct as well as embedding interfaces.

EXERCISES

The following exercises are provided to allow you to experiment with the tools and concepts presented in this lesson. For each exercise, write a program that meets the specified requirements and verify that the program runs as expected. The exercises are:

Exercise 15.1: Rectangle Sides

Exercise 15.2: Rectangle Space

Exercise 15.3: Rectangle Borders

Exercise 15.4: Triangles and Rectangles

Exercise 15.5: Circles and Other Shapes

NOTE The exercises are for your benefit. The exercises help you apply what you learn in the lessons. You are also encouraged to experiment with the code as you complete the exercises.

Exercise 15.1: Rectangle Sides

Create a struct for a rectangle similar to what is shown in Figure 15.1.

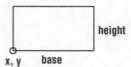

This structure can contain x, y, base, and height fields. Create a display method in your struct that displays the values for the four fields.

Create an interface called sides that lists two methods, one for updating the base and one for updating the height.

In your program, create two rectangles and assign them different values. Apply the sides interface to your rectangle and use it to double the base and height of both rectangles. Print the new values to show the update.

Exercise 15.2: Rectangle Space

Update your program from Exercise 15.1 with a second interface. This interface should be called area. Within the interface create a method to return the area of the rectangle (base times height) and a second method to display the area. You can call these methods getArea and displayArea. Add the code for the two methods using a rectangle receiver.

In your main program, apply the new interface along with the previous sides interface to your two rectangle structures. Print the information on each rectangle along with its area.

Exercise 15.3: Rectangle Borders

Continuing with the code in Exercise 15.2, create a third interface called circumference. Define it with two methods, getBorder and displayBorder. Update the main section of the program to also print the length of the border along with the area and other information for each rectangle. Once completed, you should be using three interfaces with your rectangle structure.

Exercise 15.4: Triangles and Rectangles

Create a new struct to hold a triangle. Similar to the rectangle struct, the triangle struct should contain x, y, base, and height. This structure should be added to the listing you created in Exercise 15.3.

In your main program, create two variables using your triangle struct. Using the same interfaces, display the values from the two triangles along with their area and circumference.

> **NOTE** Use the same interfaces; however, you might need to create new methods.

Exercise 15.5: Circles and Other Shapes

Update Listing 15.4 to work with other shapes. You can include a circle, an oval, and a trapezoid. Use the same interfaces.

Lesson 16
Pulling It All Together: Building a Burger Shop

In this lesson, you'll build an application to pull together many of the concepts you've learned up to this point. This lesson focuses on building an application that accepts a customer's order at a burger shop.

LEARNING OBJECTIVES

By the end of this lesson, you will be able to:

- Design appropriate structs and data structures for the burger application.
- Understand how to create a more robust application.

> **NOTE** If this program sounds familiar, it's because you were given an exercise in Lesson 11, "Organizing with Structs" to build something very similar.

REQUIREMENTS FOR OUR APPLICATION

Our burger shop application allows customers to place custom orders for hamburgers and other items. In the ordering process, you will want the customer to be able to specify what kind of food or drink they want; then you'll need to calculate and display the cost of the order and display the completed order to the user. More specifically, the completed application must be able to perform the following steps:

- Ask the customer if they want a burger, a side, a drink, or a combo that must include a burger, a side, and a drink.

- Prompt them for details about their selection, such as condiments for a burger, what kind and size of drink, and so on.

- Create the item based on their selections.

- Add the item to the order.

- Repeat these steps until the customer doesn't want to order anything else.

- Display the order details, including the total price.

- Thank the customer for their business.

- Give the customer the option to end their order at any point in the ordering process.

PLANNING THE CODE

As a first step in any development process, you begin by planning what needs to be coded in your application. The planning stage can include flowcharts or other diagrams to help you visualize how the program will be structured and what it will do. You'll start with the big picture here and then focus on smaller parts of the program as you work through the steps.

The main program itself must include the following steps:

1. Greet the customer and ask their name.

2. Ask the user what they want to order (one item at a time!).

3. Ask the user for customizations, such as burger toppings or drink size.

4. Add each item to the order as it is requested.

5. Ask the user to continue or complete their order after each item.

   When the user completes the order, the program will display the order and the total price.

The customer should be able to order any combination of the following items:

- Burger
- Drink
- Side

You also want to allow them to order a combo that includes a burger, a drink, and a side at a discount.

> **NOTE** You'll notice that the planning and design of the application includes a lot of information that seems redundant with the requirements that were mentioned. This should make sense because the objectives of the application are to meet the requirements. If your planning includes items that were not a part of the requirements, then you should consider whether they should be included or whether they are beyond the scope of your current application.

CREATING THE STRUCTS

You can identify multiple structs in this scenario. These include the following:

- The order itself
- The items the customer can order, which you know to be:
  - Burger
  - Drink
  - Side
  - Combo

You can define the order itself as a struct. You can also define each of the items that can be ordered as a struct. You can then use these structs in the main program to streamline the code.

Begin by coding the structs themselves, including the structs you've already identified:

- order
- burger
- drink
- side
- combo

Creating a *burger* Struct

The burger struct needs to track the name, price, and condiments of the burger. You can use a simple array to store the condiments. The burger struct is shown in Listing 16.1.

LISTING 16.1

The burger struct

```
type burger struct {
  name       string
  price      int
  condiments []string
}
```

The code in Listing 16.1 simply creates a burger struct with three fields: name, price, and condiments.

Having defined the burger struct, you can now implement basic methods for the struct, such as adding a condiment or returning the price of the burger. To do that, use the method in Listing 16.2.

LISTING 16.2

The getName method for burger

```
func (b *burger) getName() string {
    return b.name
}
```

In Listing 16.2, you create a method called getName, which returns the name of the burger. You can also create a basic method for getting the price, as shown in Listing 16.3.

LISTING 16.3

The computePrice method for burger

```
func (b *burger) computePrice() int {
  b.price = burgerPrice
  return b.price
}
```

You'll use several constants in your program. One will be the burger prices:

```
const burgerPrice = 6.00
```

You'll add this constant to the top of your program file. This allows you to easily change the price of the burger at any time.

The next method to add to the burger struct is addCondiment, shown in Listing 16.4. This method allows you to add a condiment to the burger.

LISTING 16.4

The addCondiment method for burger

```
func (b *burger) addCondiment(condiment string) {
  b.condiments = append(b.condiments, condiment)
}
```

As you can see, the method takes as input a condiment. You simply append it to the existing list of condiments.

Finally, you need a display method that will allow you to display the information about the burger in a user-friendly manner. In the method shown in Listing 16.5, you display each condiment. Notice that the display method takes as input a Boolean variable, which decides if the price should be displayed. This will come in handy later when the prices are being displayed in the order or in the combo. Other than that, the display method displays the name, the list of condiments, and the price of the burger if the input Boolean is true.

LISTING 16.5

The display method for burger

```
func (b *burger) display(displayPrice bool) {
  fmt.Println("Item Name: " + b.getName())
  fmt.Print("Condiments: ")
  for _, condiment := range b.condiments {
    fmt.Print(condiment + " ")
  }
```

continues

continued

```
    fmt.Println()
    if displayPrice == true {
        fmt.Printf("Item Price: $%d\n", b.computePrice())
    }

}
```

Finally, let's see the burger code in action. Add the `main` function in Listing 16.6 to your code.

LISTING 16.6

A `main` **function to test the** `burger` **struct**

```
func main() {
    var b burger
    b.name = "Burger"

    b.addCondiment("Lettuce")
    b.addCondiment("Tomato")
    b.addCondiment("Onion")
    b.addCondiment("Mayo")
    b.computePrice()
    b.display(true)
}
```

As you can see, you created a variable b of type `burger` and then added the `name` and four condiments. Finally, you use the `display` method to display the burger. When you add the code in Listing 16.6 to the previous code, you should have a program similar to Listing 16.7.

LISTING 16.7

The `burger` **struct in action**

```
package main

import "fmt"

const burgerPrice = 6.00
```

```go
type burger struct {
  name       string
  price      int
  condiments []string
}

func (b *burger) getName() string {
  return b.name
}
func (b *burger) computePrice() int {
  b.price = burgerPrice
  return b.price
}
func (b *burger) addCondiment(condiment string) {
  b.condiments = append(b.condiments, condiment)
}

func (b *burger) display(displayPrice bool) {
  fmt.Println("Item Name: " + b.getName())
  fmt.Print("Condiments: ")
  for _, condiment := range b.condiments {
      fmt.Print(condiment + " ")
  }
  fmt.Println()
  if displayPrice == true {
      fmt.Printf("Item Price: $%d\n", b.computePrice())
  }

}

func main() {
  var b burger
  b.name = "Burger"

  b.addCondiment("Lettuce")
  b.addCondiment("Tomato")
  b.addCondiment("Onion")
  b.addCondiment("Mayo")
  b.computePrice()
  b.display(true)
}
```

When you run this code, you should see the following:

```
Item Name: Burger
Item Price: $6
Condiments: Lettuce Tomato Onion Mayo
```

Creating a *drink* Struct

Drinks will have sizes associated with them, in addition to the name and price. As shown in Listing 16.8, the size is of type int and the price is also of type int. The allowed sizes will be 12, 16, and 24 oz. The corresponding prices for these sizes are, respectively, $1, $2, and $3.

LISTING 16.8

The drink struct

```
type drink struct {
  name  string
  size  int
  price int
}
```

Next, you'll create the methods supporting the drink struct. First, create the getName method, which returns the name of the drink, as shown in Listing 16.9.

LISTING 16.9

The getName method for drink

```
func (d *drink) getName() string {
    return d.name
}
```

Then, create the getSize method, which will return the size of the drink, as shown in Listing 16.10.

LISTING 16.10

The getSize method for drink

```
func (d *drink) getSize() int {
    return d.size
}
```

You will also need to create the computePrice method, as shown in Listing 16.11, which computes the price based on size and assigns it to the price field of the drink struct.

LISTING 16.11

The computePrice method for drink

```
func (d *drink) computePrice() int {
  if _, ok := drinks[d.getSize()]; ok {
    d.price = drinks[d.getSize()]
  }
  return d.price
}
```

Note that this method uses values from one map that keeps track of the sizes and associated prices. You have to define this map in your program as well. Because these are values that could change, they should be defined near the top of the listing, after the constants. The code for declaring and initializing this map is as follows:

```
var drinks = map[int]int{12: 1, 16: 2, 24: 3}
```

Finally, you'll need to create the display method, which displays the different fields of the drink struct in a user-friendly manner. The display method for drink is shown in Listing 16.12.

LISTING 16.12

The display method for drink

```
func (d *drink) display(displayPrice bool) {
  fmt.Println("Item Name: " + strings.ToUpper(d.getName()))
  fmt.Printf("Item Size: %d\n", d.size)
  if displayPrice == true {
    fmt.Printf("Item Price: $%d\n", d.computePrice())
  }
}
```

This code prints the name of the drink in uppercase followed by the size. Note that Printf is being used to print the size. With Printf, the %d indicates a number will be displayed, which will be filled in by `d.size`. Finally, if `true` was passed to the `display` function, then the price of the drink will be calculated based on the current size and then displayed using the `Printf` function as well. To see this code in action, add the code in Listing 16.13 to the `main` function.

LISTING 16.13

Code to test the `drink` functionality

```
func main() {

    var d drink
    d.name = "Sprite"
    d.size = 24
    d.display(true)
}
```

This code creates a variable named `d` of type `drink` and then assigns `name` and `size` to `drink`. You then call `computePrice`, which will determine the price based on the assigned size:

```
Item Name: SPRITE
Item Size: 24
Item Price: $3
```

Creating a *side* Struct

All the sides on our menu have the same price ($2). Listing 16.14 shows the `side` struct, which includes two fields, `name` and `price`.

LISTING 16.14

The `side` struct

```
type side struct {
  name   string
  price int
}
```

Following the same process you used for the burger and drink, let's create a few methods. The getName method returns the name of the side, as shown in Listing 16.15.

LISTING 16.15

The getName **method for** side

```
func (s *side) getName() string {
  return s.name
}
```

> **NOTE** Because the getName method is not modifying any values in the struct being passed to it, you can technically omit the *. The asterisk indicates that a pointer to the struct is being passed to the method. Omitting it indicates a copy of the struct itself is being passed. Removing the asterisk doesn't affect the execution, but doing so would mean the getName method would not be able to change the values stored in the struct and would be read-only. The same change could also be made to many of the other methods in this program.

The computePrice method assigns 2 (the dollar value) to the price of the side and returns it. This is shown in Listing 16.16.

LISTING 16.16

The computePrice **method for** side

```
func (s *side) computePrice() int {
  s.price = sidePrice
  return s.price
}
```

You'll want to define a constant for the price of a side. This should go at the top of the listing with the other defined constants:

```
const sidePrice = 2.00
```

Finally, the `display` method prints the two fields, name and price. The `display` method for `side` is shown in Listing 16.17.

LISTING 16.17

The `display` method for `side`

```go
func (s *side) display(displayPrice bool) {

    fmt.Println("Item Name: " + s.getName())
    if displayPrice == true {
        fmt.Printf("Item Price: $%d\n", s.computePrice())
    }
}
```

To see this code in action, add the code from Listing 16.18 to the `main` function.

LISTING 16.18

A `main` function to test `side`

```go
func main() {
    var s side
    s.name = "Coleslaw"
    s.display(true)
}
```

The output from running this code will look like this:

```
Item Name: Coleslaw
Item Price: $2
```

Creating a *combo* Struct

A combo is much more complicated than the other food items. While it does include both a name and a price, a combo includes multiple items as well as a discounted price based on the price of the individual items.

The code in Listing 16.19 is an example of the `combo` struct. Each combo includes a name and a price, as well as a burger, a drink, and a side.

LISTING 16.19

The combo struct

```
type combo struct {
  name   string
  burger burger
  drink  drink
  side   side
  price  int
}
```

As with the other structs you've created, you'll create a number of methods to work with the combo struct. The first is the getName method (Listing 16.20), which returns the name of the combo.

LISTING 16.20

The getName method for combo

```
func (c *combo) getName() string {
    return c.name
}
```

The computePrice method computes the price of the combo. In our case, combos will include a one-dollar discount. Thus, the price of the combo is the price of the burger, side, and drink minus one dollar. The code for the computePrice method should look like Listing 16.21.

LISTING 16.21

The computePrice method for combo

```
func (c *combo) computePrice() int {
  c.price = c.burger.computePrice() + c.drink.computePrice() +
c.side.computePrice() - comboDiscount
  return c.price
}
```

You used a constant called comboDiscount in the computePrice method for the discount instead of using one dollar, so you'll need to define the comboDiscount at the top of your program where you define the other constants. Doing so will make it easier to change later if necessary. Include the following code to define comboDiscount:

```
const comboDiscount = 1.00
```

Finally, the display method prints all the information about the combo. This includes calling the display method of the burger, side, and drink structs, as shown in Listing 16.22.

LISTING 16.22

The display method for combo

```
func (c *combo) display() {
  fmt.Println("Burger For Combo")
  c.burger.display(false)
  fmt.Println("Side For Combo")
  c.side.display(false)
  fmt.Println("Drink For Combo")
  c.drink.display(false)
  fmt.Printf("Price For Combo: $%d\n", c.computePrice())
}
```

To see the code for a combo in action, we can add the code in Listing 16.23 to the main function.

LISTING 16.23

The code to test combo

```
func main() {
    var c combo
    c.burger = b
    c.side = s
    c.drink = d
    c.display()
}
```

Creating the *order* Struct

Finally, you'll create the order struct. There are various ways to design the order struct; Listing 16.24 shows one way.

LISTING 16.24

The order struct

```
type order struct {
  name     string
  price    int
  burgers  []burger
  drinks   []drink
  sides    []side
  combos   []combo
}
```

As you can see, the order struct tracks the different menu items (burgers, drinks, side, and combos) separately. Another design option is to have a single data structure that tracks all the menu items. In our case, you are tracking the burgers, drinks, sides, and combos in slices; however, other data structures could be used.

The first method that you need to implement for order is the getName method, which returns the name on the order, as shown in Listing 16.25.

LISTING 16.25

The getName method for order

```
func (o *order) getName() string {
    return o.name
}
```

You also need to implement a method to compute the price of an order. The computePrice method, shown in Listing 16.26, iterates through all the burgers, sides, drinks, and combos in the order and adds the corresponding prices together.

LISTING 16.26

The computePrice method for order

```go
func (o *order) computePrice() int {
  var price = 0

  for _, b := range o.burgers {
    price = price + b.computePrice()
  }
  for _, s := range o.sides {
    price = price + s.computePrice()
  }
  for _, d := range o.drinks {
    price = price + d.computePrice()
  }
  for _, c := range o.combos {
    price = price + c.computePrice()

  }
  o.price = price
  return o.price
}
```

The last method you'll implement for the order struct is the display method, which displays all the details of an order. Listing 16.27 shows the display method for order.

LISTING 16.27

The display method for order

```go
func (o *order) display() {
    fmt.Println("=====================================")
    fmt.Println("===========ORDER OVERVIEW===========")
    for k, b := range o.burgers {
        fmt.Printf("=====Burger %d\n", k+1)
        b.display(true)
    }
    for k, s := range o.sides {
        fmt.Printf("=====Side %d\n", k+1)
        s.display(true)
    }
```

```
    for k, d := range o.drinks {
        fmt.Printf("=====Drink %d\n", k+1)
        d.display(true)
    }
    for k, c := range o.combos {
        fmt.Printf("=====Combo %d\n", k+1)
        c.display()
    }
    fmt.Printf("=====ORDER TOTAL: $%.2f\n", o.computePrice())
    fmt.Println("====================================")
}
```

This code leverages the display method of the burger, drink, side, and combo structs.
It includes several other print statements to provide some structure to the order,
but otherwise, most of the information is displayed with calls to the individual
struct display methods.

CREATING THE HELPER FUNCTIONS

From a user experience (UX) perspective, you'll need to create various functions that are
reusable and that will make your code less cumbersome. Create the following functions to
aid in the ordering process:

- orderBurger: This function first asks the user if they want condiments on their
  burger. If they do, it then walks the user through the list of condiments one by one
  and asks them what they want.

- orderDrink: This function first displays the list of available drinks and sizes and
  then asks the user to enter the drink they want and then enter the size of drink
  they want.

- orderSide: This function first displays the list of available sides and then asks the
  user to correctly enter their side.

- orderCombo: This function walks the user through the process of ordering a combo
  by first ordering their burger, then the side, then the drink, using the previous
  functions.

Each of the four functions will return the corresponding struct types (burger, side, drink,
or combo).

In addition to the helper functions for ordering, there are a number of values you can
declare that will make it easier for the user of the application to know what values are
available for ordering. Define the arrays shown in Listing 16.28 near the top of the program, after the constants.

LISTING 16.28

Support arrays for user choices

```
const burgerPrice = 6.00
const sidePrice = 2.00
const comboDiscount = 1.00

var burgerCondiments = []string{"Tomato", "Onion", "Lettuce", "Mayo"}
var drinkTypes = []string{"FANTA", "COKE", "SPRITE", "PEPSI"}
var drinks = map[int]int{12: 1, 16: 2, 24: 3}
var sideTypes = []string{"fries", "coleslaw", "salad"}
var possibleChoices = []string{"b", "s", "d", "c"}
```

Note that drinks and drinkTypes were shown earlier, so they might already be added to your listing. burgerCondiments defines a number of strings that provide choices that the user can select for condiments on their burger. drinkTypes is a list of drink types the user can select in the application. Similarly, sideTypes is a list of the sides that can be selected. The final array, possibleChoices, is a list of choices that the user can use to select the type of order they want. They will be able to select **b** for burger, **s** for side, **d** for drink, or **c** for combo. The possibleChoices array will be used in the menu.

In the program, there is one additional helper function, which is shown in Listing 16.29. The contains function will be used to validate if a side or drink selection the user selects is in the array of types we defined in Listing 16.28.

LISTING 16.29

The contains function

```
func contains(arr []string, choice string) bool {
   for _, v := range arr {
      if v == choice {
         return true
      }
   }
   return false
}
```

In this function, you pass two values. The first is an array of strings called arr. This is an array such as drinkTypes or sideTypes. The second is a single string (called choice), which in this case will be a value entered by the user of your program. The function then checks to see if the choice is in the array. If it is, the value of true is returned. If not, the value of false is returned.

Ordering a Burger

Let's start by creating the first function that will take a user through the process of ordering a burger. In our case, our function will return a type of burger that will contain all the data related to the user's burger. Listing 16.30 shows an example of the orderBurger function.

LISTING 16.30

The orderBurger function

```
func orderBurger() burger {
  var b burger
  b.name = "Beef Burger"
  fmt.Print("Do you want condiments on your burger? (type y for yes): ")
  var choice1 string
  fmt.Scanln(&choice1)
  if strings.ToLower(choice1) == "y" {
      for _, condiment := range burgerCondiments {
          var choice2 string
          fmt.Print("Do you want " + condiment + " on your burger? (type y for
yes): ")
          fmt.Scanln(&choice2)
          if strings.ToLower(choice2) == "y" {
              b.addCondiment(condiment)

          }
      }

  }
  return b
}
```

The function starts by asking the user if they want a condiment on their burger. If the user answers **y** (for yes), then a for loop will display the condiments one by one, and the user will be asked if they want to have that condiment. They can respond by entering **y** if they do. Once the user has indicated all the condiments they want, the burger type that was created is returned from the function.

To see this function in action, add the code in Listing 16.31 to the main function.

LISTING 16.31

The code to test ordering a burger

```
var b = orderBurger()
b.display(true)
```

Ordering a Side

The next function is the orderSide function, which walks the user through the process of ordering a side. The code in Listing 16.32 shows an example of the orderSide function.

LISTING 16.32

The orderSide function

```
func orderSide() side {
  fmt.Print("These are the available sides: ")
  fmt.Println(sideTypes)
  var choice bool = false
  var sideTypeChoice string
  for choice == false {
    fmt.Print("What side do you want? ")
    fmt.Scanln(&sideTypeChoice)
    if contains(sideTypes[:], sideTypeChoice) {
      choice = true
    } else {
      fmt.Println("Please enter a valid choice")
    }
  }
  var s side
  s.name = strings.ToLower(sideTypeChoice)
  s.computePrice()
  return s
}
```

The code begins by displaying the list of available sides to the user, and then asks the user to validate their side option. Notice that you go into a loop until the user provides you with a valid side option.

Ordering a Drink

The next function is the orderDrink function, shown in Listing 16.33. This function walks the user through the process of ordering a drink.

LISTING 16.33

The orderDrink function

```go
func orderDrink() drink {
  fmt.Print("These are the available drinks: ")
  fmt.Println(drinkTypes)
  fmt.Print("These are the available sizes: ")
  fmt.Println("[12 16 24]")

  var choice bool = false
  var drinkTypeChoice string
  var drinkSizeChoice int
  for choice == false {
    fmt.Print("What drink do you want? ")
    fmt.Scanln(&drinkTypeChoice)
    if contains(drinkTypes, strings.ToUpper(drinkTypeChoice)) {
      choice = true
    } else {
      fmt.Println("Please enter a valid drink")
    }
  }
  choice = false
  for choice == false {
    fmt.Print("What size do you want? ")
    fmt.Scanln(&drinkSizeChoice)
    if _, ok := drinks[drinkSizeChoice]; ok {
      choice = true
    } else {
      fmt.Println("Please enter a valid size")
    }
  }
  var d drink
  d.name = strings.ToLower(drinkTypeChoice)
  d.size = drinkSizeChoice
  d.computePrice() // equivalent also to d.price = drinks[drinkSizeChoice]
  return d
}
```

As mentioned earlier, there are three sizes of drinks (12, 16, and 24 oz.), which are priced at $1, $2, and $3, respectively. The code prompts the user for the type of drink and then loops until the user makes a valid entry. The program then prompts for the size and again loops until the user makes a valid entry.

Ordering a Combo

The orderCombo function is the final order function to add to our program. This function walks the user through the process of ordering a combo, as shown in Listing 16.34.

LISTING 16.34

The orderCombo function

```
func orderCombo() combo {
    var c combo
    fmt.Println("Let's get you a combo meal!")
    fmt.Println("First, let's order the burger for your combo")
    c.burger = orderBurger()

    fmt.Println("Now, let's order the drink for your combo")
    c.drink = orderDrink()

    fmt.Println("Finally, let's order the side for your combo")
    c.side = orderSide()

    return c
}
```

The orderCombo function is a combination of the three functions you just included. It creates a combo and fills the values with the results from calling orderBurger, orderDrink, and orderSide.

TYING THE CODE TOGETHER

At this point, all you have left to do is to create the main loop that will keep asking the user for their menu items and add them to the order. Listing 16.35 presents a main function that will run the burger shop using the code you've created up to this point.

LISTING 16.35

The final main function for the burger shop

```
func main() {
    var ord order
    var name string
    var done bool
    done = false
    fmt.Println("Welcome to Myriam's Burger Shop!")
    fmt.Print("May I have your name for the order?  ")
    fmt.Scanln(&name)
    ord.name = name
    fmt.Println("Let's get your order in " + name + "!")
    for done == false {
        fmt.Println("Enter b for Burger")
        fmt.Println("Enter s for Side")
        fmt.Println("Enter d for Drink")
        fmt.Print("Enter c for Combo: ")
        choice := ""
        for contains(possibleChoices[:], choice) == false {
            fmt.Scanln(&choice)
            switch choice {
            case "b":
                fmt.Println("Burger it is!")
                var b = orderBurger()
                ord.burgers = append(ord.burgers, b)
            case "s":
                fmt.Println("Side it is!")
                var s = orderSide()
                ord.sides = append(ord.sides, s)
            case "d":
                fmt.Println("Drink it is!")
                var d = orderDrink()
                ord.drinks = append(ord.drinks, d)
            case "c":
                fmt.Println("Combo it is!")
                var c = orderCombo()
                ord.combos = append(ord.combos, c)
            default:
                fmt.Println("Unknown choice")
                fmt.Println("Please enter a valid choice")
            }
        }
    }
```

continues

continued

```
        fmt.Print("Do you want to order more items? (Enter n or N to stop.):    ")
        var q1 string
        fmt.Scanln(&q1)
        if strings.ToLower(q1) == "n" {
            done = true
        }
    }
    ord.display()
}
```

Let's consider the `main` function. The code begins by displaying a friendly message to the user asking them for their name for the order. After you get the user's name, you assign it to the order. You then ask the user if they want to order a burger, side, drink, or combo. Depending on their choice, you call the appropriate helper function created earlier, which walks the user through the process of ordering their chosen menu items:

```
Welcome to Myriam's Burger Shop!
May I have your name for the order?  John
Let's get your order in John!
Enter b for Burger
Enter s for Side
Enter d for Drink
Enter c for Combo: b
Burger it is!
Do you want condiments on your burger? (type y for yes): y
Do you want Lettuce on your burger? (type y for yes): y
Do you want Tomato on your burger? (type y for yes): n
Do you want Onion on your burger? (type y for yes): y
Do you want Mayo on your burger? (type y for yes): n
Do you want to order more items? (Enter n or N to stop.):   y
Enter b for Burger
Enter s for Side
Enter d for Drink
Enter c for Combo: d
Drink it is!
These are the available drinks: [FANTA COKE SPRITE PEPSI]
These are the available sizes: [12 16 24]
What drink do you want? Sprite
What size do you want? 15
Please enter a valid size
What size do you want? 16
Do you want to order more items? (Enter n or N to stop.):   n
```

After the user enters an item, you prompt them to see if they want to order another item. If they do, the loop continues. If they don't, then you call the `display` method on the order to display the final output, which contains an overview of the order:

```
==================================
===========ORDER OVERVIEW===========
=====Burger 1
Item Name: Beef Burger
Condiments: Lettuce Onion
Item Price: $6
=====Drink 1
Item Name: SPRITE
Item Size: 16
Item Price: $2
=====ORDER TOTAL: $8
==================================
```

SUMMARY

At this point, the code should work for placing a customized order. You've created all the structs and other code needed to have a burger shop application that allows the user to place orders. Run your program a few times to make sure it works as expected (including ordering everything possible!).

Once the program works, try tweaking it a bit with the following ideas:

- How could you add more condiments (such as mustard or ketchup) to the burger?

- Can you add more drink or side options?

- What about including water at no cost?

- How about options that change the cost of a burger? For example, adding cheese might add a dollar to the price of the burger, or the customer could order a burger with two patties for a higher price.

THE FULL BURGER SHOP LISTING

The full listing is presented in Listing 16.36. This listing is very long; if something is unclear to you, return to the section where we described that portion of the listing individually.

LISTING 16.36

The complete listing

```go
package main

import (
  "fmt"
  "strings"
)

const burgerPrice = 6.00
const sidePrice = 2.00
const comboDiscount = 1.00

var burgerCondiments = []string{"Lettuce", "Tomato", "Onion", "Mayo"}
var drinkTypes = []string{"FANTA", "COKE", "SPRITE", "PEPSI"}
var drinks = map[int]int{12: 1, 16: 2, 24: 3}
var sideTypes = []string{"fries", "coleslaw", "salad"}
var possibleChoices = []string{"b", "s", "d", "c"}

type burger struct {
  name       string
  price      int
  condiments []string
}

func (b *burger) getName() string {
  return b.name
}
func (b *burger) computePrice() int {
  b.price = burgerPrice
  return b.price
}
func (b *burger) addCondiment(condiment string) {
  b.condiments = append(b.condiments, condiment)
}

func (b *burger) display(displayPrice bool) {
  fmt.Println("Item Name: " + b.getName())
  fmt.Print("Condiments: ")
  for _, condiment := range b.condiments {
    fmt.Print(condiment + " ")
  }
```

```go
      fmt.Println()
      if displayPrice == true {
          fmt.Printf("Item Price: $%d\n", b.computePrice())
      }

}

type drink struct {
  name   string
  size   int
  price int
}

func (d *drink) getName() string {
  return d.name
}
func (d *drink) getSize() int {
  return d.size
}

func (d *drink) computePrice() int {
  if _, ok := drinks[d.getSize()]; ok {
      d.price = drinks[d.getSize()]
  }
  return d.price
}

func (d *drink) display(displayPrice bool) {
  fmt.Println("Item Name: " + strings.ToUpper(d.getName()))
  fmt.Printf("Item Size: %d\n", d.size)
  if displayPrice == true {
      fmt.Printf("Item Price: $%d\n", d.computePrice())
  }
}

type side struct {
  name   string
  price int
}

func (s *side) getName() string {
  return s.name
}
func (s *side) computePrice() int {
  s.price = sidePrice
  return s.price
}
```

continues

continued

```go
func (s *side) display(displayPrice bool) {

   fmt.Println("Item Name: " + s.getName())
   if displayPrice == true {
      fmt.Printf("Item Price: $%d\n", s.computePrice())
   }
}

type combo struct {
   name   string
   burger burger
   drink  drink
   side   side
   price  int
}

func (c *combo) getName() string {
   return c.name
}

func (c *combo) computePrice() int {
   c.price = c.burger.computePrice() + c.drink.computePrice() + c.side
.computePrice() - comboDiscount
   return c.price
}

func (c *combo) display() {
   fmt.Println("Burger For Combo")
   c.burger.display(false)
   fmt.Println("Side For Combo")
   c.side.display(false)
   fmt.Println("Drink For Combo")
   c.drink.display(false)
   fmt.Printf("Price For Combo: $%d\n", c.computePrice())
}

type order struct {
   name    string
   price   int
   burgers []burger
   drinks  []drink
   sides   []side
   combos  []combo
}
```

```go
func (o *order) getName() string {
  return o.name
}

func (o *order) computePrice() int {
  var price = 0

  for _, b := range o.burgers {
    price = price + b.computePrice()
  }
  for _, s := range o.sides {
    price = price + s.computePrice()
  }
  for _, d := range o.drinks {
    price = price + d.computePrice()
  }
  for _, c := range o.combos {
    price = price + c.computePrice()

  }
  o.price = price
  return o.price
}

func (o *order) display() {
  fmt.Println("====================================")
  fmt.Println("===========ORDER OVERVIEW===========")
  for k, b := range o.burgers {
    fmt.Printf("=====Burger %d\n", k+1)
    b.display(true)
  }
  for k, s := range o.sides {
    fmt.Printf("=====Side %d\n", k+1)
    s.display(true)
  }
  for k, d := range o.drinks {
    fmt.Printf("=====Drink %d\n", k+1)
    d.display(true)
  }
  for k, c := range o.combos {
    fmt.Printf("=====Combo %d\n", k+1)
    c.display()
  }
  fmt.Printf("=====ORDER TOTAL: $%d\n", o.computePrice())
  fmt.Println("====================================")

}
```

continues

continued

```go
func contains(arr []string, choice string) bool {
  for _, v := range arr {
    if v == choice {
      return true
    }
  }
  return false
}
func orderBurger() burger {
  var b burger
  b.name = "Beef Burger"
  fmt.Print("Do you want condiments on your burger? (type y for yes): ")
  var choice1 string
  fmt.Scanln(&choice1)
  if strings.ToLower(choice1) == "y" {
    for _, condiment := range burgerCondiments {
      var choice2 string
      fmt.Print("Do you want " + condiment + " on your burger? (type y
for yes): ")
      fmt.Scanln(&choice2)
      if strings.ToLower(choice2) == "y" {
        b.addCondiment(condiment)

      }
    }

  }
  return b

}
func orderSide() side {
  fmt.Print("These are the available sides: ")
  fmt.Println(sideTypes)
  var choice bool = false
  var sideTypeChoice string
  for choice == false {
    fmt.Print("What side do you want? ")
    fmt.Scanln(&sideTypeChoice)
    if contains(sideTypes[:], sideTypeChoice) {
      choice = true
    } else {
      fmt.Println("Please enter a valid choice")
    }
  }
  var s side
  s.name = strings.ToLower(sideTypeChoice)
```

```
      s.computePrice()
      return s
}

func orderDrink() drink {
   fmt.Print("These are the available drinks: ")
   fmt.Println(drinkTypes)
   fmt.Print("These are the available sizes: ")
   fmt.Println("[12 16 24]")

   var choice bool = false
   var drinkTypeChoice string
   var drinkSizeChoice int
   for choice == false {
      fmt.Print("What drink do you want? ")
      fmt.Scanln(&drinkTypeChoice)
      if contains(drinkTypes, strings.ToUpper(drinkTypeChoice)) {
         choice = true
      } else {
         fmt.Println("Please enter a valid drink")
      }
   }
   choice = false
   for choice == false {
      fmt.Print("What size do you want? ")
      fmt.Scanln(&drinkSizeChoice)
      if _, ok := drinks[drinkSizeChoice]; ok {
         choice = true
      } else {
         fmt.Println("Please enter a valid size")
      }
   }
   var d drink
   d.name = strings.ToLower(drinkTypeChoice)
   d.size = drinkSizeChoice
   d.computePrice() // equivalent also to d.price = drinks[drinkSizeChoice]
   return d
}

func orderCombo() combo {
   var c combo
   fmt.Println("Let's get you a combo meal!")
   fmt.Println("First, let's order the burger for your combo")
   c.burger = orderBurger()
```

continues

continued

```go
    fmt.Println("Now, let's order the drink for your combo")
    c.drink = orderDrink()

    fmt.Println("Finally, let's order the side for your combo")
    c.side = orderSide()

    return c
}

func main() {
  var ord order
  var name string
  var done bool
  done = false
  fmt.Println("Welcome to Myriam's Burger Shop!")
  fmt.Print("May I have your name for the order?  ")
  fmt.Scanln(&name)
  ord.name = name
  fmt.Println("Let's get your order in " + name + "!")
  for done == false {
      fmt.Println("Enter b for Burger")
      fmt.Println("Enter s for Side")
      fmt.Println("Enter d for Drink")
      fmt.Print("Enter c for Combo: ")
      choice := ""
      for contains(possibleChoices[:], choice) == false {
        fmt.Scanln(&choice)
        switch choice {
        case "b":
            fmt.Println("Burger it is!")
            var b = orderBurger()
            ord.burgers = append(ord.burgers, b)
        case "s":
            fmt.Println("Side it is!")
            var s = orderSide()
            ord.sides = append(ord.sides, s)
        case "d":
            fmt.Println("Drink it is!")
            var d = orderDrink()
            ord.drinks = append(ord.drinks, d)
        case "c":
            fmt.Println("Combo it is!")
            var c = orderCombo()
            ord.combos = append(ord.combos, c)
```

```go
        default:
            fmt.Println("Unknown choice")
            fmt.Println("Please enter a valid choice")
        }
    }
    fmt.Print("Do you want to order more items? (Enter n or N to stop.):   ")
    var q1 string
    fmt.Scanln(&q1)
    if strings.ToLower(q1) == "n" {
        done = true
    }
}
ord.display()
}
```

PART III

Creating
Job Ready
Solutions in Go

Lesson 17
Handling Errors

Programming code, regardless of the language, can include a variety of errors, including syntax errors, logic, division by zero, and missing files, to name just a few. As a result, every programming language has built-in mechanisms to deal with errors. In this lesson, we will look at error handling in Go.

LEARNING OBJECTIVES

By the end of this lesson, you will be able to:

- Understand different types of errors.
- Capture and handle errors.
- Create your own custom error messages.
- Format your error messages.
- Create multiple custom error messages.

ERRORS IN GO PROGRAMS

It is important to point out that there are several types of errors. There are syntax errors that are generally typos made when a developer is writing the code. These can be simply a misspelled word or a coding statement that is missing a character. Syntax errors generally stop a program from compiling and running, so a programmer must fix them before the program will run. Like most languages, the Go compiler will indicate syntax errors when the program is compiled or run. Examples of common syntax errors include:

- Using the wrong capitalization such as using `println` instead of `Println`
- Failing to declare a variable before using it
- Trying to assign a value of one type to a variable of a different type

There are also logic errors. With logic errors, the code will generally compile and run but the output might not be what is expected. Like syntax errors, logic errors are generally caused by the developer. A logic error could be something such as the following:

- Checking for false when you meant to check for true
- Assigning the wrong value or variable
- The use of an incorrect business rule

There are other logic and similar errors that can cause a program to stop working. These can include errors such as:

- Dividing by zero
- Attempting to write to a file that doesn't exist
- Attempting to place a value that is too big into a numeric variable
- Using bad data that is received

These are errors that need to be caught and handled from within a Go program. For example, if a user is prompted to enter their age as an integer but they enter their name, a Go program is likely to crash if logic isn't included to handle the error.

THE GO ERROR TYPE

In Go, there is a dedicated type for errors known as the *error type*. Because error is a type, we can store errors in variables, return an error from functions, and perform any other action on an error that we can perform with a type.

As an example, Listing 17.1 contains a syntax error, which is captured.

LISTING 17.1

Capturing a syntax error

```
package main

import (
    "fmt"
```

```
    "strconv"
)

func main() {
    var str string = "10x"

    // the ParseInt function returns the parsed integer or
    // the error if the conversion failed
    nbr, error := strconv.ParseInt(str,10,8)
    fmt.Println(nbr)
    fmt.Println(error)
}
```

When you run the code, you get the following message:

```
0
strconv.ParseInt: parsing "10x": invalid syntax
```

In this case, you cannot parse the value 10x that is stored in str into an integer. Go handles the error automatically using the error parameter assigned to the ParseInt function, which provides an explanation of the error to the user. At the same time, the variable nbr receives the default value for an integer (0). The way this program is coded, it will print the integer assigned to nbr, even if ParseInt cannot perform the conversion.

NOTE Exercise 17.1 at the end of the lesson asks you to update this listing so that it doesn't generate an error. You should note the value stored in the variable error when an error is not caused by ParseInt.

To take a closer look at the error type from the ParseInt function, let's use the reflect package. We do this in Listing 17.2.

LISTING 17.2

A closer look at an error

```
package main

import (
    "fmt"
    "reflect"
    "strconv"
)
```

continues

continued

```go
func main() {
    var s string = "10x"

    i, error := strconv.ParseInt(s,10,8)
    fmt.Println(i)
    fmt.Println(error)
    fmt.Println(reflect.TypeOf(error))
}
```

In this listing, we imported the `reflect` package. We then use the `TypeOf` method of `reflect` on the `error` variable. This tells us that the type of the `error` variable is the `NumError` type defined in the `strconv` package, as can be seen from the output:

```
0
strconv.ParseInt: parsing "10x": invalid syntax
*strconv.NumError
```

> **NOTE** Each package in Go can implement its own custom error types to deal with the various errors that might arise in that particular package.

CUSTOM ERROR HANDLING

While Go has built-in error handling messages, they are not always self-explanatory or user-friendly. In the previous example, the error makes sense to a developer, but it may sound too technical to an end user. For this reason, you typically want to check for an error before displaying the value and set up Go to display a more meaningful error message.

In Listing 17.3, you use an `if–else` statement to control the output of the `ParseInt` function. You do this in order to present a friendlier message to the user if there is an error.

LISTING 17.3

Custom error handling

```go
package main

import (
    "fmt"
```

```
    "strconv"
)

func main() {
    var s string = "10x"

    i,error := strconv.ParseInt(s,10,8)

    if error == nil{
        fmt.Println(i)
    } else {
        fmt.Println("You cannot convert text into a number")
        fmt.Println(error)
    }
}
```

This time we have added a check to see if an error was generated with the call to
ParseInt. If no error occurred, then nil will be assigned to error. As such, if error is
equal to nil, then we know there wasn't an error. If error is not equal to nil, then there
was an error, so we can print a user-friendly message for the user. By using 10x in this case,
the listing will generate an error. The output from running the listing is as follows:

```
You cannot convert text into a number
strconv.ParseInt: parsing "10x": invalid syntax
```

This output is more meaningful because it tells the user what went wrong in layperson's
terms. You could even remove the fmt.Println(error) statement if you don't want it to
be displayed to the user.

ERROR METHODS

Internally, the error type is simply an interface with one single method, Error, that
returns a string:

```
type error interface {
    Error() string
}
```

For instance, the os package has a variety of error types to deal with missing files,
operating system issues, and so on. These are different from errors in the strconv
package. Both packages, however, implement the same error interface.

Any type that implements this interface is considered an error type. If you are building your own package, you can create types that implement the error interface and use custom error types specific to your application. You can implement functions and methods to errors, as shown in Listing 17.4.

LISTING 17.4

Creating a custom error method

```
package main

import (
    "errors"
    "fmt"
)

type account struct {
    number string
    balance float64
}

func(a *account) withdraw(value float64) (bool,error) {
    if a.balance >= value{
        a.balance = a.balance - value
        return true,nil
    }

    // use the errors package to display a new, custom error message
    return false, errors.New("You cannot withdraw from this account.")
}

func main() {
    acct := account{}
    acct.number = "C21345345345355"
    acct.balance = 159
    out,err := acct.withdraw(200)
    fmt.Println(out)

    // output if error
    if err != nil {
        fmt.Println(err)
        return
    }
```

```
    // output if no error
    fmt.Println("The withdrawal occurred successfully.")
    fmt.Println("Your new balance is", acct)
}
```

In Listing 17.4 you use an `account` struct similar to what you've seen in previous lessons. When you define a `withdraw` method for your `account` struct, you set it to return a Boolean as well as an error type from the `errors` package. Notice that we use the `errors.New` function from the `errors` package to create a new error type.

If the balance in the account is greater than the amount being requested (`value`), then the `withdraw` method will return `true` and `nil` as the error. Otherwise, if the balance is not greater than the requested amount, then `withdraw` will return `false` and a new error type with a custom message.

In the `main` function, we execute the `withdraw` method and check for the error. If it's not `nil`, then an error occurred, and we display that error. Because our request to withdraw 200 is greater than the balance of 159, running Listing 17.4 results in the following error:

```
false
You cannot withdraw from this account.
```

Change the withdrawal amount from 200 to 100 in the listing. When you do this, then the amount to withdraw is less than the balance, so the result is that no error message is created:

```
true
The withdrawal occurred successfully.
Your new balance is {C21345345345355 59}
```

ERRORF

The `fmt` package includes the `Errorf` function, which can create custom errors with data from the method. To understand the `Errorf` function, consider the code in Listing 17.5.

LISTING 17.5

Using `Errorf`

```
package main
```

continues

continued

```go
import (
    "fmt"
)

type account struct {
    number string
    balance float64
}

func(a *account) withdraw(value float64) (bool, error) {
    if a.balance >= value {
        a.balance = a.balance-value
        return true, nil
    }
    return false, fmt.Errorf("Withdrawal failed, because the requested amount of
%0.2f is higher than balance of %0.2f. ", value,a.balance)
}

func main() {
    acct := account{}
    acct.number = "C21345345345355"
    acct.balance = 159
    out, err :=acct.withdraw(200)
    fmt.Println(out)

    if err!=nil{
        fmt.Println(err)
        return
    }

    fmt.Println("The withdrawal occurred successfully.")
    fmt.Println("Your new balance is", acct)
}
```

The code is the same as the previous listing, except that here, the withdraw method returns an error message using the fmt.Errorf function. This allows you to add more detail to the error message by parsing the value and balance to include the exact values in play.

The Errorf function looks at the string being passed and replaces any escape sequences with the arguments that are included after the string. The escape sequences begin with a percentage sign (%) and end with a character that indicates a type. In this listing, the string passed to fmt.Errorf has two escape sequences. They are both %0.2f. The f indicates a numeric floating-point value will be inserted. The 0.2 indicates it should be presented with two numbers to the right of the decimal. In this case, the numbers stored in value and a.balance will be placed into the string. The final output looks like this:

```
false
Withdrawal failed, because the requested amount of 200.00 is higher than
balance of 159.00.
```

BLANK IDENTIFIERS

Listing 17.5 returned out and err from the a.withdraw method call. Since you aren't really using the out variable in the program, you can replace it with a blank identifier, which is an underscore (_). The blank identifier is an anonymous variable that is not bound to a value.

Listing 17.6 is an updated version of the previous example. This time you use the blank identifier as the first parameter for the withdraw function.

LISTING 17.6

Using a blank identifier

```
package main

import (
    "fmt"
)

type account struct {
    number string
    balance float64
}
func(a *account) withdraw(value float64) (bool, error) {
    if a.balance >= value{
        a.balance = a.balance-value

        return true, nil
    }
    return false, fmt.Errorf("Withdrawal failed, because the request amount of
%0.2f is higher than balance of %0.2f ", value,a.balance)
}
```

continues

continued

```
func main() {
    acct := account{}
    acct.number = "C21345345345355"
    acct.balance = 159

    // we use _ to omit out since we don't need it
    _,err := acct.withdraw(200)
    if err!=nil{
        fmt.Println(err)
        return

    }
    fmt.Println("The withdrawal occurred successfully.")
    fmt.Println("Your new balance is", acct)
}
```

Other than the change to using the blank identifier, this listing is just like the previous one and the same output is generated:

```
Withdrawal failed, because the request amount of 200.00 is higher than balance
of 159.00
```

ERROR MESSAGES WITH STRUCTS

It is possible to improve on the previous example to include more details about the errors and implement additional custom mechanisms to deal with errors. Listing 17.7 uses structs to include more details about the error.

LISTING 17.7

Generating more detailed custom error messages

```
package main

import (
    "fmt"
)

// struct for error output
type withdrawError struct {
    err string
    value float64
    balance float64
}
```

```go
type account struct {
    number string
    balance float64
}

func(a *account) withdraw(value float64) (bool, error) {
    if a.balance >= value{
        a.balance = a.balance - value
        return true,nil
    }
    return false, &withdrawError{"Withdraw Error", value, a.balance}
}

// implement the method for the withdrawError Type
func (e *withdrawError) Error() string {
    return fmt.Sprintf("%s: withdrawal failed because the requested amount of
%0.2f is higher than balance of %0.2f", e.err, e.value, e.balance)
}

func main() {
    acct := account{}
    acct.number = "C21345345345355"
    acct.balance = 159

    _, err := acct.withdraw(200)
    if err != nil{
        fmt.Println(err)
        return
    }

    fmt.Println("The withdrawal occurred successfully.")
    fmt.Println("Your new balance is", acct)
}
```

The code is mostly the same as the previous listing except for a few things:

- You create a struct, withdrawError, that includes an error message of type string as well as the balance and value. In this case, you want to record the data that led to the error itself.

- Next, you implement a method on the withdrawError type that returns a detailed message about the error.

- The next change is in the `withdraw` method. Instead of returning the standard error, you return a reference to a `withdrawError` initialized with the data that led to the error (the standard error message, balance, and value to be withdrawn).

This approach makes your code more organized while providing a more informative error message:

```
Withdraw Error: withdrawal failed because the requested amount of 200.00 is
higher than balance of 159.00
```

MULTIPLE CUSTOM ERROR MESSAGES

Let's update the previous example to handle a variety of errors that might arise when a customer withdraws money from an account, including:

- The balance of the account is 0 or negative. In this case, you cannot withdraw any money, regardless of the size of the withdrawal.
- The value to be withdrawn is 0 or negative. In this case, you cannot logically withdraw money.
- The balance is lower than the amount to be withdrawn.

Ideally, you would like the `withdraw` method to have a custom message for each of these situations. Review the updates in Listing 17.8 that have been added to the program.

LISTING 17.8

Using multiple custom error messages

```
package main

import (
    "fmt"
)

type withdrawError struct {
    err string
    value float64
    balance float64
}
```

```go
// implement the method for the withdrawError Type
func (e *withdrawError) Error() string {
    return fmt.Sprintf("%s: withdrawal failed because the requested amount of
%0.2f is higher than balance of %0.2f.", e.err,e.value, e.balance)
}

func (e *withdrawError) balanceNegativeorZero() bool {
    return e.balance <= 0
}

func (e *withdrawError) AmountNegativeorZero() bool {
    return e.value <= 0
}

func (e *withdrawError) InsufficientFunds() bool {
    return e.balance - e.value < 0
}

type account struct {
    number string
    balance float64
}

func(a *account) withdraw(value float64) (bool,error) {
    if a.balance <=0 {
        return false, &withdrawError{"Withdrawal Error", value, a.balance}
    }
    if value <=0 {
        return false, &withdrawError{"Withdrawal Error", value, a.balance}
    }
    if a.balance >= value{
        a.balance = a.balance-value
        return true, nil
    }
    return false, &withdrawError{"Withdrawal Error", value, a.balance}
}

func main() {
    acct := account{}
    acct.number = "C21345345345355"
    acct.balance = -100
```

continues

continued

```
    _, err := acct.withdraw(46)
    if err != nil{
        if err2, ok := err.(*withdrawError); ok {
            if err2.AmountNegativeorZero() {
                fmt.Println("Amount to be withdrawn is negative")
            }
            if err2.balanceNegativeorZero() {
                fmt.Println("Balance is negative")
            }
            if err2.InsufficientFunds(){
                fmt.Println("Insufficient funds")
            }
            return
        }
    }

    fmt.Println("The withdrawal occurred successfully.")
    fmt.Println("Your new balance is ")
    fmt.Println(acct)
}
```

When you run this version, you receive this output:

```
Balance is negative
Insufficient funds
```

The updated version includes three new methods for the `withdrawError` type:

- `balanceNegativeorZero`: Checks if the balance recorded in the error is 0 or negative

- `AmountNegativeorZero`: Checks if the amount recorded in the error is 0 or negative

- `InsufficientFunds`: Checks if the requested amount is higher than the balance

Next, in the `withdraw` method, you go through the issues listed here and you return an error message for each of the situations.

The real magic happens in the `main` method when you trigger an error. After checking that the error is not `nil`, you go into a series of `if` statements to determine which method triggered the error, starting with the following `if` statement:

```
if err2, ok := err.(*withdrawError); ok {
```

This might seem more complex than what you've used before; however, you are performing a two-step statement. The first part of the statement is:

```
err2, ok := err.(*withdrawError);
```

Here, you are retrieving the error. Because you know `err` is not equal to `nil` (based on the previous line in the listing), you have an error, so you will parse that error. After this statement, `err2` will contain the error that occurred, and `ok` will be a Boolean value. In the second step of the statement, `ok` is checked to determine if it is `true`. This two-step statement is equivalent to doing the following:

```
err2, ok := err.(*withdrawError)
  if ok {
```

As a result, if `ok` is `true`, then we go through the different errors to determine which occurred. In this scenario, you have a negative balance, which will trigger the negative balance error, but you also get an insufficient funds error because the balance is lower than the amount. Using this technique, you can create various scenarios for error messages in the same method while keeping the code elegant and compact.

SUMMARY

Errors happen. They are a part of programming. As a Go developer, you should work to prevent errors whenever possible. When your program needs to display an error message to the user, you should make sure the message is clear and understandable. In this lesson you learned how to capture and display errors. You also learned how to create your own custom error messages.

EXERCISES

The following exercises are provided to allow you to experiment with the tools and concepts presented in this lesson. For each exercise, write a program that meets the specified requirements and verify that the program runs as expected. The exercises are:

Exercise 17.1: Not an Error

Exercise 17.2: Greedy Withdrawal

Exercise 17.3: Extending the Banking Application

Exercise 17.4: On Your Own

NOTE The exercises are for your benefit. The exercises help you apply what you learn in the lessons. You are also encouraged to experiment with the code as you complete the exercises.

Exercise 17.1: Not an Error

Modify Listing 17.1 so that it does not cause an error. When you do this, what are the values assigned to nbr and error?

Exercise 17.2: Greedy Withdrawal

Modify Listing 17.4 to include a second check within the withdraw method. Generate a custom error message if a request to withdraw more than $1,000 is made. Test your program with the following scenarios to make sure you get the expected error messages or account balances:

- Balance is 159 and a request is made to withdraw 200
- Balance is 159 and a request is made to withdraw 100
- Balance is 159 and a request is made to withdraw 2,000
- Balance is 2,000 and a request is made to withdraw 100
- Balance is 2,000 and a request is made to withdraw 1,500
- Balance is 2,000 and a request is made to withdraw 1,000
- Balance is 2,000 and a request is made to withdraw 3,000

Exercise 17.3: Extending the Banking Application

Implement error handling for the bank application, including the following:

- Create appropriate error types for all possible errors, including withdrawals, wires, and deposits.
- Add error handling to all methods and functions in the program to make the program as user-friendly as possible.

Exercise 17.4: On Your Own

Refactor activities you have already completed in previous exercises in this book to include appropriate error handling.

Lesson 18

Concurrency

In this lesson, we'll look at the concept of *concurrency* and show you how to apply it to your Go applications. We'll spend extra time explaining concurrency concepts and parallelism before writing Go code.

LEARNING OBJECTIVES

By the end of this lesson, you will be able to:

- Understand concurrency and some of its challenges.
- Understand parallelism and some of its challenges.
- Use goroutines.
- Work with channels.
- Iterate through channels.

USING CONCURRENCY

Before we go into details about how Go handles concurrency, let's look at the concept of concurrency itself. In the early days of computing, a computer system had one processor that was responsible for executing all instructions. Because of this architecture, computer programs were written to run in a serial fashion, where the program was sequentially executed instruction by instruction in a predefined order. Figure 18.1 illustrates this use of serial programming by a computer program.

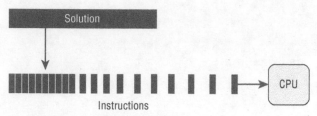

Figure 18.1: Serial programming

As computer programs became increasingly complex, the use of serial programming introduced some limitations because a program could only execute one instruction at a time. The more instructions a computer program had, the longer it would take to execute. This resulted in the need for faster and more efficient ways to execute computer programs.

The Role of the Operating System

The operating system (OS) is the component responsible for managing the different processes running on a computer. Process management can be classified into three main categories:

Multiprogramming   Multiple processes are running on the same processor, as shown in Figure 18.2.

Multiprocessing   Multiple processes are running on multiple processors, as shown in Figure 18.2.

Distributed Processing   Multiple processes are running on multiple machines.

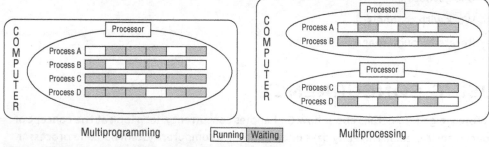

Figure 18.2: Multiprogramming as compared to multiprocessing

Independently of the type of processing, these concurrent processes must be able to cooperate with one another, compete for the same resources, and communicate with one another. The only difference is the way you execute the processes. In multiprogramming, since you have one processor, you must interleave the execution of the various processes. With multiprocessing, you need to execute the processes on the different processors.

Concurrency is the process of switching between the executions of computer programs on the same processor so that a user has the illusion that these programs are running at the same time. An example of concurrency is the OS and the applications it is running. From a user perspective, you are able to listen to music, write a document, and search the Internet at the same time. This is what we by concurrency.

Concurrency focuses on creating the illusion of simultaneity by allowing different computer programs to share the CPU of a computer. Concurrency is the computer's version of multitasking. It can only perform one task at a time, but it can switch between tasks very quickly.

Concurrency is easy to manage when the processes running on the computer are independent of one another and do not access the same resources on the computer. However, in practice, most active computer processes share and compete for the same resources. This could introduce some issues and challenges in writing concurrent software. When designing software, you must account for concurrency and the issues and challenges it introduces.

Problems with Concurrency

To illustrate the issues with concurrency, assume you have two computer processes, A and B, that access the same global variable and that the global variable is set up by the OS. If both process A and process B access the global variable at the same time, there is a chance that process A might change the value of the global variable and process B would retrieve the old value instead of the new value set up by process A. This could cause errors in the execution of processes A and B.

The following shows an example with specific numbers. Assume your global variable starts with a value of 6 and you have two processes that are each going to add to the global variable:

- Process A grabs the global variable, which has a value of 6.
- Process B grabs the global variable, which has a value of 6.
- Process A adds 3 to the value it retrieved, getting a total of 9.
- Process B adds 5 to the value it retrieved, getting a total of 11.
- Process A updates the global variable to its new total of 9.
- Process B updates the global variable to its new total of 11.

The result is that the global variable has a value of 11, when it should have a value of 14 (6 + 3 + 5). The update from process A was overwritten by the update from process B, as illustrated in Figure 18.3.

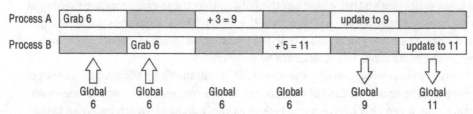

Figure 18.3: A concurrency error

In order to prevent such a scenario from happening, you need to restrict the access to the global variable to one process at a time. This is also known as *mutual exclusion*. That is, if one process is accessing a shared resource, other processes must be prevented from accessing that resource until the current process finishes its execution. Examples of shared resources between the different processes are printers, scanners, and files. Two processes that are accessing the same file at the same time might cause unexpected behavior. Mutual exclusion states that the file can be accessed by only one process at a time.

> **NOTE** You may have experienced mutual exclusion firsthand. If you have a file open (like a Microsoft Word document) and you try to delete or rename that file through the OS, you will likely receive an error message to the effect that you must close the file before completing the other action. In this case, the application using the file is process A, and the OS trying to change the file is process B. Process A must release the file before process B can act on it.

Mutual Exclusion

Concurrency poses two main challenges:

- Appropriate resource allocation to the different processes
- Sharing of global resources safely

As indicated by the earlier example, in order to share global resources safely, you must implement mutual exclusion, which states that only one process can access a shared resource at one time. There are three main ways to implement mutual exclusion:

Processes handle mutual exclusion themselves. The programmers who write the software implement the mutual exclusion in the source code of the software. This approach tends to lead to errors and unexpected behavior since the programmer can easily make programming errors or simply forget to implement mutual exclusion.

Force processes to access shared resources using special machine instructions. The machine instructions guarantee mutual exclusion.

Implement mutual exclusion in the OS and programming languages so that processes are forced to respect mutual exclusion. The OS is the component responsible for managing the different processes and thus can force processes to respect mutual exclusion and concurrency. Examples of techniques for mutual exclusion implemented by the OS include semaphores, monitors, and message passing.

Although you must use some type of mutual exclusion to ensure that only one process has access to a specific resource at any given time, there are disadvantages. For example, when process A accesses a shared resource, all other processes must wait until process A has finished its work. This introduces delays.

Another potential problem is that deadlocks can occur. A *deadlock* is the permanent blocking of a set of computer processes by the OS. In the case of deadlock, the set processes are competing for global resources and preventing one another from accessing the resources until the OS decides to block the processes. Every process in the blocked processes is waiting for a resource that is taken by another blocked process.

In order for a deadlock to happen, you need three conditions:

Mutual Exclusion Between Processes Only one process may use the resources at any given time.

Hold and Wait Any process can hold some resources while waiting for other resources to be freed.

No Preemption Any process cannot be forced to release any resources.

For instance, process A can hold one resource and wait for another resource that process B is currently using. Process B could be holding the resource process A needs but could be waiting for process C to complete before it releases the resource. Process C could itself be waiting for the resource process A is holding. This could lead to a deadlock of the different processes as they each wait for the others to complete and free their resources.

A classic analogy of a deadlock is the act of selling something on a site like eBay. Suppose Mary wants to sell a computer she no longer uses and Pete wants to buy it from her, but they live in different states. Mary won't ship the computer until she has the money from Pete, but Pete won't send the money until he receives the computer and verifies that it is what he expected. The transaction is in a state of deadlock because both Pete and Mary are waiting for the other to complete their part first.

Deadlocks lead to unexpected behavior and errors while executing different processes. However, there are techniques to avoid deadlocks. One is to implement a rule that breaks one of the three conditions we just identified. For instance, the OS can implement a rule that breaks the no preemption rule. That is, the OS can force any process to release any resource. This allows you to avoid deadlocks since no process can hold resources indefinitely. However, you cannot implement rules to break mutual exclusion because it is the essence of concurrency, and the OS must respect mutual exclusion.

Another technique for avoiding deadlocks is through detection and recovery. In this case, the OS recognizes deadlocks and recovers from them using specific rules.

PARALLELISM

Parallelism is the process of executing several tasks at once. For instance, if you have a grill that can hold six burgers, then you can cook six burgers at the same time in a parallel fashion. Parallelism assumes that the tasks are independent of one another. For example, the process of cooking one burger is independent of cooking another burger. Thus, you can execute them at the same time without having to worry about one depending on the other. Another example is laundry. If you have two washing machines, then you can wash two loads of laundry at the same time.

In terms of computing, parallelism is the process of exploiting several processors or hardware resources to execute several independent tasks at once. This is what we referred to in the previous section as multiprocessing. For instance, a quad-core processor contains four processors, which allow it to execute four computer instructions at once. Each processor is responsible for executing one instruction. Similarly, multiple processors can run one or many computer processes at the same time.

Implementing Parallelism

As computer systems continued to evolve and the prices of computer hardware decreased, computer systems started to include more than one processor. This allowed instructions to be distributed over the different processors to speed up the execution of computer programs. Figure 18.4 shows the execution of a computer program in a parallel fashion using four processors.

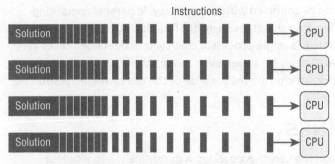

Figure 18.4: Parallel execution of a program

Parallel computing focuses on distributing tasks to several processors. Truly implementing parallel processing requires that there be more than one processor. Figure 18.5 shows an example of a CPU with multiple processors.

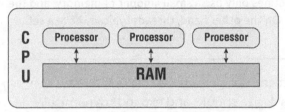

Figure 18.5: A CPU with multiple processors

As shown in Figure 18.5, the different processors share the same memory. This could lead to issues similar to those described for concurrency, so you must make sure that while processor A is accessing a memory location for a read or write operation, you prevent the other processors from accessing the same memory location until processor A is done with the operation. Another example is that two processors, A and B, could access the printer at the same time.

Preventing Problems with Parallelism

In order to prevent parallel processors from having concurrency issues, you have two possible options:

- Create completely separate resources for each processor, including the memory.
- Implement techniques similar to those used in concurrency.

Parallel computing should not be confused with concurrency. In parallel computing, there are separate processors working simultaneously but functioning independently of one another. In concurrency, there is a single processor that switches between tasks very quickly, giving the illusion of parallelism. However, even though these approaches are very different, they share some of the same problems because of the use of shared resources.

USING GOROUTINES

Go supports concurrency through the use of *goroutines*. A goroutine is a function or method that runs concurrently with another method or function.

Other programming languages rely on the concept of threads to implement concurrence. In the Go language, you don't use actual threads but instead use functions or methods, which are lightweight and more compact, to execute concurrently. This makes the resource cost of creating goroutines extremely cheap compared to executing multiple threads concurrently. In fact, goroutines only use a small amount of memory, and the usage shrinks and expands dynamically. On the other hand, threads typically have a set amount of memory they use.

> **NOTE** Being more specific and technical, goroutines cost only a few kilobytes in stack size and the stack size shrinks and expands dynamically. Threads typically have a set stack size.

> **NOTE** The Go language favors having many small lightweight functions or methods (often on the order of 100 at once) executed concurrently over having a few threads running concurrently.

The goroutines are all multiplexed (combined) to be executed in a small number of OS threads, which makes one thread able to handle thousands or more goroutines. When a goroutine is blocking the thread as it's waiting to finish its tasks, Go will automatically spin up another thread and move the other goroutines there. This is done automatically, and you do not need to worry about such details. Instead, you can use goroutines as a lightweight way to implement concurrency and let Go handle thread management. In fact, by default, the `main` function in a Go program is its own goroutine. It is called the *main goroutine*.

To understand the concept of goroutines, let's look at Listing 18.1, which implements a goroutine.

LISTING 18.1

A simple goroutine

```
package main

import (
   "fmt"
)

func goroutine() {
   fmt.Println("This is my first goroutine.")
}

func main() {
   go goroutine()

   fmt.Println("main goroutine")
}
```

In this code, you create a function goroutine called goroutine that displays a message. In the main function, you execute the function using the keyword go, which creates a goroutine out of the goroutine function call. In this case, you are instructing Go to execute the goroutine function concurrently with the main function (or main goroutine).

If you run this code, you see the following output instead of the message displayed by the goroutine function:

```
main goroutine
```

This is because when you start a goroutine, the control flow of the Go program does not wait until the routine has finished executing. Instead, it continues with the next statement in the program. The next statement in Listing 18.1 is a Println statement, which executes immediately, ending the program.

There isn't time for the goroutine function to execute before the program ends. In this case, you need a way to pause the execution of the main goroutine so that the other goroutines get to run. You can do that using the time package and the Sleep function.

Listing 18.2 is the same as the previous listing, but you include a Sleep instruction that delays the execution of the Println command.

LISTING 18.2

Pausing execution

```
package main

import (
    "fmt"
    "time"
)

func goroutine() {
    fmt.Println("This is my first goroutine.")
}

func main() {
    go goroutine()

    time.Sleep(4* time.Second)
    fmt.Println("main goroutine")
}
```

This time, when you run this program, you will see both outputs:

```
This is my first goroutine.
main goroutine
```

This program added the `time` package using an import. Also added was the call to the `time.Sleep` function, which pauses the execution for approximately 4 seconds. When you run this listing, there is a significant delay between the first output and the second output.

> **NOTE** Some of the delay in running the program is the initial startup. You can add an `fmt.Println` statement before the call to `go goroutine()` to see when the program starts executing the code in the `main` routine.

Although the `Sleep` function did the trick, this is only a basic solution, and you will need a better way to get data from goroutines to the `main` goroutine. You use channels for this purpose in Go. We'll cover channels later in this lesson. For now, let's focus on goroutines.

MULTIPLE GOROUTINES

In the previous example, you used only one goroutine (in addition to the required main goroutine), but it is possible to have as many as you need. Listing 18.3 includes two separate goroutines.

LISTING 18.3

Using multiple goroutines

```
package main

import (
    "fmt"
    "time"
)

func goroutine() {
    fmt.Println("This is my first goroutine.")
}

func anothergoroutine() {
    fmt.Println("This is my second goroutine.")
}

func main() {

    fmt.Println("Starting...")

    go goroutine()
    go anothergoroutine()

    time.Sleep(4* time.Second)
    fmt.Println("main goroutine")
}
```

In Listing 18.3, you start two goroutines that will execute concurrently. As you can see, both begin by using the go keyword and then the routine. You again include the 4-second delay for the Println instruction to allow time for both goroutines to execute before the program ends. The listing adds a simple `Println` statement so that it is clear when the main program begins to execute. The output from the listing is as follows:

```
Starting...
This is my second goroutine.
This is my first goroutine.
main goroutine
```

To better see the power of goroutines, let's implement a function that you can actually see running concurrently. In Listing 18.4, you change the two functions, `goroutine` and `anothergoroutine`, to display numbers between 0 and an input limit. The trick is that you use the `Sleep` function to print a number and message every 250 ms in the `goroutine` function and every 400 ms in `anothergoroutine`.

> **NOTE** There are almost always multiple ways to accomplish the same task. In this lesson, the `time.Sleep` function is used. It is also possible to use the `sync.WaitGroup` function in the sync package to wait for multiple goroutines to finish.

LISTING 18.4

Using two timers

```
package main

import (
    "fmt"
    "time"
)

func goroutine(limit int) {
    for i := 0;i < limit; i++ {
        time.Sleep(250 * time.Millisecond)
        fmt.Print(i)
        fmt.Println(" - calling goroutine")
    }
}
```

```
func anothergoroutine(limit int) {
    for i := 0;i < limit; i++ {
        time.Sleep(400 * time.Millisecond)
        fmt.Print(i)
        fmt.Println(" - calling anothergoroutine")
    }
}

func main() {

    fmt.Println("Starting...")
    go goroutine(10)
    go anothergoroutine(10)

    time.Sleep(6 * time.Second)
    fmt.Println("main goroutine")
}
```

The code in Listing 18.4 should be relatively easy to follow. The two goroutines do the same thing for the most part. They both use a `for` statement to loop a given number of times. Each time the loop occurs, a sequential number is printed, followed by a string indicating which goroutine is being used. As mentioned earlier, each goroutine uses a different number of milliseconds to pause. It is 250 for `goroutine` and 400 for `anothergoroutine`. When you execute the `main` function, you can see that both functions execute concurrently and display numbers in the frequency dictated by the `Sleep` function pattern:

```
Starting...
0 - calling goroutine
0 - calling anothergoroutine
1 - calling goroutine
2 - calling goroutine
1 - calling anothergoroutine
3 - calling goroutine
2 - calling anothergoroutine
4 - calling goroutine
5 - calling goroutine
3 - calling anothergoroutine
6 - calling goroutine
4 - calling anothergoroutine
7 - calling goroutine
8 - calling goroutine
5 - calling anothergoroutine
```

continues

continued

```
9 - calling goroutine
6 - calling anothergoroutine
7 - calling anothergoroutine
8 - calling anothergoroutine
9 - calling anothergoroutine
main goroutine
```

> **NOTE** As you have seen before, fmt.Println adds a newline character when printing but fmt.Print does not. That is why the string is printed on the same line as the number.

WORKING WITH CHANNELS

Goroutines allow us to implement concurrency. In this section, you will learn about *channels*. Channels act as pipes that connect goroutines with each other and allow goroutines to exchange data with other goroutines.

You can define a channel using the chan keyword when declaring a variable assigned to the channel.

Each channel is assigned a specific data type and a given channel can only transport that type of data between goroutines. In the example in Listing 18.5, you define a channel called myChannel of type int. Because myChannel is of type int, it can only transport integer data.

LISTING 18.5

Defining a channel

```
package main

import "fmt"

func main() {
    var myChannel chan int

    fmt.Println(myChannel)
}
```

The default value of a channel is `nil`. Because you have not assigned a value to the channel (`myChannel`) in your listing, the output of this program will be `<nil>`.

Creating a Channel Using *make*

You use the `make` function to create and initialize channels. Listing 18.6 contains the code to create a channel using the `make` function.

LISTING 18.6

Creating a channel using make

```
package main

import "fmt"

func main() {
    var myChannel = make(chan int)
    fmt.Printf("Channel Type is %T", myChannel)
}
```

You create a variable called `myChannel` and initialize it using the `make` function. You pass the `chan` keyword and a type to the function. In this case, you pass a type of `int`. The result is that you create and initialize `myChannel` with a type of `int`. Printing its type gives you:

```
Channel Type is chan int
```

Channels and Concurrency

As we mentioned previously, a channel is used by goroutines to send data in and out. However, while goroutines are processed automatically by the compiler, channels impose concurrency blocks that prevent the `main` goroutine from completing until all data has been appropriately transferred through the channels. Listing 18.7 presents a more concrete example.

LISTING 18.7

Using concurrent channels

```
package main

import "fmt"
```

continues

continued

```go
// a function that takes a channel as input
func message(ch chan string) {
    // we use ch followed by <- to write data to the channel
    ch <- "Hello World"
}

func main() {
    // create a channel that transports string
    ch := make(chan string)

    // execute the goroutine with input as the channel
    go message(ch)

    // read from the channel into a variable b
    b := <- ch
    fmt.Println(b)

    fmt.Println("This will execute last")
}
```

In this example, you create a function called message that takes as input a channel ch and writes to that channel using the following convention:

```
channel_name <- data_to_written
```

In this case, you can see that the string, "Hello World," is being written to ch:

```
ch <- "Hello World"
```

In the main goroutine, you create a channel ch that only accepts a string. You then execute the goroutines with input as ch. This is followed by a statement that reads from the goroutines into a variable b and then uses Println to display the message received:

```
b := <- ch
fmt.Println(b)
```

The output is:

```
Hello World
This will execute last
```

Notice that the main goroutine waited until you finished reading from the channel. It does this because writing and reading data to a channel is a *blocking call*, which means that when you send data to a channel, control is blocked in the write statement until another goroutine reads from that channel. In other words, because you are writing the message to the goroutine channel, the main goroutine is blocked during that process.

In the same way, when you are reading from a channel, the read is a blocking call until another goroutine writes to that channel. This approach means that developers don't have to use explicit locks to implement concurrency like they might have to in other programming languages.

Adding a Delay

You can use a Sleep statement to include a delay in the channel processes, allowing you to see better how the goroutines and channels function in a concurrent manner. Let's add a Sleep statement in the message goroutine as shown in Listing 18.8.

LISTING 18.8

Adding a delay

```
package main

import (
    "fmt"
    "time"
)

func message(ch chan string) {
    // add a sleep delay to the channel
    time.Sleep(6 * time.Second)
    ch <- "Hello World"
}

func main() {
    ch := make(chan string)
    go message(ch)
    b := <- ch
    fmt.Println(b)
    fmt.Println("This will execute last")
}
```

This listing is the same as the previous with many of the comments removed and a line added to the goroutine message. In this version, the goroutine message goes to sleep for 6 seconds and then writes to the channel. You are still reading from the channel in the main goroutine using:

```
b := <- ch
```

As such, the main goroutine will wait until the goroutine message writes to the channel before reading the data and finishing the program's execution. In other words, this program works exactly the same way that the previous version functions, except that you have to wait for at least 6 seconds to see the output.

CHANNELS WITH MULTIPLE GOROUTINES

Channels can execute multiple goroutines. Listing 18.9 presents an example of channels where you are executing two goroutines. The first one computes the max of an array, and the second one computes the min of an array.

LISTING 18.9

Using a channel with two goroutines

```
package main

import (
    "fmt"
)

// calculate the max
func computeMax(ch chan int, numbers [4]int) {
    max := numbers[0]
    for i := 0; i < len(numbers); i++ {
        if numbers[i] > max {
            max = numbers[i]
        }
    }
    ch <- max
}

// calculate the min
func computeMin(ch chan int, numbers [4]int) {
    min := numbers[0]
    for i := 0; i < len(numbers); i++ {
        if numbers[i] < min {
```

```
        min = numbers[i]
    }
  }
  ch <- min
}

func main() {
  numbers := [4]int{25, 64, 75, 5}
  fmt.Println(numbers)

  ch1 := make(chan int)
  go computeMax(ch1, numbers)
  b := <- ch1
  fmt.Printf("Max is: %v\n", b)

  ch2 := make(chan int)
  go computeMin(ch2, numbers)
  b = <- ch2
  fmt.Printf("Min is: %v\n", b)
}
```

In this listing, two goroutines are created that each take a channel and an array of four integers. computeMax uses a for loop to determine the largest number, which is saved in the variable max, which is then written to the channel. The computeMin routine is very similar, except it looks for the smallest value and saves it in a variable called min, which is then written to the channel.

In the main routine, an array of numbers is created and then printed to the screen. This is followed by creating a channel called ch that works with int. This channel is then passed along with the array of integers to the computeMax goroutine. The program then waits for the channel to be written to, at which point it assigns the value to the variable b, which is then printed. The same process is then repeated using the other goroutine, computeMin. The output is:

```
[25 64 75 5]
Max is: 75
Min is: 5
```

CLOSING CHANNELS

You can close channels to let receivers know that you aren't sending any more data on a particular channel. In Listing 18.10 you close the channels you are using after the min and max are sent.

LISTING 18.10

Closing channels

```go
package main

import (
    "fmt"
)

func computeMax(ch chan int, numbers [4]int) {
    max := numbers[0]
    for i := 0; i < len(numbers); i++ {
        if numbers[i] > max {
            max = numbers[i]
        }
    }
    ch <- max
    close(ch)
}

func computeMin(ch chan int, numbers [4]int) {
    min := numbers[0]
    for i := 0; i < len(numbers); i++ {
        if numbers[i] < min {
            min = numbers[i]
        }
    }
    ch <- min
    close(ch)
}

func main() {
    numbers := [4]int{25, 64, 75, 5}
    fmt.Println(numbers)

    ch1 := make(chan int)
    go computeMax(ch1, numbers)
    b, ok := <- ch1
    fmt.Printf("Channel is closed: %v\n", ok)
    fmt.Printf("Max is: %v\n", b)

    ch2 := make(chan int)
    go computeMin(ch2, numbers)
    b, ok = <- ch2
```

```
    fmt.Printf("Channel is closed: %v\n", ok)
    fmt.Printf("Min is: %v\n", b)
}
```

This listing is similar to the previous one, with a couple of new instructions added. First, after you send the data on the channel in computeMax or computeMin, you use the close function to close the channel.

You then ask the receiver to check that the channel was closed by adding an extra variable, ok, to the read statement:

```
b, ok := <- ch1
```

The variable ok will contain a Boolean. If the channel is closed, it will return true, and if the channel is open, it will return false. In this case, the output is as follows:

```
[25 64 75 5]
Channel is closed: true
Max is: 75
Channel is closed: true
Min is: 5
```

If you remove the close statement and rerun the listing, you'll see that the value of ok will be false.

ITERATING THROUGH A CHANNEL

In the previous example, you started with a fixed array of numbers, but in many cases, you don't know how many values the program will use. Take a look at the code in Listing 18.11, which reads values from a channel.

LISTING 18.11

Reading values from a channel

```
package main

import (
    "fmt"
)
```

continues

continued

```go
func numberGenerator(ch chan int,limit int) {
    for i := 0; i < limit; i++ {
        ch <- i
    }
    close(ch)
}

func main() {
    ch := make(chan int)
    go numberGenerator(ch,20)

    // read the first number
    b := <- ch
    fmt.Println("Number:", b)

    // read the second number
    b = <-ch
    fmt.Println("Number:", b)
}
```

In this example, the channel is being used to write multiple values in a row. However, in the `main` goroutines, you need to read the values one by one, which creates an excessive amount of code. While the `numberGenerator` goroutine in this example generates 20 values that it sends to the channel, the output displays only the first two, because you have only two read instructions:

```
Number: 0
Number: 1
```

Instead of reading individual values from the channel, you can use `range` to iterate through the channel, as shown in Listing 18.12.

LISTING 18.12

Using `range` with multiple values

```go
package main

import (
    "fmt"
)
```

```
func numberGenerator(ch chan int,limit int) {
    for i := 0; i < limit; i++ {
        ch <- i
    }
    close(ch)
}

func main() {
    ch := make(chan int)
    go numberGenerator(ch, 20)
    for b := range ch {
        fmt.Println("Number:", b)
    }
}
```

In this listing, you can see that a `for` loop is used with the `range` keyword to iterate through the channel and print each value. This is a much faster way to read in the values from the channel, giving you the output:

```
Number: 0
Number: 1
Number: 2
Number: 3
Number: 4
Number: 5
Number: 6
Number: 7
Number: 8
Number: 9
Number: 10
Number: 11
Number: 12
Number: 13
Number: 14
Number: 15
Number: 16
Number: 17
Number: 18
Number: 19
```

SUMMARY

In this lesson you learned about concurrency and parallelism as well as about some of the key issues that can happen if they are not programmed correctly. Of course, Go supports concurrency and takes care of a lot of the background work for you. In this lesson, you discovered how to apply concurrency to your Go applications by creating and using goroutines. You also worked with passing data back and forth to goroutines using channels. The chapter wrapped up with showing you how to easily iterate through the data returned by a channel by using the Go `range` keyword.

EXERCISES

The following exercises are provided to allow you to experiment with the tools and concepts presented in this lesson. For each exercise, write a program that meets the specified requirements and verify that the program runs as expected. The exercises are:

Exercise 18.1: Counting Up and Down

Exercise 18.2: Passing to a Goroutine

Exercise 18.3: Rolling the Die

Exercise 18.4: Rolling the Dice

> **NOTE** The exercises are for your benefit. The exercises help you apply what you learn in the lessons. You are also encouraged to experiment with the code as you complete the exercises.

Exercise 18.1: Counting Up and Down

Create a program that declares two anonymous functions.

- One function counts down from 100 to 0.
- One function counts up from 0 to 100.

Display each number with a unique identifier for each goroutine, as was done in Listing 18.4. Create goroutines from these functions. Use a timer to make sure you don't let `main` return until the goroutines complete. Run both processes in parallel.

Exercise 18.2: Passing to a Goroutine

Modify your program from Exercise 18.1 to allow your goroutines to be created with an upper and a lower bounding number. You should still display each number along with the unique identifiers to know which goroutine is displaying the values.

Exercise 18.3: Rolling the Die

Create a goroutine called diceRoll that returns a random number from 1 to 6 using a channel. From the main goroutine, call the goroutine you created 6 times. Use the values from calling the goroutine to calculate the average of the numbers. Additionally, if all six rolls of the die are the same, display the message "Winner!"

NOTE You learned about generating random values in Lesson 8, "Using Functions."

Exercise 18.4: Rolling the Dice

In Exercise 18.3, your goroutine was expected to return one random number at a time. This time, create a goroutine called playerRoll that generates 6 dice rolls when called. The main goroutine should print the values of the dice rolls. The main goroutine should also print out messages if any of the following are true:

- If all the numbers are the same, display "Winner!"
- If each die roll is different (1, 2, 3, 4, 5, and 6 are returned in any order), then display "Long Straight."
- If five numbers in the group are different, display "Short Straight."

You can also print out other combinations such as three of a kind and three pairs. You can use the range keyword to obtain values from the channel.

Lesson 19
Sorting and Data Processing

In this lesson, a number of data-related topics will be covered. In previous lessons, you've imported and used packages, such as `fmt` to do printing and the `time` package to pause your program for a period of time. You'll dig into a number of other packages provided in Go and learn how to use them to do sorting, to work with dates and times, and to perform searches in strings with regular expressions.

LEARNING OBJECTIVES

By the end of this lesson, you will be able to:

* Sort strings and other values.
* Get the current date and time.
* Work with dates and times.
* Perform math operations using times values.
* Apply regular expressions.

SORTING

Go includes the sort package, which allows you to perform sorting operations on comparable data types such as numbers and strings. In Listing 19.1 you define a slice storing integers. You then use the Ints function from the sort package to sort the values in the slice.

LISTING 19.1

Sorting integers

```
package main

import (
    "fmt"
    "sort"
)

func main() {
    // define a slice
    numbers := []int{67, 18, 62, 60, 25, 64, 75, 5, 17, 55}
    fmt.Println("Original Numbers:", numbers)

    // use the sort.Ints function to sort the values in the slice
    sort.Ints(numbers)

    fmt.Println("Sorted Numbers:", numbers)

}
```

In this listing, we use the sort package to execute the Ints function, which sorts the slice in ascending order. This is done by passing the name of the slice to the function:

```
sort.Ints(numbers)
```

The sorted values are stored back into the original slice, replacing the original order of the values. The result is a sorted slice, as you can see in the output:

```
Original Numbers: [67 18 62 60 25 64 75 5 17 55]
Sorted Numbers: [5 17 18 25 55 60 62 64 67 75]
```

You can also use the sort package to sort strings alphabetically, as shown in Listing 19.2.

LISTING 19.2

Sorting strings

```
package main

import (
    "fmt"
    "sort"
)

func main() {
    // define a slice
    words := []string{"camel", "zebra", "horse", "dog", "elephant", "giraffe"}
    fmt.Println("Original slice:", words)

    // sort the values in the slice
    sort.Strings(words)
    fmt.Println("Sorted slice:", words)
}
```

This program uses the same logic as the previous example, but with strings instead of numbers. To sort strings, the Strings function of the sort package is used. Again, the sorted values replace the original values in the slice. The output is as follows:

```
Original slice: [camel zebra horse dog elephant giraffe]
Sorted slice: [camel dog elephant giraffe horse zebra]
```

Checking Sorted Values

To determine whether a slice or an array of strings is sorted, you can use the StringsAreSorted function from the sort package. StringsAreSorted will return true if the input is sorted or false otherwise. The example in Listing 19.3 shows how to use the StringsAreSorted function.

LISTING 19.3

Verifying if values are sorted

```go
package main

import (
    "fmt"
    "sort"
)

func main() {
    // define a slice
    words := []string{"camel", "zebra", "horse", "dog", "elephant", "giraffe"}
    fmt.Println("Original slice:", words)
    fmt.Println("The original values are sorted:", sort.StringsAreSorted(words))

    // sort the values in the slice
    sort.Strings(words)
    fmt.Println("Sorted slice:", words)
    fmt.Println("The values are sorted:", sort.StringsAreSorted(words))
}
```

In this listing, you create an array of words, which you print to the screen. You then check using sort.StringsAreSorted to see if the words are already sorted. In this case, you know they are not, so the returned value will be false. Using sort.Strings, you then sort the words before again printing them and checking to see if they are sorted.

Note that you checked to see if the words are sorted twice, once for the original slice and again after you have sorted the values in the slice. The final output looks like this:

```
Original slice: [camel zebra horse dog elephant giraffe]
The original values are sorted: false
Sorted slice: [camel dog elephant giraffe horse zebra]
The values are sorted: true
```

To determine if other data types are sorted, you can use a function similar to StringsAreSorted. The function would be named similarly, using the following format:

```
sort.DatatypeAreSorted( slice )
```

where Datatype is replaced with the type of the data to be sorted. For example, integers would use sort.IntsAreSorted and float64 values would use sort.Float64sAreSorted. The slice passed would need to contain values of the corresponding type.

Custom Sort Functions

If you want to sort data based on a specific criterion, you can build your own functions and embed them in the sort package for your use. For instance, imagine that you want to sort a set of words based on the number of characters in each word rather than alphabetically. The sort package includes the Sort interface, which you can implement with your own logic to create custom sorting algorithms.

The sort interface includes three methods that you need to implement:

- Len: The Len function returns the length of the data type in the context of sorting. In this case, you want to sort words based on their length so that the Len function will return the length of the input words.

- Swap: The sort package uses the Swap function internally to swap items in a slice or array during sorting. The function takes as input two indexes, and it swaps the values in those indexes.

- Less: The Less function provides the logic for comparing two items in a slice or array. Because you want to compare based on length, this function will take the indexes of the two items you want to compare in the slice or array, and it will return true if the length of the first word (stored in the first index) is higher than the length of the second word (stored in the second index).

Listing 19.4 implements the three methods of the sort package to sort the string values based on the length of the string.

LISTING 19.4

Sorting by length

```
package main

import (
    "fmt"
    "sort"
)

// create an alias type
type mytype []string

// implement the Len method
func (s mytype) Len() int {
    return len(s)
}
```

continues

continued

```go
// implement the Swap method
func (s mytype) Swap(i, j int) {
    s[i], s[j] = s[j], s[i]
}

// implement the Less method
func (s mytype) Less(i, j int) bool {
    return len(s[i]) < len(s[j])
}

func main() {
    // create a slice of strings
    fruits := []string{"pear", "pineapple", "mango", "banana", "fig"}
    fmt.Println("Original slice:", fruits)

    // create a mytype variable
    myfruits := mytype(fruits)

    sort.Sort(myfruits)
    fmt.Println("Sorted by length:", myfruits)
}
```

In order to implement the interface, you need your own custom type, so the first thing you do is create your own alias type, mytype, based on a slice of strings:

```go
type mytype []string
```

Remember that in Go, the definition of the receiver type must be in the same package as the method. This means that you cannot use an array of strings as the receiver type for the methods since it is not in the same package as the method. Thus, you need to create your own alias type.

Next, you implement the three methods Len, Swap, and Less, with each function performing a specific action on the array. In the main function, you create a slice of strings that you then convert into your own data type (mytype).

Finally, you use the Sort function from the sort package to sort the list of words based on length. When you run the listing, you can see that the set of strings is indeed sorted by length:

```
Original slice: [pear pineapple mango banana fig]
Sorted by length: [fig pear mango banana pineapple]
```

Reversing the Sort Order

Go also provides a method for reversing the sort order of a slice that has used the sort interface. The method for reversing the sort order is sort.Reverse. Listing 19.5 shows the sort order of an array of integers being reversed.

LISTING 19.5

Reversing the sort order

```
package main

import (
    "fmt"
    "sort"
)

func main() {
    // define a slice
    numbers := []int{67, 18, 62, 60, 25, 64, 75, 5, 17, 55}
    fmt.Println("Original Numbers:", numbers)

    sort.Ints(numbers)
    fmt.Println("Sorted Numbers:", numbers)

    sort.Sort(sort.Reverse(sort.IntSlice(numbers)))
    fmt.Println("Sorted Numbers:", numbers)
}
```

In this listing, you use the numbers slice that you used in Listing 19.1. The primary difference is that you added the last two lines to the main function, with the key line of code being:

```
sort.Sort(sort.Reverse(sort.IntSlice(numbers)))
```

In this line of code, the numbers slice is sorted into reverse order. Specifically, you are passing your slice, numbers, to sort.IntSlice. This in turn is passed to sort.Reverse, which is the function that will reverse the sort order. To do the sort, however, you pass all of this to sort.Sort. The end result is that the order of the numbers is reversed, as shown in the output:

```
Original Numbers: [67 18 62 60 25 64 75 5 17 55]
Sorted Numbers: [5 17 18 25 55 60 62 64 67 75]
Reversed Numbers: [75 67 64 62 60 55 25 18 17 5]
```

If you want to reverse the order of data of a different data type, you can swap out IntSlice with an interface based on the type you want to sort. The format of the interface would be:

```
sort.datatypeSlice( slice )
```

For example, to reverse the order of slice of strings called MyStrings, you'd use the following:

```
sort.Sort(sort.Reverse(sort.StringSlice(MyStrings)))
```

> **NOTE** The actual format for the interface being used in the previous example is:
>
> ```
> sort.datatypeSlice(x []datatype)
> ```
>
> where *datatype* is the type of data being sorted such as Int, Float64, or String, and *x* is the slice containing the data values.

> **NOTE** You might wonder why you can pass a slice of integers to sort.Ints but you can't do the same with sort.Reverse, and why you have to mess with sort.Sort(sort.Reverse(sort.IntSlice())). The answer is that sort.Ints is just a wrapper around sort.IntSlice. The developers of Go created the helper function, sort.Ints, as a convenience, but did not see the need to create a helper function like sort.ReverseInts. You can see the code at https://cs.opensource.google/go/go/+/refs/tags/go1.18:src/sort/sort.go.

TIME AND DATE OPERATIONS

Go includes a robust time package that you can use to manipulate date and time values. As an example, you can use the Now functions shown in Listing 19.6 to retrieve the current date and time, based on system values.

LISTING 19.6

Getting the current date and time

```
package main

import (
    "fmt"
    "time"
)

func main() {
    // display current time
    now := time.Now()
    fmt.Println("Today's date and time:", now)
    fmt.Println("Current year:", now.Year())
    fmt.Println("Current month:", now.Month())
    fmt.Println("Current day:", now.Day())
    fmt.Println("Current hour:", now.Hour())
    fmt.Println("Current minute:", now.Minute())
    fmt.Println("Current second:", now.Second())
```

continues

continued

```
    fmt.Println("Current nanosecond:", now.Nanosecond())
    fmt.Println("Current location:", now.Location())
        // now.Zone() returns 2 values
    zone, zoneOffset := now.Zone()
    fmt.Println("Current zone:", zone)
    fmt.Println("Current zone offset:", zoneOffset)
    fmt.Println("Current weekday:", now.Weekday())
}
```

Listing 19.6 imports the `time` package to gain access to a number of date and time functions. Using a variety of functions, the program prints the requested information based on the local system clock. While the actual outputs will change, it should look something like the following:

```
Today's date and time: 2022-04-13 12:27:36.0247625 -0400 EDT m=+0.006465401
Current year: 2022
Current month: April
Current day: 13
Current hour: 12
Current minute: 27
Current second: 36
Current nanosecond: 24762500
Current location: Local
Local:  2022-04-13 12:27:36.0247625 -0400 EDT
Current zone: EDT
Current zone offset: -14400
Current weekday: Wednesday
```

In the first line of output, now is printed. As you can see, it contains the date, time, and more. This is followed by calls to individual functions that return various pieces of the current date and time. You can review the listing to see the functions that are used. Several of the available functions are listed in Table 19.1.

Table 19.1 Time functions

Function	Description
Year()	Displays the year as a four-digit value
Month()	Displays the textual representation of a month, such as "January"
Day()	Displays the numeric day of the month
Hour()	Displays the numeric representation of the hour
Minute()	Displays the numeric representation of the minutes
Second()	Displays the numeric representation of the seconds
Nanosecond()	Displays the numeric representation of the nanoseconds
Weekday()	Displays the textual representation of the day of the week, such as "Monday"

Function	Description
YearDay()	Displays the numeric representation for the day within the year
Local()	Displays the current time value adjusted to local time
Location()	Displays information about the time zone associated with the current time variable
Zone()	Returns two values: first, a textual representation of the time zone such as "EST," and second, a numeric value for the duration offset (in seconds) from GMT

Defining a Time

It is often useful to retrieve date and time values from the system, but you can also define a date/time value and analyze that value. Listing 19.7 defines a specific date and time and then retrieves values from that definition.

LISTING 19.7

Getting parts of a date or time

```
package main

import (
    "fmt"
    "time"
)

func main() {
    // create custom time
    customTime := time.Date(
        2025, 05, 15, 15, 20, 00, 0, time.Local)
    fmt.Println("Custom date and time:", customTime)

    fmt.Println("Custom year:", customTime.Year())
    fmt.Println("Custom month:", customTime.Month())
    fmt.Println("Custom day:", customTime.Day())
    fmt.Println("Custom weekday:", customTime.Weekday())
    fmt.Println("Custom hour:", customTime.Hour())
    fmt.Println("Custom minute:", customTime.Minute())
    fmt.Println("Custom second:", customTime.Second())
    fmt.Println("Custom nanosecond:", customTime.Nanosecond())
    fmt.Println("Custom location:", customTime.Location())
    // Zone() returns 2 values
```

continues

continued

```
    zone, zoneOffset := customTime.Zone()
    fmt.Println("Custom zone:", zone)
    fmt.Println("Custom zone offset:", (zoneOffset/3600))
}
```

In this listing, instead of using the current time (now), you are creating a date and time, which you assign to a variable called customTime. You initialize your custom time with values when you create it:

```
customTime := time.Date( 2025, 05, 15, 15, 20, 00, 0, time.Local)
```

The arguments you pass also include time.Local to indicate that the values should be based on the local location. Once your custom time has been created, you can display the pieces in the same manner you did for the current time in the previous listing. The output showing customTime and the various pieces is as follows:

```
Custom date and time: 2025-05-15 15:20:00 -0400 EDT
Custom year: 2025
Custom month: May
Custom day: 15
Custom weekday: Thursday
Custom hour: 15
Custom minute: 20
Custom second: 0
Custom nanosecond: 0
Custom location: Local
Custom zone: EDT
Custom zone offset: -4
```

Note that if you are located in a different time zone than EDT, then you will have slightly different values showing for the Custom date and time, Custom zone, and Custom zone offset values. The output shown here is based on the program being run in the EDT time zone. Also notice that the code divided the zone offset by 3,600. This is simply taking the return value saved in zoneOffset and converting it to hours instead of seconds. There are 3,600 seconds in an hour.

Comparing Times

You can ask Go to compare two times and determine which one occurs earlier. In Listing 19.8 you compare a custom time to the current time to determine which one is earlier. You can do this using functions provided by the time package.

LISTING 19.8

Comparing time

```go
package main

import (
    "fmt"
    "time"
)

func main() {
    // display current time
    now := time.Now()
    fmt.Println("Current date and time:", now)

    // create custom time
    customTime := time.Date(
        2025, 05, 15, 15, 20, 00, 0, time.Local)
    fmt.Println("Custom date and time:", customTime)

    // comparisons
    fmt.Println("The custom time is before now:", customTime.Before(now))
    fmt.Println("The custom time is after now:", customTime.After(now))
    fmt.Println("The custom time is equal to now:", customTime.Equal(now))
}
```

This listing creates two time variables. The first is called now and contains the current time. The second is called customTime and contains a date in 2025. The last three lines of code call three functions to compare the times. The Before, After, and Equal functions return Boolean values based on comparing the associated time (customTime in this case) to the time passed to the function (now in this case). The output from this listing at the time this lesson was written is as follows:

```
Current date and time: 2022-01-21 16:30:24.8709676 -0500 EST m=+0.010002901
Custom date and time: 2025-05-15 15:20:00 -0400 EDT
The custom time is before now: false
The custom time is after now: true
The custom time is equal to now: false
```

Note that you could reverse what's done in Listing 19.8 and call these functions on now with the customTime being passed, as shown in Listing 19.9.

LISTING 19.9

Comparing times again

```
package main

import (
    "fmt"
    "time"
)

func main() {
    // display current time
    now := time.Now()
    fmt.Println("Current date and time:", now)

    // create custom time
    customTime := time.Date(
        2025, 05, 15, 15, 20, 00, 0, time.Local)
    fmt.Println("Custom date and time:", customTime)

    // comparisons
    fmt.Println("The current time is before the custom time:", now.Before
(customTime))
    fmt.Println("The current time is after the custom time:", now.After
(customTime))
    fmt.Println("The current time is equal to the custom time:", now.Equal
(customTime))
}
```

The result of flipping the time variables is what should be expected. The before and after results flip:

```
Current date and time: 2022-01-21 16:35:10.8787301 -0500 EST m=+0.016997501
Custom date and time: 2025-05-15 15:20:00 -0400 EDT
The current time is before the custom time: true
The current time is after the custom time: false
The current time is equal to the custom time: false
```

Time Math

You can also use the time package to perform calculations such as subtracting dates from each other, adding dates together, and adding values to a date.

Determining Date Differences

Using subtraction, you can determine the difference between two dates. When you subtract one time value from another time value, Go returns the duration of time between those two values. You can see this in action in Listing 19.10.

LISTING 19.10

Subtracting dates

```
package main

import (
    "fmt"
    "time"
)

func main() {
    // display current time
    now := time.Now()
    fmt.Println("Current date and time:", now)

    // create custom time
    customTime := time.Date(
        2025, 05, 15, 15, 20, 00, 0, time.Local)
    fmt.Println("Custom date and time:", customTime)

    // subtract two times to return a duration in hours,
    // minutes, seconds
    diff := now.Sub(customTime)
    fmt.Println("Time between now and custom time:", diff)

    fmt.Println("Hours between now and custom time:", diff.Hours())
    fmt.Println("Minutes between now and custom time:", diff.Minutes())
    fmt.Println("Seconds between now and custom time:", diff.Seconds())
    fmt.Println("Nanoseconds between now and custom time:", diff.Nanoseconds())
}
```

The use of the Sub function allows one time that is passed as an argument to be subtracted from the current time. In the listing, the instruction:

```
diff := now.Sub(customTime)
```

subtracts the `customTime` value from `now` and stores the difference in the `diff` variable. In this example, the custom date is after the current date, so the result is negative. If you are running this listing after May 15, 2025, then the numbers will be positive.

The `diff` variable contains the overall difference in time between the two dates. The third `Println` statement prints the value of `diff`:

```
Time between now and custom time: -27074h19m13.3341849s
```

You can see that the value contains several components, including hours, minutes, and seconds, with a decimal place. Each of these components of the time difference can be accessed by using functions with the `diff` variable. This is done in the last four `Println` statements within the listing. These lines get the components using `diff.Hours()`, `diff.Minutes()`, `diff.Seconds()`, and `diff.Nanoseconds()`. The full output is dependent on the current date but should be similar to the following:

```
Current date and time: 2022-04-13 13:00:46.6658151 -0400 EDT m=+0.007016301
Custom date and time: 2025-05-15 15:20:00 -0400 EDT
Time between now and custom time: -27074h19m13.3341849s
Hours between now and custom time: -27074.320370606918
Minutes between now and custom time: -1.624459222236415e+06
Seconds between now and custom time: -9.74675533341849e+07
Nanoseconds between now and custom time: -97467553334184900
```

> **NOTE** You might be wondering why it doesn't provide the number of days. Simply stated, if you want the number of days, divide the number of hours by 24!

Adding a Duration to a Date/Time

You can also add a specific amount of time to a date/time value and return the date/value that results. For example, you may want to calculate a date two weeks later or one month earlier than a given date. Listing 19.11 builds on the earlier example and uses the duration between the current time and the custom time as the value in an `Add` function.

LISTING 19.11

Adding a duration

```
package main

import (
```

```
    "fmt"
    "time"
)

func main() {
    // display current time
    now := time.Now()
    fmt.Println("Current date and time:", now)

    // create custom time
    customTime := time.Date(
        2025, 05, 15, 15, 20, 00, 0, time.Local)
    fmt.Println("Custom date and time:", customTime)

    // time operations
    // subtract two times to return a duration in hours, minutes, seconds
    diff := now.Sub(customTime)
    fmt.Println("Time between now and custom time:", diff)

    fmt.Println(customTime.Add(diff))
    fmt.Println(customTime.Add(-diff))
}
```

In this listing, the duration between the current date (now) and the custom date, which is May 15, 2025, is determined using the Sub function, as shown in the previous listing. The result of this duration of time is stored in the diff variable. When this lesson was written, the custom time was in the future, so diff was a negative number:

```
Time between now and custom time: -27074h9m47.2688778s
```

The value for the difference is then added to the custom time and printed, followed by subtracting the difference:

```
fmt.Println(customTime.Add(diff))
fmt.Println(customTime.Add(-diff))
```

If you run this listing prior to May 15, 2025, then when you add the difference, it will result in the current date and time, whereas adding the negative of the difference will result in a date in the future past May 15, 2025. If you run the listing after May 15, 2025, then adding the difference will result in a date in the future, and adding the negative of the difference will result in the current date and time.

Using as the current date the date this lesson was written (which is prior to May 15, 2025), the output looks like this:

```
Current date and time: 2022-04-13 13:10:12.7311222 -0400 EDT m=+0.006706501
Custom date and time: 2025-05-15 15:20:00 -0400 EDT
Time between now and custom time: -27074h9m47.2688778s
2022-04-13 13:10:12.7311222 -0400 EDT
2028-06-16 17:29:47.2688778 -0400 EDT
```

Adding Hours, Minutes, and Seconds

While the previous listings have shown how to get the difference between two dates and how to use that difference to adjust an existing date, that's not always practical. Sometimes we just want to add a given number of hours, minutes, or seconds. This can also be done using the Add function along with constants, as shown in Listing 19.12.

LISTING 19.12

Adding seconds, minutes, hours, and weeks

```go
package main

import (
    "fmt"
    "time"
)

func main() {

    // Declaring time in UTC
    myTime := time.Date(2025, 5, 15, 12, 0, 0, 0, time.Local)

    date1 := myTime.Add(time.Second * 6)
    date2 := myTime.Add(time.Minute * 6)
    date3 := myTime.Add(time.Hour * 6)
    date4 := myTime.Add(time.Hour * 24 * 7)

    // Print the date/time output
    fmt.Println(myTime)
    fmt.Println(date1)
    fmt.Println(date2)
    fmt.Println(date3)
    fmt.Println(date4)
}
```

In this listing, you create a Time type called myTime that is initialized to May 15, 2025, at 12:00:00. This date is then used to create four new dates that will have the time component adjusted.

For date1 the Add function is used to add 6 seconds to the date and time stored in myTime. To add the 6 seconds, you multiply 6 by the constant time.Seconds. You then create date2 and date3 in a similar manner; however, with date2 you are adding 6 minutes, which is done by multiplying 6 by the constant time.Minute. With date3 you are adding 6 hours using 6 multiplied by the constant time.Hour.

For date4, you are adding a week. There is no function for adding a week, so instead you add the number of hours that are in a week, which would be 24 (the number of hours in a day) times 7 (the number of days in a week). You again multiply this by the time.Hour constant.

With our new date variables created, you print each to the screen to verify that the original date was indeed changed as expected:

```
2025-05-15 12:00:00 -0400 EDT
2025-05-15 12:00:06 -0400 EDT
2025-05-15 12:06:00 -0400 EDT
2025-05-15 18:00:00 -0400 EDT
2025-05-22 12:00:00 -0400 EDT
```

> **NOTE** The time zone displayed in the output will be dependent on the local time zone where the program is run.

Adding Years, Months, and Days

While the previous listings have shown how to get the difference between two dates and how to add time components, sometimes you just want to add a given number of days, months, or years to a date and you don't want to have to calculate the number of hours as you did in the previous listing to add a week. Fortunately, you can do that with the AddDate function.

The AddDate function can be applied to a time variable. The format of the function is:

```
AddDate(years, months, days)
```

Each of the arguments is a variable of type int. To add two weeks to a time variable called customDate, as you do in Listing 19.13, use this:

```
customDate.AddDate(0, 0, 14)
```

LISTING 19.13

Adding years, months and/or days to a date

```
package main

import (
    "fmt"
    "time"
)

func main() {
    // display current time
    now := time.Now()
    fmt.Println("Current date and time:", now)

    newDate := now.AddDate(0, 0, 14)
    fmt.Println("Two weeks in the future:", newDate)

    // Using a custom date
    customDate := time.Date(
        2025, 05, 15, 15, 20, 00, 0, time.Local)
    fmt.Println("Custom date and time:", customDate)

    newCustomDate := customDate.AddDate(0, 0, 14)
    fmt.Println("Two weeks after custom date:", newCustomDate)
}
```

In this listing, you create a variable called now that holds the current date and time. You then use the AddDate function to add two weeks (14 days) to now and save the resulting date in a new variable called newDate. This is followed by printing the newDate, which will be two weeks from the current time.

The listing then does the same thing again, but it starts with a custom date that was created. The approach works the same and the result is that a date two weeks in the future from your custom date is printed.

> **NOTE** The signature of the AddDate function shows that it is a function that is associated to a Time type. The signature also shows that the function receives three ints and returns a Time as well. The signature is as follows:
>
> ```
> func (t Time) AddDate(years int, months int, days int) Time
> ```

Parsing Time

With Go, you can parse strings into time values using the `time.Parse` function. This would allow you, for example, to accept date values as strings through user input or from a data file and then be able to convert those values into time values as needed. Listing 19.14 takes a string representing a time and parses it into individual parts of the date/time the string represents.

LISTING 19.14

Parsing time

```
package main

import (
    "fmt"
    "time"
)

func main() {

    myDate := "2025-05-21T12:50:41+00:00"
    fmt.Println(myDate)

    t1, e := time.Parse(
        time.RFC3339,
        myDate)

    fmt.Println(t1)
    fmt.Println(t1.Day())
    fmt.Println(t1.Month())

    // error if there is an error during parsing;
    // nil if there is no error
    fmt.Println(e)
}
```

This listing creates a variable called `myDate` and assigns it a string value that contains what appears to be a date. This string is then passed to the `time.Parse` function to be converted into an actual date, which will be placed in `t1`. The `Parse` function also does error handling, so you include the variable `e` to catch any errors that might occur.

The `Parse` function also takes two parameters. The first one indicates the format of the date you will be parsing. The second parameter is the string to be parsed.

In the listing, once you call `Parse`, you print the resulting date followed by the day and the month. You also print the value captured by e, which will show an error if one happened during the parsing or `nil` if there was no error. In our case, there was no error, as you can see in the output:

```
2025-05-21 12:50:41 +0000 +0000
21
May
<nil>
```

As mentioned, the first parameter passed to `Parse` indicates the format the date within the string is expected to follow. In this case, we used RFC3339, which assumes a string uses the following format:

```
"2006-01-02T15:04:05Z07:00"
```

Table 19.2 lists many of the formats that are defined by the `time` package. You can pass to `Parse` either the constant, as we did in Listing 19.14, or the literal form.

Table 19.2 Date format constants

Constant	Literal format
ANSIC	"Mon Jan _2 15:04:05 2006"
UnixDate	"Mon Jan _2 15:04:05 MST 2006"
RubyDate	"Mon Jan 02 15:04:05 -0700 2006"
RFC822	"02 Jan 06 15:04 MST"
RFC822Z	"02 Jan 06 15:04 -0700"
RFC850	"Monday, 02-Jan-06 15:04:05 MST"
RFC1123	"Mon, 02 Jan 2006 15:04:05 MST"
RFC1123Z	"Mon, 02 Jan 2006 15:04:05 -0700"
RFC3339	"2006-01-02T15:04:05Z07:00"
RFC339Nano	"2006-01-02T15:04:05.999999999Z07:00"
Kitchen	"3:04PM"
Stamp	"Jan _2 15:04:05"
StampMilli	"Jan _2 15:04:05.000"
StampMicro	"Jan _2 15:04:05.000000"
StampNano	"Jan _2 15:04:05.000000000"

Working with Unix Time

You can also use a Unix representation of time in Go time functions. You can learn more about Unix time at https://pubs.opengroup.org/onlinepubs/9699919799/xrat/V4_xbd_chap04.html#tag_21_04_16. Listing 19.15 shows two ways to display time in a Unix format.

LISTING 19.15

Using Unix time

```
package main

import (
    "fmt"
    "time"
)

func main() {
    now := time.Now()
    unixtime := now.Unix() // Unix time
    unixnanotime := now.UnixNano() // Unix nano time

    fmt.Println(now)
    fmt.Println(unixtime)
    fmt.Println(unixnanotime)
}
```

This listing starts by creating a variable and assigning the current time using the Now function as you've done before. It then uses the Unix and UnixNano functions from the time package to create two variables containing the current Unix times. The output looks like this:

```
2020-06-02 13:00:33.5876249 -0400 EDT m=+0.005984001
1591117233
1591117233587624900
```

Formatting Standard Times

Another option for displaying dates is to use standard time formats that are user-friendlier. Listing 19.16 formats the date using the RFC 1123 Z standard.

LISTING 19.16

Working with other standards

```go
package main

import (
    "fmt"
    "time"
)

func main() {
    now := time.Now()
    fmt.Println(now.Format(time.RFC1123Z))
}
```

In this listing, you use the `Format` function to format a time. In this case you are formatting the time stored in your variable `now`, which is the current time. You are formatting it based on the pattern in the `time.RFC1123Z` constant. This is the same constant presented earlier in Table 19.2. The output is:

```
Sun, 02 Jan 2022 13:01:53 -0400
```

In addition to using the `time.RFC1123Z` format, any of the other formats presented in Table 19.2 can be used. For example, if the `Println` statement in Listing 19.15 is changed to the following:

```go
fmt.Println(now.Format(time.Kitchen))
```

then the output would be:

```
1:01PM
```

NOTE You can pass either the time constant listed in Table 19.2 or the literal string to the `time.Format` function. As such, `Format(time.Kitchen)` works the same as `Format("3:04PM")`. The string must match the string literal in Table 19.2. Custom strings will not work.

REGULAR EXPRESSIONS

Regular expressions (also commonly referred to as *regex* or *regexp*) is a general tool that is widely used across computer languages. It includes standard search patterns that allow us to search for specific string values inside larger string patterns.

Go includes a package dedicated to regular expressions, regexp, that allows us to perform regex searches in strings. Listing 19.17 shows two examples of using the MatchString function within basic regexp within searches.

> **NOTE** In Go, you can use back-tick single quotes (`` ` ``) to create a raw string literal. This means that special characters such as a double quote will be included as part of the string. For example, `` `"hello Mr. O'Connel"` `` would be a string that includes the double and single quotes: `"hello Mr. O'Connel"`.

LISTING 19.17

Using regexp

```
package main

import (
    "fmt"
    "regexp"
)

func main() {
    // check if string starts with C and ends with n
    m1,err1 := regexp.MatchString("^C([a-z]+)n$", "Catelyn")
    fmt.Println(m1)
    fmt.Println(err1)

    // check if string contains at least one digit
    m2,err2 := regexp.MatchString("[0-9]", "jonathan6smith")
    fmt.Println(m2)
    fmt.Println(err2)
}
```

In the first example, you use the following pattern as the search string:

```
C([a-z]+)n
```

The `regexp` package interprets this as a string that starts with C, contains any number of letters, and ends in n. The name `Catelyn` meets this pattern, so the program returns `true`. You can see that the `MatchString` function includes error checking, so you capture the return value of `true` or `false` in `m1` as well as any error conditions returned to `err1`.

In the second example, you use this pattern:

```
[0-9]
```

This tells the program to search for any numeric character anywhere in the string. Because the username `jonathan6smith` includes a numeric character, this also returns `true`. The full output from running the listing is:

```
true
<nil>
true
<nil>
```

> **NOTE** You can research regular expressions online to find some search patterns that it includes. The following sites are good starting points, but because regex is a standard tool, there are many other resources as well:
>
> - GoLang package `regexp`—https://pkg.go.dev/regexp
> - Regular Expression Library—https://regexlib.com
> - Geeks for Geeks, How to write Regular Expressions—www.geeksforgeeks.org/write-regular-expressions

Instead of using the `MatchString` function, you can use the `Compile` function to parse a regular expression and then use the result to perform matching. Listing 19.18 shows how the `Compile` function can be used.

LISTING 19.18

Using `regexp` **compile**

```
package main

import (
```

```
        "fmt"
        "regexp"
)

func main() {
    r, _ := regexp.Compile("[0-9]")
    fmt.Println("Search term:", r)

    // check if the string contains digits
    fmt.Println("S54366456SDfhdgstf7986:", r.MatchString("S54366456SDfhdgstf7986"))
    fmt.Println("It's five o'clock now:", r.MatchString("It's five o'clock now"))

    // return the first match
        fmt.Println("The phone number is 555-9980:",
        r.FindString("The phone number is 555-9980"))
    fmt.Println("Alexander Hamilton:", r.FindString("Alexander Hamilton"))
}
```

You use Compile to define the search term separately from the search operation, and you save the operation to a variable. You can then reuse the variable with any string, without having to redefine the search for each operation. In this case, you pass the following expression to Compile:

```
[0-9]
```

As mentioned earlier, this will match any numeric digit from 0 to 9. This expression is assigned to the variable r. When you print r, you see that it contains this range as its search term.

The MatchString function returns a Boolean based on whether the search is successful. In this listing, you use MatchString with r. Unlike in the previous listing, you only include the string to be searched. The search pattern is already known as a part of r. When you search the string "S54366456SDfhdgstf7986", you will find a number, so the returned value is true. When you search the string "It's five o'clock now", you do not find a number, so false is returned.

You also use the FindString function in the listing. The FindString function returns the first matching instance of the search, regardless of the number of times the search term may appear in the original string, and it returns nothing if the search is not successful. In the output, you see the results from the searches using the MatchString and FindString functions with the search pattern in r:

```
Search term: [0-9]
S54366456SDfhdgstf7986: true
```

continues

continued

```
It's five o'clock now: false
The phone number is 555-9980: 5
Alexander Hamilton:
```

SUMMARY

In this lesson, we covered a number of prebuilt routines that can be used by importing the sort, time, or regex packages. By importing these packages, you gain access to functions that will let data be easily sorted, allow you to use a variety of date and time functions, and allow you to incorporate regular expression searches.

EXERCISES

The following exercises are provided to allow you to experiment with the tools and concepts presented in this lesson. For each exercise, write a program that meets the specified requirements and verify that the program runs as expected. The exercises are:

Exercise 19.1: Sorting Floats

Exercise 19.2: Sorting Student Grades

Exercise 19.3: Knowing What Time It Is

Exercise 19.4: Working with Dates

Exercise 19.5: String Searching

Exercise 19.6: More String Searching

Exercise 19.7: Date-Time Calculator

> **NOTE** The exercises are for your benefit. The exercises help you apply what you learn in the lessons. You are also encouraged to experiment with the code as you complete the exercises.

Exercise 19.1: Sorting Floats

You learned in the lesson that you can use sort.Ints to sort integers and sort.Strings to sort strings. You can use the sort method Float64s to sort Float64 values. Create a program that uses sort.Float64s to sort 10 floating-point numbers. Only call the sort function if the values are not already in sorted order.

Exercise 19.2: Sorting Student Grades

The following is a struct called Student that contains fields for the student's name and a student grade:

```
Type Student struct {
    Name string
    Grade int
}
```

Create a program that includes the Student struct and declares a collection of Students:

```
type Students []Student
```

Within the program, create an array of students in a class and assign each a name and a grade. Create a custom sort that sorts the students based on their grades, sorting from highest to lowest. The sort should be on the slice of students you create.

Exercise 19.3: Knowing What Time It Is

Write a program to display the following:

- Current date and time
- Current year
- Current month
- Week number of the year
- Weekday of the week
- Day of the year
- Day of the month
- Day of the week

Exercise 19.4: Working with Dates

Write a program that starts with a date and then does each of the following:

- Prints the dates for yesterday, today, and tomorrow.
- Prints the date for the next five days, starting from today.
- Adds 5 seconds to the current time and displays the result.

- Computes the number of days between your date and January 1st, 2000. (Make sure your result is a positive number.)
- Determines if the date entered is in the same year as a leap year.

Exercise 19.5: String Searching

Starting with a string of your choice, create a program that searches for at least five different string patterns in the original string. Include the following patterns:

- Find two or more variations on the same word, for example, *gray* or *grey*.
- Find a properly formatted email address.
- Find any three-letter words that start with the same letter and end with the same letter, but that might have a different letter in between, such as *cat* or *cot*.
- Find words that contain any of a defined set of characters, such as the values a, e, i, o, u.
- Find words that contain double letters.

Be sure to test for strings that don't exist in the original string as well as for strings that do exist. Feel free to include additional features, such as prompting the user for the original string as well as for search terms and including appropriate feedback messages if the search fails.

Exercise 19.6: More String Searching

Write a program that lets the user enter a string. Using regular expressions, check the string and print a response indicating which of the following cases are true for the string:

- String contains only letters and numbers (*a–z, A–Z, 0–9*).
- String includes the letter *i* followed by zero or more instances of the letter *n*.
- String includes the letter *i* followed by one or more instances of the letter *n*.
- String includes the letter *i* followed by one or two instances of the letter *n*.
- String contains only numbers (0–9).
- String contains only letters (a–z, A–Z).

Exercise 19.7: Date-Time Calculator

This exercise is a bigger challenge that will require you to use much of what you've learned up to this point from this book. In this exercise, you should build several different date-time calculators, each of which performs a different calculation. Each calculator should accept appropriate user input for that calculator and perform the specified calculation using that input.

For each calculator:

- You may define the format that the user should use to enter the values, but that format must be very clear to the user.
  - If the user does not enter data in the expected format, the program should display an appropriate message and prompt the user to try again.
- Create appropriate functions, classes, and methods to simplify your code.
- The user must be able to clear all input at any time to start over again.
- The user must be able to exit the program at any time.

User input can be simplified by breaking it up into discrete values. For example, instead of asking the user to enter a complete date (which could have a variety of formats), the program can prompt for separate date, month, and year values. This creates more work on the backend because your program will have to be able to convert the distinct values into a date, but it can make the program less error-prone.

Put all the following calculators in a single program and allow the user to choose the one they wish to use.

Calculator 1: Time Duration

Add or subtract two different lengths of time.

- The calculator must include days, hours, minutes, and seconds.
- The user must be able to specify addition or subtraction between the two different input times.
- The output must display the results in multiple ways:
  - The number of days, hours, minutes, and seconds
  - The number of days
  - The number of hours
  - The number of minutes
  - The number of seconds

For example, if the user enters one value of 3 days, 5 hours, 15 minutes, and 0 seconds, and adds a value of 7 days, 20 hours, 50 minutes, and 10 seconds, the result will be:

- 11 days 2 hours 2 minutes 10 seconds
- 11.084838 days

- 266.03611 hours
- 15,962.167 minutes
- 957,730 seconds

As a challenge, after the initial version of the calculator works as expected, include weeks as an additional unit for the input values and the output result.

Calculator 2: Add Time to or Subtract Time from a Date

Given a date and time, add or subtract an input length of time and display the date and time of the result.

- The calculator must include days, hours, minutes, and seconds for input and output.
- The user must be able to choose between addition and subtraction.

For example, if the user enters December 1, 2021, 12:04:00 PM, and wants to subtract 5 days, 3 hours, and 30 minutes, the result would be November 25, 2021, 08:34:00 PM.

As a challenge, include the day of the week (Monday, Tuesday, etc.) in the output.

Calculator 3: Age Calculator

Given a start date and an end date, calculate the amount of time that has passed between the dates, displayed in years, months, days, hours, minutes, and seconds. For example, given the start date September 1, 1994 and the end date December 1, 2021, the results would be:

- 25 years 3 months 10 days
- 303 months 10 days
- 1,318 weeks 6 days
- 9,232 days
- 221,568 hours
- 13,294,080 minutes
- 797,644,800 seconds

As a challenge, update the calculator to include a specific time with each date.

Lesson 20

File I/O and OS Operations

U p to this point, we've been working with data within our programs that we either created in our code or have had users enter. It is also important to be able to save and retrieve data. In this lesson, we will cover file functionality provided in Go that will let us input data into and output it from our programs. We will also add coverage of working with directories. For an added bonus, we will cover the use of command-line arguments with our Go programs.

LEARNING OBJECTIVES

By the end of this lesson, you will be able to:

- Read data from a file into memory.
- Seek data from specific areas within a file.
- Use a buffered reader when working with files.
- Apply the Go `defer` statement.
- Work with directories in a computer system.
- Access and use command-line arguments.

READING A FILE

You can perform standard input and output (I/O) operations on a file using the `io/ioutil` package in Go. This package provides routines to perform standard I/O operations such as reading and writing to files. The example in Listing 20.1 reads a file called `flatland01.txt` into memory and displays its contents as a string.

> **NOTE** Code examples in this lesson use a file called `flatland01.txt`. This sample file is an extract from Edwin A. Abbott's novel *Flatland*, as downloaded from Project Gutenberg (`www.gutenberg.org`). It is distributed in the public domain. You can download a copy from:
>
> `https://the-software-guild.s3.amazonaws.com/golang/v1-2006/data-files/flatland01.txt`
>
> We have also included a copy of the file in the data folder of `JRGoSource.zip`, which you can download from the `Wiley.com` site to follow along. You are also welcome to use a different text file of your choice.

LISTING 20.1

Reading an entire file into memory

```
package main

import (
    "fmt"
    "io/ioutil"
)

func main() {
    // use the ReadFile from ioutil package to read the
    // entire file in memory

    data, err := ioutil.ReadFile("flatland01.txt")

    // feedback message in case of error
    if err != nil {
        fmt.Println(err)
    }
```

```
   // convert the file contents to a string and display them
   fmt.Print(string(data))
}
```

For this listing to work, you must download the `flatland01.txt` file to the same folder as your source file. Reviewing this code, you can see that it is relatively straightforward. You start by importing the `io/ioutil` package that includes the I/O functions you want to use.

You then read the file `flatland01.txt` from the current directory on your system. Note that it is possible to read a file from another location as well. You can include a relative or absolute path in the string you pass to the `ReadFile` function. Go does, however, require the use of forward slashes (/) to separate directories. For example, the following would read the file from a subfolder called `datafiles`:

```
data, err := ioutil.ReadFile("./datafiles/flatland01.txt")
```

The call to `ReadFile` includes error handling. Any errors will be returned to the second variable, `err`. The file data itself will be returned to the first variable, called `data` here.

In the listing, after calling the `ReadFile` function, you do a test to see if there is an error while reading. If the file is read without any issues, then the error value (`err`) will be set to `nil`. If `err` is not `nil`, then you display the error given when reading from the file.

Finally, you convert the file contents to a string and display the string to the user. Assuming that the path to the file is correct, the output looks like this:

```
FLATLAND

PART 1

THIS WORLD

SECTION 1  Of the Nature of Flatland

I call our world Flatland, not because we call it so, but to make its
nature clearer to you, my happy readers, who are privileged to live in
Space.

Imagine a vast sheet of paper on which straight Lines, Triangles,
Squares, Pentagons, Hexagons, and other figures, instead of remaining
fixed in their places, move freely about, on or in the surface, but
without the power of rising above or sinking below it, very much like
shadows--only hard with luminous edges--and you will then have a pretty
correct notion of my country and countrymen.  Alas, a few years ago, I
should have said "my universe:"  but now my mind has been opened to
higher views of things.
```

continues

continued

In such a country, you will perceive at once that it is impossible that
there should be anything of what you call a "solid" kind; but I dare
say you will suppose that we could at least distinguish by sight the
Triangles, Squares, and other figures, moving about as I have described
them. On the contrary, we could see nothing of the kind, not at least
so as to distinguish one figure from another. Nothing was visible, nor
could be visible, to us, except Straight Lines; and the necessity of
this I will speedily demonstrate.

The *panic* Function

When you are working with files, it is important to be aware that problems can happen,
such as not finding a file where it is expected. You can use the panic function to signal
an error or an unexpected behavior in the program. panic is mostly used to signal to the
program to fail when there are errors that you aren't sure how to handle. For example, in
Listing 20.2 you use the ReadFile function to read a file using a filename. You then use the
panic function to fail the program.

LISTING 20.2

Using the panic function

```
package main

import (
    "os"
    "fmt"
)

func main() {
    data, err := ioutil.ReadFile("badFileName.txt")
    if err != nil {
        panic(err)
    }

    // Won't get here if there is an error reading file
    fmt.Print(string(data))
}
```

The output will look something like this:

```
panic: open badFileName.txt: The system cannot find the file specified.

goroutine 1 [running]:
main.main()
        C:/Users/User/Documents/GoLang/abc.go:14 +0x97
exit status 2
```

Essentially, a program does not necessarily stop running when it encounters an error. You use the panic function to force the program to stop, allowing the program to exit gracefully.

Reading a Subset of a File

In many cases, you don't want to use the entire file. Go gives you options for retrieving only parts of a file. In modern computer systems, each string character is represented by a byte. You can use this unit to retrieve sets of characters from a text file.

In Listing 20.3, instead of reading an entire file, you retrieve the first five letters from your file. Note that you are again using the flatland01.txt file in the same folder as your Go program.

LISTING 20.3

Reading bytes from a file

```
package main

import (
    "fmt"
    "os"
)

func main() {
    f, err := os.Open("flatland01.txt")

    if err != nil {
        fmt.Println(err) // if there is an error, print it
    }
```

continues

continued

```
    // create a slice of bytes
    b1 := make([]byte, 5)
    data, err := f.Read(b1)

    // feedback message in case of error; otherwise nil
    if err != nil {
        fmt.Println(err) // if there is an error, print it
    }

    // display the slice
    fmt.Println(string(b1[:data]))

    // close the file after completing the operations
    f.Close()
}
```

If you didn't have any errors opening or reading the file, then the output will look something like this:

```
FLATL
```

There are some differences here from the example in Listing 20.1. First, you are using the os library rather than the io/ioutil library. The os library includes file management tools. You see this in the call to open the file:

```
f, err := os.Open("flatland01.txt")
```

In this listing, you are retrieving the first 5 bytes of data from the file. Because this is a text file, those bytes are characters in the file. In the listing, you create a slice of five items of type byte, which you name b1. You then use this slice to read from your file:

```
b1 := make([]byte, 5)
data, err := f.Read(b1)
```

With the file read, you then check to see if there was an error (err != nil). If so, the error is printed. After checking for an error, you then display the contents of the slice.

The final operation is to close the file that you opened. You do so by calling the close method on the file:

```
f.Close()
```

When you execute the listing using the flatland01.txt file, the first five characters are displayed as follows:

```
FLATL
```

The *defer* Statement

In Listing 20.3, the file was closed before exiting the program. It is important when you open a file that you also close it. In longer listings, however, something could happen between the time that you open a file and when you get to the close statement that could cause your program to prematurely exit. This would mean the file didn't get closed, which might cause an issue with it. To help ensure that a file gets closed, you can use the defer statement.

A defer statement postpones the execution of a function until the surrounding function returns, either normally or through panic. This means that the delayed function will execute last in the main function, regardless of the order in which the functions appear in the program. Listing 20.4 presents a simple example of using defer.

LISTING 20.4

Using *defer*

```
package main

import (
    "fmt"
)

func main() {
    defer fmt.Println("Hello")
    fmt.Println("World")
}
```

Because the Println command for "Hello" is deferred, the output looks like this:

```
World
Hello
```

By using the defer statement, you can add a file close statement after you open or create a file rather than later in the listing. This will make sure the file then gets closed if something unexpected happens. You'll see this in use in the later listings in this lesson.

Reading a File from a Specific Starting Point

While the first few characters of a file may be useful for identifying the contents of a file, you often need to retrieve specific parts of a file. The Seek function allows you to specify a start location in a file and go from there. Listing 20.5 uses the os.Seek function to do a 100-byte offset. You then read 20 characters starting from that point.

LISTING 20.5

Using the *Seek* function

```
package main

import (
    "fmt"
    "os"
)

func main() {
    f, err := os.Open("flatland01.txt")
    if err != nil {
        fmt.Println(err)
    }

    // Close the file when program is done
    defer f.Close()

    // skip the first 100 bytes
    s, err := f.Seek(100, 0)

    if err != nil {  // if there is an error, print it
        fmt.Println(err)
    }

    // display the offset
    fmt.Println(s)
```

```
// read 20 bytes starting from the offset
data := make([]byte, 20)
n, err := f.Read(data)

if err != nil {  // if no error, then err is nil
    fmt.Println(err) // if there is an error, print it
}

fmt.Println("Bytes read", n)
fmt.Println("Reading starting from byte >>", s, ":", string(data[:n]))
}
```

If there were no errors, then the output is:

```
100
bytes read 20
Reading starting from byte 100>> : d, not because we ca
```

This program moves to the 100th byte (or character, in this case) by using the Seek function. By passing the value of 100 to Seek, you will move 100 characters forward in the file. By passing 0 for the second parameter of the Seek function, you indicate that Seek should shift from the beginning of the file.

After calling the Seek function, you verify there was no error. If there was, you print the error. You then print the value of s that was returned from the Seek function. This indicates the current offset from within the file, in this case, 100. With your position shifted in the file, you then call the Read function to read into your variable called data that you defined. Finally, you print the information before closing your file and ending the program.

Note that by passing 0 to the Seek function as the second parameter, you shifted from the beginning of the file. You could also have moved from your current location by passing 1, or from the end of the file by passing 2.

Buffered Reader

When you're working with very large files, it can be useful to buffer data as it is read from one place to another place, such as from one file to another. This allows you to put the read data in a safe place while you wait for the CPU to move the data. Buffering operations are in the bufio package in Go.

Listing 20.6 uses the bufio.NewReader function to create a buffered reader. It then uses the Peek function to access the first five characters in the data file.

LISTING 20.6

Using a buffered reader

```
package main

import (
    "bufio"
    "fmt"
    "os"
)

func main() {
    f, err := os.Open("flatland01.txt")
    if err != nil {
        panic(err)
    }

    br := bufio.NewReader(f)  // create a buffered reader
    data, err2 := br.Peek(5)  // read 5 bytes

    if err2 != nil {
        fmt.Println(err)
    }

    // display the peeked data
    fmt.Println(string(data))
}
```

Peeking at data is a way to take a quick look at a file without having to open the file completely. In this listing, you open your file again but then create a buffered reader by passing your file handle to bufio.NewReader. You can then use the Peek function with this buffered reader to read from the file. In this case, you pass 5 to br.Peek, which reads the first 5 bytes. You then print:

```
FLATL
```

Reading a File Line by Line

You can also analyze the data in a file using lines. A line is a string of text from one edge of the file to the other edge. In normal text files, lines are often arbitrary in that they correspond mainly to the width of the editor window used to create the file. For other file types, lines can be significant. For example, in a CSV file, each line typically corresponds to a record of data.

Listing 20.7 includes steps to read data from an existing file line by line using the `bufio.ScanLines` function, which stores the lines in a slice. You then read the contents of the slice to see the lines.

LISTING 20.7

Reading lines

```
package main

import (
    "bufio"
    "fmt"
    "os"
)

func main() {
    file, err := os.Open("flatland01.txt")
    if err != nil {
        // if error is not nil, panic
        panic("File not found")
    }

    // Close the file when program is done
    defer file.Close()


    // create a scanner to read from file and split text based on lines
    scanner := bufio.NewScanner(file)
    scanner.Split(bufio.ScanLines)

    // create a slice, which will contain the lines read from file
    var lines []string

    // use Scan to iterate through the file
    for scanner.Scan() {
        // append the current line to the slice lines
        lines = append(lines, scanner.Text())
    }
```

continues

continued

```
  // iterate through lines
  for _, line := range lines {
    fmt.Println("line:", line)
  }
}
```

The output from running this listing is as follows:

```
line: FLATLAND
line:
line: PART 1
line:
line: THIS WORLD
line:
line: SECTION 1  Of the Nature of Flatland
line:
line: I call our world Flatland, not because we call it so, but to make its
line: nature clearer to you, my happy readers, who are privileged to live in
line: Space.
line:
line: Imagine a vast sheet of paper on which straight Lines, Triangles,
line: Squares, Pentagons, Hexagons, and other figures, instead of remaining
line: fixed in their places, move freely about, on or in the surface, but
line: without the power of rising above or sinking below it, very much like
line: shadows--only hard with luminous edges--and you will then have a pretty
line: correct notion of my country and countrymen.  Alas, a few years ago, I
line: should have said "my universe:" but now my mind has been opened to
line: higher views of things.
line:
line: In such a country, you will perceive at once that it is impossible that
line: there should be anything of what you call a "solid" kind; but I dare
line: say you will suppose that we could at least distinguish by sight the
line: Triangles, Squares, and other figures, moving about as I have described
line: them.  On the contrary, we could see nothing of the kind, not at least
line: so as to distinguish one figure from another.  Nothing was visible, nor
line: could be visible, to us, except Straight Lines; and the necessity of
line: this I will speedily demonstrate.
```

NOTE In the output, lines with no content are read as separate lines.

In this code, you again use the os.Open function to open your file and create a handle called file to use to access the file. Because you are going to read the file line by line, you create a scanner to read from the file. You do this by passing your open file handle to the `bufio.NewScanner` function. You then take your scanner and split it into lines by calling the `Split` function and passing `bufio.ScanLines`:

```
scanner.Split(bufio.ScanLines)
```

With your file now broken into lines, you can read each line by calling the `Scan` function on your scanner. Within the listing, you use a `for` loop to iterate through the file, scanning for each line and adding it to the slice called `lines` that you created. After adding all the lines from the file to the `lines` slice, you close the file. You end the listing by doing another `for` loop that iterates through your new `lines` slice and prints each line with the text `line:` before it.

WRITING TO A FILE

In addition to reading existing files, you often need to write data to a new file. You use the `ioutil.WriteFile` function for this purpose. Listing 20.8 starts with a string, converts the characters of the string to UTF-8 byte representations, writes the data to a new file, and reads the new file.

LISTING 20.8

Writing to a file

```
package main

import (
    "fmt"
    "io/ioutil"
)

func main() {
    // create a slice of bytes (UTF-8 code) from an input string
    data := []byte("Hello, world!")

    fmt.Println(data) // display the slice
```

continues

continued

```go
    // feedback message in case of error
    err := ioutil.WriteFile("new_file.txt", data, 0644)
    if err != nil {
        panic("cannot write file: " + err.Error())
    }

    new_file, err := ioutil.ReadFile("new_file.txt")

    // feedback message in case of error
    if err != nil {
        panic("cannot read file: " + err.Error())
    }

    // convert the file contents to a string and display them
    fmt.Print(string(new_file))
}
```

There are a few things to note about this code. First, you create a slice called data. This slice includes only UTF-8 byte values to represent the characters in the original string. When you print the data slice, you see the values of the characters:

```
[72 101 108 108 111 44 32 119 111 114 108 100 33]
```

You use the WriteFile function to create a file with the specified path. If the file does not already exist, it will be created. If the file does exist, the existing file will be overwritten. In the function, you specify data as the source, so Go will write the values from data into the new file. You also need to include 0644 as the permission setting on the file. It will grant read/write access to the current user but read-only access for any other user.

NOTE You can find more information on file permissions in Appendix, "File Permissions and Access Rights."

You then read the new file into a variable called new_file. Note that the UTF-8 bytes are reconverted to string characters when you read the file. When you print new_file as a string, you see the contents of your file. The full output from the listing should be as follows:

```
[72 101 108 108 111 44 32 119 111 114 108 100 33]
Hello, world!
```

> **NOTE** This listing assumes that the file is being written to an existing folder
> or directory. Since you are writing to the current folder, you know the folder
> exists. If you try to write the file to a folder that does not exist, an error will
> be given. For example, if the subfolder `datafiles` didn't exist and you tried
> to do the following, you'd get an error:
>
> ```
> err := ioutil.WriteFile("./datafiles/new_file.txt", data, 0644)
> ```
>
> We'll show you how to create a directory later in this lesson.

Creating a New File

In the previous example, you used the `WriteFile` function to both create a new file and
write data to that file in the same operation. In some cases, you simply want to create a
new file that you can add data to later. You can use the `os.Create` function for this purpose. In Listing 20.9 you create a new file and write data into that file as a separate step.

LISTING 20.9

Creating and writing separately

```go
package main

import (
    "fmt"
    "os"
)

func main() {
    data := "Hello, world!"
    fmt.Println("data string:", data)

    // create a new file
    f, err := os.Create("another_file.txt")

    // display the new file
    if err != nil {
        panic("cannot create file: " + err.Error())
    }
```

continues

continued

```
    // Close the file when program is done
    defer f.Close()

    fmt.Println("new file:", f)

    // write the string to the new file
    n, err := f.WriteString(data)
    if err != nil {
        panic("cannot write to file: " + err.Error())
    }
    fmt.Println("characters in file:", n)
}
```

In this example, the `os.Create` function creates a new, empty file in the named path. If there is already a file with that name in the same location, the existing file is truncated and replaced. This function automatically assigns permission 0666 to the new file.

You then write data to the file after the file has been created. In this case, you are writing a string to the file by passing the string called `data` to the `WriteString` function. The output is as follows:

```
data string: Hello, world!
new file: &{0xc0000cc780}
characters in file: 13
```

> **NOTE** The value printed for new file will be an address, so what you see will be different from the output shown here.

Buffered Writer

As you have learned, you can use a buffer to hold read data temporarily while you transfer data from one place to another. You can also buffer data that will be written. In Listing 20.10 you create a string and a new file, and then use a buffered writer to add the string to the file.

LISTING 20.10

Using a buffered writer

```
package main

import (
```

```go
    "bufio"
    "fmt"
    "os"
    "io/ioutil"
)

func main() {
    data :="Hello, world!!!"
    fmt.Println("original string:", data)

    // create a new file
    f, err := os.Create("another_file.txt")
    if err != nil {
        panic("cannot create file: " + err.Error())
    }

    // Close the file when program is done
    defer f.Close()

    // create a buffered writer that we can use to write data to the new file
    bw := bufio.NewWriter(f)

    // write the data to the buffered writer
    n, err := bw.WriteString(data)

    if err != nil {
        panic("cannot write string: " + err.Error())
    }

    // display the number of bytes written
    fmt.Println("bytes written:", n)

    // flush flushes/submits the data to the underlying io.Writer
    bw.Flush()

    newFile, err := ioutil.ReadFile("another_file.txt")

    // feedback message in case of error
    if err != nil {
        panic("cannot read file: " + err.Error())
    }

    // convert the file contents to a string and display it
    fmt.Print("file contents: ", string(newFile))
}
```

When this listing is executed, the output should be as follows:

```
original string: Hello, world!!!
bytes written: 15
file contents: Hello, world!!!
```

In this program you create a string called `data` and assign it a value. You then display that string to confirm that it has been assigned to your variable.

You then create the file calling `os.Create`. As you've done before, if there is an error, you will display it and exit the program. You then create a buffered writer using `bufio.NewWriter` and passing your file handle, `f`. Your buffered writer is then used to write data using the `WriteString` function. In this case, you pass your string stored in `data` to the function:

```
n, err := bw.WriteString(data)
```

At this point, the string is written to the buffer. The `WriteString` function will return the number of characters written and an error code (or `nil` if there is no error). You display the number of characters written, which is 15 in this case. Finally, you use `Flush` to transfer the data from the buffer to the new file.

In the rest of the listing, you read the file using `ReadFile` and display the contents to confirm that the information was indeed written to the file.

NOTE It is important to understand that by using buffering, no data is added to the new file until the `Flush` function is executed.

WORKING WITH DIRECTORIES

In addition to creating files, the `os` package allows you to work with directories. You can do a variety of actions, including the following:

- Creating a directory
- Deleting a directory
- Creating a directory tree
- Listing directory contents
- Changing a directory

In this section, we'll cover examples of each of these. We will then pull the information all together into an example.

Creating a Directory

Let's start by covering how to create a new directory or folder. This can be done with the os.Mkdir function. In Listing 20.11 you create a new directory in the current directory.

> **NOTE** The words "folder" and "directory" may be used interchangeably.

LISTING 20.11

Creating a directory

```
package main

import (
    "os"
)

func main() {
    // create a directory
    err := os.Mkdir("./test_directory", 0755) // will throw an error if the
directory exists

    // if there is an error then panic to fail program
    if err != nil {
        panic(err)
    }
}
```

In this listing, you use the os.Mkdir function to create a directory called *test_directory* that will be located within the current directory. You assign the 0755 permissions to the new directory. If you build and run this code, you will see the new directory in your computer's file management system.

It is important to note, however, that you cannot use Mkdir to overwrite an existing directory. If you run this program a second time, you will encounter an error:

```
panic: mkdir ./test_directory: Cannot create a file when that file already
exists.
```

> **NOTE** You are creating a directory within the current directory. As mentioned at the beginning of the lesson, you can use a different path to create a directory as well. For example, you could add a directory to your documents folder to hold files by passing the path to your documents folder, such as /Users/*username*/Documents/new_directory, where *username* is your username.

Deleting a Directory

You can delete an existing directory using os.RemoveAll, which removes the directory and all its contents. If you add this command at the beginning of the previous program, you can run the program as many times as you wish, because it will delete the directory before re-creating it. Listing 20.12 includes this change.

LISTING 20.12

Deleting an existing directory

```
package main

import (
    "os"
)

func main() {
    // delete directory and all contents
    os.RemoveAll("./test_directory")

    // create a directory
    err := os.Mkdir("./test_directory", 0755)

    // if there is an error then panic to fail program
    if err != nil {
        panic(err)
    }
}
```

This listing is the same as Listing 20.10, with the addition of the following line:

```
os.RemoveAll("./test_directory")
```

This line removes the directory that is passed, which in this case is ./test_directory, if it exists. If the directory doesn't exist, the program simply continues.

NOTE With great power comes great responsibility. When you remove a directory, its contents will be removed as well. You should make sure you are aware of what you are removing.

Creating a Directory Tree

You saw how to create a single new directory earlier. You can also create a series of nested directories by using the os.MkdirAll function. This is illustrated in Listing 20.13.

LISTING 20.13

Making a series of directories

```go
package main

import (
    "os"
)

func main() {
    // delete directory and all contents
    os.RemoveAll("./test_directory")

    // create a directory
    err := os.Mkdir("./test_directory", 0755)
    // if there is an error then panic to fail program
    if err != nil {
        panic(err)
    }
```

continues

continued

```
    // MkdirAll creates a tree of directories
    err = os.MkdirAll("./test_directory/another_directory/third_directory", 0755)
    // if there is an error then panic to fail program
    if err != nil {
        panic(err)
    }
}
```

After running this program, check your computer for the tree of nested directories created here. You should have the directories added within the directory where the program is executed.

Listing Directory Contents

The function ioutil.ReadDir retrieves a list of items in a directory/folder. Listing 20.14 shows the ReadDir in action to list the files in the *test_directory* you've been creating in this lesson.

LISTING 20.14

Listing a directory's contents

```
package main

import (
    "os"
    "io/ioutil"
    "fmt"
)

func main() {
    // delete directory and all contents
    os.RemoveAll("./test_directory")

    // create a directory
    err := os.Mkdir("./test_directory", 0755)
    // if there is an error then panic to fail program
    if err != nil {
        panic(err)
    }
```

```
// MkdirAll creates a tree of directories
err = os.MkdirAll("./test_directory/another_directory/third_directory", 0755)
// if there is an error then panic to fail program
if err != nil {
    panic(err)
}

// list content of a directory
content, err := ioutil.ReadDir("./")
// if there is an error then panic to fail program
if err != nil {
  panic(err)
}
// iterate through content
for _, item := range content {
  fmt.Println(" ", item.Name(), item.IsDir())
}
}
```

In this example, the first part of the listing is what was done In the previous listing. After removing and creating directories, you then add a call to `ioutil.ReadDir`. You pass the path of the current directory (`./`); however, you could pass the path of any directory on your system. You save the list that is returned from reading the directory into a variable called content, and you then use a `for` loop to display the individual items. In addition to displaying the individual items using the `Name` function, you use a call to the function `IsDir` to determine if the item is a directory. This is a Boolean check that will return `true` or `false` depending on whether or not the item is a directory. Here's an example of the output:

```
another_file.txt false
datafiles true
flatland01.txt false
new_file.txt false
test_directory true
```

Changing a Directory

Most of the examples up to this point have used the current, active directory as the starting point for writing files or creating directories. You can use `os.Chdir` to change the active directory in use in a program, as shown in Listing 20.15.

LISTING 20.15

Changing the active directory

```go
package main

import (
  "os"
  "io/ioutil"
  "fmt"
)

func main() {
  // delete directory and all contents
  os.RemoveAll("./test_directory")

  // MkdirAll creates a tree of directories
  if err := os.MkdirAll("./test_directory/another_directory/third_directory",
0755); err != nil {
    panic(err)    // if there is an error then panic to fail program

  }

  // change the working directory
  if err := os.Chdir("./test_directory/another_directory/third_directory");
err != nil {
    panic(err)     // if there is an error then panic to fail program

  }

  // create a file in this directory
  data := []byte("Hello, world!")
  if err := ioutil.WriteFile("new_file.txt", data, 0644); err != nil {
    panic(err)   // if there is an error then panic to fail program
  }

  // list content of a directory
  content, err := ioutil.ReadDir("./")
  // if there is an error then panic to fail program
  If err != nil {
    panic(err)     // if there is an error then panic to fail program

  }
  // iterate through content
  for _, item := range content {
```

```
    fmt.Println(" ", item.Name(), item.IsDir())
  }
}
```

This listing uses a lot of what was covered earlier in this lesson. You start by removing your `test_directory` and anything contained within it. This is followed by creating a directory tree as you've done before. You then, however, use `os.Chdir` to change to the subdirectories you created. The result is that you change to the `third_directory` folder that is below `another_directory`, which is below our `test_directory`.

While this illustrates at this point in the code that you changed directories, the listing continues by creating a file called `new_file.txt` using `WriteFile`. If you use your computer's file manager, this new file will indeed be found in `third_directory`.

In the listing, you continue by then listing the files in the directory in the same way you did earlier. The result is that the new file you just created will be shown. Because you just created this directory and navigated to it, the new file will be the only thing listed:

```
new_file.txt false
```

Temporary Files and Directories

In the previous listing, you created a test file. Because you don't really need the file after the listing runs, you could have added another call to `os.RemoveAll` at the end of the listing to remove the directories and file you created:

```
os.RemoveAll("./test_directory")
```

Creating temporary files like this is common in programs. Because it is so common, there is a way to create temporary files and directories that are handled by the operating system. The operating system will automatically delete these temporary files based on system settings.

Listing 20.16 shows an example of `ioutil.TempFile`, which creates a temporary file, and of `ioutil.TempDir`, which creates a temporary directory.

LISTING 20.16

Creating a temporary file and a temporary directory

```
package main

import (
```

continues

continued

```go
    "fmt"
    "io/ioutil"
    "os"
)

func main() {
    // create a new temporary file
    f, err := ioutil.TempFile("./", "file")
    if err != nil {
        panic(err)
    }

    // The OS will clean up this temporary file by itself
    // at some point but we can do it anyway for safety
    defer os.Remove(f.Name())

    // we can see the pattern added to the end of the temp filename
    fmt.Println("File name:", f.Name())

    // add data to the file
    f.WriteString("Hello!\n")
    f.WriteString("This file will be deleted once the program is done executing.\n")
    f.WriteString("The advantage of using temp files is that they don't pollute
the file system.\n")
    f.WriteString("Don't use temp files to persist data because they will be
deleted by the OS at some point.\n")

    // read the new file
    tempContents, _ := ioutil.ReadFile(f.Name())
    fmt.Print(string(tempContents))

    // create a new temporary directory
    d, err := ioutil.TempDir("./", "tempdir")
    if err != nil {
        panic(err)
    }

    // The OS will delete temp directory at some point but we
    // can do it anyway
    defer os.RemoveAll(d)

    // print the temporary directory name
    fmt.Println("Directory name:", d)
}
```

`TempFile` creates a new temporary file in the named path and opens the file for reading and writing. The filename is generated using the format of the word `file` followed by a random string of numbers to the end. You can use this file as you would any other file, including adding new content and reading that content.

`TempDir` creates a new temporary directory using very similar steps to those used to create a temporary file, including the use of a naming structure. In this case, the names will start with `"tempdir"` followed by a string of numbers.

Because these items are created as temporary objects, the OS will automatically delete them at some point in time. However, you include deferred `Remove` and `RemoveAll` functions to make sure they are deleted when you no longer need them.

If you build and run this program, you will see output that looks like this:

```
File name: ./file623023391
Hello!
This file will be deleted once the program is done executing.
The advantage of using temp files is that they don't pollute the file system.
Don't use temp files to persist data because they will be deleted by the OS at
some point.
Directory name: ./tempdir824820722
```

COMMAND-LINE ARGUMENTS

Many programs allow the user to include specific arguments when they run the program. These arguments can control how the program runs but are not included in the program itself. Common examples include running a program as an admin (rather than as the default user) or specifying a working directory or other external variables for the program to use, such as the location of a stored file.

You typically use the command line to run a program that supports additional arguments. Listing 20.17 shows an example of a program that includes command-line arguments, which are defined using the os.Args function.

LISTING 20.17

Using command-line arguments

```
package main

import (
```

continues

continued

```
    "fmt"
    "os"
)

func main() {
    args := os.Args
    programName := args[0]
    arguments := args[1:]
    fmt.Println(programName)
    fmt.Println(arguments)
}
```

This program is set up to handle command-line arguments. In the listing, you grab the arguments using os.Args and place them in a slice. The slice will contain the name of the program itself and an additional argument whose value will be passed into the program at runtime.

In the listing, you assign the first element of the args slice to a variable called programName, since you know it contains the program name along with its path. Any remaining command-line arguments from the slice will be in args from index position 1 to the end of the slice. You assign these to a variable called arguments and then print the values from your two variables.

If you run this program from the command line with no arguments, the output will show the program name. To fully test it, run it with several arguments from the command line using a statement like this:

```
go run program_name.go argument1 argument2 argument3
```

In this case, program_name.go should be the name you give your program. Go will map the arguments (starting with the program name) in the order provided and use the values when it runs the program. The output in this case will be something similar to the following:

```
C:\Users\username\AppData\Local\Temp\go-build1651887209\b001\exe\
program_name.exe
[argument1 argument2 argument3]
```

SUMMARY

This lesson showed you how to read and write to files, how to work with directories and files within the operating system, how to create and use temporary files, and how to use command-line arguments with your programs. It is by being able to persist data to a file that you can make your Go programs more useful and user-friendly. Of course, one thing to remember with working with directories and folders is that you don't overwrite or delete something you intend to keep. As such, it is important to make sure you test your code.

EXERCISES

The following exercises are provided to allow you to experiment with the tools and concepts presented in this lesson. For each exercise, write a program that meets the specified requirements and verify that the program runs as expected. The exercises are:

Exercise 20.1: Text Filing

Exercise 20.2: Jumping Around

Exercise 20.3: Counting Letters

Exercise 20.4: Copying a File

Exercise 20.5: Copying a File, Take 2

Exercise 20.6: Burger Shop

> **NOTE** The exercises are for your benefit. The exercises help you apply what you learn in the lessons. You are also encouraged to experiment with the code as you complete the exercises.

Exercise 20.1: Text Filing

Find or create a text file and practice reading it using the various methods learned in this lesson:

- Add a prompt that allows the user to enter the file path when the program runs.
- Apply string functions (such as changing the case) to the text and write the data to a new file.
- Try to read a non-text file and see what is displayed.
- Experiment with other text-only file formats, such as CSV and JSON.

> **NOTE** Project Gutenberg (located at www.gutenberg.org) is an excellent site for text files that are in the public domain, especially if you just want to experiment with data processing. Many of the files are rather large, however, so you may want to edit them down to a more manageable size.

Exercise 20.2: Jumping Around

Rewrite Listing 20.4 to accomplish each of the following. Each task can be a separate program:

- Read 20 characters starting 200 positions from the beginning of the file.
- Read 20 characters from 100 positions into the file, but then also read 20 more characters from the 200th position in the file. For the second read, seek from the current position (after reading the 20 characters) rather than from the beginning of the file. Do the second 20 characters match what you returned from the previous bullet?
- Read 20 characters starting 100 positions from the end of the file.
- Read the first 10 characters of the file, then skip the next 10 characters. Do this through the entire file to where every group of 10 characters is being displayed.

Exercise 20.3: Counting Letters

Create a program to read the flatlands01.txt file. After reading the file, print out the number of times each character in the alphabet is used. Ignore case, so that "a" and "A" are counted together. The results should list each letter of the alphabet and its number of occurrences.

Exercise 20.4: Copying a File

Create a program called copyfile that takes one command-line argument. The argument should be the name of a file. The program should read the file and write a copy of the file. The copy should use the same name, but include the extension .copy. For example, if you ran the program passing the flatland01.txt file:

```
Copyfile flatland01.txt
```

then you should have an additional new file called flatland01.txt.copy after the program runs. The new file should be an exact copy of the original.

Exercise 20.5: Copying a File, Take 2

Modify the listing in the previous exercise so that if two filenames are passed on the command line, the new file uses the second filename passed.

Exercise 20.6: Burger Shop

Modify the Burger Shop program from Lesson 16, "Pulling It All Together: Building a Burger Shop," so that it saves all completed orders to a file called OrderHistory.txt. Before writing each order to the file, write a line that indicates a new order is starting. This can be done with something similar to the following:

```
<NEWORDER_#####_DateAndTime>
```

You can replace the ##### with a sequential number that is one more than the last order number used in the file. You can replace *DateAndTime* with the current date and time when the order was initially saved.

Lesson 21
Pulling It All Together: Word Analysis in Go

I n this lesson, you will apply what you've learned up to this point to perform a common text analysis process using Go. Specifically, you will build a program that takes a dataset of e-commerce reviews and analyzes them to calculate the number of times each word appears.

LEARNING OBJECTIVES

By the end of this lesson, you will be able to build a project that can:

- Read a JSON file that contains a list of online e-commerce reviews.
- Tokenize each review in the dataset.
- Compute word count in each review in the dataset.

EXAMINING THE DATA

When you start any data analysis process, the first step is to ensure that the data is in a format that your system can use and ensure that the data is available for use. For our project, you will need to download the data. You'll use the Digital Music review set from Julian McAuley's Amazon product data website, which can be found at http://jmcauley.ucsd.edu/data/amazon. This file, reviews.json, can also be found in the downloadable zip file for this book, which can be found at www.wiley.com/go/jobreadygo. The data is in the file reviews_Digital_Music_5.json.gz and will need to be extracted.

> **NOTE** You must extract the downloaded file before you can use it. In macOS or Linux, open the file and it will extract automatically. For Windows users, we recommend using 7-zip to extract the file; you'll find 7-zip at www.7-zip.org.

This file is in a modified JSON format. If you open the extracted file using any text editor, the first two records look like this:

```
{"reviewerID": "A3EBHHCZO6V2A4", "asin": "5555991584", "reviewerName":
"Amaranth \"music fan\"", "helpful": [3, 3], "reviewText": "It's hard to
believe \"Memory of Trees\" came out 11 years ago;it has held up well over
the passage of time.It's Enya's last great album before the New Age/pop of
\"Amarantine\" and \"Day without rain.\" Back in 1995,Enya still had her
creative spark,her own voice.I agree with the reviewer who said that this
is her saddest album;it is melancholy,bittersweet,from the opening title
song.\"Memory of Trees\" is elegaic&majestic.;\"Pax Deorum\" sounds like it
is from a Requiem Mass,it is a dark threnody.Unlike the reviewer who said
that this has a \"disconcerting\" blend of spirituality&sensuality;,I don't
find it disconcerting at all.\"Anywhere is\" is a hopeful song,looking to
possibilities.\"Hope has a place\" is about love,but it is up to the listener
to decide if it is romantic,platonic,etc.I've always had a soft spot for
this song.\"On my way home\" is a triumphant ending about return.This is
truly a masterpiece of New Age music,a must for any Enya fan!", "overall":
5.0, "summary": "Enya's last great album", "unixReviewTime": 1158019200,
"reviewTime": "09 12, 2006"}
{"reviewerID": "AZPWAXJG9OJXV", "asin": "5555991584", "reviewerName":
"bethtexas", "helpful": [0, 0], "reviewText": "A clasically-styled and
introverted album, Memory of Trees is a masterpiece of subtlety.  Many of
the songs have an endearing shyness to them - soft piano and a lovely, quiet
voice.  But within every introvert is an inferno, and Enya lets that fire
```

explode on a couple of songs that absolutely burst with an expected raw power. If you've never heard Enya before, you might want to start with one of her more popularized works, like Watermark, just to play it safe. But if you're already a fan, then your collection is not complete without this beautiful work of musical art.", "overall": 5.0, "summary": "Enya at her most elegant", "unixReviewTime": 991526400, "reviewTime": "06 3, 2001"}

Each record is enclosed in curly brackets ({}), and the records are separated by new lines. In standard JSON, each record would be enclosed in square brackets ([ ]). Your code will need to take this into account when you import the data to be analyzed.

The fields in each record include a name and value using a colon (:) as the separator:

"reviewerID": "A3EBHHCZO6V2A4"

The fields are separated by commas:

"reviewerID": "A3EBHHCZO6V2A4", "asin": "5555991584"

For this analysis, we are most interested in the reviews themselves. The review of the first record looks like the following:

"reviewText": "It's hard to believe \"Memory of Trees\" came out 11 years ago;it has held up well over the passage of time.It's Enya's last great album before the New Age/pop of \"Amarantine\" and \"Day without rain.\" Back in 1995,Enya still had her creative spark,her own voice. I agree with the reviewer who said that this is her saddest album;it is melancholy,bittersweet,from the opening title song.\"Memory of Trees\" is elegaic&majestic.;\"Pax Deorum\" sounds like it is from a Requiem Mass,it is a dark threnody.Unlike the reviewer who said that this has a \"disconcerting\" blend of spirituality&sensuality;,I don't find it disconcerting at all.\"Anywhere is\" is a hopeful song,looking to possibilities.\"Hope has a place\" is about love,but it is up to the listener to decide if it is romantic,platonic,etc.I've always had a soft spot for this song.\"On my way home\" is a triumphant ending about return.This is truly a masterpiece of New Age music,a must for any Enya fan!"

You can see that in addition to words, the text includes punctuation. While you can use spaces as one option for separating and identifying distinct words in the data, you can also use punctuation.

Because the focus of our project is to count the number of times a word appears, you have another problem with the raw data. Some words are capitalized and others are not. Keeping in mind that Go is case-sensitive, you also want to normalize the text so that it is all in lowercase, so that both *hope* and *Hope* are considered the same word.

READING THE REVIEW DATA

Now that you have looked at the data and identified what you want your code to do, you're ready to start writing code.

In the previous lessons, you didn't have to know how to read a JSON file, but the concept is fairly similar to our use case. Let's look at the function `read_json_file` in Listing 21.1.

LISTING 21.1

The `read_json_file` function

```
func read_json_file( filepath string) {
   // read the json file using the os package
   content, err := os.Open(filepath)
   // if we have an error, we log the error and exit the program
   if err != nil {
      log.Fatal(err)
   }
   // defer closing the file until the read_json_file function finishes
   defer content.Close()
   // create a scanner variable that we will use to iterate through the reviews
   scanner := bufio.NewScanner(content)
   // split the content of the file based on lines (each line is a review)
   scanner.Split(bufio.ScanLines)
}
```

The `read_json_file` function takes as an input the file path. The function uses the `os` package to read the file using the `Open` function.

Next, the code checks to see if an error occurred. If that's the case, you log/display the error and the program is terminated. Otherwise, the file is valid, and you can proceed to read it.

Because you are opening a file, you also want to make sure it gets closed. The listing defers closing the file until the function finishes executing.

To read the file, you will leverage the NewScanner function from the bufio package to create a scanner called scanner. If you look closely, our JSON file is structured in a way where each review in the JSON file is on a separate line. Thus, you will need to split the text based on lines using the Split function from scanner.

At this point, all the function does is read the file and split the JSON file based on new lines. The next step will be to iterate and scan the lines in the text. Add the code shown in Listing 21.2 to the same read_json_file function.

LISTING 21.2

Expanding read_json_file

```go
func read_json_file(filepath string) {
    // read the json file using the os package
    content, err := os.Open(filepath)
    // if we have an error, we log the error and exit the program
    if err != nil {
        log.Fatal(err)
    }
    // defer closing the file until the read_json_file function finishes
    defer content.Close()
    // create a scanner variable that we will use to iterate
    //    through the reviews
    scanner := bufio.NewScanner(content)
    // split the content of the file based on lines (each line is a review)
    scanner.Split(bufio.ScanLines)
    for scanner.Scan() {
        // We can iterate through and display each review
        //fmt.Println(scanner.Text()) // This is commented; otherwise, it will
                                    // print the entire file, which will take
                                    // a while. Uncomment if you want to see
                                    // the content of the file.
    }
}
```

The code adds a `for` loop that iterates and scans each line using the `Scan` function, and then it prints each line. Note that in the listing, you have commented out the `Println` function. You will need to uncomment it (remove the //) to see the data actually print. The entire contents of the file will be printed, which can take a while.

It's important to remember that at this point, you are still reading each review as a string. The string represents the bulk of the JSON version of the review. You will have to convert that string into a valid representation where you can access all the attributes of the review easily. In this case, using structs sounds like the best choice. Go ahead and model the JSON review using structs, as shown in Listing 21.3.

LISTING 21.3

Structs for modeling our JSON

```
type Review struct {
    ReviewerID     string   `json:"reviewerID"`
    Asin           string   `json:"asin"`
    ReviewerName   string   `json:"reviewerName"`
    Helpful        [2]int   `json:"helpful"`
    ReviewText     string   `json:"reviewText"`
    Overall        float32  `json:"overall"`
    Summary        string   `json:"summary"`
    UnixReviewTime int64    `json:"unixReviewTime"`
    ReviewTime     string   `json:"reviewTime"`
}
```

As Listing 21.3 shows, the `Review` struct represents the different fields in the JSON review. For each field, you use the appropriate data type. For instance, the `helpful` field must be `[2]int` to be parsed correctly. (If you choose `string`, then the JSON won't parse.)

Going back to the reviews, each review is defined as:

```
var review Review
```

The goal now is to take the string representation of the JSON review and convert it into the `Review` struct that you've defined. This is where the `json` package comes into play. The `json` package allows you to encode and decode JSON objects. In our example, it will allow you to convert the string into a valid review represented by the `Review` struct in Listing 21.3.

To do that we will need to use the `Unmarshal` function, which has the following format:

```
json.Unmarshal(data []byte, v interface{}) error
```

As it can be seen, the `Unmarshal` function takes as input the data that we want to unmarshal. The function will parse the JSON data and store the results in the value of v. In our case, v is the review (or the struct defined earlier in this case). The type of v is an interface that is empty (called *empty interface*). The *empty interface* type is an interface that implements at least zero or more methods and is defined as `interface{}`.

> **NOTE** In Go, to marshal is the process of generating a JSON string based on Go objects. To unmarshal is the process of parsing JSON into a Go object.

Since all types in Go implement zero (or more methods), we can use the struct type of the review we defined earlier as input to the `Unmarshal` function (some similarity with object-oriented programming [OOP] concepts in this case).

One thing to notice is that the data must be a slice of bytes, so you will need to convert the string representation of the review into the equivalent byte representation. Conveniently, you can do that by passing the text data during initialization of the byte slice, as shown here:

```
[]byte(scanner.Text())
```

Going back to the `Unmarshal` function, you can parse the review into the struct defined earlier by using the following code:

```
var review Review
json.Unmarshal([]byte(scanner.Text()), &review)
```

This code will parse the JSON-encoded review into the variable of type `Review`. Note that to use the `json.Unmarshal` function, you have to add `"encoding/json"` to the current list of imports in the listing:

```
import (
    "bufio"
    "encoding/json"
    "fmt"
    "log"
    "os"
)
```

Going back to the `read_json_file` function, you have to perform this process for each line of text. Listing 21.4 adds this process to the function.

LISTING 21.4

Adding the unmarshaling to the `read_json_file` function

```
func read_json_file(filepath string) {
    // read the json file using the os package
    content, err := os.Open(filepath)
    // if we have an error, we log the error and exit the program
    if err != nil {
        log.Fatal(err)
    }
    // defer closing the file until the read_json_file function finishes
    defer content.Close()
    // create a scanner variable that we will use to iterate through the reviews
    scanner := bufio.NewScanner(content)
    // split the content of the file based on lines (each line is a review)
    scanner.Split(bufio.ScanLines)
    for scanner.Scan() {
        // We can iterate through and display each review
        //fmt.Println(scanner.Text()) // Remove comment to print
        var review Review
        err := json.Unmarshal([]byte(scanner.Text()), &review)
        if err != nil {
            log.Fatal(err)
            return
        }
    }
}
```

Listing 21.4 adds a few lines within the for loop so that the code will scan and convert each line to a type Review. It also checks for errors returned by the Unmarshal function, and in case an error occurs, it logs the error and exits the function.

At this point, you can display individual attributes of the review/map by adding the code shown in Listing 21.5.

LISTING 21.5

Displaying individual attributes in the `read_json_file` function

```
func read_json_file(filepath string) {
    // read the json file using the os package
```

```
    content, err := os.Open(filepath)
    // if we have an error, we log the error and exit the program
    if err != nil {
        log.Fatal(err)
    }
    // defer closing the file until the read_json_file function finishes
    defer content.Close()
    // create a scanner variable that we will use to iterate through the reviews
    scanner := bufio.NewScanner(content)
    // split the content of the file based on lines (each line is a review)
    scanner.Split(bufio.ScanLines)
    for scanner.Scan() {
        // We can iterate through and display each review
        //fmt.Println(scanner.Text()) // Remove comment to print review line
        var review Review
        err := json.Unmarshal([]byte(scanner.Text()), &review)
        if err != nil {
            log.Fatal(err)
            return
        }
        fmt.Println(review.Asin)
    }
}
```

In Listing 21.5, you are simply displaying the asin attribute of each review. Let's see the code in action. Listing 21.6 presents a full listing using the read_json_file function.

LISTING 21.6

Our full listing at this point

```
package main

import (
    "fmt"
    "os"
    "bufio"
    "encoding/json"
    "log"
)

func main() {
    read_json_file("./Digital_Music_5.json")
}
```

continues

continued

```go
type Review struct {
    ReviewerID     string  `json:"reviewerID"`
    Asin           string  `json:"asin"`
    ReviewerName   string  `json:"reviewerName"`
    Helpful        [2]int  `json:"helpful"`
    ReviewText     string  `json:"reviewText"`
    Overall        float32 `json:"overall"`
    Summary        string  `json:"summary"`
    UnixReviewTime int64   `json:"unixReviewTime"`
    ReviewTime     string  `json:"reviewTime"`
}

func read_json_file(filepath string) {
    // read the json file using the os package
    content, err := os.Open(filepath)
    // if we have an error, we log the error and exit the program
    if err != nil {
        log.Fatal(err)
    }
    // defer closing the file until the read_json_file function finishes
    defer content.Close()
    // create a scanner variable that we will use to iterate through the reviews
    scanner := bufio.NewScanner(content)
    // split the content of the file based on lines (each line is a review)
    scanner.Split(bufio.ScanLines)
    for scanner.Scan() {
        // We can iterate through and display each review
        //fmt.Println(scanner.Text()) // Remove comment to print review line
        var review Review
        err := json.Unmarshal([]byte(scanner.Text()), &review)
        if err != nil {
            log.Fatal(err)
            return
        }
        fmt.Println(review.Asin)
    }
}
```

NOTE Remember to change the filename in the main function to match the file you downloaded at the beginning of this lesson. If you downloaded the digital music 5-core file, then the name (Digital_Music_5.json) should match the listing.

When you execute the listing, the code will read the file, iterate through each line, parse the data from the line into a type Review, and display the asin attribute. Note that you pass the location of the review file to the read_json_file function. In Listing 21.6, the JSON file is in the same directory as the Go program. If you saved the JSON file in a different directory, then you will need to adjust the path accordingly. If you downloaded a different review file from Amazon, then you'll want to change the JSON filename to match as well.

Returning the Reviews

At this point, let's discuss what the read_json_file function should return. Ideally, you want to return a slice of reviews. In other words, the read_json_file should return the following type:

```
[]Review
```

As you can see, the slice holds elements where each element is of type Review. By doing so, you can iterate through the file, parse each review, append it to the slice of reviews, and return the slice when the function is done.

Listing 21.7 makes a few changes to the code.

LISTING 21.7

Adjusting read_json_file to return the slice of reviews

```
func read_json_file(filepath string) []Review {
    // read the json file using the os package
    content, err := os.Open(filepath)
    // if we have an error, we log the error and exit the program
    if err != nil {
        log.Fatal(err)
    }
    // defer closing the file until the read_json_file function finishes
    defer content.Close()
    // create a scanner variable that we will use to iterate through the reviews
    scanner := bufio.NewScanner(content)
    // split the content of the file based on lines (each line is a review)
    scanner.Split(bufio.ScanLines)
```

continues

continued

```
    var reviews []Review
    for scanner.Scan() {
        // We can iterate through each review
        var review Review
        err := json.Unmarshal([]byte(scanner.Text()), &review)
        if err != nil {
            log.Fatal(err)
        }
        reviews = append(reviews, review)
    }
    return reviews
}
```

Listing 21.7 adds a few things to the read_json_file function:

- The returned type in the function signature. The function read_json_file now returns a slice where each element is of type Review.

- You created a slice named reviews, which will hold all the reviews from the JSON file.

- Within the for loop, once you parse a review, you append it to the slice of reviews.

- Return the slice of reviews once you finish iterating through the file.

It is time now to see this code in action. Update the main function with the code shown in Listing 21.8. Again, remember to adjust your filename and path if necessary.

LISTING 21.8

A new main function to print the first two reviews

```
func main() {
    reviews := read_json_file("./Digital_Music_5.json")
    fmt.Println(reviews[0].ReviewText)
    fmt.Println("----------")
    fmt.Println(reviews[1].ReviewText)
}
```

This new main function reads the JSON file using your latest read_json_file and stores the output in a slice named reviews. Next, you display the first two reviews in the file with a set of dashes between them to provide some separation. The output should look like this:

It's hard to believe "Memory of Trees" came out 11 years ago;it has held up well over the passage of time.It's Enya's last great album before the New Age/pop of "Amarantine" and "Day without rain." Back in 1995,Enya still had her creative spark,her own voice.I agree with the reviewer who said that this is her saddest album;it is melancholy,bittersweet,from the opening title song."Memory of Trees" is elegaic&majestic.;"Pax Deorum" sounds like it is from a Requiem Mass,it is a dark threnody.Unlike the reviewer who said that this has a "disconcerting" blend of spirituality&sensuality;,I don't find it disconcerting at all."Anywhere is" is a hopeful song,looking to possibilities."Hope has a place" is about love,but it is up to the listener to decide if it is romantic,platonic,etc.I've always had a soft spot for this song."On my way home" is a triumphant ending about return.This is truly a masterpiece of New Age music,a must for any Enya fan!

A clasically-styled and introverted album, Memory of Trees is a masterpiece of subtlety. Many of the songs have an endearing shyness to them - soft piano and a lovely, quiet voice. But within every introvert is an inferno, and Enya lets that fire explode on a couple of songs that absolutely burst with an expected raw power.If you've never heard Enya before, you might want to start with one of her more popularized works, like Watermark, just to play it safe. But if you're already a fan, then your collection is not complete without this beautiful work of musical art.

> **NOTE** The review data being used in these examples comes from text that people have posted online. The text has not been modified, so it might contain grammatical and other issues.

TOKENIZING AN INPUT STRING

You need to split the reviews into individual words so that the words can be counted. A function to tokenize any input string is a simple approach in terms of input for accomplishing this. The function can accept as input a string and returns a list that represents the words in the string with the order preserved. This function should split the string into words based on spaces or punctuation.

You can simplify the problem by first identifying each punctuation mark and replacing it with a space. You can then split based solely on spaces. For example, consider the following:

```
"Hello, Sean! —How are you?"
```

The first step is to replace the punctuation with a space. This results in the following string:

```
Hello  Sean   How are you
```

Next, you can use the `split` function to split the string based on spaces and get the list of words in the string, which will be the following:

```
[hello sean how are you]
```

The logic of this function is as follows:

1. Identify and replace punctuation with a space in the string.
2. Convert the input text string to lowercase.
3. Split the string into words based on spaces.

Identifying and Replacing Punctuation with a Space

First, let's focus on step 1. To identify/replace punctuation with a space in the string, you will leverage *regular expressions*, or *regex*, which you learned about in Lesson 19, "Sorting and Data Processing." Regex is a standard that developers use frequently for searching through strings. In fact, most modern search engines use regex as a standard part of their matching process. You will leverage regex to identify and replace punctuation with a space.

NOTE It is beyond the scope of this book to cover regular expressions in detail. You can find other books on regular expressions such as *Beginning Regular Expressions,* by Andrew Watt (Wiley, 2005), or you can review online resources such as `www.regexlib.com` or `https://github.com/google/re2/wiki/Syntax`.

In our example, you will use the `regexp` package from Go to search for punctuation marks and the `ReplaceAllString` function to substitute spaces for those punctuation marks. Let's consider the code in Listing 21.9.

LISTING 21.9

Using `regexp`

```go
package main

import (
    "fmt"
    "regexp"
)

func main() {
    text := "Hello, Sean! -How are you?"
    fmt.Println("original string: " + text)

    // The following is regex for the punctuation list. This
    // means that any of the punctuation in the list will be
    // replaced by a space.
    re := regexp.MustCompile(`[.,!?\-_#^()+=;/&'"]`)

    // Use the ReplaceAllString to replace any punctuation with a space
    w := re.ReplaceAllString(text, " ")

    fmt.Println("string after replacing punctuation with a space: " + w)
}
```

First, you use the `MustCompile` function, to which you pass a regex expression. This regex expression will then be used automatically for the subsequent operations that are done with the `regexp` package. Note that if you need to apply other regex expressions, then you must compile again. In this listing, your regex is a list of all the possible punctuation that you want to replace with a space (`[.,!?\-_#^()+=;/&'"]`).

Keep in mind that `MustCompile` will panic if the input regular expression is not a valid expression. That means you should double-check your regex if it throws an error.

The next step is to use the `ReplaceAllString` function to replace any identified punctuation with a space. Since you compiled the regex in the previous step, you don't need to specify the regex expression to `ReplaceAllString`.

Finally, you display both strings so that you can compare the results. As you can see, you are able to replace any punctuation with a space. The results should look like the following:

```
original string: Hello, Sean! -How are you?
string after replacing punctuation with a space: Hello  Sean   How are you
```

> **NOTE** In the regex expression in Listing 21.9, the specific characters are
> listed that we want to replace presented as a raw string between backticks
> (`` ` ``). A simpler alternative would be to use a punctuation class, as follows:
>
> ```
> re := regexp.MustCompile(`[[:punct:]]`)
> ```
>
> The `` `[[:punct:]]` `` regex expression would match the following characters:
>
> ```
> ! " # $ % & ' ( ) * + , - . / : ; < = > ? @ [ \ ] ^ _ ` { | } ~
> ```

Converting Input Text to Lowercase

The next step in the tokenization process is to convert the string to lowercase.
Listing 21.10 adds this code to your `main` function.

LISTING 21.10

Converting input to lowercase

```go
package main

import (
    "fmt"
    "regexp"
    "strings"
)

func main() {
    text := "Hello, Sean! -How are you?"
    fmt.Println("original string: " + text)

    re := regexp.MustCompile(`[[:punct:]]`)

    w := re.ReplaceAllString(text, " ")

    fmt.Println("string after replacing punctuation with a space: " + w)

    w = strings.ToLower(w)  // convert to lowercase
}
```

This listing introduces an additional line that calls the ToLower function of strings. In order to use this, you will also need to import the strings package into your program. The strings.ToLower function converts the received string (w in this case) to lowercase and returns it. In our example, you return the string back to w as well. You also added the punctuation class mentioned in the previous note for the regex expression.

Splitting the String into Words

Finally, you need to split the string at spaces and retrieve the slice of strings, which represents the different words (in order). To do that, you can use the built-in function, Fields, from the strings package.

The Fields function splits an input string around each instance of one or more consecutive whitespace characters. It is important to note that there could be multiple spaces grouped together. Since you are replacing punctuation with a space, if you have two consecutive punctuation marks, then you will have double spaces. The Fields function allows you to split based on any number of consecutive spaces. Let's add another instruction to the previous code, as shown in Listing 21.11.

LISTING 21.11

Splitting our string

```
package main

import (
    "fmt"
    "regexp"
    "strings"
)

func main() {
    text := "Hello, Sean! --How are you?"
    fmt.Println("original string: " + text)

    re := regexp.MustCompile(`[[:punct:]]`)

    w := re.ReplaceAllString(text, " ")

    fmt.Println("string after replacing punctuation with a space: " + w)
```

continues

continued

```
w = strings.ToLower(w)        // convert to lowercase
// Use the Fields function from the strings package to split
// the string w around each instance of one or more consecutive
// whitespace characters
tokens := strings.Fields(w)

fmt.Print("Tokens: ")
fmt.Println(tokens)
}
```

In this code, the call to the Fields function has been added to split the string w into a slice of strings representing the different words/tokens in the string. Finally, the tokens are displayed from the input string. Running the code should produce the following results:

```
original string: Hello, Sean! --How are you?
string after replacing punctuation with a space: Hello  Sean   How are you
Tokens: [hello sean how are you]
```

CREATING A TOKENIZE FUNCTION

Now that you have a working code, you can create a function that will leverage the code you've seen to tokenize any input string. Create a function called tokenize, as shown in Listing 21.12.

LISTING 21.12

The tokenize **function**

```
func tokenize(text string) []string {

    // Set up the regexp to use a punctuation list
    re := regexp.MustCompile(`[[:punct:]]`)

    // use the ReplaceAllString to replace any punctuation with a space
    w := re.ReplaceAllString(text, " ")

    w = strings.ToLower(w)        // convert to lowercase

    // Use the Fields function from the strings package to split
    // the string w around each instance of one or more consecutive
    // whitespace characters
    tokens := strings.Fields(w)
```

```
    // return the slice, which represents the list of tokens in
    // order from the input string
    return tokens
}
```

In this listing, you wrap the previous code into a function called tokenize that takes as input a string and returns a slice of strings that represent the different tokens/words in the input string.

Tokenizing an Input Review

Let's leverage the tokenize function to tokenize a review from the JSON file. Replace the main function you used in Listing 21.8 with the code in Listing 21.13.

LISTING 21.13

A new main function for our reviews program

```
func main() {
    reviews := read_json_file("./Digital_Music_5.json")
    tokens := tokenize(reviews[0].ReviewText)
    fmt.Print("tokens: ")
    fmt.Println(tokens)

}
```

In this code, you use the read_json_file function to read the JSON file containing the reviews. Next, you call the tokenize function to tokenize the text of the first review and display the token.

Note that in addition to updating the main function with the code in Listing 21.13, you also have to add the tokenize function from Listing 21.12 to your program as well as include "strings" and "regexp" in your list of imported packages. With the updated code, the output produced should be similar to the following:

```
tokens: [it s hard to believe memory of trees came out 11 years ago it has
held up well over the passage of time it s enya s last great album before
the new age pop of amarantine and day without rain back in 1995 enya still
had her creative spark her own voice i agree with the reviewer who said that
this is her saddest album it is melancholy bittersweet from the opening title
song memory of trees is elegaic majestic pax deorum sounds like it is from a
requiem mass it is a dark threnody unlike the reviewer who said that this has
```

continues

continued

```
a disconcerting blend of spirituality sensuality i don t find it disconcerting
at all anywhere is is a hopeful song looking to possibilities hope has a
place is about love but it is up to the listener to decide if it is romantic
platonic etc i ve always had a soft spot for this song on my way home is a
triumphant ending about return this is truly a masterpiece of new age music a
must for any enya fan]
```

Tokenizing the Entire Dataset

The last step is to implement the code that will iterate through the entire dataset and tokenize each review. First, let's start with the basic code in Listing 21.14.

LISTING 21.14

Tokenizing the entire dataset

```
func main() {

    reviews := read_json_file("./Digital_Music_5.json")

    for i := range reviews {
        tokenize(reviews[i].ReviewText) // tokenize review
    }
}
```

Here we open and read the JSON file, and then iterate through all the reviews and tokenize each of them. There is no output at this time.

COUNTING THE WORDS IN EACH REVIEW

Now that each review in the dataset is tokenized, you can proceed to compute the word count in each review. The word count is the frequency of occurrence of each unique word in the review.

In order to achieve this, you will adopt the same logic as the tokenize step. That is, you will build a function that computes the word count of an input list of words. This function, shown in Listing 21.15, takes as input a list of words and iterates through them and computes the frequency of occurrence of each unique word in the input list.

LISTING 21.15

Word count for an input list of words

```
func count_words(words []string) map[string]int {

    word_count := make(map[string]int)

    for i := range words {
        if _, ok := word_count[words[i]]; ok {
            word_count[words[i]] = word_count[words[i]] + 1
        } else {
            word_count[words[i]] = 1
        }
    }

    return word_count
}
```

The count_word function takes a slice of strings as input, and it returns a map. In the returned map, the keys are strings, which represent the unique words in the slice, and the values are integers, which represent the frequency of occurrence of the corresponding unique word.

In the count_words function, you create an empty map that will hold the unique words/frequency of occurrence. You then iterate through the slice of words. First, you check if the current word in the slice already exists in the map:

```
if _, ok := word_count[words[i]]; ok {
```

If the word is in the map, then you have seen this word before, so you need to increase the current count by 1:

```
word_count[words[i]] = word_count[words[i]] + 1
```

If the word doesn't exist in the map already, that means that this is the first time you see this word. In this case, you will need to initialize the count to 1:

```
word_count[words[i]] = 1
```

After looping through the entire slice, you return the word_count map.

> **NOTE** In the following line, the word count is being incremented by 1:
>
> ```
> word_count[words[i]] = word_count[words[i]] + 1
> ```
>
> This line could be simplified by using the incremental operator:
>
> ```
> word_count[words[i]]++
> ```

TOKENIZING AND COUNTING THE REVIEWS

With the word_count function written, you can add it to your reviews listing along with the tokenize function. Listing 21.16 pulls all the code you've written into a single listing.

LISTING 21.16
Tokenizing and counting words per review

```go
package main

import (
    "os"
    "bufio"
    "encoding/json"
    "log"
    "regexp"
    "strings"
)

func main() {

    reviews := read_json_file("./Digital_Music_5.json")

    for i := range reviews {
        tokens := tokenize(reviews[i].ReviewText) // tokenize review
        count_words(tokens)
    }
}

type Review struct {
    ReviewerID    string    `json:"reviewerID"`
    Asin          string    `json:"asin"`
```

```go
    ReviewerName    string   `json:"reviewerName"`
    Helpful         [2]int   `json:"helpful"`
    ReviewText      string   `json:"reviewText"`
    Overall         float32  `json:"overall"`
    Summary         string   `json:"summary"`
    UnixReviewTime  int64    `json:"unixReviewTime"`
    ReviewTime      string   `json:"reviewTime"`
}

func read_json_file(filepath string) []Review {
    // read the json file using the os package
    content, err := os.Open(filepath)
    // if we have an error, we log the error and exit the program
    if err != nil {
        log.Fatal(err)
    }
    // defer closing the file until the read_json_file function finishes
    defer content.Close()
    // create a scanner variable that we will use to iterate through the reviews
    scanner := bufio.NewScanner(content)
    // split the content of the file based on lines (each line is a review)
    scanner.Split(bufio.ScanLines)

    var reviews []Review
    for scanner.Scan() {
        // We can iterate through each review
        var review Review
        err := json.Unmarshal([]byte(scanner.Text()), &review)
        if err != nil {
            log.Fatal(err)
        }
        reviews = append(reviews, review)
    }
    return reviews
}

func tokenize(text string) []string {

    // Set up the regexp to use a punctuation list
    re := regexp.MustCompile("[.,!?\\\\-_#^()+=;/&'\"]")

    // use the ReplaceAllString to replace any punctuation with a space
    w := re.ReplaceAllString(text, " ")

    w = strings.ToLower(w)        // convert to lowercase
```

continues

continued

```
    // Use the Fields function from the strings package to split
    // the string w around each instance of one or more consecutive
    // whitespace characters
    tokens := strings.Fields(w)

    // return the slice, which represents the list of tokens in
    // order from the input string
    return tokens
}

func count_words(words []string) map[string]int {

    word_count := make(map[string]int)

    for i := range words {
        if _, ok := word_count[words[i]]; ok {
            word_count[words[i]] = word_count[words[i]] + 1
        } else {
            word_count[words[i]] = 1
        }
    }

    return word_count
}
```

The only code in this listing that is different from what you've seen before is in the main function. In the main function you can see that the tokenization and word counting operations have been combined in the code.

When this listing is executed, nothing is shown on the screen; however, each review is being read and broken into tokens, and the word count of each word in each review is being counted.

> **NOTE** If you want to see something happening while the listing is executing, then you can add the fmt package to the imports and include a few lines in the main function to print feedback. The following update to the main function shows when the processing starts and stops and prints a dot each time a review is read and tokenized:
>
> ```
> func main() {
>     fmt.Println("Starting")
>
>     reviews := read_json_file("./Digital_Music_5.json")
> ```

```
        for i := range reviews {
            fmt.Print(".")
            tokens := tokenize(reviews[i].ReviewText) // tokenize review
            count_words(tokens)
        }
        fmt.Println("Complete")
    }
```

DESIGNING IMPROVEMENTS

The code you have so far performs all the necessary tasks that you set out to do. However, you can give it a few tweaks to make it more elegant and reusable. Here are some changes you can make:

- Improve the structs
- Add custom error and exception handling
- Improve tokenizing
- Improve word counting

Improvement 1: Improving the Structs

If you look closely, so far you didn't store the tokens or the word count anywhere. It will be beneficial to keep track of that data. To do that, you will leverage structs. First, let's modify the Review struct, as shown in Listing 21.17.

LISTING 21.17

Modified Review struct

```
type Review struct {
    ReviewerID     string  `json:"reviewerID"`
    Asin           string  `json:"asin"`
    ReviewerName   string  `json:"reviewerName"`
    Helpful        [2]int  `json:"helpful"`
    ReviewText     string  `json:"reviewText"`
    Overall        float32 `json:"overall"`
    Summary        string  `json:"summary"`
    UnixReviewTime int64   `json:"unixReviewTime"`
```

continues

continued

```
ReviewTime       string    `json:"reviewTime"`
Tokens           []string
WordCount        map[string]int
}
```

In this updated Review struct, you include two additional fields, Tokens and WordCount. This means that you will have a place to store the tokens and word count of each review in the review variable itself.

Next, add the Dataset struct shown in Listing 21.18.

LISTING 21.18

The Dataset struct

```
type Dataset struct {
    filepath string
    reviews  []Review
}
```

The Dataset struct includes two attributes:

- filepath: This represents the file path to the dataset.
- reviews: This is a slice where each element is of type Review.

Update *read_json_file*

With these two structs, you can make some modifications to your code base. You can refactor the read_json_file to have a receiver of type Dataset. For instance, let's consider the read_json_file function presented in Listing 12.19. Because they have different signatures, you can add this read_json_file function to the same file (for now) where the existing read_json_file function is.

LISTING 21.19

A **second** read_json_file

```
func (dataset *Dataset) read_json_file() {
    // read the json file using the os package
    content, err := os.Open(dataset.filepath)
    // if we have an error, we log the error and exit the program
    if err != nil {
```

```
    log.Fatal(err)
  }

  // defer closing the file until the read_json_file function finishes
  defer content.Close()

  // create a scanner variable that we will use to iterate
  // through the reviews
  scanner := bufio.NewScanner(content)

  // split the content of the file based on lines (each line is a review)
  scanner.Split(bufio.ScanLines)
  for scanner.Scan() {
    // we can iterate through and display each review
    // fmt.Println(scanner.Text()) // This is commented otherwise, it
    // will print the entire file, which will take a while. Uncomment
    // if you want to see the content of the file.
     var review Review
     err := json.Unmarshal([]byte(scanner.Text()), &review)
     if err != nil {
        log.Fatal(err)
     }
     dataset.reviews = append(dataset.reviews, review)
  }
}
```

The code in this new read_json_file function is similar to the original read_json_file function except for the following:

- The function includes a receiver of type Dataset, which will allow you to execute this function (now called a method) through Dataset types.

- We append the review variable to the list of reviews in the dataset.

Let's see the new read_json_file function in action. In the main function, add the code shown in Listing 21.20.

LISTING 21.20

Updated main function

```
func main() {
    dataset := Dataset{filepath: "./Digital_Music_5.json"}
    dataset.read_json_file()
    fmt.Println(dataset.reviews[1].ReviewText)
    fmt.Println(dataset.reviews[2].ReviewText)
}
```

In the code, you create a variable of type Dataset and initialize the filepath with the JSON file that you want to read. Next, you execute the read_json_file function, which populates the field reviews within the dataset type with the raw reviews from the JSON file. Finally, you display the second and third reviews from the dataset.

Update to Tokenize

Similar to the read_json_file, we can implement a tokenize function that will allow you to tokenize the entire dataset. Let's look at the tokenize function presented in Listing 21.21. Note that you can keep the other tokenize function for now.

LISTING 21.21

tokenize function using a dataset

```
func (dataset *Dataset) tokenize() {
   for i := range dataset.reviews {
      dataset.reviews[i].Tokens = tokenize(dataset.reviews[i].ReviewText)
   }
}
```

The tokenize function is very simple. First, it includes a receiver in the signature of type Dataset. The body of the function includes a for loop that iterates through the reviews and tokenizes each review using the tokenize function you built earlier.

main Function Update

Listing 21.22 adds more code to the main function so that you can see the new tokenize function in action.

LISTING 21.22

Updated main function to use new tokenize function

```
func main() {
   dataset := Dataset{filepath: "./Digital_Music_5.json"}
   dataset.read_json_file()
   dataset.tokenize()
   fmt.Println(dataset.reviews[1].ReviewText)
   fmt.Println("---")
   fmt.Println(dataset.reviews[1].Tokens)
```

```
    fmt.Println("---")
    fmt.Println(dataset.reviews[2].ReviewText)
    fmt.Println("---")
    fmt.Println(dataset.reviews[2].Tokens)
}
```

In this updated code, you first read the dataset using the read_json_file function, and then you execute the tokenize function, which tokenizes the entire dataset. Finally, you display the second and third reviews as well as their corresponding tokens. The output should show the review text and then the tokens:

A clasically-styled and introverted album, Memory of Trees is a masterpiece of subtlety. Many of the songs have an endearing shyness to them – soft piano and a lovely, quiet voice. But within every introvert is an inferno, and Enya lets that fire explode on a couple of songs that absolutely burst with an expected raw power.If you've never heard Enya before, you might want to start with one of her more popularized works, like Watermark, just to play it safe. But if you're already a fan, then your collection is not complete without this beautiful work of musical art.

[a clasically styled and introverted album memory of trees is a masterpiece of subtlety many of the songs have an endearing shyness to them soft piano and a lovely quiet voice but within every introvert is an inferno and enya lets that fire explode on a couple of songs that absolutely burst with an expected raw power if you ve never heard enya before you might want to start with one of her more popularized works like watermark just to play it safe but if you re already a fan then your collection is not complete without this beautiful work of musical art]

I never thought Enya would reach the sublime heights of Evacuee or Marble Halls from 'Shepherd Moons.' 'The Celts, Watermark and Day...' were all pleasant and admirable throughout, but are less ambitious both lyrically and musically. But Hope Has a Place from 'Memory...' reaches those heights and beyond. It is Enya at her most inspirational and comforting. I'm actually glad that this song didn't get overexposed the way Only Time did. It makes it that much more special to all who own this album.

[i never thought enya would reach the sublime heights of evacuee or marble halls from shepherd moons the celts watermark and day were all pleasant and admirable throughout but are less ambitious both lyrically and musically but hope has a place from memory reaches those heights and beyond it is enya at her most inspirational and comforting i m actually glad that this song didn t get overexposed the way only time did it makes it that much more special to all who own this album]

Word Count Update

Finally, let's implement the count_words function for the Dataset struct. This function will allow you to count the unique words in each review in the entire dataset.

Let's consider the simple implementation of the count_words function in Listing 21.23. This function iterates through the reviews in the dataset and performs a word count for each review.

LISTING 21.23

Doing a word count for each review in a dataset

```go
func (dataset *Dataset) count_words() {
    for i := range dataset.reviews {
        dataset.reviews[i].WordCount = count_words(dataset.reviews[i].Tokens)
    }
}
```

With this code, you can update your main function to execute the count_words function on your dataset of reviews. Update the code to use the main function shown in Listing 21.24.

LISTING 21.24

Updated main using word counts

```go
func main() {
    dataset := Dataset{filepath: "./Digital_Music_5.json"}
    dataset.read_json_file()
    dataset.tokenize()
    dataset.count_words()
    fmt.Println(dataset.reviews[1].ReviewText)
    fmt.Println("---")
    fmt.Println(dataset.reviews[1].Tokens)
    fmt.Println("---")
    fmt.Println(dataset.reviews[1].WordCount)
    fmt.Println("----------")

    fmt.Println(dataset.reviews[2].ReviewText)
    fmt.Println("---")
    fmt.Println(dataset.reviews[2].Tokens)
```

```
    fmt.Println("---")
    fmt.Println(dataset.reviews[2].WordCount)
}
```

As the listing shows, you add the execution of the count_words method, and then display the word_count for the second and third reviews.

Improvement 2: Adding Custom Error and Exception Handling

So far, you've implemented minimal error and exception handling. Let's investigate improving our program in the way it handles unexcepted errors and exceptions.

First, to add the appropriate errors for your methods, replace the existing read_json_file method with the code in Listing 21.25.

LISTING 21.25

Updated read_json_file method with error handling

```
func (dataset *Dataset) read_json_file() (bool, error) {
    // read the json file using the os package
    content, err := os.Open(dataset.filepath)
    // if we have an error, we log the error and exit the program
    if err != nil {
        return true, err
    }

    // defer closing the file until the read_json_file function finishes
    defer content.Close()

    // create a scanner variable that we will use to iterate
    // through the reviews
    scanner := bufio.NewScanner(content)

    // split the content of the file based on lines (each line is a review)
    scanner.Split(bufio.ScanLines)

    for scanner.Scan() {
        // we can iterate through and display each review
        //fmt.Println(scanner.Text()) // This is commented; otherwise, it
                                      // will print the entire file, which
                                      // will take a while. Uncomment if you
                                      // want to see the content of the file.
```

continues

continued

```
    var review Review
    err := json.Unmarshal([]byte(scanner.Text()), &review)
    if err != nil {
        return true, err
    }
    dataset.reviews = append(dataset.reviews, review)
}
return false, nil
}
```

Compared to the previous implementation of read_json_file, nothing much has changed. The first change is that the method now returns a Boolean and an error type. The Boolean is true if there is an error, and it is false if there is no error. The error type returns an error description if an error occurs. Next, you need to identify where possible errors might occur. In our example, there are two possible exceptions.

The first exception might occur if you can't open the file because it's corrupted or the path is erroneous:

```
if err != nil {
    return true, err
}
```

The second exception might occur when you are parsing the JSON data into the struct type due to an erroneous JSON file. The second exception might occur when umarshaling the JSON data into Go objects.

The Unmarshal function returns an error type, so it is a matter of propagating the error:

```
err := json.Unmarshal([]byte(scanner.Text()), &review)
if err != nil {
    return true, err
}
```

Finally, if the function finishes executing (meaning everything went well), then you simply return no error:

```
return false, nil
```

Improvement 3: Improving Tokenizing

What if you execute the tokenize method before reading JSON data? That means you are tokenizing an empty dataset. In our example, if someone executes the tokenize function without reading the JSON data first, you want to show them an error function.

To do that, first add the method shown in Listing 21.26. The method called empty checks if the dataset is empty by checking whether or not the reviews slice is empty.

LISTING 21.26

The empty function

```
func (dataset *Dataset) empty() bool {
    if len(dataset.reviews) == 0 {
        return true
    }
    return false
}
```

With this function added to your program, you then need to update the tokenize method. Listing 21.27 contains the new code.

LISTING 21.27

Updated tokenize function with empty check

```
func (dataset *Dataset) tokenize() (bool, error) {
    if dataset.empty() {
        return true, errors.New("Dataset is empty. Please read data from
json first.")
    }

    for i := range dataset.reviews {
        dataset.reviews[i].Tokens = tokenize(dataset.reviews[i].ReviewText)
    }
    return false, nil
}
```

In this update, you have added a few things to the tokenize method. First, you now return a Boolean and an error type. Additionally, before you perform any tokenization, you check if the dataset is empty. If that's the case, then you return true and a custom message instructing the user to read the data before performing tokenization. If there's no error, you perform the tokenization on the dataset. At the end of the method, you return false and nil, which means no error occurred.

To see these custom errors in action, update the main function with the code in Listing 21.28. You must also include the errors package, so add "errors" to the imports in the listing.

LISTING 21.28

Testing our new tokenize code

```
func main() {
    dataset := Dataset{filepath: "./Digital_Music_5.json"}
    _, err := dataset.tokenize()
    if err != nil {
        log.Fatal(err.Error())
    }
}
```

If you look at the code in Listing 21.28, you will notice that the tokenize method is being executed before reading any data, which is erroneous. This should trigger the custom exception handling, which you implemented in the previous listing:

```
2022/02/09 19:16:53 Dataset is empty. Please read data from json first.
exit status 1
```

Improvement 4: Improving Word Counting

If you execute the count_words method before executing the tokenize method, it means that the tokens aren't computed and so you would be performing a word count on empty slices, which is not what you want. For instance, look at the code in Listing 21.29.

LISTING 21.29

Not tokenizing before counting

```
func main() {
    dataset := Dataset{filepath: "./Digital_Music_5.json"}
    _, err := dataset.read_json_file()
    if err != nil {
        log.Fatal(err.Error())
    }
```

```
//dataset.tokenize()

dataset.count_words()

fmt.Println(dataset.reviews[1].ReviewText)
fmt.Println(dataset.reviews[1].Tokens)
fmt.Println(dataset.reviews[1].WordCount)
}
```

This code will execute without any issues. However, you are running count_words before performing any tokenization. This results in the code running the word count on empty slices, which returns an empty word_count. You can see this in the output:

```
A clasically-styled and introverted album, Memory of Trees is a masterpiece of
subtlety.  Many of the songs have an endearing shyness to them — soft piano
and a lovely, quiet voice.  But within every introvert is an inferno, and Enya
lets that fire explode on a couple of songs that absolutely burst with an
expected raw power.If you've never heard Enya before, you might want to start
with one of her more popularized works, like Watermark, just to play it safe.
But if you're already a fan, then your collection is not complete without this
beautiful work of musical art.
[]
map[]
```

Let's fix the situation by checking first if the token slice is empty. If that's the case, you will execute the tokenization (just in case it didn't run before). This will effectively make word_count able to perform tokenization with or without calling the tokenize method. Update the count_words method with the code in Listing 21.30.

LISTING 21.30

Updated count_words to check for tokenize issue

```
func (dataset *Dataset) count_words() (bool, error) {
    if dataset.empty() {
        return true, errors.New("Dataset is empty. Please read data from
json first.")
    }

    for i := range dataset.reviews {
        if len(dataset.reviews[i].Tokens) == 0 {
```

continues

continued

```
        dataset.reviews[i].Tokens = tokenize(dataset.reviews[i].ReviewText)
    }
    dataset.reviews[i].WordCount = count_words(dataset.reviews[i].Tokens)
  }
  return false, nil
}
```

Now you simply check if the dataset is empty. If that's the case, you return an error message. Otherwise, you iterate through each review, first determining if you have any tokens doing the following check:

```
if len(dataset.reviews[i].Tokens) == 0 {
}
```

If the number of tokens is 0, it means that you didn't run any tokenization yet. In this case, you force the method to perform the tokenization prior to performing a word count:

```
if len(dataset.reviews[i].Tokens) == 0 {
    dataset.reviews[i].Tokens = tokenize(dataset.reviews[i].ReviewText)
}
```

POSSIBLE FURTHER IMPROVEMENTS

At this point, you have a working program that reads a JSON file and tokenizes the data as well as counts the words. We've gone through a few improvements that could made; however, there are many more that could be applied as well. Additional changes could include:

- Adding support to read reviews from CSV files.
- Performing a word count on the entire dataset. This means that after the word count for each review is completed, the results could then be combined into one single count for the entire dataset.

FINAL CODE LISTING

Your final code is going to be dependent on how you added the various suggestions throughout this lesson. Listing 21.31 contains a complete listing that includes both versions of tokenize and count_words.

LISTING 21.31

The complete reviews listing

```go
package main

import (
    "fmt"
    "os"
    "bufio"
    "encoding/json"
    "log"
    "regexp"
    "strings"
    "errors"
)

type Review struct {
    ReviewerID     string    `json:"reviewerID"`
    Asin           string    `json:"asin"`
    ReviewerName   string    `json:"reviewerName"`
    Helpful        [2]int    `json:"helpful"`
    ReviewText     string    `json:"reviewText"`
    Overall        float32   `json:"overall"`
    Summary        string    `json:"summary"`
    UnixReviewTime int64     `json:"unixReviewTime"`
    ReviewTime     string    `json:"reviewTime"`
    Tokens         []string
    WordCount      map[string]int
}

type Dataset struct {
    filepath string
    reviews  []Review
}

func (dataset *Dataset) empty() bool {
    if len(dataset.reviews) == 0 {
        return true
    }
    return false
}
```

continues

continued

```go
func (dataset *Dataset) read_json_file() (bool, error) {
    // read the json file using the os package
    content, err := os.Open(dataset.filepath)
    // if we have an error, we log the error and exit the program
    if err != nil {
        return true, err
    }

    // defer closing the file until the read_json_file function finishes
    defer content.Close()

    // create a scanner variable that we will use to iterate
    // through the reviews
    scanner := bufio.NewScanner(content)

    // split the content of the file based on lines (each line is a review)
    scanner.Split(bufio.ScanLines)

    for scanner.Scan() {
        // we can iterate through and display each review
        //fmt.Println(scanner.Text())  // This is commented; otherwise, it
                                        // will print the entire file, which
                                        // will take a while. Uncomment if you
                                        // want to see the content of the file.
        var review Review
        err := json.Unmarshal([]byte(scanner.Text()), &review)
        if err != nil {
            return true, err
        }
        dataset.reviews = append(dataset.reviews, review)
    }
    return false, nil
}

func tokenize(text string) []string {
    // Set up the regexp to use a punctuation list
    re := regexp.MustCompile(`[[:punct:]]`)

    // use the ReplaceAllString to replace any punctuation with a space
    w := re.ReplaceAllString(text, " ")

    w = strings.ToLower(w)          // convert to lowercase

    // Use the Fields function from the strings package to split
    // the string w around each instance of one or more consecutive
    // whitespace characters
    tokens := strings.Fields(w)
```

```go
    // return the slice, which represents the list of tokens in
    // order from the input string
    return tokens
}

func (dataset *Dataset) tokenize() (bool, error) {
    if dataset.empty() {
        return true, errors.New("Dataset is empty. Please read data from
json first.")
    }

    for i := range dataset.reviews {
        dataset.reviews[i].Tokens = tokenize(dataset.reviews[i].ReviewText)
    }
    return false, nil
}

func count_words(words []string) map[string]int {
    word_count := make(map[string]int)

    for i := range words {
        if _, ok := word_count[words[i]]; ok {
            word_count[words[i]] = word_count[words[i]] + 1
        } else {
            word_count[words[i]] = 1
        }
    }

    return word_count
}

func (dataset *Dataset) count_words() (bool, error) {
    if dataset.empty() {
        return true, errors.New("Dataset is empty. Please read data from
json first.")
    }
    for i := range dataset.reviews {
        if len(dataset.reviews[i].Tokens) == 0 {
            dataset.reviews[i].Tokens = tokenize(dataset.reviews[i].ReviewText)
        }
        dataset.reviews[i].WordCount = count_words(dataset.reviews[i].Tokens)
    }
    return false, nil
}
```

continues

continued

```go
func main() {
    dataset := Dataset{filepath: "./Digital_Music_5.json"}
    _, err := dataset.read_json_file()
    if err != nil {
        log.Fatal(err.Error())
    }

    _, err = dataset.tokenize()
    if err != nil {
        log.Fatal(err.Error())
    }

    dataset.count_words()

    fmt.Println(dataset.reviews[0].ReviewText)
    fmt.Println("---")
    fmt.Println(dataset.reviews[0].Tokens)
    fmt.Println("---")
    fmt.Println(dataset.reviews[0].WordCount)
}
```

Running this listing will tokenize the JSON file and print the first review. The review will be printed, followed by its tokens, followed by the word counts.

SUMMARY

In this lesson, you applied what you've learned up to this point to implement a tokenizer/word counter from scratch using built-in Go packages. Tokenization and word count are both important concepts used in many data analysis tasks such as topic detection. In this lesson you created a program that did the following:

- Read a JSON file that contains a list of online e-commerce reviews.
- Tokenized each review in the dataset.
- Computed word counts in each review in the dataset.

PART IV

Advanced Topics for Go Development

Lesson 22
Testing

In order to make sure your Go applications are "job ready," you should test them to make sure they work correctly. In this lesson, we not only present information on test-driven development, but we introduce behavior-driven development as well. As an added bonus, we walk through an example of a test-driven case.

LEARNING OBJECTIVES

By the end of this lesson, you will be able to:

- Apply the basics of test-driven development.
- Know the four testing levels.
- Understand the test-driven development workflow.
- Use a testing package.
- Define behavior-driven development processes.
- Compare the behavior-driven development process to the test-driven development process.
- Identify tools that teams can use to support behavior-driven development processes.
- Define user stories that could be used in behavior-driven development processes.

TEST-DRIVEN DEVELOPMENT

The traditional coding process involves writing code and then running and testing the code to see what happens. If the code fails, you rewrite the program and try it again. If it doesn't fail, you move on to the next program. However, this approach can lead to wasted time because you typically spend a lot of time writing code before testing it, and if the code fails, it takes more time to find and correct the errors. In many respects, it makes more sense to test code as you write it so that you can make corrections as soon as the errors are found.

TESTING LEVELS

There are multiple testing levels that can be used to test software. These levels are designed to allow software developers to test all units in a program, from the smallest units to bigger and more complex units.

The four main testing levels are:

- Unit testing
- Integration testing
- System testing
- Acceptance testing

Unit testing deals with testing units, the smallest components in a software program that can be compiled and executed. When you are designing and developing a large, complex software package, the development processes typically involve dividing the software into components, each of which can be developed individually by separate teams of developers. As teams develop these units, it is important to test each unit. This type of testing is done by developers throughout the development of the software and before handing the software to the testing team. The goal of unit testing is to isolate each unit in the software and test it separately.

The next step in the development process is to integrate the separate components into a single, final solution. During this integration process, it is crucial to use *integration testing* to determine how well the individual components work together.

System testing deals with testing the entire software as a whole. After integrating the different units into one final package, the next step is to test the integrated program to make sure it behaves as expected. System testing is the first level of testing where the software is tested as a whole.

Finally, the quality assurance (QA) team will perform *acceptance testing* to ensure that the requirements established in the early steps of the software development life cycle (SDLC) are met. At this point, the tests focus on quality and performance requirements, using prewritten test cases to make sure that the software behaves as expected.

> **NOTE** In smaller organizations, the developer might also be the quality
> assurance team.

Testing Pyramid

Another approach to testing is the Testing Pyramid, which includes lots of
testing during the development cycles but less testing at higher levels. See
Ham Vocke's article "The Practical Test Pyramid" for more information about
this approach to test-driven development: `https://martinfowler.com/articles/
practical-test-pyramid.html`.

THE TDD WORKFLOW

When you use tests throughout the software development process, you are using an
approach referred to as test-driven development (TDD), a workflow that involves writing
test units first and then writing the simplest code possible to pass those tests. When the
code passes the unit tests, you typically go back and refactor code to make it more efficient while ensuring it still passes those tests.

TDD is the process of developing and executing automated tests prior to the development of the application (before writing any code). For this reason, TDD is also known as
test-first development.

The goal of TDD is to focus on requirements rather than writing and validating code
(testing). In fact, TDD allows developers to focus on the requirements before writing any
functional code. The process of TDD starts with designing and implementing tests for
every block of code, function, class, and so on. In other words, the tests are developed
first to validate what the code will do, and the code is written only after the tests have
been designed.

TDD is different from traditional testing in many ways, including:

- TDD allows developers to feel more confident about the system under development because they build the code to meet requirements.

- TDD focuses on creating production-quality code, while traditional testing focuses
  more on test case design.

- Using TDD, you can achieve 100 percent test coverage: every line in the code can
  be tested.

The TDD Process

TDD revolves around the same set of standard steps for each part of a program under development:

1. Before implementing any code, you write an automated test for the code that you intend to write. To write the automated test, you must identify all possible aspects of what the code will do, including inputs, errors, and outputs.

2. Run the automated test, which will fail because you haven't written any code yet.

3. Implement the code that will pass the automated test.

   If the test continues to fail, the code is not complete or correct. You must fix and retest the code until it passes the test.

4. After the code passes the automated test, you can start the refactoring step, where the goal is to improve the quality of the code while still passing the automated test.

5. Once you are satisfied with the quality of the code (and the code passes the automated test), you can move on to the next set of requirements and repeat the whole process again.

Advantages of TDD

TDD offers the following advantages over the traditional approach of testing only after the code is written:

- Developers are forced to understand the expected outcome before developing the code.

- Developers are forced to complete one component in a program before moving to the next because they can't move on to the next step as long as the current test fails.

- Unit tests run at each step in the development process, which provides constant feedback to developers that all code is working correctly. If one component breaks because of a new component, the developer will receive instant feedback because the unit test will fail.

- Developers can refactor code at any time in the development process and the test units ensure the software is still working.

- Developers can create tests to identify defects and then modify the code to pass the test units.

- Because testing is an integral part of the development process, the testing step in the SDLC is typically shorter.

THE TESTING PACKAGE

Go provides a testing package that includes a variety of tools you can use to write unit tests. As a first step, when you want to execute a Go file as a test unit, you should use the convention of adding _test to the end of the filename. For instance, if you have a file called Hello.go, you will need to create a file named Hello_test.go for the tests.

This file contains the tests for the main program. The test file essentially defines the output you expect the program itself to generate, and it compares the expected output with the actual output.

Creating the Program

Let's create a program that will calculate the square of an input number. Begin by creating a file named **Square.go** and add the code shown in Listing 22.1.

LISTING 22.1

The Square.go **program**

```
package main

import "fmt"

// calculate the square of input value
func Square(a int) int {
    return a * a
}

func main(){
    fmt.Println("main function")
    fmt.Println(Square(2))
}
```

This is a short listing that computes the square of an input number using a function called Square that takes a number of type int and returns the resulting square also as an int.

Writing the Test

With the program written, you can now create a test file. Enter the code in Listing 22.2 and save it as **Square_test.go** in the same directory as Square.go.

LISTING 22.2

The `Square_test.go` **test program**

```go
package main

import (
    "fmt"
    "testing"
)


// test if the Square function produces the correct output
//    for a particular scenario a = 2
// *testing.T is a type passed to Test functions to manage
//    test state and support formatted test logs

func TestSquare(t *testing.T) {
    ans := Square(2)
    if ans != 4 {
        // we use t to record the testing error
        t.Errorf("Square(2) = %d; Should be 4", ans)
    }
}


// use table-driven testing to test the function in various
//    situations

func TestSquareTableDriven(t *testing.T) {
    var tests = []struct {
        a int
        expect int
    }{
        // the first input is a = 0 and the expected output is 0
        {0, 0},
        // the second input is a = 1 and the expected output is 1 * 1 = 1
        {1, 1},
        // the third input is a = 2 and the expected output is 2 * 2 = 4
        {2, 4},
        {6, 36},
        {5, 25},
    }

    // iterate through each test table entry
    for _, tt := range tests {
        // display the value to be tested
```

```
testname := fmt.Sprintf("%d", tt.a)
// use t.Run method to execute the test for the current table entry
t.Run(testname, func(t *testing.T){
    // The second argument of Run is a function that simply calls the
    // Square function and compares it against the expected output
    ans := Square(tt.a)
    if ans != tt.expect {
        // use t (type testing.T) to record the error.
        t.Errorf("got %d, want %d", ans, tt.expect)
    }
})
    }
}
```

The program includes two tests: TestSquare and TestSquareTableDriven. By convention, the name of any function used for testing purposes starts with Test.

In TestSquare, you test the function for a single input. The TestSquare takes as input a pointer of type testing.T. This is a built-in type in the testing package that allows you to manage testing states and record errors during testing.

TestSquareTableDriven is a more robust test that uses table-driven testing, where you provide various scenarios/expected output. We recommend that you use this type of testing whenever possible. In the table-driven test, you create a struct (called tests) that contains the various scenarios you want to test and their expected output.

The struct includes two fields, named a and expect in this example. a represents a possible input value, and expect represents the expected output based on a. You provide several scenarios and corresponding expected output in the initialization of the struct. You can add as many scenarios as needed.

The test iterates through the struct table, comparing input to expected output. If it encounters an error, it outputs an appropriate message.

Running the Test

You have two choices for running the tests from the command line. The first is to run the following at the command line:

```
go test
```

This option runs the tests and gives a simple PASS/FAIL response for the program as a whole. It can tell you that the program is working as expected, but it only displays FAILs, without displaying PASSes.

For example, in the program you have at this point, the output for go test is:

```
PASS
ok      _/C_/Users/username/Documents/Go/testing    3.935s
```

Note that if the program and its testing program are in the same folder as other programs, you will need to name the files when running the tests:

```
go test Square.go Square_test.go
```

If you want a more verbose output, you can include the –v switch:

```
go test –v
```

This option will provide feedback for each test, whether it passes or fails, like so:

```
=== RUN    TestSquare
--- PASS: TestSquare (0.00s)
=== RUN    TestSquareTableDriven
=== RUN    TestSquareTableDriven/0
=== RUN    TestSquareTableDriven/1
=== RUN    TestSquareTableDriven/2
=== RUN    TestSquareTableDriven/6
=== RUN    TestSquareTableDriven/5
--- PASS: TestSquareTableDriven (0.01s)
    --- PASS: TestSquareTableDriven/0 (0.00s)
    --- PASS: TestSquareTableDriven/1 (0.00s)
    --- PASS: TestSquareTableDriven/2 (0.00s)
    --- PASS: TestSquareTableDriven/6 (0.00s)
    --- PASS: TestSquareTableDriven/5 (0.00s)
PASS
ok      _/C_/Users/username/Documents/Go/testing      0.070s
```

Again, if the program and its testing program are in the same folder as other programs, you will need to name the files when running the tests:

```
go test –v Square.go Square_test.go
```

TUTORIAL: TEST-DRIVEN DEVELOPMENT

We've shown you a basic example of test-driven development. Let's take a step back and apply what you've learned to a larger example. In the following sections, you will implement Dollar objects that represent the dollar currency using test-driven development.

To develop software using TDD, follow these guidelines:

- Try not to read or think ahead.
- Work incrementally, doing only one task at a time.

In this short tutorial, you will add requirements as we go through the example, making it easy to focus on one step at a time. This particular example will seem simple in its solution, but keep in mind that you are focusing on the process, not the solution, so that you can get a glimpse of how to develop using TDD.

First Test: String Representation of Dollar Amount

With TDD, you start by defining what you want to test, and then you build the code that you want to test. So, your first step is to create the test. This allows you to focus on what you want the program to do first, and then you can write code that meets your expectations. If you start with a well-defined outcome, it takes less time to write the code that produces that outcome.

Add a Test

The first requirement in your solution is that you need to be able to create Dollar objects and get string representations for them, like "USD 2.00". To do this you will write the test program shown in Listing 22.3 and name it Dollar_test.go.

LISTING 22.3

Dollar_test.go

```go
package main

import (
    "testing"
)
func TestFormatAmount(t *testing.T) {
    ans := FormatAmount(2.00)
    if ans != "USD 2.00" {
        // we use t to record the testing error
        t.Errorf("FormatAmount(2.00) = %s; Should be 2.00", ans)
    }
}
```

This test defines how the number output should be formatted (as *USD 2.00*). If the output does not have this format, the test will fail.

Write the Program

Now you are ready to write the `Dollar.go` program that will be tested by the test. This program is shown in Listing 22.4.

LISTING 22.4

Dollar.go

```
package main

import "fmt"

// function formats the output
func FormatAmount(a float64) string {
    return "USD 2.00"
}

func main(){
    fmt.Println("main function")
    fmt.Println(FormatAmount(2.00))
}
```

This program is very simple in that it contains a function called `FormatAmount` that returns a `float64` value formatted as a string. The `main` function prints a message and then formats and prints the value of `2.00`.

At this point, you have implemented enough code to pass the test you created in Listing 22.3, which is the only test that you have created so far. The dollar amount is hard-coded into the program, and you can easily guess that it will fail given a different amount.

Run the Test

Let's run the test to see what happens. This can be accomplished by entering the following on the command line where the program listings are located:

```
go test -v Dollar.go Dollar_test.go
```

Because there is only one possible outcome to our program and the test tests for that outcome, it isn't a surprise that the program passes the test:

```
=== RUN    TestFormatAmount
--- PASS: TestFormatAmount (0.00s)
PASS
ok      command-line-arguments  1.214s
```

Second Test: Test with Other Values

You have now established that the output USD 2.00 created by the FormatAmount function is equal to USD 2.00 defined in the test. However, it's important to test that the functions also fail when you expect them to fail. Let's see what happens if we have another value instead of 2.00.

Add a Test

Let's add another test to the Dollar_test.go program. Listing 22.5 contains an updated version.

LISTING 22.5

Dollar_test.go **with a second test added**

```
package main

import (
    "testing"
)

func TestFormatAmount(t *testing.T) {
    ans := FormatAmount(2.00)
    if ans != "USD 2.00" {
        t.Errorf("FormatAmount(2.00) = %s; Should be 2.00", ans)
    }
}

func TestFormatAmount2(t *testing.T) {
    ans := FormatAmount(4.00)
    if ans != "USD 4.00" {
        t.Errorf("FormatAmount(2.00) = %s; Should be 2.00", ans)
    }
}
```

In this update you add a second function called TestFormatAmount2 to see if the result of your call to FormatAmount is equal to "USD 4.00". You expect the program to fail this test, because 2.00 is not equal to 4.00. This is confirmed when you run the test again:

```
=== RUN    TestFormatAmount
--- PASS: TestFormatAmount (0.00s)
=== RUN    TestFormatAmount2
```

continues

continued

```
    TestFormatAmount2: Dollar_test.go:17: FormatAmount(2.00) = USD 2.00;
Should be 2.00
--- FAIL: TestFormatAmount2 (0.00s)
FAIL
FAIL    command-line-arguments  1.725s
FAIL
```

> **NOTE** If you are not sure why the testing failed in the previous listing, then remember that the FormatAmount program you are testing in Dollar.go only returns "USD 2.00" at this point regardless of what value is passed to it.

Reconfigure the Test

Before addressing the failure, you first need to reconfigure the test to handle decimal values. Let's add a third test called TestFormatAmount3 that will test for a decimal value. Update the Dollar_test.go program with the added test shown in Listing 22.6.

LISTING 22.6

Dollar_test.go **with a third test added**

```go
package main

import (
    "testing"
)

func TestFormatAmount(t *testing.T) {
    ans := FormatAmount(2.00)
    if ans != "USD 2.00" {
        t.Errorf("FormatAmount(2.00) = %s; Should be 2.00", ans)
    }
}

func TestFormatAmount2(t *testing.T) {
    ans := FormatAmount(4.00)
    if ans != "USD 4.00" {
        t.Errorf("FormatAmount(4.00) = %s; Should be 4.00", ans)
    }
}
```

```
func TestFormatAmount3(t *testing.T) {
    ans := FormatAmount(5.10)
    if ans != "USD 5.10" {
        t.Errorf("FormatAmount(5.10) = %s; Should be 5.10", ans)
    }
}
```

The TestFormatAmount3 test is similar to the previous two tests. This time, however, a value of 5.10 is passed to the FormatAmount function for testing.

Reconfigure the Program

The FormatAmount function in the Dollar.go program must be able to handle any appropriate dollar amount, so you need to update it to be more flexible. Specifically, you want it to take any float64 and express that value with the prefix USD and rounded to two decimal places. The fmt.Sprintf function will be used, which converts the number to a string, with the format specifier %.2f, which rounds the original value to two decimal places. Update the Dollar.go listing with the changes to FormatAmount shown in Listing 22.7.

LISTING 22.7

Updated FormatAmount in Dollar.go

```
package main

import (
    "fmt"
)

func FormatAmount(a float64) string {
    // use %.2f for precision 2 which is adequate to represent
    // dollar amounts for now
    return "USD " + fmt.Sprintf("%.2f", a)
}

func main(){
    fmt.Println("main function")
    fmt.Println(FormatAmount(2.00))
}
```

You can see that the change in the listing is to the return value in the FormatAmount function. You are using "%.2f" to indicate that you want a precision of two decimal places, which is enough to represent dollar amounts for now. You are formatting the value of a that is passed into the function using this precision. You are no longer returning the value of `"USD 2.00"`.

Run the Test

Run the tests again to verify that each test passes. The following should be shown:

```
=== RUN    TestFormatAmount
--- PASS: TestFormatAmount (0.00s)
=== RUN    TestFormatAmount2
--- PASS: TestFormatAmount2 (0.00s)
=== RUN    TestFormatAmount3
--- PASS: TestFormatAmount3 (0.00s)
PASS
ok      command-line-arguments  1.246s
```

You have successfully written the test to allow for any `float64` value that you may have in the program. You can change the value in the program to test this.

Third Test: Operation Output

You want your program to do more than just format the number. You also want it to be able to perform a mathematical operation on two numbers and format the output of that operation. Since you are using TDD, you will start by writing the test for this new functionality.

Add a Test

Update `Dollar_test.go` with the new test shown in Listing 22.8.

LISTING 22.8

`Dollar_test.go` **with the new test for** SubtractFormatAmount

```go
package main

import (
    "testing"
)
```

```go
func TestFormatAmount(t *testing.T) {
    ans := FormatAmount(2.00)
    if ans != "USD 2.00" {
        t.Errorf("FormatAmount(2.00) = %s; Should be 2.00", ans)
    }
}
func TestFormatAmount2(t *testing.T) {
    ans := FormatAmount(4.00)
    if ans != "USD 4.00" {
        t.Errorf("FormatAmount(4.00) = %s; Should be 4.00", ans)
    }
}

func TestFormatAmount3(t *testing.T) {

    ans := FormatAmount(5.10)
    if ans != "USD 5.10" {
        t.Errorf("FormatAmount(5.10) = %s; Should be 5.10", ans)
    }
}

func TestSubtractFormatAmount(t *testing.T) {
    ans := SubtractFormatAmount(4.00, 2.00)
    if ans != "USD 2.00" {

        t.Errorf("FormatAmount(4.00, 2.00) = %s; Should be USD 2.00", ans)
    }
}
```

The new test performs the SubtractFormatAmount function from Dollar.go using two hard-coded values and the formatted result you should see using those values. However, if you run the test at this point, it will fail because you haven't yet created the SubtractFormatAmount function. But keep in mind that this is the whole point of TDD: you write tests, you fail them, you implement minimal code to pass them, you refactor, you pass the tests, and repeat.

Reconfigure the Program

Let's implement minimal code to pass the new test that was created. Listing 22.9 updates the Dollar.go program with a very basic SubtractFormatAmount function.

LISTING 22.9

Dollar.go **with** SubtractFormatAmount

```go
package main

import (
    "fmt"
)

func FormatAmount(a float64) string {
    // use %.2f for precision 2 which is adequate to represent
    // dollar amounts for now
    return "USD " + fmt.Sprintf("%.2f", a)
}

func SubtractFormatAmount(a, b float64) string {
    return "USD 2.00"
}

func main(){
    fmt.Println("main function")
    fmt.Println(FormatAmount(2.00))
    fmt.Println(SubtractFormatAmount(2.00, 1.14))
}
```

Note that the SubtractFormatAmount function doesn't actually perform subtraction at this point. The listing is using a minimal viable output that can pass the test to make sure that the test works with a valid input.

Run the Test

Run the test to check that it passes. You should see output similar to the following:

```
=== RUN    TestFormatAmount
--- PASS: TestFormatAmount (0.00s)
=== RUN    TestFormatAmount2
--- PASS: TestFormatAmount2 (0.00s)
=== RUN    TestFormatAmount3
--- PASS: TestFormatAmount3 (0.00s)
=== RUN    TestSubtractFormatAmount
--- PASS: TestSubtractFormatAmount (0.00s)
PASS
ok      command-line-arguments  1.294s
```

Test the Test

Remember that you also want to check that the test will fail when you expect it to. To this end, add another test to Dollar_test.go that will fail, as shown in Listing 22.10.

LISTING 22.10

Dollar_test **updated with a test for failure**

```go
package main

import (
    "testing"
)

func TestFormatAmount(t *testing.T) {
    ans := FormatAmount(2.00)
    if ans != "USD 2.00" {
        t.Errorf("FormatAmount(2.00) = %s; Should be 2.00", ans)
    }
}
func TestFormatAmount2(t *testing.T) {
    ans := FormatAmount(4.00)
    if ans != "USD 4.00" {
        t.Errorf("FormatAmount(4.00) = %s; Should be 4.00", ans)
    }
}

func TestFormatAmount3(t *testing.T) {

    ans := FormatAmount(5.10)
    if ans != "USD 5.10" {
        t.Errorf("FormatAmount(5.10) = %s; Should be 5.10", ans)
    }
}

func TestSubtractFormatAmount(t *testing.T) {
    ans := SubtractFormatAmount(4.00, 2.00)
    if ans != "USD 2.00" {
        t.Errorf("FormatAmount(4.00,2.00) = %s; Should be USD 2.00", ans)
    }
}
```

continues

continued

```
func TestSubtractFormatAmount2(t *testing.T) {
    ans := SubtractFormatAmount(3.00, 1.12)
    if ans != "USD 1.88" {
        t.Errorf("FormatAmount(3.00,1.12) = %s; Should be USD 1.88", ans)
            // we use t to record the testing error.
    }
}
```

This test verifies that subtracting 1.12 from 3.00 using the SubtractFormatAmount function returns a proper result of 1.88. Run the test. Because you know SubtractFormatAmount returns a hard-coded value of "USD 2.0" at this time, you expect the most recent test to fail at this point. When the test runs, you should see that it, indeed, does fail:

```
=== RUN    TestFormatAmount
--- PASS: TestFormatAmount (0.00s)
=== RUN    TestFormatAmount2
--- PASS: TestFormatAmount2 (0.00s)
=== RUN    TestFormatAmount3
--- PASS: TestFormatAmount3 (0.00s)
=== RUN    TestSubtractFormatAmount
--- PASS: TestSubtractFormatAmount (0.00s)
=== RUN    TestSubtractFormatAmount2
    TestSubtractFormatAmount2: Dollar_test.go:38: FormatAmount(3.00,1.12) =
USD 2.00; Should be USD 1.88
--- FAIL: TestSubtractFormatAmount2 (0.00s)
FAIL
FAIL    command-line-arguments  1.262s
FAIL
```

Refactor *SubtractFormatAmount*

Next, you want to refactor the SubtractFormatAmount function to use the format settings you added to the FormatAmount function so that it will work with any float64 value. This update is shown in Listing 22.11.

LISTING 22.11

Dollar.go **update to** SubtractFormatAmount

```
package main

import (
    "fmt"
)
```

```
func FormatAmount(a float64) string {
    // use %.2f for precision 2 which is adequate to represent
    // dollar amounts for now
    return "USD " + fmt.Sprintf("%.2f", a)
}

func SubtractFormatAmount(a, b float64) string {
    return "USD " + fmt.Sprintf("%.2f", a - b)
}

func main(){
    fmt.Println("main function")
    fmt.Println(FormatAmount(2.00))
    fmt.Println(SubtractFormatAmount(2.00, 1.14))
}
```

Run the Test

After making this latest update, run the test again to check that it passes. You should see that it does:

```
=== RUN    TestFormatAmount
--- PASS: TestFormatAmount (0.00s)
=== RUN    TestFormatAmount2
--- PASS: TestFormatAmount2 (0.00s)
=== RUN    TestFormatAmount3
--- PASS: TestFormatAmount3 (0.00s)
=== RUN    TestSubtractFormatAmount
--- PASS: TestSubtractFormatAmount (0.00s)
=== RUN    TestSubtractFormatAmount2
--- PASS: TestSubtractFormatAmount2 (0.00s)
PASS
ok        command-line-arguments   1.222s
```

Examining the Tests

Sometimes just running a test (even with the verbose option) doesn't tell you everything you need to know. For example, you may want to know how much of the code is being tested, and you may want to share that information with others on your team.

Test Coverage

You can get the test coverage by using the –cover flag when running the test program from the command line:

```
go test -cover Dollar.go Dollar_test.go
```

You should see a result that looks like this:

```
ok      command-line-arguments  0.051s  coverage: 40.0% of statements
```

In this example, 40 percent of the code is tested. This value should be as high as possible, but it is not always necessary to achieve 100 percent coverage. Test coverage is computed as follows:

Test coverage = (B / A) × 100

where A is the total lines of code in the piece of software you are testing, and B is the number of lines of code all test cases currently execute.

Coverage Reports

Detailed coverage reports can be created as well by using the following commands:

```
go test -cover -coverprofile=c.out Dollar.go Dollar_test.go
go tool cover -html=c.out -o coverage.html
```

The first command creates a text file with references to the test coverage, including which lines were tested and which lines weren't. The second command formats that file as an HTML file, making the information easier to see. Both files will appear in the directory identified in the command prompt similar to what is shown in Figure 22.1.

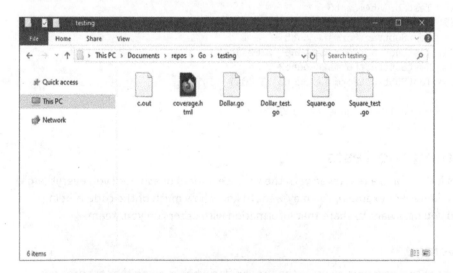

Figure 22.1: The Windows folder includes the files c.out, coverage.html, Dollar.go, Dollar_test.go, Square.go, and Square_test.go

The HTML file looks something like Figure 22.2.

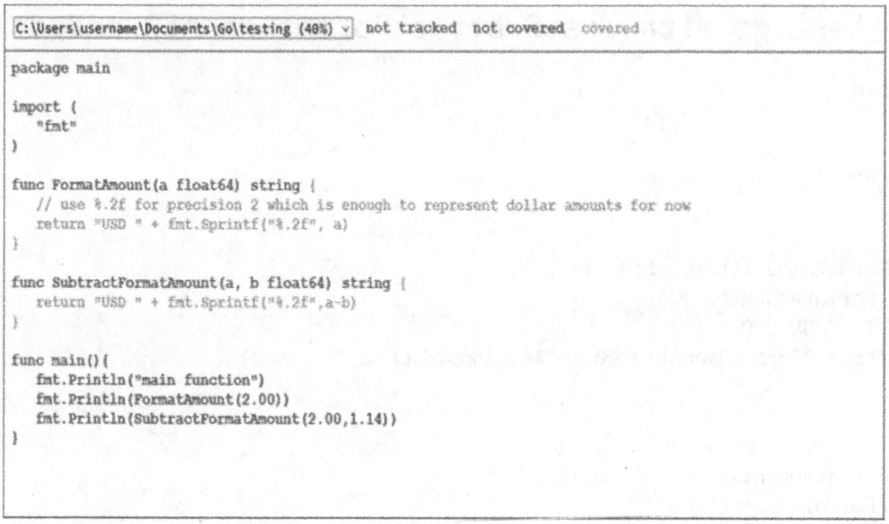

```
C:\Users\username\Documents\Go\testing (40%) v    not tracked  not covered  covered

package main

import (
    "fmt"
)

func FormatAmount(a float64) string {
    // use %.2f for precision 2 which is enough to represent dollar amounts for now
    return "USD " + fmt.Sprintf("%.2f", a)
}

func SubtractFormatAmount(a, b float64) string {
    return "USD " + fmt.Sprintf("%.2f",a-b)
}

func main(){
    fmt.Println("main function")
    fmt.Println(FormatAmount(2.00))
    fmt.Println(SubtractFormatAmount(2.00,1.14))
}
```

Figure 22.2: The web page color-codes the lines of code. The results are summarized next.

The original CSS settings use black backgrounds, making the content hard to read. You can edit this file to remove the background styles and improve its appearance. Additionally, the code not tracked, not covered, and covered are each presented in a different color to make it easy to see the coverage.

As shown in this report, only the lines inside the functions were covered, which you expect. The test ignores the entirety of the main function, as well as the import statements.

Fourth Test: Include Subtraction

Now let's get back to our program and continue developing the test. Specifically, you want SubtractFormatAmount to include a subtraction operation.

Add a Test

Test to see what happens when you subtract values and a < b. You expect this value to be negative (even if you don't want it to be negative in the context of money). Add the test to the Dollar_test.go file, as shown in Listing 22.12.

LISTING 22.12

`Dollar_test.go` **with** `TestSubtractFormatAmount3` **added**

```go
package main

import (
    "testing"
)

func TestFormatAmount(t *testing.T) {
    ans := FormatAmount(2.00)
    if ans != "USD 2.00" {
        t.Errorf("FormatAmount(2.00) = %s; Should be 2.00", ans)
    }
}

func TestFormatAmount2(t *testing.T) {
    ans := FormatAmount(4.00)
    if ans != "USD 4.00" {
        t.Errorf("FormatAmount(4.00) = %s; Should be 4.00", ans)
    }
}

func TestFormatAmount3(t *testing.T) {
    ans := FormatAmount(5.10)
    if ans != "USD 5.10" {
        t.Errorf("FormatAmount(5.10) = %s; Should be 5.10", ans)
    }
}

func TestSubtractFormatAmount(t *testing.T) {
    ans := SubtractFormatAmount(4.00, 2.00)
    if ans != "USD 2.00" {
        t.Errorf("FormatAmount(4.00,2.00) = %s; Should be USD 2.00", ans)
    }
}

func TestSubtractFormatAmount2(t *testing.T) {
    ans := SubtractFormatAmount(3.00, 1.12)
    if ans != "USD 1.88" {
```

```
        t.Errorf("FormatAmount(3.00,1.12) = %s; Should be USD 1.88", ans)
    }
}

func TestSubtractFormatAmount3(t *testing.T) {
    ans := SubtractFormatAmount(1.00, 1.12)
    if ans != "Impossible operation" {
        t.Errorf("FormatAmount(1.00, 1.12) cannot be performed")
    }
}
```

Refactor the Program

If you run the test now, the new test will fail since your SubtractFormatAmount is not set up to handle cases where a < b. Fix that by updating your SubtractFormatAmount function as shown in Listing 22.13.

LISTING 22.13

Dollar.go **with updated** SubtractFormatAmount

```go
package main

import (
    "fmt"
)

func FormatAmount(a float64) string {
    // use %.2f for precision 2 which is adequate to represent
    // dollar amounts for now
    return "USD " + fmt.Sprintf("%.2f", a)
}

func SubtractFormatAmount(a, b float64) string {
    if a >= b{
        return "USD " + fmt.Sprintf("%.2f",a - b)
    }
    return "Impossible operation"
}
```

continues

continued

```
func main(){
    fmt.Println("main function")
    fmt.Println(FormatAmount(2.00))
    fmt.Println(SubtractFormatAmount(2.00,1.14))
}
```

As you can see, the SubtractFormatAmount function now checks to make sure that a is greater than or equal to b before returning the formatted string. If a doesn't pass the check (it should be less than b), then the message Impossible operation is returned instead.

Run the Test

Let's test the updates with coverage. Remember, you do this with the following command:

```
go test -v -cover Dollar.go Dollar_test.go
```

The results show that you have increased the coverage:

```
=== RUN    TestFormatAmount
--- PASS: TestFormatAmount (0.00s)
=== RUN    TestFormatAmount2
--- PASS: TestFormatAmount2 (0.00s)
=== RUN    TestFormatAmount3
--- PASS: TestFormatAmount3 (0.00s)
=== RUN    TestSubtractFormatAmount
--- PASS: TestSubtractFormatAmount (0.00s)
=== RUN    TestSubtractFormatAmount2
--- PASS: TestSubtractFormatAmount2 (0.00s)
=== RUN    TestSubtractFormatAmount3
--- PASS: TestSubtractFormatAmount3 (0.00s)
PASS
coverage: 57.1% of statements
ok      command-line-arguments   0.069s  coverage: 57.1% of statements
```

Final Tests: Look at Input Values

Testing helps you identify places where a program can go wrong, and you want most of the code to be tested. Let's look at other ways you can improve the testing and increase the coverage.

Add a Test

You normally want to use positive numbers when manipulating values that represent money. How would you handle a case where one of the input values is negative? You should consider the same when using FormatAmount. If the input a is negative, you should handle it properly as well.

Update the Tests

The code in Listing 22.14 shows the updates necessary to handle situations of negative values.

LISTING 22.14

Dollar_test.go **with negative value tests added**

```go
package main

import (
    "testing"
)

func TestFormatAmount(t *testing.T) {
    ans := FormatAmount(2.00)
    if ans != "USD 2.00" {
        t.Errorf("FormatAmount(2.00) = %s; Should be 2.00", ans)
    }
}

func TestFormatAmount2(t *testing.T) {
    ans := FormatAmount(4.00)
    if ans != "USD 4.00" {
        t.Errorf("FormatAmount(4.00) = %s; Should be 4.00", ans)
    }
}

func TestFormatAmount3(t *testing.T) {
    ans := FormatAmount(5.10)
    if ans != "USD 5.10" {
        t.Errorf("FormatAmount(5.10) = %s; Should be 5.10", ans)
    }
}
```

continues

continued

```go
// test if input value is negative
func TestFormatAmount4(t *testing.T) {
    ans := FormatAmount(-5.10)
    if ans != "Impossible operation" {
        t.Errorf("FormatAmount(-5.10) cannot be performed")
    }
}

func TestSubtractFormatAmount(t *testing.T) {
    ans := SubtractFormatAmount(4.00, 2.00)
    if ans != "USD 2.00" {
        t.Errorf("FormatAmount(4.00,2.00) = %s; Should be USD 2.00", ans)
    }
}

func TestSubtractFormatAmount2(t *testing.T) {
    ans := SubtractFormatAmount(3.00, 1.12)
    if ans != "USD 1.88" {
        t.Errorf("FormatAmount(3.00,1.12) = %s; Should be USD 1.88", ans)
    }
}

func TestSubtractFormatAmount3(t *testing.T) {
    ans := SubtractFormatAmount(1.00, 1.12)
    if ans != "Impossible operation" {
        t.Errorf("FormatAmount(1.00, 1.12) cannot be performed")
    }
}

// test if both input values are negative
func TestSubtractFormatAmount4(t *testing.T) {
    ans := SubtractFormatAmount(-1.00, -1.12)
    if ans != "Impossible operation" {
        t.Errorf("FormatAmount(-1.00, -1.12) cannot be performed")
    }
}

// test if b is negative
func TestSubtractFormatAmount5(t *testing.T) {
    ans := SubtractFormatAmount(1.00,-1.12)
    if ans != "Impossible operation" {
        t.Errorf("FormatAmount(1.00, -1.12) cannot be performed")
    }
}
```

In this update, you've added a few tests for scenarios where negative values are entered. Two test cases were added, TestSubtractFormatAmount4 and TestSubtractFormatAmount5. Each checks for negative numbers.

Refactor the Program

Now you will update the program itself to handle these situations. Listing 22.15 presents the updated program that handles negative results.

LISTING 22.15

Dollar.go with final additions

```
package main

import (
    "fmt"
)

func FormatAmount(a float64) string {
    // handle when a is negative
    if a < 0 {
        return "Impossible operation"
    }
    // use %.2f for precision 2 which is adequate to represent dollar
amounts for now
    return "USD " + fmt.Sprintf("%.2f", a)
}

func SubtractFormatAmount(a, b float64) string {
    // if a is negative
    if a < 0 {
        return "Impossible operation"
    }
    // if b is negative
    if b < 0 {
        return "Impossible operation"
    }
    if a >= b {
        return "USD " + fmt.Sprintf("%.2f", a - b)
    }
```

continues

continued

```
    // if 0 < a < b
    return "Impossible operation"
}

func main(){
    fmt.Println(FormatAmount(0.00))
    fmt.Println(FormatAmount(-10.00))

    fmt.Println(SubtractFormatAmount(0.03 , 0.42))
    fmt.Println(SubtractFormatAmount(-0.03 , -0.42))
}
```

There are a couple of things to note with this updated listing. In the function SubtractFormatAmount, you have separate statements to determine if a or b is negative. You could use a single OR statement instead:

```
    if ((a < 0) || (b < 0))...
```

In the same function, you also simplify the code a bit using if statements for each possible combination of values less than 0, and you perform the function only if a is greater than or equal to b. You have a default return that runs only if a is less than b but neither value is less than 0.

Run the Test

After updating both the program and the tests, run the test again. All tests should pass, and the coverage amount should be even higher.

```
=== RUN     TestFormatAmount
--- PASS: TestFormatAmount (0.00s)
=== RUN     TestFormatAmount2
--- PASS: TestFormatAmount2 (0.00s)
=== RUN     TestFormatAmount3
--- PASS: TestFormatAmount3 (0.00s)
=== RUN     TestFormatAmount4
--- PASS: TestFormatAmount4 (0.00s)
=== RUN     TestSubtractFormatAmount
--- PASS: TestSubtractFormatAmount (0.00s)
=== RUN     TestSubtractFormatAmount2
```

```
--- PASS: TestSubtractFormatAmount2 (0.00s)
=== RUN   TestSubtractFormatAmount3
--- PASS: TestSubtractFormatAmount3 (0.00s)
=== RUN   TestSubtractFormatAmount4
--- PASS: TestSubtractFormatAmount4 (0.00s)
=== RUN   TestSubtractFormatAmount5
--- PASS: TestSubtractFormatAmount5 (0.00s)
PASS
coverage: 71.4% of statements
ok      command-line-arguments  0.468s  coverage: 71.4% of statements
```

BEHAVIOR-DRIVEN DEVELOPMENT

Behavior-driven development (BDD) focuses on user requirements of the software throughout the development process, using plain language and user stories rather than programming code to define what the software should do and to verify that the software meets expectations as it is developed.

Goals of Behavior-Driven Development

Behavior-driven development is a methodology that arose from test-driven development, where the focus is on testing software as the code is developed by first defining what the code should do, creating a test for those requirements, and finally writing code that passes the tests.

BDD employs user stories to describe the behavior of the software under development. These stories are written in plain language that can be understood by all parties involved in the development process, including those with no coding experience. For example, a starting point for a BDD rule might be something like, "The user must be able to update their address when they move."

BDD has the following goals:

- Promote a better understanding of the customer, the product, and the requirements.
- Promote continuous communication between customers and developers.
- Bridge communication gaps between team members.

These goals are accomplished by using tools and resources that reinforce communication between the different parties involved in the software development process.

Avoiding Failure

One of the most common ways that a software development project can fail is when various teams or individuals have different understandings of how the software should behave. The importance of identifying the correct requirements is emphasized in BDD by:

- Deriving examples of different behaviors of the software

- Allowing developers to write these examples in plain language that everyone involved in the process can understand, including the customer

- Verifying the examples with the customers to make sure the requirements are correct

- Focusing on the examples (or requirements) throughout the development process

- Using examples as tests to ensure that the requirements are implemented correctly into the software

- Implementing only behaviors that contribute directly to the business outcomes

As mentioned earlier, BDD is an extension of TDD. As with TDD, in BDD, you write test units first and then implement the code to pass that test. However, BDD is different from TDD in the following aspects:

- Tests are first written in plain English, so everyone can understand them.

- Tests are explained as behaviors of the application under development.

- Tests are more user-focused.

- Examples are used to clarify requirements.

- There is more focus on behavior than on tests.

Development teams can use tools like Cucumber (`https://cucumber.io`), SpecFlow (`https://specflow.org`), and behave (`https://behave.readthedocs.io`) when using a BDD approach to software development. These tools allow the development team to write software specifications and requirements in a business-readable, domain-specific language, which developers can then translate into unit tests in programming languages like Java and .NET. Writing requirements in a business-readable language means that non-technical parties such as project managers and external clients can understand and verify them throughout the development process.

These specifications serve as documentation as well. As a result, BDD tools solve problems related to identifying requirements, creating automated testing, and producing documentation in a single step, which saves time and development costs.

Behavior Specifications

Unlike TDD, BDD heavily relies on tools like Cucumber and SpecFlow, which use DSL (domain-specific language) to describe the behavior of the software under development. Behavior specifications are written using a standard Agile framework of a user story. A typical syntax for these user stories looks like this:

```
As a [role] I want [feature] so that [benefit]
```

Acceptance criteria are written in the form of scenarios:

```
Given [initial context] when [event occurs], then [outcomes]
```

To better understand the principles of BDD, let's look at a specific example. Imagine that you are building a user portal where users can view various information such as weather, stock market reports, news, and similar content. Users from all over the world will be using this software, so the software must support the different languages of the users themselves. You need to test the language to make sure that the selected language for each user is correct. For the sake of simplicity, let's assume that users will speak only one of two languages: English and French.

As a starting point, let's look at the site's login functionality. When the user fails to log in, you should be able to display an error message in their native language:

- English: Invalid Login
- French: Le login est invalide

Let's consider these three users:

- Kate from the United States (Language: English)
- Brittney from the United Kingdom (Language: English)
- Jean from France (Language: French)

Story: Failed Login

Feature: As a user, I want to see information in my own language, so I can understand the information.

Now let's consider the following scenarios. Note the use of Given, When, and Then to define each step of the validation process:

Scenario: Failed Login

Given: Failed login by Kate

When: The website sends the error message
Then: The error message should be "Invalid Login"

Scenario: Failed Login
Given: Failed login by Jean
When: The website sends the error message
Then: The error message should be "Le login est invalide"

Tools like the Given-When-Then scenario in Cucumber (named for the first word in each line following the scenario definition) make it relatively straightforward to define scenarios like this and test to be sure that each scenario is satisfied appropriately in the code.

Defining User Stories

Typically, BDD includes two main activities: specification workshops and executable specifications.

Specification Workshops

The purpose of specification workshops is to gather the teams involved in the development of the software and agree on a common understanding of how the software should behave. During these workshops, the teams involved in the meetings create user stories like the one presented previously, along with concrete examples that describe the business rules and acceptance criteria.

These examples define how the software will behave. By conducting specification workshops, teams help avoid any confusion or misunderstanding about the behavior or requirements of the software. Moreover, specification workshops allow business stakeholders to make sure that the developers understand the requirements of the software before they start building the software.

Executable Specifications

Once the teams have identified the specifications, the next step is to transform these specifications into executable software specifications (unit tests), which will verify that the implemented software is behaving the same way as the identified behavior in the specification workshops.

Cucumber is an example of a tool that can transform specifications into executable specifications. In this case, we simply provide the Given-When-Then scenarios (like the ones in the login example earlier) and Cucumber will create executable specifications. These executable specifications provide developers with instant feedback throughout the development process, which reduces the chances of defects.

SUMMARY

This was one of the longest lessons in the book, but a lot was covered. Testing is an important part of doing "job ready" development because it helps ensure your applications work properly. In this lesson you learned about test-driven development (TDD) and how it can be used to create testing along with your code. You also learned about behavior-driven development (BDD), which is similar to TDD but with a focus on requirements.

EXERCISES

The following exercises are provided to allow you to experiment with the tools and concepts presented in this lesson. For each exercise, write a program that meets the specified requirements and verify that the program runs as expected. The exercises are:

Exercise 22.1: Breaking the Square

Exercise 22.2: Adding More to Dollar

> **NOTE** The exercises are for your benefit. The exercises help you apply what you learn in the lessons. You are also encouraged to experiment with the code as you complete the exercises.

Exercise 22.1: Breaking the *Square*

The code presented in Listing 22.1 and Listing 22.2 does what you want it to do, so all the tests pass. Build both programs (in the same folder) and verify that the program passes all the tests. Once this is working, change the Square function In the main program so that it performs a different calculation, such as addition instead of multiplication. Save the change and run the tests again to see the results.

After changing and testing the function in the main program, change the tests to match the expected output for the new function, and run the tests again.

Exercise 22.2: Adding More to *Dollar*

Update the Dollar program and test to include a function that adds the input values and formats the result in the same format used in the current program. Write appropriate tests that apply to that function as well.

Once you have a complete working program that passes all tests, refactor the program to include:

- User inputs for a and b.
- Allow the program to apply other currency formats to the output, based on user input.

> **NOTE** For this exercise, you can start with Listing 22.14 and Listing 22.15.

Lesson 23
API Development Tutorial

This lesson is a tutorial in which you will create a fully working REST API that uses GET, POST, PUT, and DELETE HTTP requests to perform CRUD (create, read, update, and delete) operations on a dataset. As a tutorial, the focus will be on writing code to develop a working solution.

LEARNING OBJECTIVES

By the end of this lesson, you will be able to:

- Understand the basics of REST and related terminology.
- Create a return handler.
- Create a request handler.
- Work with GET, POST, PUT, and DELETE actions.
- Use REST to perform create, read, update, and delete operations on a dataset.

OVERVIEW AND REQUIREMENTS

REST stands for Representational State Transfer. A REST can be used to expose information from a web application and to allow other applications to access that information. REST basically is an architecture that can be used to let web applications access resources and information about the state of a resource on another system. By using REST application programming interfaces (RESTful APIs), you can interact with other servers and systems.

In this lesson, you will learn how to create a number of elements that help make working with remote processes possible:

Requests – In the context used in this lesson, a request is an HTTP request. All requests within the API are in the form of an HTTP request.

Handlers – A handler is a function that processes or handles incoming requests from clients. Each type of request should have an appropriate handler that processes that request and provides a response to that request.

Routers – A router is a function that maps the endpoints of your API to the corresponding handler that will handle it.

Your goal is to create a fully working RESTful API that uses GET, POST, PUT, and DELETE HTTP requests to create, read, update, and delete (CRUD) data. The CRUD actions correspond to HTTP requests as follows:

POST – Add new data to the dataset

GET – Retrieve existing data

PUT – Update existing data

DELETE – Delete existing data

This tutorial uses Postman, an app used to build and use APIs. If you do not already have Postman installed on your computer, you can download and install it from Postman.com/downloads. Postman asks you to set up a free user account; however, an account is not required to download or use Postman. The installation is straightforward once you've requested the download.

> **NOTE** In this lesson we are using the Microsoft Windows version of the Postman app. There is also a web version that you can use as well as desktop clients for both macOS and Linux.

STEP 1: CREATE THE DATASET AND A SIMPLE API

The first step is to plan the basic elements and add them to the program. To build the API, you'll need the following packages:

- encoding/json: This package helps parse JSON data that you receive from requests into Go data, and vice versa.

- `log`: The log package allows you to implement logging capabilities for your API, such as logging errors in requests.
- `net/http`: This package allows you to receive, parse, and send HTTP requests.

Create a new program and add the required packages, as shown in Listing 23.1.

LISTING 23.1

The new program with the required imported packages

```
package main

import (
    "encoding/json"
    "fmt"
    "log"
    "net/http"
)
```

The listing also includes the `fmt` package, which you will use for output.

Defining the Dataset

The next step is to define the dataset that you will perform the CRUD operations on. For this simple example, you want the following fields as a starting point:

- `Number` – The account number
- `Balance` – The current account balance
- `Desc` – The type of account

This definition of a dataset will work as a basic representation, but you can include additional fields if necessary. You will map these fields to appropriate fields in a JSON dataset. Add the struct in Listing 23.2 to the code you created in Listing 23.1 following the `import` statements.

LISTING 23.2

An `Account` struct

```
type Account struct {
    Number string   `json:"AccountNumber"`
```

continues

continued

```
    Balance string `json:"Balance"`
    Desc string    `json:"AccountDescription"`
}
```

You will also create a dataset of accounts, which you'll store in a slice. You want several different functions to access this dataset, so you'll define it as a global variable, outside of the main function. Add the variable immediately after the struct:

```
var Accounts []Account
```

Another option is to create the Accounts dataset as a local variable and then pass it to every function, but the global option is fine for this tutorial and is generally more efficient than local variables are.

The *homePage* Function

The homePage function shown in Listing 23.3 takes as an input http.ResponseWriter and a pointer to an HTTP request. A function that takes as arguments a ResponseWriter and an HTTP request, such as homePage, is called a *handler*. This is because Handler is an inter-face in Go, represented as follows:

```
type Handler interface {
    ServeHTTP(http.ResponseWriter, *http.Request)
}
```

As you can see, the interface Handler includes one method called ServeHTTP. This method has the purpose of answering/responding to an HTTP request. The method has the same signature as the homePage function. In the example, you are implementing the ServeHTTP method in the homePage function, which makes homePage a handler.

In homePage, you use http.ResponseWriter to create an initial message for your appli-cation. The API returns something right off the bat to the client (see Listing 23.3).

LISTING 23.3

The homePage function

```
func homePage(w http.ResponseWriter, r *http.Request){
    fmt.Fprintf(w, "Welcome to our bank!")
    fmt.Println("Endpoint: /")
}
```

Return Handler

You want your app to return the accounts in the dataset in a JSON format, so create the `returnAllAccounts` function to handle this process. As you can see in Listing 23.4, the `returnAllAccounts` function is also a handler.

LISTING 23.4

The `returnAllAccounts` function

```
func returnAllAccounts(w http.ResponseWriter, r *http.Request){
    json.NewEncoder(w).Encode(Accounts)
}
```

In this function, you use the `Encode` function to convert the Accounts in `Json Encoding` into a JSON object.

Handling and Routing Incoming Requests

Next, you need a way to handle the incoming HTTP requests and route them to the appropriate handler (the two you've created so far). If the client sends a request to access all the accounts, you will route the request to the appropriate handler. In other words, you are mapping the endpoints of your API to the corresponding handle. In the example, you have two endpoints so far (/ and /accounts). You'll use a `handleRequests` function for this, as shown in Listing 23.5.

LISTING 23.5

The `handleRequests` function

```
func handleRequests() {
  http.HandleFunc("/", homePage)
  http.HandleFunc("/accounts", returnAllAccounts)
  log.Fatal(http.ListenAndServe(":10000", nil))
}
```

The `handleRequests` function assigns handlers for the different endpoints in our API. An API typically includes different endpoints that it can support, and you will need to call the appropriate handler, depending on the input request, that will handle the request and return the appropriate response/data that should be sent back to the client.

In our example, so far the API can handle only two requests (two endpoints). The first one is the homepage, which is similar to a landing page for your API and allows the client to know that the API is up and running and ready to accept requests. The second request is /accounts, which is used to retrieve the list of accounts available. The handleRequests function uses the HandleFunc function to assign the appropriate handler. As you develop more handlers, you'll add them here to support incoming requests.

You use the log package to log errors related to the API. The http package includes the function ListenAndServe, which you use to listen to incoming requests on port 10000. The nil relates to using a custom router—more on this later.

With this function, you can reach the API at the address http://localhost:10000 while the program is running.

Adding Data

In the main function, you create fictional data for the Accounts dataset and execute the handleRequests function. Listing 23.6 presents a main function that can be used as a starting point.

LISTING 23.6

Creating test data

```
func main() {
    Accounts = []Account{
        Account{Number: "C45t34534", Balance: "24545.5", Desc: "Checking
Account"},
        Account{Number: "S3r53455345", Balance: "444.4", Desc: "Savings Account"},
    }
}
```

Executing the Request Handler

As a last step, you execute the request handler as shown in the updated main function in Listing 23.7. This launches the API, and you can access it using the URL defined for localhost.

LISTING 23.7

Executing the request handler

```
func main() {
  // initialize the dataset
   Accounts = []Account{
      Account{Number: "C45t34534", Balance: "24545.5", Desc: "Checking
Account"},
      Account{Number: "S3r53455345", Balance: "444.4", Desc: "Savings Account"},
   }

   handleRequests()
}
```

At this point, your program should be similar to Listing 23.8.

LISTING 23.8

Our complete listing to this point

```
package main

import (
    "encoding/json"
    "fmt"
    "log"
    "net/http"
)

type Account struct {
    Number string `json:"AccountNumber"`
    Balance string `json:"Balance"`
    Desc string `json:"AccountDescription"`
}

var Accounts []Account
```

continues

continued

```go
func homePage(w http.ResponseWriter, r *http.Request){
    fmt.Fprintf(w, "Welcome to our bank!")
    fmt.Println("Endpoint: /")
}

func returnAllAccounts(w http.ResponseWriter, r *http.Request){
    json.NewEncoder(w).Encode(Accounts)
}

func handleRequests() {
  http.HandleFunc("/", homePage)
  http.HandleFunc("/accounts", returnAllAccounts)
  log.Fatal(http.ListenAndServe(":10000", nil))
}

func main() {
  // initialize the dataset
  Accounts = []Account{
      Account{Number: "C45t34534", Balance: "24545.5", Desc: "Checking
Account"},
      Account{Number: "S3r53455345", Balance: "444.4", Desc: "Savings Account"},
  }

  handleRequests()
}
```

Running the Program

After you've added all the code, check that everything works. Run the program as you normally would. Because this program uses HTTP GET requests to display information (rather than sending output directly to the console), you should use Postman to check the results.

After running the program and without closing the command-line interface, open Postman so that you can create a request to your application. You do this in Postman by clicking the Create a request link on the right, as shown in Figure 23.1.

> **NOTE** You can toggle on and off the left part of the Postman screen by selecting Toggle Sidebar from the View menu.

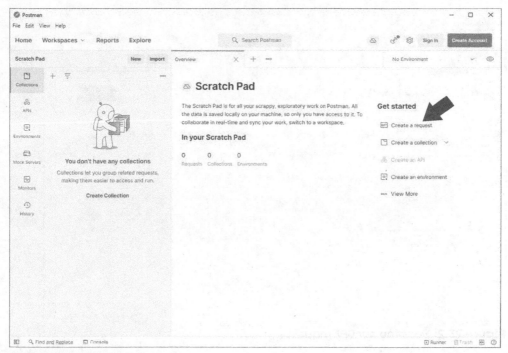

Figure 23.1: Creating a request

With Postman open and on the request page, you can send a GET request to the address `http://localhost:10000`. You do so by entering the URL in the location shown in Figure 23.2 and clicking Send.

Postman will connect to the API, which will execute the `handleRequests` function. Because you are using the root address for the API, it will return the definition for the home page. Note the following from what is shown in Figure 23.2:

- You see a GET request to the URL at the top of the window. The Send button sends the request through the API.

- The API returns the text you defined for the home page, and you see that text in the Body tab in the lower part of the window.

This tells you that the API is running on your machine and that Postman can reach it. But you really want to see the data in the dataset. Update the GET request to `http://localhost:10000/accounts` and send the request again, as shown in Figure 23.3.

Figure 23.2: Sending our GET request

Figure 23.3: A GET request for the account information

The Body tab now displays the records you added to the dataset in the `main` function, with each record in JSON format.

Verify that your program works as expected at this point. You should be able to use Postman to retrieve both the home page and the account list. You may also wish to add a couple more records to the dataset to verify that the `GET` request retrieves all data in the dataset. When you are ready to go to the next step, you can stop the current API by pressing Ctrl+C at the same command window where you started the application.

STEP 2: ADD A ROUTER: GORILLA MUX

So far, you have been using built-in functions in the `handleRequests` function to route incoming requests to the appropriate handler that will process those requests and construct the response for them. This is fine for each request without any input data.

Our API doesn't accept any input data from the client for now. For instance, it would be great if when the client sent an account ID that the API would return the data for that particular account (if it exists). This is where the `gorilla/mux` package comes into play.

Gorilla Mux makes it easy to create a router type that will map your request to the appropriate handler as well as parse input data from client requests.

To install Gorilla Mux, run the following command at a command prompt:

```
go get -u github.com/gorilla/mux
```

This will retrieve the `gorilla/mux` package from its GitHub repository and install it in your Go package. After installing the package, add the following to your imported packages in your program:

```
"github.com/gorilla/mux"
```

Finally, you want to update the `handleRequests` function to include the Gorilla Mux router. Update that function to match Listing 23.9.

LISTING 23.9

The updated handleRequests function

```
func handleRequests() {
    // create a router to handle our requests from the mux package.
    router := mux.NewRouter().StrictSlash(true)
    router.HandleFunc("/", homePage)
```

continues

continued

```
    router.HandleFunc("/accounts", returnAllAccounts)
    log.Fatal(http.ListenAndServe(":10000", router))
}
```

Look at the new code. Note that `StrictSlash` defines the trailing slash behavior for new routes. The initial value is `false`. When `true`, if the route path is "/path/", accessing "/path" will perform a redirect to the former, and vice versa. Essentially, this guarantees that your application will always see the path as specified in the route.

As you can see, Listing 23.9 uses the `NewRouter` function from the `gorilla/mux` package to create a router type that will hold all the mappings of your API.

You use the new `router` variable to handle requests to the API, rather than using the built-in `http` package. You also update the code to use the `mux` router as a custom handler for the `ListenAndServe` function.

After updating the code, run the updated program and troubleshoot it as necessary. Listing 23.10 contains the full program for reference. You should still be able to send a `GET` command to both the home page and the accounts list and retrieve the same data you saw at the end of the previous step.

> **NOTE** Additional comments were added to Listing 23.10.

LISTING 23.10

The full listing with the router added

```go
package main

import (
    "encoding/json"
    "fmt"
    "log"
    "net/http"
    "github.com/gorilla/mux"
)

// create a type Account that will be used to represent a bank account
type Account struct {
    Number string  `json:"AccountNumber"`
    Balance string `json:"Balance"`
    Desc string    `json:"AccountDescription"`
}
```

```
// we use Accounts as a global variable because it is used by
// several functions in the code
var Accounts []Account

// implement the homePage
// we use the ResponseWriter w to display some text when
// we visit the home page
func homePage(w http.ResponseWriter, r *http.Request){
    fmt.Fprintf(w, "Welcome to our bank!")
  // we can use a print command to log the request or we
  // can log it to a file, etc.
    fmt.Println("Endpoint: /")
}

// return the dataset Accounts in a JSON format
func returnAllAccounts(w http.ResponseWriter, r *http.Request){
    // we use the Encode function to convert the Account slice into a json object
    json.NewEncoder(w).Encode(Accounts)
}

// handleRequests will process HTTP requests and redirect them to
// the appropriate Handle function
func handleRequests() {
    // create a router to handle our requests from the mux package.
    router := mux.NewRouter().StrictSlash(true)
    // access root page
    router.HandleFunc("/", homePage)
    // returnAllAccounts
    router.HandleFunc("/accounts", returnAllAccounts)
    // define the localhost
    log.Fatal(http.ListenAndServe(":10000", router))
}

func main() {
  // initialize the dataset
    Accounts = []Account{
        Account{Number: "C45t34534", Balance: "24545.5", Desc: "Checking
Account"},
        Account{Number: "S3r53455345", Balance: "444.4", Desc: "Savings Account"},
    }

  // execute handleRequests, which will kick off the API
  // we can access the API using the URL defined above
    handleRequests()
}
```

STEP 3: RETRIEVE A RECORD

Now you want to start using the API to manage the data in the dataset, including creating new data, retrieving existing data, updating data, and deleting data. As mentioned earlier, the CRUD actions correspond to HTTP requests as follows:

GET – Retrieve existing data

POST – Add new data to the dataset

PUT – Update existing data

DELETE – Delete existing data

You will include additional functions from gorilla/mux to help parse the data in these processes.

Retrieving a Specific Record

In this step, you will modify the API so that you can retrieve the record associated with a specific account number. For example, if you send a GET request to the URL http://localhost:10000/account/C45t34534, you should get back only the data associated with that account.

Add a new global function, called returnAccount, to the program, as shown in Listing 23.11. This function should be added after the returnAllAccounts function.

LISTING 23.11

The returnAccount function

```
func returnAccount(w http.ResponseWriter, r *http.Request){
    vars := mux.Vars(r)
    key := vars["number"]
    for _, account := range Accounts {
        if account.Number == key {
```

```
        json.NewEncoder(w).Encode(account)
    }
  }
}
```

This function does a number of things. First, it accesses the variables sent in the request (r) from the mux router and assigns them to vars. The function then accesses the account number value that was sent by the HTTP request. The convention here is that the parameter's name is "number". Finally, the function iterates through the dataset, and when the account with the corresponding account number is found, you encode that account in JSON format and write the data to the HTTP ResponseWriter named w.

You also need to update the handleRequests function to include the new function. This update is shown in Listing 23.12.

LISTING 23.12

The updated handleRequests function

```
func handleRequests() {
    router := mux.NewRouter().StrictSlash(true)
    router.HandleFunc("/", homePage)
    router.HandleFunc("/accounts", returnAllAccounts)
    router.HandleFunc("/account/{number}", returnAccount)
    log.Fatal(http.ListenAndServe(":10000", router))
}
```

Here, you've added a new HandleFunc call to handle retrieving an account. Using mux makes it much easier to reference specific parts of a record.

Testing the Updates

Test the updates by sending a new GET request to http://localhost:10000/account/C45t34534 using Postman. If everything is set up correctly, you should see a single record that corresponds to the account number in the URL, as shown in Figure 23.4. You may also want to test with the other account created in the program.

The complete code (with added comments) at this point is shown in Listing 23.13.

Figure 23.4: Testing the request for a specific record

LISTING 23.13

The complete code at this point

```
package main

import (
    "encoding/json"
    "fmt"
    "log"
    "net/http"
    "github.com/gorilla/mux"
)

// we create a type Account that will be used to represent a bank account
type Account struct {
    Number string `json:"AccountNumber"`
    Balance string `json:"Balance"`
    Desc string `json:"AccountDescription"`
}
```

```go
// we use Accounts as a global variable because it is used by
// several functions in the code
var Accounts []Account

// implement the homePage
// we use the ResponseWriter w to display some text when we visit the home page
func homePage(w http.ResponseWriter, r *http.Request){
    fmt.Fprintf(w, "Welcome to our bank!")
  // we can use a print command to log the request or we can log it to a
file, etc.
    fmt.Println("Endpoint: /")
}

// handleRequests will process HTTP requests and redirect them to
// the appropriate Handle function
func handleRequests() {
    // create a router to handle our requests from the mux package.
    router := mux.NewRouter().StrictSlash(true)
    // access root page
    router.HandleFunc("/", homePage)
    // returnAllAccounts
    router.HandleFunc("/accounts", returnAllAccounts)
    // return requested account
    router.HandleFunc("/account/{number}", returnAccount)
    // define the localhost
    log.Fatal(http.ListenAndServe(":10000", router))
}

// return the dataset Accounts in a JSON format
func returnAllAccounts(w http.ResponseWriter, r *http.Request){
    // we use the Encode function to convert the Account slice into a json object
    json.NewEncoder(w).Encode(Accounts)
}

func returnAccount(w http.ResponseWriter, r *http.Request){
    vars := mux.Vars(r)
    key := vars["number"]
    for _, account := range Accounts {
        if account.Number == key {
            json.NewEncoder(w).Encode(account)
        }
    }
}

func main() {
    // initialize the dataset
```

continues

continued

```
    Accounts = []Account{
        Account{Number: "C45t34534", Balance: "24545.5", Desc: "Checking
Account"},
        Account{Number: "S3r53455345", Balance: "444.4", Desc: "Savings Account"},
    }

    // execute handleRequests, which will kick off the API
    // we can access the API using the URL defined above
    handleRequests()
}
```

STEP 4: ADD A NEW RECORD

In this step, you will implement the POST functionality, which will allow you to create new accounts and add them to the Accounts dataset. Because you are writing new data, you must add the io/ioutil package to the import statements at this point. The import statements should then look like the following:

```
import (
    "encoding/json"
    "fmt"
    "log"
    "net/http"
    "github.com/gorilla/mux"
    "io/ioutil"
)
```

You then create a handler function named createAccount that will handle the steps required to create a new account and add the account to the dataset. This function is shown in Listing 23.14. Add the new function after the returnAccount function.

LISTING 23.14

The createAccount function

```
func createAccount(w http.ResponseWriter, r *http.Request) {
    reqBody, _ := ioutil.ReadAll(r.Body)
    var account Account
    json.Unmarshal(reqBody, &account)
    Accounts = append(Accounts, account)
    json.NewEncoder(w).Encode(account)
}
```

The createAccount function performs several steps. It starts by getting the body of your POST request calling ioutil.ReadAll and passing r.Body. This returns the string response containing the request body, which is stored in reqBody. After creating an Account variable called account, you convert the JSON into the account type using the json.Unmarshal function. This is followed by appending the new account to the global list of accounts. In the final line of createAccount, the new account is returned as a response.

The final step of adding a new record is to update the handleRequests function to include the new request type. The update is shown in Listing 23.15.

LISTING 23.15

The updated handleRequests function

```
func handleRequests() {
    router := mux.NewRouter().StrictSlash(true)
    router.HandleFunc("/", homePage)
    router.HandleFunc("/accounts", returnAllAccounts)
    router.HandleFunc("/account/{number}", returnAccount)
    router.HandleFunc("/account", createAccount).Methods("POST")
    // our API will be accessible at http://localhost:10000/
    // we add the router as a handler in the ListenAndServe function
    log.Fatal(http.ListenAndServe(":10000", router))
}
```

This will instruct the mux router to handle the new service and forward it to the createAccount function. If all updates were added correctly, you should be able to add a new record to the dataset.

Run the updated version of the application and use a GET request in Postman to view all accounts and verify the connection. You should see both existing records, just as you did in earlier steps.

To test that you can add a new record, within Postman do the follow steps:

- Change the request type in Postman to POST (instead of GET).

- Set the URL to http://localhost:10000/account (singular for one account, no slash at the end).

- Under the address bar, click the Body tab.

- On that tab, select the raw option.

- Because we are providing the new record in JSON format, select JSON from the drop-down menu that will appear to the right of the binary option.

- On the first line in the Body pane, add the following record:

```
{"AccountNumber": "C3234535", "Balance": "100.5", "AccountDescription":
"Checking Account"}
```

At this point (before clicking Send), the Postman window should look like Figure 23.5. When all the settings appear to be correct, click Send. If everything works as expected, Postman will return the new record in the return pane at the bottom of the window (Figure 23.6), and you should see the Status message 200 OK.

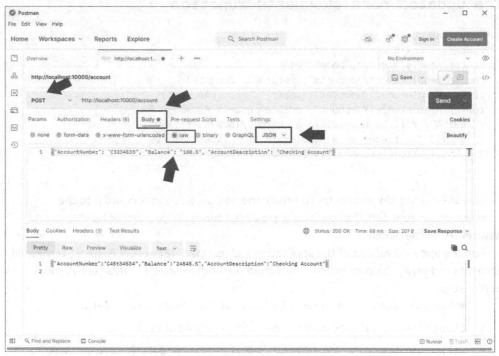

Figure 23.5: Setting up Postman to POST a new account

Figure 23.6: The return pane in Postman

Run the GET request as shown in Figure 23.7 to see the new dataset and verify that it includes the new record.

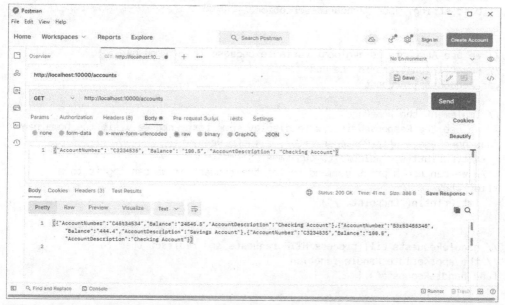

Figure 23.7: Running a GET request to verify record was added

At this point, Listing 23.16 presents all the code you've created with added comments. You should confirm that your code runs correctly. If you have issues, compare your code to this listing.

LISTING 23.16

The full code listing at this point

```
package main

import (
    "encoding/json"
    "fmt"
    "log"
    "net/http"
    "github.com/gorilla/mux"
    "io/ioutil"
)

// we create a type Account that will be used to represent a bank account
type Account struct {
    Number string `json:"AccountNumber"`
    Balance string `json:"Balance"`
    Desc string `json:"AccountDescription"`
}

// we use Accounts as a global variable because it is used by
// several functions in the code
var Accounts []Account

// implement the homePage
// we use the ResponseWriter w to display some text when we visit the home page
func homePage(w http.ResponseWriter, r *http.Request){
    fmt.Fprintf(w, "Welcome to our bank!")
    // we can use a print command to log the request or we can log it to a
file, etc.
    fmt.Println("Endpoint: /")
}

// handleRequests will process HTTP requests and redirect them to
// the appropriate Handle function
func handleRequests() {
```

```go
    // create a router to handle our requests from the mux package.
    router := mux.NewRouter().StrictSlash(true)
    // access root page
    router.HandleFunc("/", homePage)
    // returnAllAccounts
    router.HandleFunc("/accounts", returnAllAccounts)
    // return requested account
    router.HandleFunc("/account/{number}", returnAccount)
    // create new account
    router.HandleFunc("/account", createAccount).Methods("POST")
    // define the localhost
    log.Fatal(http.ListenAndServe(":10000", router))
}

// return the dataset Accounts in a JSON format
func returnAllAccounts(w http.ResponseWriter, r *http.Request){
    // we use the Encode function to convert the Account slice into a json object
    json.NewEncoder(w).Encode(Accounts)
}

// return a single account
func returnAccount(w http.ResponseWriter, r *http.Request){
    vars := mux.Vars(r)
    key := vars["number"]
    for _, account := range Accounts {
        if account.Number == key {
            json.NewEncoder(w).Encode(account)
        }
    }
}

// create a new account
func createAccount(w http.ResponseWriter, r *http.Request) {
    reqBody, _ := ioutil.ReadAll(r.Body)
    var account Account
    json.Unmarshal(reqBody, &account)
    Accounts = append(Accounts, account)
    json.NewEncoder(w).Encode(account)
}

func main() {
    // initialize the dataset
    Accounts = []Account{
        Account{Number: "C45t34534", Balance: "24545.5", Desc: "Checking
Account"},
```

continues

continued

```
    Account{Number: "S3r53455345", Balance: "444.4", Desc: "Savings Account"},
}

// execute handleRequests, which will kick off the API
// we can access the API using the URL defined above
handleRequests()
}
```

STEP 5: DELETE A RECORD

Now you need to update the program so that you can delete data in the dataset through the API. You first need a new function that will delete a record. Add the global function deleteAccount shown in Listing 23.17 to your program.

LISTING 23.17

The deleteAccount function

```
func deleteAccount(w http.ResponseWriter, r *http.Request) {
    // use mux to parse the path parameters
    vars := mux.Vars(r)
    // extract the account number of the account we wish to delete
    id := vars["number"]
    // we then need to loop through the dataset
    for index, account := range Accounts {
        // if our id path parameter matches one of our
        // account numbers
        if account.Number == id {
            // updates our dataset to remove the account
            Accounts = append(Accounts[:index], Accounts[index + 1:]...)
        }
    }
}
```

In this function, you see the following:

- As with the CREATE function, you use mux to parse the path parameters.

- You want to use the account number to identify the account to delete, so you use the parser to identify that value in the dataset.

- You loop through the dataset until you find the requested account number.

- When the loop finds the account number, update the dataset to remove the account number.

As you've done before, you also need to add the function to the `handleRequests` function. You can see the `deleteAccount` function added to `handleRequests` in Listing 23.18.

LISTING 23.18

The updated `handleRequests` function

```go
func handleRequests() {
    router := mux.NewRouter().StrictSlash(true)
    router.HandleFunc("/", homePage)
    router.HandleFunc("/accounts", returnAllAccounts)
    router.HandleFunc("/account/{number}", returnAccount)
    router.HandleFunc("/account", createAccount).Methods("POST")
    router.HandleFunc("/account/{number}", deleteAccount).Methods("DELETE")
    log.Fatal(http.ListenAndServe(":10000", router))
}
```

With the new code added, you can go back to Postman and make sure you can delete an account. To do this, from within Postman, follow these steps:

1. Set the request to DELETE (instead of GET or POST).

2. Enter a URL for an existing account:

   http://localhost:10000/account/C3234535

3. Send the request.

If everything works as expected, you will see a status 200 OK message, but the body will no longer contain account C3234535. If you have an issue, you can compare your code to Listing 23.19, which is the final listing containing all the code added in this lesson, plus additional comments.

LISTING 23.19

The final full code listing

```go
package main

import (
    "encoding/json"
    "fmt"
```

continues

continued

```go
    "log"
    "net/http"
    "github.com/gorilla/mux"
    "io/ioutil"
)

// we create a type Account that will be used to represent a bank account
type Account struct {
    Number string `json:"AccountNumber"`
    Balance string `json:"Balance"`
    Desc string `json:"AccountDescription"`
}

// we use Accounts as a global variable because it is used by
// several functions in the code
var Accounts []Account

// implement the homePage
// we use the ResponseWriter w to display some text when we visit the home page
func homePage(w http.ResponseWriter, r *http.Request){
    fmt.Fprintf(w, "Welcome to our bank!")
    // we can use a print command to log the request or we can log it to a
file, etc.
    fmt.Println("Endpoint: /")
}

// handleRequests will process HTTP requests and redirect them to
// the appropriate Handle function
func handleRequests() {
    // create a router to handle our requests from the mux package
    router := mux.NewRouter().StrictSlash(true)
    // access root page
    router.HandleFunc("/", homePage)
    // returnAllAccounts
    router.HandleFunc("/accounts", returnAllAccounts)
    // return requested account
    router.HandleFunc("/account/{number}", returnAccount)
    // create requested account
    router.HandleFunc("/account", createAccount).Methods("POST")
    // delete requested account
    router.HandleFunc("/account/{number}", deleteAccount).Methods("DELETE")
    // define the localhost
    log.Fatal(http.ListenAndServe(":10000", router))
}
```

```go
// return the dataset Accounts in a JSON format
func returnAllAccounts(w http.ResponseWriter, r *http.Request){
    // we use the Encode function to convert the Account slice into a json object
    json.NewEncoder(w).Encode(Accounts)
}

func returnAccount(w http.ResponseWriter, r *http.Request){
    vars := mux.Vars(r)
    key := vars["number"]
    for _, account := range Accounts {
        if account.Number == key {
            json.NewEncoder(w).Encode(account)
        }
    }
}

func createAccount(w http.ResponseWriter, r *http.Request) {
    reqBody, _ := ioutil.ReadAll(r.Body)
    var account Account
    json.Unmarshal(reqBody, &account)
    Accounts = append(Accounts, account)
    json.NewEncoder(w).Encode(account)
}

func deleteAccount(w http.ResponseWriter, r *http.Request) {
    // use mux to parse the path parameters
    vars := mux.Vars(r)
    // extract the account number of the account we wish to delete
    id := vars["number"]
    // we then need to loop through the dataset
    for index, account := range Accounts {
        // if our id path parameter matches one of our
        // account numbers
        if account.Number == id {
            // updates our dataset to remove the account
            Accounts = append(Accounts[:index], Accounts[index + 1:]...)
        }
    }
}

func main() {
    // initialize the dataset
    Accounts = []Account{
```

continues

continued

```
     Account{Number: "C45t34534", Balance: "24545.5", Desc: "Checking
Account"},
     Account{Number: "S3r53455345", Balance: "444.4", Desc: "Savings Account"},
   }

   // execute handleRequests, which will kick off the API
   // we can access the API using the URL defined above
   handleRequests()
}
```

SUMMARY

This lesson was a tutorial where you were able to walk step by step through creating an application that uses REST to create an application that can create, read, update, and delete (CRUD) data from a remote data source. You created HTTP request handlers and used custom routing to route incoming requests to your API to those appropriate handlers.

EXERCISES

The following exercises are provided to allow you to experiment with the tools and concepts presented in this lesson. For each exercise, write a program that meets the specified requirements and verify that the program runs as expected. The exercises are:

Exercise 23.1: Students

Exercise 23.2: Student Name

Exercise 23.3: Going Local

NOTE The exercises are for your benefit. The exercises help you apply what you learn in the lessons. You are also encouraged to experiment with the code as you complete the exercises.

Exercise 23.1: Students

Replicate what you did in this lesson, but instead of using an Account struct, use a Students struct. Make sure you include the ability to add or delete as well as retrieve one or all students. Your struct should contain fields for the following items:

- Student number
- First name
- Last name
- Grade average
- Grade level

Exercise 23.2: Student Name

Modify your solution to Exercise 23.1 to retrieve a student by their name instead of their student number.

Exercise 23.3: Going Local

The application presented in this lesson used a global data source. The Account struct and the Accounts list were both global variables, which made it easier to access from the various functions.

Declaring data and data sources globally is often not the best solution. Rather, you should localize them and pass references for their use. Update the code from this lesson so that Account and Accounts are both declared within the main function. Then pass the appropriate variables to the various functions within the listing as needed.

Lesson 24
Working with gRPC

In the last decade, REST APIs have become the standard option for applications and systems to communicate with each other. However, in 2015, Google introduced the concept of a modern open source remote procedure call, gRPC, which provides the same functionality of REST APIs with faster, lighter, and more flexible services and communications. As a result, Google Remote Procedure Call, or gRPC, is now supported by most programming languages. In this lesson, you'll learn about gRPC in the context of Go.

LEARNING OBJECTIVES

By the end of this lesson, you will be able to:

- Work with gRPC.
- Create a gRPC server.
- Build a chat service.
- Create a client.
- Execute your server and client together.

WORKING WITH gRPC

In the simplest terms, gRPC is a modern, open source remote procedure call (RPC) framework that can run anywhere. An RPC is a function within an application that can be executed remotely by another application. RPCs are particularly common in distributed systems where one computer wants to invoke methods or functions hosted on another machine in the distributed system.

gRPC is similar to a REST API in that you are exposing services hosted on a server to clients. There are a few differences between gRPC and REST:

- gRPC uses HTTP/2 whereas REST uses HTTP 1.1. This allows gRPC to leverage capabilities of HTTP/2 such as server-side and client-side streaming.

- gRPC uses the Protocol Buffers (Protobuf) data format whereas REST uses JSON.

- In a traditional REST API setting, a client communicates with a server using standard HTTP requests (GET, POST, PUT, and DELETE), whereas gRPC uses a level of abstraction through Protobuf to allow more flexible communication.

To illustrate all these concepts in more detail, in this lesson you will implement a chat service using gRPC. Specifically, you will create a gRPC server and a gRPC client and use Protobuf to create a chat service between both parties.

SETTING UP THE SERVICES

This lesson requires additional services that are not included in a typical Go installation. You will need to download and install the following applications as well as create a user directory:

- Git
- gRPC
- Protobuf
- Protoc

Git

Git is a distributed version control tool. You can verify if Git is installed on your computer by entering the following command at a command-line prompt:

```
git --version
```

If Git is installed on your system, this command will return the current version. If your system does not already have Git available, download and installation instructions are available through Git's downloads page at https://git-scm.com/downloads.

> **NOTE** Go also uses Git behind the scenes, so you might not always be aware of when it is being used.

gRPC

You will also need to install gRPC on your system. You can install the gRPC services from a command line using the following command:

```
go get -u google.golang.org/grpc
```

If successful, when you run this command you won't see anything at the command prompt. Figure 24.1 shows that the current Microsoft Windows system has Git installed and also shows installing gRPC. There isn't much to see when installing these services.

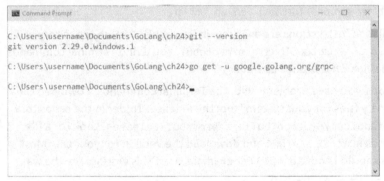

Figure 24.1: Verifying Git and installing gRPC in Go

Protobuf

Protobuf is an open source cross-platform mechanism developed by Google that is used to serialize structured data. You can think of Protobuf as a lighter and faster version of XML. As with XML, you can decide the structure of your data (using proto files; more on this later), then use Protobuf to read and write structured data into a variety of streams. Typically, Protobuf is used by programs to store data or to communicate with other applications.

Install the protocol compiler plug-in for Go (`protoc-gen-go`) using the following command:

```
go get github.com/golang/protobuf/protoc-gen-go
```

This Go `get` instruction will download and save the files to a new directory on your computer. If you are using macOS or Linux, you can enter the following command to set a path so that the plug-in can find the code files:

```
export PATH="$PATH:$(go env GOPATH)/bin"
```

This setting should already be in place if you are using Windows and you installed Go using the provided MSI file.

Next, check to make sure that the files are installed. You can do so by navigating to that directory and looking in the `pkg/mod` subdirectory. The default directories are:

- Windows: `C:\Users\%USERNAME%\Go`
- macOS or Linux: `Users/<username>/go`

Protoc

Install the protocol buffer compiler (protoc), version 3 or later:

- Detailed installation instructions are available in Protobuf's GitHub repository at `https://github.com/protocolbuffers/protobuf`. You'll find Terminal commands for macOS and Linux on this page as well.

- For Windows, or if you have problems with the Terminal commands, download the appropriate binary files for your system from the Releases folder in the repository at `https://github.com/protocolbuffers/protobuf/releases`. Look for a file whose name ends in `win32` or `win64` and download the version for your OS. (Most Windows users should choose `win64`.) For example, as of this writing, the file was named `protoc-3.19.4-win64.zip`.

After downloading the file, open the compressed folder and copy the `bin` and `include` subdirectories to your *user*/Go folder. This will add protoc to your Go installation. You'll see an existing `bin` subdirectory in Go; paste the new version to the same location. Select Merge, if necessary, to merge the folders.

User Directory

For this lesson, all program files should be saved to the usr/Go/src location created by downloading the files.

- In Linux or macOS, a possible location is /usr/local/go/src.

- In Windows, this should be C:\Users\%*USERNAME*%\Go\src.

Verify this folder is on your computer. Also check that the bin subdirectory includes two files:

- protoc.exe

- protoc-gen-go.exe

CREATING A SERVER

Once you have everything set up and you've confirmed your user directories are created and contain the appropriate files, then you are ready to continue. In the first step, you will create a simple server using the net package that will listen for TCP connections on port 10000. This is the most basic version of a server.

Create a new file named **server.go** and save it to your src folder. Add the code in Listing 24.1 to the new file.

LISTING 24.1

go/src/server.go

```
package main

import (
    "fmt"
    "log"
    "net"
)

func main() {
    listener, err := net.Listen("tcp", ":10000")
    fmt.Println(listener)
```

continues

continued

```
    if err != nil {
        log.Fatalf("failed to listen: %v", err)
    }
}
```

At this point the code does not do much. It listens on the local network address using the net.Listen function. The first input of net.Listen is the network (tcp in this case), and the second parameter is the port or address, in this case 10000. Note that the network must be one of the following values:

- "tcp"
- "tcp4"
- "tcp6"
- "unix"
- "unixpacket"

The program should run without error and open a server connection. It will print the value for the listener similar to the following, but nothing else will happen:

```
C:\Users\MRBRADLEYL\go\src>go run server.go
&{0xc00014ea00 {<nil> 0}}
```

CREATING A gRPC SERVER

Now you will modify the server as a gRPC server using the grpc package you downloaded earlier. This is shown in Listing 24.2.

LISTING 24.2

go/src/server.go **with the gRPC package added**

```
package main

import (
    "fmt"
    "google.golang.org/grpc" // import the grpc package
    "log"
    "net"
)
```

```
func main() {
    fmt.Println("Our first gRPC server ")
    listener, err := net.Listen("tcp", ":10000")

    if err != nil {
        log.Fatalf("failed to listen: %v", err)
    }

    // create a new grpc server
    grpcServer := grpc.NewServer()
    err = grpcServer.Serve(listener)

    if err != nil {
        log.Fatalf("failed to serve: %s", err)
    }
}
```

The server.go program shown in Listing 24.2 has now been updated with a few changes. First, you add the grpc package to the import statements. You also add some output text that will indicate you are making a connection to the server. Finally, you create the gRPC server using grpc.NewServer and register the endpoints you want to expose before serving this over the existing TCP connection, using the listener you created earlier.

At this point, if you save and run the program, you should see the print output to confirm the connection:

```
Our first gRPC server
```

> **NOTE** To stop the server, press Ctrl+C in the Terminal or command window.

CREATING THE CHAT SERVICE

So far, our server is still not useful. You need to expose some services that clients can use to communicate with the server. As we mentioned earlier, gRPC uses the Protocol Buffers (Protobuf) data format to allow applications to communicate with each other. In the previous step, you created the gRPC server application. In this step, you will create a Protobuf file that you'll use to define how other applications can communicate with the server you just created.

Create a file named `chat.proto` (proto is the extension for Protobuf files) and include the code shown in Listing 24.3. Save this file in the same folder as your server file from Listing 24.2.

LISTING 24.3

go/src/chat.proto

```
syntax = "proto3";
package chat;
option go_package=".;chat";

message Message {
  string body = 1;
}

service ChatService {
  rpc SayHello(Message) returns (Message) {}
}
```

The proto file exposes the services that your gRPC will provide. First, you define the syntax used in the file. In our example, you are using proto3:

```
syntax = "proto3";
```

> **NOTE** Details about the proto3 language are outside the scope of this lesson, but its use should be easy to understand. For more information about proto3, see Google's Language Guide for proto3 at `https://developers.google.com/protocol-buffers/docs/proto3`.

You then define the name of the package that you want to create. In our example, the package name is `chat`:

```
package chat;
```

Next, you identify the location where the new service will be hosted—in this case, a subdirectory named `chat`, which you'll create momentarily. Finally, you define a message type named `Message` and a `service` called `ChatService`. This service calls `rpc` of `SayHello`, which takes as input a `Message` and returns the message.

You then add a subdirectory named chat to the current directory (where the code files are) and then, from the command prompt, run the following command:

```
protoc --go_out=plugins=grpc:chat chat.proto
```

After you execute this command, you should see a file named chat.pb.go in the chat subdirectory. There will be no output to the command window itself.

UPDATING THE SERVER CODE TO INCLUDE THE CHAT SERVICE

Now that you have the necessary files for your chat service, you need to instruct the gRPC server to expose that service. Update your server program to include the new code shown in Listing 24.4.

LISTING 24.4

go/src/server.go **with chat service**

```go
package main

import (
    "fmt"
    "google.golang.org/grpc" // import the grpc package
    "log"
    "net"
    "chat" // call the chat service that was defined
)

func main() {
    fmt.Println("Our first gRPC server ")
    listener, err := net.Listen("tcp", ":10000")

    if err != nil {
        log.Fatalf("failed to listen: %v", err)
    }

    // create a new grpc server
    grpcServer := grpc.NewServer()
```

continues

continued

```
ch := chat.Server{}
chat.RegisterChatServiceServer(grpcServer, &ch)

// register the endpoints you want to expose before serving this
// over the existing TCP connection defined above
err = grpcServer.Serve(listener)

//display error in case of an error
if err != nil {
    log.Fatalf("failed to serve: %s", err)
}
}
```

The new code creates a chat server and exposes the service to the gRPC server. The RegisterChatServiceServer function references a function in the autogenerated chat.pb.go file you created using protoc in the previous step. The fact that protoc automatically generates the required functions is an advantage to using this tool.

If you try to run this program, you will receive feedback messages that chat is undefined:

```
# command-line-arguments
.\server.go:22:10: undefined: chat.Server
```

Let's create chat next.

CREATING THE *CHAT* PACKAGE

In this step, you will implement the SayHello method that you defined in the proto3 file in Listing 24.3. This method will accept messages from clients.

In the chat subdirectory, create a file named chat.go with the code in Listing 24.5.

LISTING 24.5

go/src/chat/chat.go

```
package chat

import (
  "log"
  "golang.org/x/net/context"
)
```

```
type Server struct {

}

func (s *Server) SayHello(ctx context.Context, in *Message) (*Message, error) {
  log.Printf("Receive message body from client: %s", in.Body)
  return &Message{Body: "Hello from the Server!"}, nil
}
```

This code performs several steps. First, you create a chat package that you can reference from other programs. You then import the log and context packages. You use log
to log incoming messages from the clients. You include the package context because the
SayHello function will take as input a Context type and a Message type, which are provided in this package.

You then create a struct type, Server, with no fields. This Server type represents the
receiver argument for the SayHello method. At runtime, that will be the gRPC server.

The SayHello method takes as input a Message type and returns a Message type as
well. It also returns an error type in case of an error. Within the SayHello method, you log
the message that you received (in is the variable of type Message and in.Body is the text).

Each time you receive a message, ideally you will want to send a message back to the
client. In this example, you return a new message variable with the text "Hello from the
Server!" and you return the error as nil.

Essentially, this code will send the message "Hello from the Server!" back to the
client each time the server receives a message. You could implement further services
by adding their definitions in the proto file and then implementing them in the chat.go
function using the same pattern.

CREATING A CLIENT

With a server built, now you need to build the client. In this step, you'll create a client
that can communicate with the server you created earlier. The code for client.go is in
Listing 24.6.

LISTING 24.6

go/src/client.go

```
package main

import (
  "chat"
```

continues

continued

```
    "google.golang.org/grpc"
    "log"
    "golang.org/x/net/context"
)

func main() {

    var conn *grpc.ClientConn
    conn, err := grpc.Dial(":10000", grpc.WithInsecure())
    if err != nil {
        log.Fatalf("did not connect: %s", err)
    }
    defer conn.Close() // this will execute last

    c := chat.NewChatServiceClient(conn)

    response, err := c.SayHello(context.Background(), &chat.Message{Body: "Hello
from the Client!"})
    if err != nil {
        log.Fatalf("Error when calling SayHello: %s", err)
    }

    // display the response from the server
    log.Printf("Response from server: %s", response.Body)

}
```

The code in client.go performs a number of tasks. It starts by creating a client connection variable called conn:

```
    var conn *grpc.ClientConn
```

The variable is then used to create a connection to the local address on port 10000 by calling the grpc.Dial method:

```
    conn, err := grpc.Dial(":10000", grpc.WithInsecure())
```

Error checking verifies that the connection is created and that an error is not returned. If an error is returned (err is not equal to nil), then the error is logged using the log .lFatalf function. You then provide the code to make sure you close the connection. The closing is deferred so that the closing won't happen until you are done using your connection.

With the connection established, you next create a client from the chat service. The NewChatServiceClient function is autogenerated from the proto file. You pass it your connection, conn. This establishes your client as c.

You send a message from this client (c) to the server using SayHello. The message you are sending says, "Hello from the Client!". In calling SayHello, you are also passing context.Background() for the first argument as a context. Background() means Background returns a non-nil, empty Context. It is never canceled, has no values, and has no deadline. It is typically used by the main function, initialization, and tests, and as the top-level Context for incoming requests.

Another context that can be used is context.Package(). The package context defines the Context type, which carries deadlines, cancelation signals, and other request-scoped values across API boundaries and between processes. Incoming requests to a server should create a Context, and outgoing calls to servers should accept a Context.

After sending the "Hello from the Client!" message with SayHello, you receive the response in the variable response and an error code. You then print this response from the server.

RUNNING THE SERVER AND THE CLIENT

On one terminal, run the server and look for it to display the message so that you know it is running. Then run the client in a separate Terminal window to see the applications communicate with each other. You should see results similar to Figure 24.2.

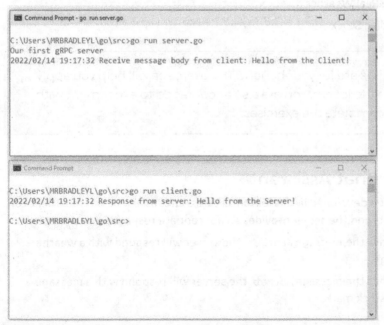

Figure 24.2: Running both the server and the client

SUMMARY

In this lesson, we presented an example of how to use gRPC to have a server and client share messages. As you saw, gRPC is lightweight and more flexible than REST services. gRPC is supported by most programming languages, including Go. With the code from this lesson, you now have the foundation to build your own servers and clients that can interact.

> **NOTE** The exercises for this lesson will ask you to expand what you've learned to create a program that is more useful!

EXERCISES

The following exercises are provided to allow you to experiment with the tools and concepts presented in this lesson. For the exercises, write a program that meets the specified requirements and verify that the program runs as expected. The exercises are:

Exercise 24.1: Chat Assistant

Exercise 24.2: The Real Weather

Exercise 24.3: Adding Stock

> **NOTE** The exercises are for your benefit. The exercises will help you apply what you learn in the lesson. You are also encouraged to experiment with the code as you complete the exercises.

Exercise 24.1: Chat Assistant

Using the code that you developed in this lesson, create a chat assistant where a client can send keyword requests and the server provides an appropriate response. For example:

- If the client sends the message weather, the server will respond with a weather-related message.
- If the client sends the message market, the server will respond with a message related to the stock market.

As a first attempt, focus on a single function and do that well. You can build in additional functions later.

Exercise 24.2: The Real Weather

Update your solution from Exercise 24.1. Using the REST API lesson, add a functionality so that when the client asks about the weather, the server will query the weather API found at www.weatherapi.com.

Exercise 24.3: Adding Stock

Update your solution from Exercise 24.1 by adding real stock quotes. Use publicly available APIs to access individual stock prices. When the client sends an index as a message, the server should return the price.

Lesson 25

Pulling It All Together: Using Smart Data

Welcome to the final Pulling It All Together project. In this lesson you will pull together all you have learned to create a robust application using Go. You will be building an API that will allow users to retrieve data from third-party APIs.

LEARNING OBJECTIVES

By the end of this lesson, you will be able to:

- Build an application to access third-party APIs.
- Work with geolocation data via RPCs and an API.
- Access stock information via an API.
- Apply gRPC to a real-world solution.

PROJECT OVERVIEW

In this lesson, you'll build an API to work with geolocation and finance information. Specifically, you and users of your application will have the following functionality:

Geolocation   When you send a physical address (anywhere in the world), the API will respond with the latitude/longitude of the input address as well as other geocoding information.

Finance   When you send a symbol for a stock, mutual fund, exchange-traded fund (ETF), and so forth, the API will respond with a quote of the input symbol.

At a high level, the application might seem complicated since you don't have a database for latitude/longitude relative to addresses. Moreover, you don't have a real-time database that is able to provide you with accurate financial quotes. Luckily, third-party websites offer an easy way to access this information through APIs.

For creating API functions to access geolocation data, the Google Maps API allows you to retrieve latitude/longitude data given an input address. For accessing financial data, the Yahoo Finance API allows you to retrieve a quote given an input symbol.

In other words, our API will leverage other third-party APIs to aggregate different types of data such as map data and finance data. An example where this API would be useful is for building a dashboard application where users can see current information about the stocks they follow, their current location, and various other relevant information. Other examples of possible functionalities for the API are the ability to retrieve weather data given an input address or the ability to retrieve a list of new articles given a list of interests.

For now, let's focus on the two functionalities that we established earlier (geolocation and finance). We'll continue with the design of our API.

DESIGNING OUR API

As mentioned earlier, you'll be creating two services in our API by leveraging two different third-party APIs (Yahoo and Google). Both APIs are easy to use. However, as you'll see later, the two APIs provide different ways to retrieve data from their API.

> **NOTE** The APIs being used are from third-party sources. You might need to adjust the information provided in this lesson if the APIs changed after this lesson was written.

Our API must retrieve data from two other APIs, so you should look at isolating the interaction of our API with each of the two other APIs. In other words, our API should delegate retrieving both the geolocation and the finance data to another application. By doing so, our API will focus primarily on handling input requests from clients and delegating the retrieval of the information to two other applications that will respectively query the Yahoo Finance API and the Google Maps API. This will allow you to have two different applications for interacting with the Yahoo Finance API and Google Maps API, respectively. Each application is completely separate from the other. Since you are relying on third-party APIs, it is important to separate the two so that, if one application goes down, you can still retrieve data from the second API. At a high level, the architecture of our application will look like Figure 25.1.

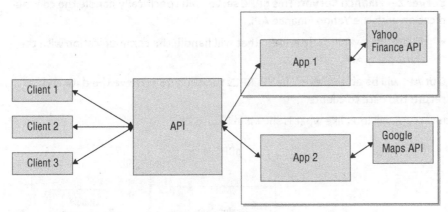

Figure 25.1: Architecture of our smart data app

Clients will be able to send requests to our API for geolocation and finance data. Our API will handle the input request from the client and delegate the request to the appropriate application that will handle the interaction with the third-party API.

This is where gRPCs come into play. The App 1 and App 2 applications shown in Figure 25.1 could be implemented using gRPCs. That way, you will have a server for each application that will handle communication with the third-party API. This will also allow you to implement each server separately while running both servers under the same gRPC server.

To recap, you are looking to implement the following applications:

- **API**—The API application will have three endpoints:
  - **Home:** This is a simple landing endpoint for our API.
  - **Retrieve Geolocation:** This endpoint will handle requests related to geolocation.
  - **Retrieve Quote:** This endpoint will handle requests related to financial data.
- **gRPC Server**—The gRPC server will handle communication with the third-party APIs.
  - **Server 1—Geolocation Server:** This gRPC server will specifically handle the communication with the Google Maps API.
    - This server will include an RPC that will handle the communication with the third-party API.
  - **Server 2—Finance Server:** This gRPC server will specifically handle the communication with the Yahoo Finance API.
    - This server will include an RPC that will handle the communication with the third-party API.
  - Our API will be able to execute the RPCs remotely to retrieve the data and return the data to clients.

Our architecture will look like what is shown in Figure 25.2.

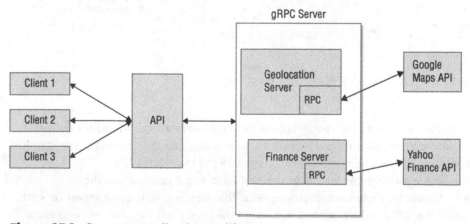

Figure 25.2: Our new application architecture

As Figure 25.2 shows, external clients will be able to send requests to our API. Additionally, our API will then connect to the gRPC server and remotely execute the RPCs that will allow you to retrieve data from the Google Maps API and the Yahoo Finance API. As expected, the gRPC server will include our two servers, the Geolocation server and the Finance server.

IMPLEMENTING THE gRPC SERVER

Let's start by looking at how to implement the gRPC server. Although the two underlying servers will serve two different types of data and the implementation between the two is different, the design step is similar.

Roughly, you will use the following steps:

1. Create a basic gRPC server.

2. Create the Geolocation server and register it to the gRPC server.

    a. Visit the Google Maps API website and gain access to the API as well as get familiar with the API.

    b. Implement the necessary code in the RPC of the geolocation server to call the Google Maps API and retrieve the geolocation information.

3. Create the Finance server and register it to the gRPC server.

    a. Visit the Yahoo Finance API website and gain access to the API as well as get familiar with the API.

    b. Implement the necessary code in the RPC of the finance server to call the Yahoo Finance API and retrieve the quote information.

> **NOTE** We covered creating gRPCs in Lesson 24, "Working with gRPC," and you will use them again in this lesson.

As discussed, you will have a single gRPC server where both the Geolocation and the Finance servers are registered. You will be able to register both servers to listen on our gRPC server for incoming requests. Leveraging the code from Lesson 24, Listing 25.1 is a first look at what our gRPC server code looks like. Save this code as `main.go` in the root directory for this project.

LISTING 25.1

`main.go`—A first look at our gRPC server

```
package main

import (
  "fmt"
  "google.golang.org/grpc"
  "log"
  "net"
)

func main() {
  fmt.Println("Smart Data Server ")
  listener, err := net.Listen("tcp", ":9997")
  if err != nil {
    log.Fatalf("failed to listen: %v", err)
  }
  grpcServer := grpc.NewServer()
  err = grpcServer.Serve(listener)
  if err != nil {
    log.Fatalf("failed to serve: %s", err)
  }
}
```

In this code, you create a gRPC server listening on port 9997 for incoming requests. Because the code doesn't do much yet, let's make it more useful.

We mentioned that you will implement two servers, one for geolocation and one for finance data. The Geolocation server will handle communication with the Google Maps API, and the Finance server will handle communication with the Yahoo Finance API. Each server is completely independent from the other. Let's first create the shells for both servers.

The Geolocation Server Shell

To create the Geolocation shell, let's first create the proto file shown in Listing 25.2 in the root directory for our project. As you can see in the code, you are simply defining the `GeoLocationService`, which includes one RPC method called `getGeoLocationData`. This method will be handling the requests with the Google API and communicating back to the gRPC server you created in Listing 25.1.

LISTING 25.2

geolocation.proto

```
syntax = "proto3";
package geolocation;
option go_package="./geolocation";
message Message {
  string body = 1;
}
service GeoLocationService {
  rpc getGeoLocationData(Message) returns (Message) {}
}
```

Next, you create a new directory under the root directory named `geolocation`. Run the following command in the root directory to generate the boilerplate code for the Geolocation server:

```
protoc --go_out=plugins=grpc:geolocation geolocation.proto
```

This command will generate a file, `geolocation.pb.go`, under `geolocation/geolocation`. This code includes the boilerplate code for our Geolocation server and client.

Let's register the server you just created by adding it to the `main.go` file you created in Listing 25.1. The update is shown in Listing 25.3.

LISTING 25.3

Updated `main.go` **registering the new server**

```
package main

import (
  "./geolocation/geolocation"
  "fmt"
  "google.golang.org/grpc"
  "log"
  "net"
)
```

continues

continued

```go
func main() {
  fmt.Println("Smart Data Server ")
  listener, err := net.Listen("tcp", ":9997")
  if err != nil {
     log.Fatalf("failed to listen: %v", err)
  }
  grpcServer := grpc.NewServer()
  // adding geolocation server
  ch1 := geolocation.Server{}
  geolocation.RegisterGeoLocationServiceServer(grpcServer, &ch1)

  err = grpcServer.Serve(listener)
  if err != nil {
     log.Fatalf("failed to serve: %s", err)
  }
}
```

If you look closely, the main.go file didn't change except for two added instructions. In the first instruction, you create a geolocation server called ch1. In the second instruction, you register it as part of our gRPC. Keep in mind that at this point, the main.go code will throw errors if you want to run it because you need to implement the RPC method from the proto file as well as the Server struct.

In the geolocation directory where the geolocation.pb.go file is located, add the code from Listing 25.4 into a new geolocation.go file.

LISTING 25.4

The geolocation.go **file in the** geolocation **directory**

```go
package geolocation

import (
  "golang.org/x/net/context"
  "log"
)

type Server struct {
}

func (s *Server) GetGeoLocationData(ctx context.Context, in *Message)
(*Message, error) {
  log.Println("Incoming GeoLocation Request")
  return &Message{Body: "Hello"}, nil
}
```

Here you are simply creating an empty struct for our `Server` type, and you implemented a very basic implementation for the RPC `GetGeoLocationData`. In our example, you are returning a `"Hello"` message. At this point, all the errors in the `main.go` file should disappear.

> **NOTE** You will use "function" and "RPC" interchangeably to call `GetGeoLocationData` because the implementation of the RPC in Go is done using functions.

To see everything in action, create a basic client for our gRPC. In the root directory, create a `client_geolocation.go` file and add the code from Listing 25.5.

LISTING 25.5

`client_geolocation.go` **in the root directory**

```go
package main

import (
  "./geolocation/geolocation"
  "golang.org/x/net/context"
  "google.golang.org/grpc"
  "log"
)

func main() {
  var conn *grpc.ClientConn
  conn, err := grpc.Dial(":9997", grpc.WithInsecure())
  if err != nil {
    log.Fatalf("did not connect: %s", err)
  }
  defer conn.Close()
  c := geolocation.NewGeoLocationServiceClient(conn)
  response, err := c.GetGeoLocationData(context.Background(), &geolocation.
Message{Body: "Hello"})
  if err != nil {
    log.Fatalf("Error when retrieving GeoLocation Data: %s", err)
  }
  // display the response from the server
  log.Printf("Response from server: %s", response.Body)

}
```

In this code, you've leveraged the same code from the previous lesson to create a basic client. The client connects to port 9997 and then creates a new Geolocation service client (using the boilerplate code that was generated in geolocation.pb.go). Finally, you execute the RPC GetGeoLocationData on the gRPC server. Here, you are sending a message, "Hello" (and you will receive "Hello" back as well). Finally, you log the response from the gRPC server.

First, run the main.go file, then run the client_geolocation.go file. If everything goes well, you should be seeing "Hello" from the gRPC server, as shown in Figure 25.3.

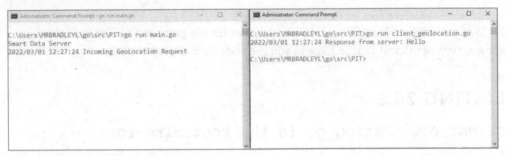

Figure 25.3: Our client and server in action

Accessing Google Location Data

At this point, you have implemented a very basic gRPC server that doesn't do much yet. Let's change that. As discussed, the Geolocation RPC will receive (from the client) an address, and it will query the Google Maps API to retrieve geographic information about the input address.

First, let's get access to the Google Maps API. In other words, in order to query the maps API, you need to generate an API key that will grant you access to the API and allow you to interact with it. To generate an API key, go to https://developers.google.com/maps/get-started#api-key and follow the steps to generate an API key.

Keep the API key secret and safe (we won't share ours here). The API key generated will grant access to the Google Maps API. Requests to the maps API cost money, so you need to keep your API key safe. As of this writing, signing up for a Google Cloud account came with a $200 credit.

Now that you have an API key, let's inspect how you can programmatically interact with the maps API from Go (in other words, from our RPC). Luckily, Go provides support for the Google Maps API through a package, googlemaps.github.io/maps. To see examples of how to use the package on GitHub, go to https://github.com/googlemaps/google-maps-services-go.

You can download the package using go get. Enter the following on the command line:

```
go get googlemaps.github.io/maps
```

Updating *geolocation.go*

Next, let's update the geolocation.go file with the code shown in Listing 25.6.

LISTING 25.6

Updated geolocation.go **file with Google Maps API call**

```
package geolocation

import (
  "encoding/json"
  "errors"
  "golang.org/x/net/context"
  "googlemaps.github.io/maps"
  "log"
)

type Server struct {
}

var GOOGLE_API_KEY string = "XXXXXXXXXXXXXXXXXXXXXXXXXXXXXXXXXXXXXXXX"
var STD_ERROR = errors.New("Unable to retrieve GeoLocation Data from the Google
Maps API. Please check the address or try again later.")

func (s *Server) GetGeoLocationData(ctx context.Context, in *Message)
(*Message, error) {
  log.Println("Incoming GeoLocation Request")
  c, err := maps.NewClient(maps.WithAPIKey(GOOGLE_API_KEY))
  if err != nil {
    return &Message{Body: "Error"}, STD_ERROR
  }
  r := &maps.GeocodingRequest{
    Address: in.GetBody(), // you retrieve the address from the
                           // Message in body
  }
```

continues

continued

```
geocode, err := c.Geocode(context.Background(), r)
if err != nil {
    return &Message{Body: "Error"}, STD_ERROR
}
if len(geocode) < 1 { // the geocode result returned is empty due
                      // to erroneous address
    return &Message{Body: "Error"}, STD_ERROR
}
geocodeJson, err := json.Marshal(geocode) // convert the geocode result to
                                          // json string so you can return it.
if err != nil {
    return &Message{Body: "Error"}, STD_ERROR
}
return &Message{Body: string(geocodeJson)}, nil
}
```

> **NOTE** The string highlighted in Listing 25.6 will need to be replaced with the key you obtained earlier.

Listing 25.6 added several things that we'll discuss step by step. First, you import the maps package, which will allow you to interact with the Google Maps API.

Next, you create two variables. The first is for the API key, where you hard-code the API key you generated from the maps API in the previous step. You'll need to replace the string assigned to GOOGLE_API_KEY with your own key. The second variable is for a standard error. One thing to keep in mind is that our RPC will mostly be receiving requests from our own API (that you will develop later) and then communicating with the Google Maps API to get the data needed for the request and sending it back to our API. To isolate errors from the Google Maps API to our own API, you will return a standard message to our API if something is not working correctly.

In the GetGeoLocationData method, you do a number of things. First, you initiate a new maps client using our API key. This client will allow you to query the maps API (given that the API key is valid). If you catch an error from the client (*API key invalid* or *Maps API down*), you return a message with the body Error and the standard error you created earlier.

Next in the GetGeoLocationData method, you create a geocoding request using the maps client. The input address is stored in the body of the input message. You simply pass that value to the GeocodingRequest function from the maps client.

In the next step, you execute the geocoding request using the Geocode function. This function will send the request to the API and retrieve the data associated with the input address and return it as a response. As usual, you check if there are any errors. If that's the case, you return an error message.

Continuing through the code, you next check for an empty geocode result (in case of an invalid address). If that's the case, then you return the standard error. If no errors are thrown, you encode the geocode result into a JSON string so that you can return to the body of the message. If any errors occur due to marshaling data, you return the standard error.

Finally, you return the valid message with the body, including the results from geocoding.

Updating *client_geolocation.go*

At this point, let's update `client_geolocation.go` to include a real address in the body of the message that you will send to the RPC. Update `client_geolocation.go` with the code in Listing 25.7.

LISTING 25.7

Updating `client_geolocation.go` to include mapping info

```
package main

import (
  "./geolocation/geolocation"
  "golang.org/x/net/context"
  "google.golang.org/grpc"
  "log"
)

func main() {
  var conn *grpc.ClientConn
  conn, err := grpc.Dial(":9997", grpc.WithInsecure())
  if err != nil {
    log.Fatalf("did not connect: %s", err)
  }
  defer conn.Close()
  c := geolocation.NewGeoLocationServiceClient(conn)
  response, err := c.GetGeoLocationData(context.Background(), &geolocation.
Message{Body: "123 Main Street Louisville"})
  if err != nil {
    log.Fatalf("Error when retrieving GeoLocation Data: %s", err)
  }
```

continues

continued

```
// display the response from the server
log.Printf("Response from server: %s", response.Body)

}
```

Little has changed in this code from the previous version. You replace sending a Message having a Body of "Hello" with the actual address that you want to geocode. In our example you are sending the address "123 Main Street Louisville". That way, the RPC will access the address and query the maps API and then return the geocode results in a response message.

Let's test everything out by first running the main.go file then running the client_geolocation.go file. The results of running the client are shown here. As you can see, you were able to receive the geocode results in a JSON format:

```
2022/02/19 18:38:01 Response from server:
[{"address_components":[{"long_name":"123","short_name":"123","types":
["street_number"]},{"long_name":"West Main Street","short_name":"W Main
St","types":["route"]},{"long_name":"Downtown","short_name":"Downtown",
"types":["neighborhood","political"]},{"long_name":"Louisville","short_
name":"Louisville","types":["locality","political"]},{"long_
name":"Jefferson County","short_name":"Jefferson County","types":["admin
istrative_area_level_2","political"]},{"long_name":"Kentucky","short_nam
e":"KY","types":["administrative_area_level_1","political"]},{"long_
name":"United States","short_name":"US","types":["country","politi
cal"]},{"long_name":"40202","short_name":"40202","types":["postal_
code"]},{"long_name":"1343","short_name":"1343","types":["postal_code_
suffix"]}],"formatted_address":"123 W Main St, Louisville, KY 40202, USA","ge
ometry":{"location":{"lat":38.2564611,"lng":-85.7526251},"location_type":"ROO
FTOP","bounds":{"northeast":{"lat":38.2566211,"lng":-85.7525723},"southwest":
{"lat":38.2563198,"lng":-85.752714}},"viewport":{"northeast":{"lat":38.257751
9302915,"lng":-85.75129416970849},"southwest":{"lat":38.2550539697085,"lng":-
85.75399213029151}},"types":null},"types":["premise"],"place_id":"ChIJodFBbbxya
YgRwIcceIGSRWI","partial_match":false,"plus_code":{"global_code":"","compound_
code":""}}]
```

If you replace the input address with an invalid address (for example, replace the Louisville address with "Hello how are you"), you should see the following error message:

```
2022/02/19 18:43:31 Error when retrieving GeoLocation Data: rpc error: code =
Unknown desc = Unable to retrieve GeoLocation Data from the Google Maps API.
Please check the address or try again later.
exit status 1
```

At this point, you have a basic gRPC server that is able to query the Google Maps API and retrieve geocode results for an input address. You can enter additional addresses in the code to see it in action.

Trouble Running the Program?

If you have trouble getting the program to run with the geolocation data, then the first thing to do is confirm that your code matches the listings in this lesson. If they match, then make sure you are using your API key and not the "Xs" shown in the listing.

  If you have a key and are still having trouble (such as an unauthorized app error), then make sure that you have enabled the Google account you used to get your API. You will need to make sure that you have activated billing. This includes adding billing information, although Google states they will not charge you. If you are still having trouble, make sure the Google Geocoding API is enabled in the dashboard on the Google account set up to get an API.

The Finance Server Shell

Next, you will do the same steps for the Finance server. First, in the root directory, create the `finance.proto` file shown in Listing 25.8. In this code you are defining the `FinanceService` function, which includes one `rpc` method called `getQuoteData`. This method will be handling the requests with the Yahoo Finance API and communicating back to the gRPC server you created earlier.

LISTING 25.8

`finance.proto`

```
syntax = "proto3";
package finance;
option go_package="./finance";
message Message {
 string body = 1;
}
service FinanceService {
  rpc getQuoteData(Message) returns (Message) {}
}
```

Next, create a new directory under the root directory. Name the new directory **finance**. With the directory in place, run the following command to generate the boiler-plate code for the Finance server:

```
protoc --go_out=plugins=grpc:finance finance.proto
```

This command will generate the file `finance.pb.go` under `finance/finance`. This code includes the boilerplate code for our server.

You can now add the server you just created to the `main.go` file you created previously. Update `main.go` with the code in Listing 25.9.

LISTING 25.9

Updated `main.go` **with the Finance server code added**

```go
package main

import (
  "./finance/finance"
  "./geolocation/geolocation"
  "fmt"
  "google.golang.org/grpc"
  "log"
  "net"
)

func main() {
  fmt.Println("Smart Data Server ")
  listener, err := net.Listen("tcp", ":9997")
  if err != nil {
    log.Fatalf("failed to listen: %v", err)
  }
  grpcServer := grpc.NewServer()
  // adding geolocation server
  ch1 := geolocation.Server{}
  geolocation.RegisterGeoLocationServiceServer(grpcServer, &ch1)
  // adding finance server
  ch2 := finance.Server{}
  finance.RegisterFinanceServiceServer(grpcServer, &ch2)
  err = grpcServer.Serve(listener)
  if err != nil {
    log.Fatalf("failed to serve: %s", err)
  }
}
```

This update to `main.go` added two more instructions. In the first instruction, you are creating a finance server and in the second instruction, you are registering that server in the gRPC. Notice that at this point, both the Finance server and the Geolocation server are registered in our gRPC servers.

Keep in mind that at this point, `main.go` will throw errors if you run it because you need to implement the `rpc` method from the proto file and the `Server` struct.

In the `finance` directory, add the code from Listing 25.10 into a new `finance.go` file.

LISTING 25.10

`finance.go`

```
package finance

import (
  "golang.org/x/net/context"
  "log"
)

type Server struct {
}

func (s *Server) GetQuoteData(ctx context.Context, in *Message) (*Message,
error) {
  log.Println("Incoming Quote Request")
  return &Message{Body: "Hello"}, nil
}
```

This code implements the `Server` struct, which is empty, and provides a basic implementation for `GetQuoteData`. In our example, you are returning a simple `"Hello"` message from `GetQuoteData`.

At this point, all the errors in the `main.go` file should disappear. To see everything in action, create a basic client for our second RPC. In the root directory, create a `client_finance.go` file and add the code from Listing 25.11.

LISTING 25.11

`client_finance.go`

```
package main

import (
  "./finance/finance"
```

continues

continued

```
    "golang.org/x/net/context"
    "google.golang.org/grpc"
    "log"
)

func main() {
    var conn *grpc.ClientConn
    conn, err := grpc.Dial(":9997", grpc.WithInsecure())
    if err != nil {
        log.Fatalf("did not connect: %s", err)
    }
    defer conn.Close()
    c := finance.NewFinanceServiceClient(conn)
    response, err := c.GetQuoteData(context.Background(), &finance.
Message{Body: "Hello"})
    if err != nil {
        log.Fatalf("Error when retrieving the Quote Data: %s", err)
    }
    // display the response from the server
    log.Printf("Response from server: %s", response.Body)
}
```

In client_finance.go, you create a basic client. The client connects to port 9997 and then creates a new Finance service client (using the boilerplate code that was generated in finance.pb.go). Finally, you execute the RPC GetQuoteData on the gRPC server. In our example, you are sending a message "Hello" (and you will receive "Hello" back as well). Finally, you log the response from the gRPC server.

First, run the main.go file, then run the client_finance.go file. If everything goes well, you should be seeing "Hello" from the gRPC server.

Accessing Yahoo Finance Quotes

The Finance server doesn't do much yet, so let's figure out how to add the necessary code to allow GetQuoteData to query the Yahoo Finance API and retrieve the information of an input symbol. For instance, if GetQuoteData sends "AAPL" to the Yahoo Finance API, it should return all the relevant stock information about the company Apple.

In order to do that, you first need to understand how the Yahoo Finance API works. You can do that by going to www.yahoofinanceapi.com, as shown in Figure 25.4.

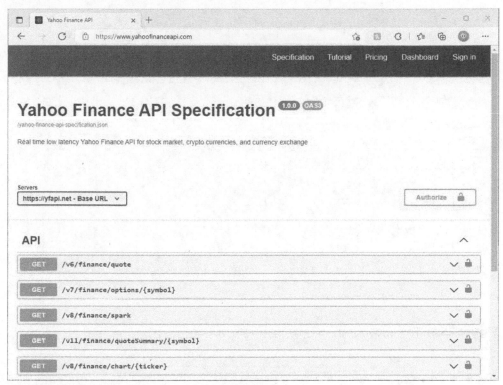

Figure 25.4: Yahoo Finance API Specification

You should see a page similar to Figure 25.4, which shows how the Yahoo Finance API works and includes links to the API. Click /v6/finance/quote to expand the section, as shown in Figure 25.5.

If you see a Try it out button, as shown in Figure 25.5, then click it. This will open the endpoints so that you can change them. The quote endpoint allows you to retrieve quotes given a list of symbols, region, and language. For simplicity, you will focus on U.S. and English for region and language, but feel free to experiment with other regions and languages to see the results.

In the symbols field, remove all symbols except for AAPL, as shown in Figure 25.6. Then click Execute.

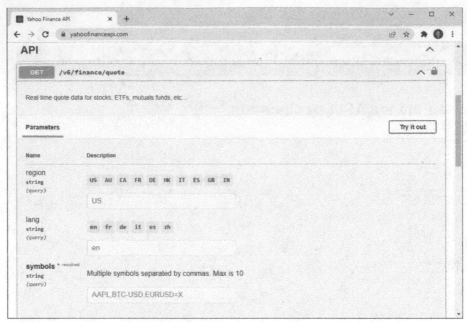

Figure 25.5: The expanded /v6/finance/quote option

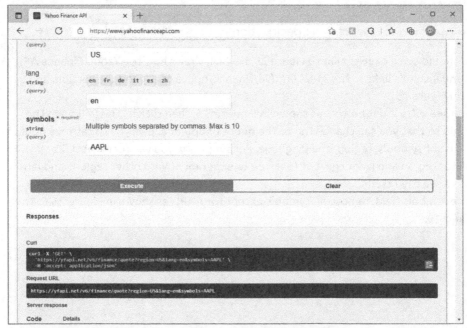

Figure 25.6: Changing symbols to just AAPL

As you can see, the curl (which is like a command-line version of Postman) request to make the API call is shown. You might need to scroll down to see the curl statement:

```
curl -X 'GET' \
  'https://yfapi.net/v6/finance/quote?region=US&lang=en&symbols=AAPL' \
  -H 'accept: application/json'
```

You can also see the request URL:

```
https://yfapi.net/v6/finance/quote?region=US&lang=en&symbols=AAPL
```

This URL is the request you made to the API and it's of type GET. If you enter this URL now, you will receive a message from the API similar to the following:

```
{"message":"Forbidden","hint":"Sign up for API key
www.yahoofinanceapi.com/tutorial"}
```

In order to use the API, you need to create a key with Yahoo. Before you do that, you can scroll down further to see an example of a response that the API will return.

Signing Up for a Yahoo Finance API Key

To use the Yahoo Finance API, you will need a key. You must sign up to create one. As of this writing, you could use your key to make up to 100 requests per day at no cost. For the purpose of this lesson, that should suffice.

To create a key, you must create an account. You can do so by clicking the Sign In button and then selecting the Create Account tab. You will be asked to enter a username (email address) and password with confirmation. Once you confirm the new account, you will be presented with a page showing your API key with a Basic plan, as shown in Figure 25.7. (The API key is blocked in this image.)

NOTE Once you generate your API key, keep it safe and handy so that you can use it within your RPC.

Querying the Yahoo Finance API Programmatically

The next step is to figure out how to query the Yahoo Finance API programmatically from our RPC. In the geolocation RPC, you leverage the maps package implemented in Go to query the Google Maps API. Unfortunately, you don't have such a thing for the Yahoo Finance API, so you will need to get creative.

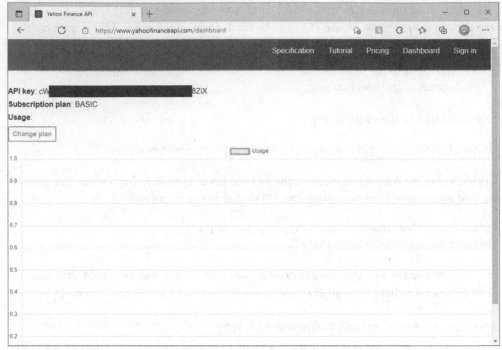

Figure 25.7: The Basic subscription for the Yahoo Finance API

As discussed earlier, you were given the `curl` command for the Yahoo Finance request to retrieve a quote about the Apple stock. If you go back to the page (www.yahoofinanceapi.com and expand the /v6/finance/quote API again) and execute the request to get the AAPL symbol quote, this time you will see that the `curl` command has been updated to include your key:

```
curl -X 'GET' \
  'https://yfapi.net/v6/finance/quote?region=US&lang=en&symbols=AAPL' \
  -H 'accept: application/json' \
  -H 'X-API-KEY: XXXXXXXXXXXXXXXXXXXXXXXXXXXXXXXXXXXXXXXXX'
```

> **NOTE** You will need to replace the string XXXXXXXXXXXXXXXXXXXXXXXXXXXXXXXX XXXXXXXXX with your own key.

Additionally, if you change the symbol to just the AAPL symbol quote again and click Execute, this time you will see the actual response displayed by calling the API, as shown in Figure 25.8, instead of just an example.

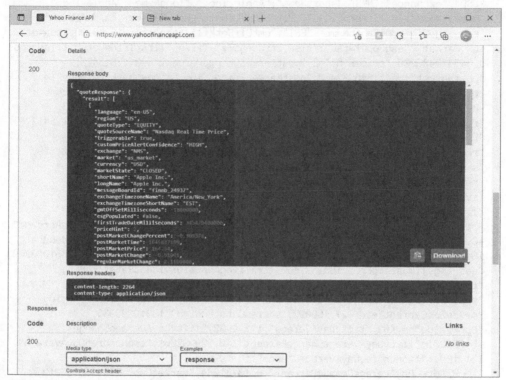

Figure 25.8: The browser JSON response from the RPC call to the quote API

The output in Figure 25.8 is what you will receive from the Yahoo Finance API. This response from the quote API endpoint is adequate to use in our program. From our RPC, you will send the symbol to the Yahoo Finance API, and you will retrieve from the browser the quote in the JSON format similar to the example in Figure 25.8.

If you have `curl` installed on your terminal (for macOS or Linux) or PowerShell (for Microsoft Windows), you can run the `curl`/HTTP command from a terminal, and you will receive the following JSON results:

```
User % curl -X 'GET' \
   'https://yfapi.net/v6/finance/quote?region=US&lang=en&symbols=AAPL' \
   -H 'accept: application/json' \
```

continues

continued

```
   -H 'X-API-KEY: XXXXXXXXXXXXXXXXXXXXXXXXXXXXXXXXXXXXXX'
```

```
{"quoteResponse":{"result":[{"language":"en-US","region":"US","quoteType":
"EQUITY","quoteSourceName":"Delayed Quote","triggerable":true,"currency":
"USD","exchange":"NMS","shortName":"Apple Inc.","longName":"Apple Inc.",
"messageBoardId":"finmb_24937","exchangeTimezoneName":"America/New_York",
"exchangeTimezoneShortName":"EST","gmtOffSetMilliseconds":-18000000,"market":
"us_market","esgPopulated":false,"tradeable":false,"firstTradeDateMilliseconds
":345479400000,"priceHint":2,"postMarketChangePercent":-0.47818473,
"postMarketTime":1645232400,"postMarketPrice":166.5,"postMarketChange":
-0.80000305,"regularMarketChange":-1.5800018,"regularMarketChangePercent":
-0.93557656,"regularMarketTime":1645218002,"regularMarketPrice":167.3,
"regularMarketDayHigh":170.5413,"regularMarketDayRange":"166.19 - 170.5413",
"regularMarketDayLow":166.19,"regularMarketVolume":82772674,
"regularMarketPreviousClose":168.88,"bid":166.37,"ask":166.59,"bidSize":9,
"askSize":8,"fullExchangeName":"NasdaqGS","financialCurrency":"USD",
"regularMarketOpen":169.82,"averageDailyVolume3Month":101533156,
"averageDailyVolume10Day":77665000,"fiftyTwoWeekLowChange":51.090004,
"fiftyTwoWeekLowChangePercent":0.4396352,"fiftyTwoWeekRange":"116.21
- 182.94","fiftyTwoWeekHighChange":-15.639999,"fiftyTwoWeekHighChangePercent":
-0.08549251,"fiftyTwoWeekLow":116.21,"fiftyTwoWeekHigh":182.94,"dividendDate":
1644451200,"earningsTimestamp":1643301000,"earningsTimestampStart":1651003200,
"earningsTimestampEnd":1651521600,"trailingAnnualDividendRate":0.865,
"trailingPE":27.8138,"trailingAnnualDividendYield":0.00512198,
"epsTrailingTwelveMonths":6.015,"epsForward":6.56,"epsCurrentYear":6.16,
"priceEpsCurrentYear":27.159092,"sharesOutstanding":16319399936,
"bookValue":4.402,"fiftyDayAverage":172.4622,"fiftyDayAverageChange":
-5.162201,"fiftyDayAverageChangePercent":-0.029932361,"twoHundredDayAverage":
151.1004,"twoHundredDayAverageChange":16.1996,
"twoHundredDayAverageChangePercent":0.10721084,"marketCap":2730235789312,
"forwardPE":25.50305,"priceToBook":38.005455,"sourceInterval":15,
"exchangeDataDelayedBy":0,"pageViewGrowthWeekly":0.052849803,
"averageAnalystRating":"1.8 - Buy","marketState":"CLOSED",
"displayName":"Apple","symbol":"AAPL"}],"error":null}}%
                                                      User %
```

You can use Go to construct an HTTP request that does the same thing as this `curl` command. You can leverage the `net` package to construct your own HTTP request and query the Yahoo Finance API. To understand what you need to do, take a look at the `BuildYahooRequest` function in Listing 25.12.

LISTING 25.12

The `BuildYahooRequest` function

```
var YAHOO_API_KEY string = "XXXXXXXXXXXXXXXXXXXXXXXXXXXXXXXXXXXXXXXXX"
var URL = "https://yfapi.net/v6/finance/quote?region=US&lang=en&symbols="
```

```go
func BuildYahooRequest(symbol string) (*http.Response, error) {
  req, err := http.NewRequest("GET", URL+symbol, nil)
  if err != nil {
    return nil, err
  }
  req.Header.Set("Accept", "application/json")
  req.Header.Set("X-Api-Key", YAHOO_API_KEY)
  resp, err := http.DefaultClient.Do(req)
  if err != nil {
    return nil, err
  }
  return resp, nil

}
```

Listing 25.12 introduces the BuildYahooRequest function, which takes a symbol as input. The function returns an HTTP response and an error type. Before creating the function, hard-code your Yahoo API key generated from the previous step as well as the URL of the Yahoo Finance API minus the symbol. You will want to replace the string being assigned to YAHOO_API_KEY with your own API key.

Using the http.NewRequest, you create a GET HTTP request (similar to the generated curl command) using the Yahoo Finance API web address. You are also appending the symbol to the URL when you are creating the new request. If any error is detected, you return nil and the error is generated.

Next, in the header of the new request, add the other parameters of the request. In this example, you are specifying that JSON can be accepted as output. You are also adding the API key you defined in the constant YAHOO_API_Key, which is the key you generated earlier in this lesson.

Next, you execute the HTTP request using the Do function, and you receive a response type as well as an error type. If the error returned is nil, the function returns nil as well as the error. If the error is NOT nil, then you return the response from the HTTP request you sent to the Yahoo Finance API.

This version of the BuildYahooRequest function in Listing 25.12 is very minimal, but it should be able to retrieve the quote as an input symbol.

Updating *GetQuoteData*

Let's go back to the finance.go file and make the necessary updates to the GetQuoteData function to start querying the Yahoo Finance API. Replace finance.go with the code in Listing 25.13.

LISTING 25.13

Updated `finance.go` **file with an updated** GetQuoteData
function

```go
package finance

import (
  "errors"
  "golang.org/x/net/context"
  "io/ioutil"
  "log"
  "net/http"
)

type Server struct {
}

var YAHOO_API_KEY string = "XXXXXXXXXXXXXXXXXXXXXXXXXXXXXXXXXXXXXXXX"
var URL = "https://yfapi.net/v6/finance/quote?region=US&lang=en&symbols="
var STD_ERROR = errors.New("Unable to retrieve quote from the Yahoo API. Please
check the symbol or try again later.")

func BuildYahooRequest(symbol string) (*http.Response, error) {
  req, err := http.NewRequest("GET", URL+symbol, nil)
  if err != nil {
    return nil, err
  }
  req.Header.Set("Accept", "application/json")
  req.Header.Set("X-Api-Key", YAHOO_API_KEY)
  resp, err := http.DefaultClient.Do(req)
  if err != nil {
    return nil, err
  }
  return resp, nil

}

func (s *Server) GetQuoteData(ctx context.Context, in *Message)
(*Message, error) {
  log.Println("Incoming Quote Request")
  symbol := in.GetBody()
  resp, err := BuildYahooRequest(symbol)
  if err != nil {
    return &Message{Body: "Error"}, STD_ERROR
```

```
  }
  body, err := ioutil.ReadAll(resp.Body)
  if err != nil {
    return &Message{Body: "Error"}, STD_ERROR
  }
  return &Message{Body: string(body)}, nil
}
```

In Listing 25.13 you are doing a number of things. You add the BuildYahooRequest function to the file. You also update the GetQuoteData function with the new code that will have the RPC send a request to the Yahoo Finance API (using the BuildYahooRequest function).

In the GetQuoteData function, you first start by retrieving the symbol from the input message's body. You then provide the parsed symbol to the BuildYahooRequest function to query the Yahoo Finance API, which returns a response type as well as an error. If there is an error, you return a standard error message; otherwise, you continue within the function.

Next, you read the body from the response (resp.Body) into a variable called body that is of type []byte. If there is an error during this operation, you return a standard error message. If there is no error, you continue within the function.

Finally, you return a message with the body that you retrieved in the previous step. Notice that you are using string() to convert the values in body from a slice of bytes to a string.

Testing Our Quote RPC

At this point, you are ready to test everything. First, let's update client_finance.go to send a valid symbol (instead of a "Hello" message). Update client_finance.go with the code in Listing 25.14.

LISTING 25.14

Updated client_finance.go file to send a stock symbol

```
package main

import (
  "./finance/finance"
  "golang.org/x/net/context"
  "google.golang.org/grpc"
```

continues

continued

```go
   "log"
)

func main() {
    var conn *grpc.ClientConn
    conn, err := grpc.Dial(":9997", grpc.WithInsecure())
    if err != nil {
        log.Fatalf("did not connect: %s", err)
    }
    defer conn.Close()
    c := finance.NewFinanceServiceClient(conn)
    response, err := c.GetQuoteData(context.Background(), &finance.
Message{Body: "AAPL"})
    if err != nil {
        log.Fatalf("Error when retrieving the Quote Data: %s", err)
    }
    // display the response from the server
    log.Printf("Response from server: %s", response.Body)
}
```

Nothing much changed in `client_finance.go` except for sending the symbol for the Apple company stock ("AAPL") for the Body of the message. To see the code in action, run the `main.go` file, and then run `client_finance.go` (in a separate Terminal window). If everything is correct, you should see results similar to the following, although you won't see the same values:

2022/02/19 20:28:03 Response from server: {"quoteResponse":{"result":[{"lang
uage":"en-US","region":"US","quoteType":"EQUITY","quoteSourceName":"Delayed
Quote","triggerable":true,"currency":"USD","firstTradeDateMilliseconds":3454
79400000,"priceHint":2,"postMarketChangePercent":-0.47818473,"postMarketTime
":1645232400,"postMarketPrice":166.5,"postMarketChange":-0.80000305,"regular
MarketChange":-1.5800018,"regularMarketChangePercent":-0.93557656,"regularMa
rketTime":1645218002,"regularMarketPrice":167.3,"regularMarketDayHigh":170.5
413,"regularMarketDayRange":"166.19 - 170.5413","regularMarketDayLow":166.19
,"regularMarketVolume":82772674,"regularMarketPreviousClose":168.88,"bid":16
6.37,"ask":166.59,"bidSize":9,"askSize":8,"fullExchangeName":"NasdaqGS","fin
ancialCurrency":"USD","regularMarketOpen":169.82,"averageDailyVolume3Month"
:101533156,"averageDailyVolume10Day":77665000,"fiftyTwoWeekLowChange":51.09
0004,"fiftyTwoWeekLowChangePercent":0.4396352,"fiftyTwoWeekRange":"116.21 -
182.94","fiftyTwoWeekHighChange":-15.639999,"fiftyTwoWeekHighChangePercent":-
0.08549251,"fiftyTwoWeekLow":116.21,"fiftyTwoWeekHigh":182.94,"dividendDate":1
644451200,"marketState":"CLOSED","tradeable":false,"exchange":"NMS","shortName
":"Apple Inc.","longName":"Apple Inc.","messageBoardId":"finmb_24937","exchang
eTimezoneName":"America/New_York","exchangeTimezoneShortName":"EST","gmtOffSet
Milliseconds":-18000000,"market":"us_market","esgPopulated":false,"earningsTim
estamp":1643301000,"earningsTimestampStart":1651003200,"earningsTimestampEnd":

1651521600,"trailingAnnualDividendRate":0.865,"trailingPE":27.8138,"trailingA
nnualDividendYield":0.00512198,"epsTrailingTwelveMonths":6.015,"epsForward":6
.56,"epsCurrentYear":6.16,"priceEpsCurrentYear":27.159092,"sharesOutstanding"
:16319399936,"bookValue":4.402,"fiftyDayAverage":172.4622,"fiftyDayAverageCha
nge":-5.162201,"fiftyDayAverageChangePercent":-0.029932361,"twoHundredDayAvera
ge":151.1004,"twoHundredDayAverageChange":16.1996,"twoHundredDayAverageChangeP
ercent":0.10721084,"marketCap":2730235789312,"forwardPE":25.50305,"priceToBook
":38.005455,"sourceInterval":15,"exchangeDataDelayedBy":0,"
pageViewGrowthWeekly":0.052849803,"averageAnalystRating":"1.8 - Buy",
"displayName":"Apple","symbol":"AAPL"}],"error":null}}

As you can see, the client is able to successfully execute the RPC `GetQuoteData` from our gRPC server.

CREATING THE API

In the previous sections, you created the gRPC servers needed for our application. To recap, you want to build an API that includes two endpoints:

- The first endpoint will receive geolocation requests from external clients. The API will leverage the Geolocation server you created previously to retrieve the data. In other words, our API will be a client of our gRPC server.

- The second endpoint will receive quote requests from external clients. The API will leverage the finance server you created earlier to retrieve the data. Again, our API will be a client of our gRPC.

Let's go ahead and create the API, which will expose to the outside world the functionalities you built previously. In the root directory of your project, create another file, `api.go`. This file will contain all the code needed for our API, as shown in Listing 25.15.

LISTING 25.15

The initial `api.go` file

```
package main

import (
  "fmt"
  "github.com/gorilla/mux"
  "log"
  "net/http"
)
```

continues

continued

```go
func homePage(w http.ResponseWriter, r *http.Request) {
  fmt.Fprintf(w, "Welcome to our API for Smart Data!")
  fmt.Println("Endpoint: /")
}


func getGeoLocationData(w http.ResponseWriter, r *http.Request) {
  log.Println("Incoming API GeoLocation Request")

}
func getQuote(w http.ResponseWriter, r *http.Request) {
  log.Println("Incoming API Quote Request")
}


// handleRequests will process HTTP requests and redirect them to
// the appropriate Handle function
func handleRequests() {
  // create a router to handle our requests from the mux package.
  router := mux.NewRouter().StrictSlash(true)
  // access root page
  router.HandleFunc("/", homePage)
  router.HandleFunc("/getGeoLocationData/{address}", getGeoLocationData)
  router.HandleFunc("/getQuote/{symbol}", getQuote)
  log.Fatal(http.ListenAndServe(":11112", router))
}
func main() {
  handleRequests()
}
```

This is minimal code, but it does stand up our API with three endpoints. First, let's look at the handleRequests function. This function leverages the mux router you used in previous lessons to create a router for our API. Notice that you have endpoints:

/   This is a simple landing page for our API.

/getGeoLocationData   This endpoint will be the one that will handle incoming geolocation requests. This endpoint requires an input address.

/getQuote   This endpoint will be the one that will handle incoming finance requests. This endpoint requires an input symbol.

In the last line of the handleRequests function, the server is connected to port 11112.

Next, let's look at the homePage function. This function is very simple and displays a welcome message. The other two functions (getGeoLocationData and getQuote) are mostly empty. You are logging that there is an incoming request every time you receive one. The next step will be to implement these two functions.

Implementing the *getGeoLocationData* Endpoints

The last step of our project is to implement the two endpoints, getGeoLocationData and getQuote. As discussed earlier, these two endpoints will call their corresponding RPC on the gRPC server you developed previously. Specifically, getGeoLocationData will call the GeoLocation RPC from our gRPC server. In other words, our API endpoint will act as a client to the gRPC server. Thus, you can leverage the client code you built earlier (client_geolocation.go) to create the code for getGeoLocationData. The code in Listing 25.16 shows an example of the getGeoLocationData function.

LISTING 25.16

The getGeoLocationData function

```
func getGeoLocationData(w http.ResponseWriter, r *http.Request) {
  log.Println("Incoming API GeoLocation Request")
  vars := mux.Vars(r)
  address := vars["address"]
  var conn *grpc.ClientConn
  conn, err := grpc.Dial(":9997", grpc.WithInsecure())
  defer conn.Close()
  if err != nil {
    fmt.Fprintln(w, "Error. Please try again later")
    return
  }
  c := geolocation.NewGeoLocationServiceClient(conn)
  response, err := c.GetGeoLocationData(context.Background(),
&geolocation.Message{Body: address})
  if err != nil {
    fmt.Fprintln(w, err)
    return
  }
  fmt.Fprintln(w, response.Body)
}
```

Here you have done a few things. First, you use the mux package to read the address from the incoming request, r. Second, you establish a connection with the gRPC server. Note that you defer closing the connection until the function completes. You check for errors, and if you find an error, you return a standard error in the response w and then return.

If you don't have any errors, you create a Geolocation client using the function NewGeoLocationServiceClient. You execute the RPC GetGeoLocationData. It is important that GetGeoLocationData is an RPC (it is defined as a function in Go but it is still considered an RPC; check the definition in the proto file): a remote procedure (on our gRPC server) that you are executing from the client (our API).

Notice that you are passing the address you parsed previously in the body of the input message. You check for errors from executing the RPC, and if there are any issues, you return an error message in the response w of the endpoint.

Finally, you write the results returned by the RPC call (the geolocation data from Google Maps API) in the response of your endpoint getGeoLocationData.

Implementing the *getQuote* Endpoint

The getQuote function will call the GetQuoteData RPC from our gRPC server. In other words, our API endpoint will act as a client to the gRPC server. Thus, you can leverage the client code you built previously (client_finance.go) to create the code for getQuote. The code in Listing 25.17 shows an example of the getQuote function.

LISTING 25.17

The getQuote function

```
func getQuote(w http.ResponseWriter, r *http.Request) {
  log.Println("Incoming API Quote Request")
  vars := mux.Vars(r)
  symbol := vars["symbol"]
  var conn *grpc.ClientConn
  conn, err := grpc.Dial(":9997", grpc.WithInsecure())
  defer conn.Close()
  if err != nil {
    // issues with connecting to gRPC
    fmt.Fprintln(w, "Error. Please try again later") //provide standard
                            // error messages instead of technical errors
    return
  }
  c := finance.NewFinanceServiceClient(conn)
  response, err := c.GetQuoteData(context.Background(), &finance.Message{Body:
symbol})
  if err != nil {
    // issues with the symbol (symbol doesn't exist) or the Yahoo
    // API is not working.
```

```
        fmt.Fprintln(w, err)
        return
    }
    fmt.Fprintln(w, response.Body) //return the quote in the body of the response
}
```

This code follows the same logic as the previous endpoint (getGeoLocationData). You first parse the input symbol that will be used to retrieve the quote. Next, you establish a connection with the gRPC server. In case of any issues, you return an error in the response.

If there is no error, then you continue within the function and establish a new client that will be used to execute the RPC GetQuoteData. You retrieve the response from the gRPC and pass the body of the response from the gRPC to the response w of your endpoint getQuote.

Updating the *api.go* File

Update the api.go file with the code from the previous two listings. The final api.go code should look like Listing 25.18.

LISTING 25.18

The **updated** `api.go` **file**

```
package main

import (
    "./finance/finance"
    "./geolocation/geolocation"
    "fmt"
    "github.com/gorilla/mux"
    "golang.org/x/net/context"
    "google.golang.org/grpc"
    "log"
    "net/http"
)


func homePage(w http.ResponseWriter, r *http.Request) {
    fmt.Fprintf(w, "Welcome to our API for Smart Data!")
    fmt.Println("Endpoint: /")
}
```

continues

continued

```go
func getGeoLocationData(w http.ResponseWriter, r *http.Request) {
  log.Println("Incoming API GeoLocation Request")
  vars := mux.Vars(r)
  address := vars["address"]
  var conn *grpc.ClientConn
  conn, err := grpc.Dial(":9997", grpc.WithInsecure())
  defer conn.Close()
  if err != nil {
    fmt.Fprintln(w, "Error. Please try again later")
    return
  }
  c := geolocation.NewGeoLocationServiceClient(conn)
  response, err := c.GetGeoLocationData(context.Background(),
&geolocation.Message{Body: address})
  if err != nil {
    fmt.Fprintln(w, err)
    return
  }
  fmt.Fprintln(w, response.Body)
}
func getQuote(w http.ResponseWriter, r *http.Request) {
  log.Println("Incoming API Quote Request")
  vars := mux.Vars(r)
  symbol := vars["symbol"]
  var conn *grpc.ClientConn
  conn, err := grpc.Dial(":9997", grpc.WithInsecure())
  defer conn.Close()
  if err != nil {
    // issues with connecting to gRPC
    fmt.Fprintln(w, "Error. Please try again later") //provide standard
                                // error messages instead of technical errors
    return
  }
  c := finance.NewFinanceServiceClient(conn)
  response, err := c.GetQuoteData(context.Background(), &finance.Message{Body:
symbol})
  if err != nil {
    // issues with the symbol (symbol doesn't exist) or the Yahoo API is
not working.
    fmt.Fprintln(w, err)
    return
  }
  fmt.Fprintln(w, response.Body) //return the quote in the body of the response
}
```

```
// handleRequests will process HTTP requests and redirect them to
// the appropriate Handle function
func handleRequests() {
  // create a router to handle our requests from the mux package.
  router := mux.NewRouter().StrictSlash(true)
  // access root page
  router.HandleFunc("/", homePage)
  router.HandleFunc("/getGeoLocationData/{address}", getGeoLocationData)
  router.HandleFunc("/getQuote/{symbol}", getQuote)
  log.Fatal(http.ListenAndServe(":11112", router))
}
func main() {
  handleRequests()
}
```

That's it. At this point, run the `main.go` program first, which kicks off the gRPC server. Then, run the `api.go` file in a separate Terminal window, as shown in Figure 25.9.

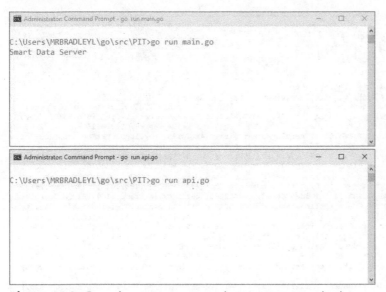

Figure 25.9: Running our programs in separate terminals

Next, you will use a browser (or Postman) to send a request to the API. First, let's try the landing endpoint, as shown in Figure 25.10. You should see this by loading your browser with the default localhost URL with the specified port from our code, `localhost:11112`.

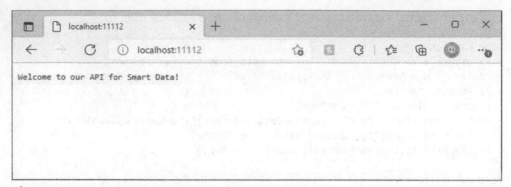

Figure 25.10: The landing endpoint for our API

You can also tap our `getQuote` endpoint with input `"AAPL"`. You can see the JSON response in the browser when you enter the URL `localhost:11112/getQuote/AAPL`, as shown in Figure 25.11.

Figure 25.11: Using the `getQuote` endpoint

You can change the URL to include other symbols as well. Figure 25.12 shows the result of changing the symbol to TSLA (for Tesla). The returned JSON from the URL (`localhost:11112/getQuote/TSLA`) will have the TSLA information.

{"quoteResponse":{"result":[{"language":"en-US","region":"US","quoteType":"EQUITY","quoteSourceName":"Nasdaq Real Time Price","triggerable":true,"customPriceAlertConfidence":"HIGH","currency":"USD","exchange":"NMS","shortName":"Tesla, Inc.","longName":"Tesla, Inc.","messageBoardId":"finmb_27444752","exchangeTimezoneName":"America/New_York","exchangeTimezoneShortName":"EST","gmtOffSetMilliseconds":-18000000,"market":"us_market","esgPopulated":false,"financialCurrency":"USD","regularMarketOpen":869.68,"averageDailyVolume3Month":26483503,"averageDailyVolume10Day":26281300,"fiftyTwoWeekLowChange":323.06012,"fiftyTwoWeekLowChangePercent":0.59882504,"fiftyTwoWeekRange":"539.49 - 1243.49","fiftyTwoWeekHighChange":-380.93988,"fiftyTwoWeekHighChangePercent":-0.30634737,"fiftyTwoWeekLow":539.49,"fiftyTwoWeekHigh":1243.49,"earningsTimestamp":1643213340,"earningsTimestampStart":1650916800,"earningsTimestampEnd":1651262400,"trailingAnnualDividendRate":0.0,"trailingPE":175.99472,"trailingAnnualDividendYield":0.0,"epsTrailingTwelveMonths":4.901,"epsForward":12.73,"epsCurrentYear":10.48,"priceEpsCurrentYear":82.304405,"marketState":"REGULAR","firstTradeDateMilliseconds":1277818200000,"priceHint":2,"regularMarketChange":-7.879883,"regularMarketChangePercent":-0.90528625,"regularMarketTime":1646159170,"regularMarketPrice":862.5501,"regularMarketDayHigh":889.88,"regularMarketDayRange":"856.6952 - 889.88","regularMarketDayLow":856.6952,"regularMarketVolume":17820763,"regularMarketPreviousClose":870.43,"bid":866.44,"ask":867.99,"bidSize":12,"askSize":10,"fullExchangeName":"NasdaqGS","sharesOutstanding":1033510016,"bookValue":29.225,"fiftyDayAverage":961.4346,"fiftyDayAverageChange":-98.88446,"fiftyDayAverageChangePercent":-0.10285095,"twoHundredDayAverage":834.2065,"twoHundredDayAverageChange":28.343628,"twoHundredDayAverageChangePercent":0.033976752,"marketCap":891454160896,"forwardPE":67.75728,"priceToBook":29.514118,"sourceInterval":15,"exchangeDataDelayedBy":0,"pageViewGrowthWeekly":0.2936184,"averageAnalystRating":"2.6 - Hold","tradeable":false,"displayName":"Tesla","symbol":"TSLA"}],"error":null}}

Figure 25.12: Getting a TSLA quote with getQuote

You can also try the other endpoint, getGeoLocationData. The results of calling getGeoLocationData using the address 19 rue jean jaures paris are shown in Figure 25.13. You can see that you used the same URL structure to call the endpoint, localhost:11112/getGeoLocationData/19 rue jean jaures paris.

[{"address_components":[{"long_name":"19","short_name":"19","types":["street_number"]},{"long_name":"Avenue Jean Jaurès","short_name":"Av. Jean Jaurès","types":["route"]},{"long_name":"Paris","short_name":"Paris","types":["locality","political"]},{"long_name":"Département de Paris","short_name":"Département de Paris","types":["administrative_area_level_2","political"]},{"long_name":"Île-de-France","short_name":"IDF","types":["administrative_area_level_1","political"]},{"long_name":"France","short_name":"FR","types":["country","political"]},{"long_name":"75019","short_name":"75019","types":["postal_code"]}],"formatted_address":"19 Av. Jean Jaurès, 75019 Paris, France","geometry":{"location":{"lat":48.883696,"lng":2.3728883},"location_type":"ROOFTOP","bounds":{"northeast":{"lat":0,"lng":0},"southwest":{"lat":0,"lng":0}},"viewport":{"northeast":{"lat":48.8849547302915,"lng":2.374293880291502},"southwest":{"lat":48.8822567697085,"lng":2.371595919708498}},"types":null},"types":["street_address"],"place_id":"ChIJ2Zdtjr9lt5kcRqSHctlfU18O","partial_match":false,"plus_code":{"global_code":"8FW4V9MF+F5","compound_code":"V9MF+F5 Paris, France"}}]

Figure 25.13: Calling the getGeoLocationData endpoint

As one last example, Figure 25.14 also presents results for calling getGeoLocationData. This time, an address in Louisville, Kentucky, is used, and the JSON results are presented.

Figure 25.14: Calling the getGeoLocationData endpoint

SUMMARY

A lot was accomplished in this lesson. You built a gRPC server that includes two servers. The first server handles geolocation data through the Google Maps API. The second server handles finance data through the Yahoo Finance API.

You built an API that exposes the services you built to the outside world. The API leverages the gRPC to get real-time data about geolocation and finance data.

If you want to build other servers that handle other types of data, the process is pretty much the same, which is to design and develop the server and the RPC that will handle the data on the gRPC server. Then, you add another endpoint to the API that will handle external requests and delegate them to the gRPC server.

You could have built the API without the gRPC server and directly retrieved the data from Yahoo and Google through our API itself. However, this process could be tedious and not scalable for extremely large projects where different teams are working on the API. In this case, having the API independent from the underlying work you do to get data from third-party APIs will allow you to divide the work between different developers/teams. Moreover, the process of how you built our two servers (Geolocation and Finance) is pretty similar (although they have different implementations), which allows you to develop a standard process for developing new servers and to expand the functionality of the API.

Lesson 26
Using Modules

Modules are important because they allow you to organize related code files into the same package and organize the code in a way that promotes simplicity and reusability. In this lesson, you'll learn the steps needed to set up and use modules.

LEARNING OBJECTIVES

By the end of this lesson, you will be able to:

- Create a Go module containing your own functions.
- Test the functions in your Go module.
- Call the functions in your Go module from other programs.

GETTING STARTED WITH MODULES

From a code perspective, a module is a collection of Go packages and files along with a file called go.mod. In the following steps, you'll learn how to create a module and then use it.

STEP 1: CREATE THE PROJECT DIRECTORY

First, create a directory with the same name that will be used for your module. In our example, you use the module and directory name `mymodule`. Create this directory under

$GOPATH/src. On our system, this is /opt/homebrew/Cellar/go/1.17.6/libexec/src/ mymodule. You can create a directory on Linux by entering the following commands on the command line:

```
user src % mkdir mymodule
user src % cd mymodule
user mymodule % ls
user mymodule %
```

On a Windows system, in a command window, you can create the new mymodule directory as follows:

```
C:\User\YourName\go\src> md mymodule
C:\User\YourName\go\src> cd mymodule
C:\User\YourName\go\src> dir
Directory of C:\Users\YourName\go\src\mymodule

04/20/2022  11:22 AM    <DIR>          .
04/20/2022  11:22 AM    <DIR>          ..
```

STEP 2: CREATE YOUR PROGRAM(S)

Next, create a file named utilities.go with the code shown in Listing 26.1. This is a sample file we are using to help illustrate the use of modules.

LISTING 26.1

utilities.go

```
package mymodule

func RepeatString(text string, count int) string {
  if count < 2 { //even if user enters negative value or 0, we return the text
by default
    return text
  }
  out := ""
  for i := 0; i < count; i++ {
    out = out + text
  }
  return out
}
```

Listing 26.1 defines a function called RepeatString that takes as input a string called text and an int called count. The function creates a new string with the original text repeated the number of times stated in count. For example, if the string contains "Help" and count is 3, then the value returned would be HelpHelpHelp.

STEP 3: CREATE A TEST PROGRAM

In the same directory, create a file that will contain a test of the function you just implemented in utilities.go. Create a file called utilities_test.go in the same directory with the code shown in Listing 26.2.

LISTING 26.2

utilities_test.go

```
package mymodule

import "testing"

func TestRepeatString(t *testing.T) {
  expected := "AA"
  result := RepeatString("A", 2)
  if result != "AA" {
    t.Errorf("Error: Expected = %s, Result = %s", expected, result)
  }
}
```

In Listing 26.2, the RepeatString function is being tested to make sure the output is correct. In this example, the RepeatString function is being sent the letter A along with the count of 2. The expected result should be the string "AA". If the function is correct, it should pass this test.

STEP 4: CREATE THE *GO.MOD* FILE

Next, create a go.mod file in the same directory using the following command:

```
go mod init mymodule
```

This command will create a file called go.mod in the same directory with the following content:

```
module mymodule

go 1.17
```

> **NOTE** The 1.17 is the version of Go being currently used. You might see a different version number.

STEP 5: TEST THE MODULE

Run the test to make sure everything is working correctly. You can do this by running the command **go test** on the command line, which should then indicate that the test passed, as shown here:

```
haythem@Haythems-Air mymodule % go test
PASS
ok      mymodule      0.102s
```

STEP 6: USING THE MODULE

Finally, create another project where the module you created can be imported and used. Create a new directory called project outside of the src directory. Within the project directory create a Go program that will call the module you created in step 2. You can include the code shown in Listing 26.3.

LISTING 26.3

Test program to call the module

```
package main

import (
  "fmt"
  "mymodule"
)
```

```
func main() {

    fmt.Println(mymodule.RepeatString("Hello", 5))

}
```

As you can see, the package mymodule that you created in step 3 is being called. The RepeatString function is being used from the mymodule module to display the string "Hello" five times. The output is as follows:

```
HelloHelloHelloHelloHello
```

NAMING MODULE FUNCTIONS

It is important to pay attention to the naming of functions when you're working with Go modules. Only functions that have names that start with an uppercase letter can be accessed by other programs. For example, if you had named the function in step 2 repeatString using a lowercase r instead of uppercase, then when you tried to use the function from the module in step 6, you would have received an error similar to the following:

```
# command-line-arguments
.\myprog.go:10:15: cannot refer to unexported name mymodule.repeatString
```

This assumes you renamed the repeatString function in all three listings to use the lowercase r version.

SUMMARY

In this lesson you saw how to create your own modules in Go as well as how to test and use them. You should now be able to create your own modules following these steps and then use the functions in the modules within your programs. Your modules can contain any functions you are likely to share.

EXERCISES

The following exercises are provided to allow you to experiment with the tools and concepts presented in this lesson. For each exercise, write a program that meets the specified requirements and verify that the program runs as expected. The exercises are:

Exercise 26.1: Shouting Text

Exercise 26.2: Shouting Correctly

> **NOTE** The exercises are for your benefit. The exercises help you apply what you learn in the lessons. You are also encouraged to experiment with the code as you complete the exercises.

Exercise 26.1: Shouting Text

Writing text in all uppercase letters is considered shouting when posting on social media or in text messages. Update the `utilities.go` program you created in Listing 26.1 to include a second function called `ShoutText` that receives a string and returns the string in all uppercase letters.

Exercise 26.2: Shouting Correctly

Create a testing function called `TestShoutText` that confirms that the `ShoutText` function works correctly. Add this new testing function to the code created in Listing 26.2. Run the test to confirm it works correctly.

Exercise 26.3: Shout It!

Create a program in a different directory that uses the new `ShoutText` function. Call the function multiple times and include the following text strings:

- How now brown cow?
- Let's count from 1 to 10
- I AM ALREADY SHOUTING!
- 1 2 3 4 5 6 7 8 9 10

Exercise 26.4: On Your Own

Take a look throughout the lessons in this book and identify some of the functions you've created. Add those that you find that could be useful to a new module.

Appendix
File Permissions and
Access Rights

In Lesson 20, "File I/O and OS Operations," we covered the use of files. A part of that use involved setting file permissions. In this appendix, we provide additional information about file permissions and access rights.

In general, each file has associated permissions that define how a user can interact with the file. In a Unix-like OS such as Linux, for example, there are three different access rights for files:

Read   Allows the user to read the file without making any changes.

Write   Allows the user to make changes to the file, including deleting the file itself. To have write privileges on a file, the user must have write privileges on the parent directory as well.

Execute   Allows the user to execute binary files and shell commands.

The access rights for each file are defined for three categories of users:

The Owner of the File   This is typically the user who created the file, although ownership can be transferred between users. The owner is represented by the letter *u* (for *user*).

The Group to which the User Belongs   In Linux, you can create a group of users who should all have the same access rights. For example, you can define a group for administrators who need to be able to execute commands and another group for users who only need to be able to view files on the server. Groups are represented by the letter *g* (for *group*).

All Other Users   Other users are represented by the letter *o* (for *other*).

In Linux, you can display the access right for each user by using the `ls` command. Use the `ls` command with the `-l` option to display user access rights to each object in the current directory. To see how this works, Figure A.1 shows an example of a Linux file named `file.txt` in the root directory. This shows the result of entering the following command at the root command line:

```
ls -l
```

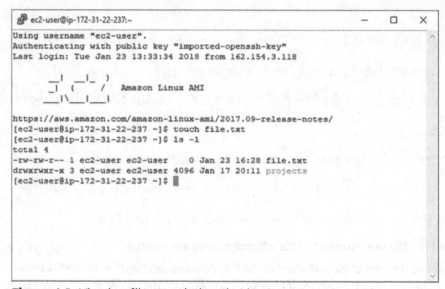

Figure A.1: Viewing file permissions in Linux

To the left of the filename in Figure A.1, you will see the file permissions defined as follows:

```
-rw-rw-r--
```

The first dash refers to a file type. A plain file is represented by a – (hyphen) and directories are represented by d. The character c is used for character-device files, b is used for block-device files, s is for a local socket, p represents a named pipe, and l represents a symbolic link.

The –rw–rw–r–– values represent read, write, execute for the three types of users mentioned earlier:

```
–rw– rw– r––
uuu ggg ooo
```

rw- (uuu)   Read, write, execute for the owner of the file or directory. In this case, the user can read and write, represented by r and w, and the dash indicates that the user does not have execute rights.

rw- (ggg)   Read, write, execute for the group that the owner belongs to. In this case, the group has read and write, represented by r and w, and does not have execute rights, indicated by the final dash.

r-- (ooo)   Read only. Both write and execute are represented by a dash.

CHANGING OTHER USER ACCESS RIGHTS IN LINUX

In Linux, the chmod command can be used to change the access permission for files and directories. This command can be used to remove all access rights to other users by providing the empty access right for o (others), as evidenced by the change from –rwxr––r–– to –rwxr–––––. With this change, file.txt can no longer be accessed by other users.

You can also combine access rights for different types of users. For example, the following command can be entered for the results shown in Figure A.2:

```
chmod og=r file.txt
```

In this example, we assigned read access rights to the group and to other users. Note that the permission settings on file.txt change from –rwxr–––––– to –rwxr––r––.

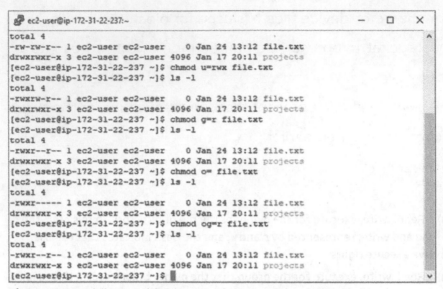

Figure A.2: Adding multiple types of access rights in Linux

DIGITAL REPRESENTATION FOR PERMISSIONS

You can use a digit representation of the permissions using the values shown in Table A.1. For instance, the permissions –rw–rw–r–– of the text file can be represented as 664:

- 6 for the permission for the current user (read and write: rw–)

- 6 for the permission of the group that the user belongs to (read and write: rw–)

- 4 for the permission of all the other users (read: r––)

Table A.1: Permission representations

Number	Permission	Symbol
0	No permission	–––
1	Execute	––x
2	Write	–w–
3	Execute+Write	–wx
4	Read	r––
5	Read+Execute	r–x
6	Read+Write	rw–
7	Read+Write+Execute	rwx

Index